LINCOLN AND THE TOOLS OF WAR

Hon. Sec. of War.

Sir.

I have examined, and seen tried, the "Raphael Repeater" and consider it a decided improvement upon what was called the "Coffee Mill gun" in these particulars, that it dispenses with the great cost, and liability to loss, of the steel cartridges, and that it is better guarded to prevent the escape of gas— Other advantages are claimed for it upon which I can not so well speak. While I do not order it into the service, I think it well worthy the attention of the Ordnance Bureau, and should be rather pleased, if it should be decided to put it into the service—

Yours truly

A. Lincoln

National Archives

LINCOLN CHAMPIONS A MACHINE GUN

LINCOLN
and
the Tools of War

ROBERT V. BRUCE

Foreword by BENJAMIN P. THOMAS

UNIVERSITY OF ILLINOIS PRESS
Urbana and Chicago

Preface © 1989
by the Board of Trustees of the University of Illinois
Manufactured in the United States of America
1 2 3 4 5 C P 5 4 3 2 1
This book is printed on acid-free paper.

Library of Congress Cataloging-in-Publication Data

Bruce, Robert V.
    Lincoln and the tools of war / by Robert V. Bruce : foreword by
Benjamin P. Thomas.
        p.   cm.
    Reprint. Originally published: Indianapolis : Bobbs-Merrill, 1956.
    Bibliography: p.
    Includes index.
    ISBN 0-252-01665-3 (cloth : alk. paper). — ISBN 0-252-06090-3 (paper :
alk. paper)
    1. United States—History—Civil War, 1861–1865—Equipment and
supplies.   2. United States—Armed Forces—Ordnance and ordnance
stores—History—19th century.   3. Lincoln, Abraham, 1809–1865—
Military leadership.   I. Title.
E491.B7   1989
973.7′092—dc20   89-4830
                                                            CIP

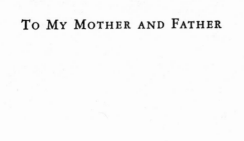

To My Mother and Father

Preface to 1989 Edition

WRITING this new preface gives me pleasure in more ways than one. It says something about the book's staying power after a third of a century. It also calls to mind the rapture I felt in my first active engagement with the American past. During the summer of 1952, as a graduate student working on my dissertation, I discovered the treasure cave known as the National Archives Building. There in its cool immensity I could free a dusty bundle of letters from the red tape that had bound them since the Civil War, and Abraham Lincoln would speak to me from a long-buried endorsement. Crusty old General Ripley would snap back; Captain Dahlgren, the lean, earnest embodiment of technical expertise, would chime in; and a picturesque and picaresque crowd of inventors would have their fervid say. I was captivated by the drama of their dreams and disappointments, triumphs and fiascos, and I surrendered to it joyously from nine in the morning till ten at night, darting out across Pennsylvania Avenue only for quick meals amid buildings, now swept away, that had looked down at Lincoln's first inaugural procession. I should like to think that something of my youthful excitement can still be savored in the book that resulted.

But what of the book otherwise, in the light of all these years gone by? Only one error of fact has come to light: it now appears to have been merely a legend that the Confederate double cannon killed its crew (p. 142).[1] Not all my conclusions have gone unquestioned. A few readers felt that I was sometimes too hard on General Ripley. But even those conceded that I stated the case for his defense fairly, albeit summarily (pp. 32–34). Besides, as my brief for him pointed out, this book deals primarily with a single aspect of his record, and that one the most vulnerable to criticism.

One reviewer took issue more particularly with my conjecture that Ripley could have shortened the war if he had been receptive to the adoption of breechloading rifles.[2] But a later study, examining that proposition in greater depth and detail, supports my view.[3] And I still stand by it.

This book can lay claim to survival in adding something to our knowledge and understanding of Abraham Lincoln, one of the enduringly central figures in American—indeed in world—history. My findings, for example, figure prominently in a chapter of Richard N. Current's classic *The Lincoln Nobody Knows*.[4] But it is not only the Lincoln connection that gives this book some title to longevity. The implications of technology for the fate of the human species loom even larger and more urgently today than they did when the book first appeared, and so their historical background has continuing relevance. As evidence of that, I shall turn directly from this preface to writing a paper, by invitation, for a symposium on "Science Advice to the President: The First 200 Years" at the 1989 meeting of the American Association for the Advancement of Science, my part being, of course, to deal with Lincoln and the Civil War.

Taking the larger view, I ventured to close the book with a prophecy: "The very power of weapons" might enforce "a lasting peace among nations" and thus further vindicate Lincoln's concern for the tools of war. To be sure, that forecast was a no-lose proposition for me, since the few survivors of a contrary outcome would have other matters on their minds than pointing the finger of scorn. Nevertheless, it is most gratifying of all to see that expressed hope, though still far from a certainty, not only alive after a third of a century but even stronger than before.

ROBERT V. BRUCE
Madbury, New Hampshire
December 27, 1988

Notes

1. Jones M. Drewry, "The Double-Barrelled Cannon of Athens, Georgia," *Georgia Historical Quarterly,* December 1964, pp. 443–46.
2. Harold J. Bingham, *Mississippi Valley Historical Review,* December 1956, pp. 495–96.
3. Carl L. Davis, *Arming the Union: Small Arms in the Civil War* (Port Washington, N.Y., 1973), pp. 122–45, 153–63, 173–76.
4. Richard N. Current, *The Lincoln Nobody Knows* (New York, 1958), pp. 176–81, 185–86.

"The Ordnance Department . . . functionary . . .
exclaimed, 'What does Lincoln know about a gun?' "

—The *Scientific American*
September 19, 1863

Foreword

BEHIND the solemn, furrowed countenance of Abraham Lincoln was an inquisitive mind. It ranged over the abstract and the infinite, the absolute and the immediate. It was philosophical, and at the same time intensely practical.

On the practical level Lincoln's curiosity directed itself, among other things, to mechanical devices. A fellow lawyer remembered that whenever Lincoln encountered a new piece of farm machinery on his rounds of the old Eighth Circuit, "he would carefully examine it all over, first generally and then critically; he would 'sight' it to determine if it was straight or warped; if he could make a practical test of it, he would do that; he would turn it over or around and stoop down, or lie down, if necessary, to look under it; he would examine it closely, then stand off and examine it at a little distance; he would shake it, lift it, roll it about, up-end it, overset it, and thus ascertain every quality and utility which inhered in it, so far as acute and patient investigation could do it."

As a young man seeking to improve his education, Lincoln acquired a fondness for mathematics. The months he spent surveying roads, bounding farms and platting town sites taught him to respect the exactness and precision of the trained engineer. His taste for mechanics carried over into the law, making him proficient in handling patent cases. He took out a patent of his own on a device for lifting vessels over shoals. He prepared and delivered a lecture on "Discoveries and Inventions." Living on the periphery of the machine age in America, he was keenly aware of the technological advances that were taking place about him. He pondered on the impact of those advances on mankind.

The war came, and Lincoln the President, in whatever time he could spare from other duties, turned his mechanical bent to the improvement of the tools of war. The subject, though touched upon by students, has never been adequately explored. In developing it fully, Robert V. Bruce has written an original and exciting book, one which probes new recesses of Lincoln's mind and personality. And there is a great deal more to the story than has been supposed.

Seldom do author and subject mesh so perfectly, for Bruce combines a sure grasp of history and the demands of historical method with expertness in technology. A New England Yankee, with the Yankee's predilection for mechanical contrivances, he originally intended to become an engineer, and studied for two years at Massachusetts Institute of Technology. Then war broke out and he was called to military service with the Enlisted Reserve Corps. The army assigned him to the University of New Hampshire, where he acquired a B.S. in mechanical engineering, and then sent him to the Pacific theater with the combat engineers. He had always enjoyed history, sometimes more than engineering, though he regarded it merely as a hobby. Gaining a new perspective in the far reaches of the Pacific, he decided that it was his true interest in life, and determined to make it his profession. At war's end he entered the graduate school at Boston University, where he received an A.M. in history in 1947, and after an interval of teaching, was awarded a Ph.D. in 1953. He is now a member of the history department at that institution.

A tireless and enthusiastic researcher, he has ransacked the manuscript collections of the Library of Congress and the National Archives, including the complete Civil War files of both the Army and Navy Ordnance Bureaus, reading hundreds of documents and unknotting the faded red tape from bundled letters undisturbed for many years. He has used the Robert Todd Lincoln Collection of Abraham Lincoln's papers and the recently published *Collected Works of Abraham Lincoln,* and has turned up some thirty Lincoln notes, letters and endorsements relating to ordnance, which are not included in the *Collected Works.* He has brought to light an important and hitherto unknown journal kept by Mrs. Gustavus Vasa Fox, wife of the Assistant Secretary of the Navy.

The search led him on to other repositories of manuscript material: the Massachusetts Historical Society, the Springfield Armory Library, the New York Public Library, the New York Historical Society and numerous university libraries. Files of yellowing newspapers, obscure magazine articles, bulky congressional documents yielded additional facts. His findings in sum total unveil a new aspect of the Civil War and of Lincoln's role as commander in chief.

Eager to utilize the North's superiority in the mechanical arts as a factor in winning the war, Lincoln made ordnance one of his special concerns during the first two years of his presidency. Thereafter, when it seemed less likely that new devices might be developed quickly enough to affect the outcome of the conflict and with weapons experiments entrusted at last to men of boldness and vision, he devoted less time to the subject, though his vigilance never flagged.

Lincoln's interest in new or improved instruments of combat embraced small arms, light and heavy artillery, rockets, projectiles, explosives, flame throwers, submarines, naval armor and mines. He was responsible for introducing machine guns and breech-loading rifles into the Union army. Wishing to render the United States independent of niter from India in the event of war with Great Britain, he by-passed the War and Navy Departments and set up a secret project, under his personal control, to develop a new explosive using a chlorate as a base. He favored the development of rifled cannon. On one occasion he narrowly escaped death or serious injury when an experimental rocket exploded in its launcher while he stood watching near by.

That many of these devices failed does not mean that Lincoln was naïve or absurdly visionary. In many instances he was on the right track but simply ahead of his time. The ideas with which he experimented were often sound, as modern warfare has demonstrated. But only with technological progress would they become practicable.

Men whose part in the war effort was important but unspectacular take on new shadings and dimensions under Bruce's scrutiny: hidebound, hotheaded General James W. Ripley, Chief of Army Ordnance, and his successors, earnest but bumbling General George D.

Ramsay and General Alexander B. Dyer, abler than the others but a late-comer to the office. The President developed close relations with General Joseph G. Totten, Chief of the Army Engineer Corps, and Lieutenant Henry A. Wise of the Navy Ordnance Bureau. Over at the Smithsonian Institution was the celebrated Dr. Joseph Henry, one of Lincoln's learned cronies, who marveled at the President's grasp of scientific matters. Between them they made possible the first successful air force in America—Professor Lowe's balloons.

Up at West Point, Lincoln discovered a young, forward-looking ordnance officer, Stephen Vincent Benét, grandfather of the poet; he tested arms for Lincoln when higher officialdom thwarted the President. Playing a strong outstanding role was keen, wiry Captain John A. Dahlgren, the Navy's leading ordnance expert. The only man in the President's entourage, at the beginning, who combined the requisites of intelligence, special training and an open mind toward new weapons, he won Lincoln's affections as well as his esteem, and his office at the Washington Navy Yard became a sort of presidential hideaway.

Moving frequently into the forefront of the story with Lincoln are devious, trigger-tempered Edwin M. Stanton, Secretary of War, and his able, hard-working assistant, Peter H. Watson, who had learned the intricacies of machines through his extensive patent law practice. And providing color and frequently a comic touch is the parade of inventors, many of them strange specimens of the human breed. Rebuffed by government functionaries, they would often write to Lincoln. Many of their letters never reached the President; his secretaries tossed them in the wastebasket. And yet they seem to have fared better on the whole than the other White House mail, for Bruce discovered more than two hundred of them, some with notations made by Lincoln, in the National Archives.

In many cases the inventors beset Lincoln in his office, often bringing their contraptions along. He listened to them patiently, amused by their eccentricities but alert for new ideas, and whenever a device showed promise, he arranged for it to be tried. Often he turned up in person at these tests, and he sometimes tried out new weapons himself in the Treasury Park behind the White House.

Besides finding a fresh theme in the much-tilled Lincoln field, Bruce has presented it delightfully. His style is facile. His characters breathe. He explains technical matters with such simple ease that they cease to be technical. The world's frantic search for new weapons in our day adds to the book's significance.

I can vouch at first hand for Bruce's expertness in tracking down elusive facts, because for some six months, more than two years ago, he worked for me in Washington as a research assistant on one of my own projects. From my first acquaintance with him at that time I have hopefully watched this book in gestation. I am pleased and proud to help give it a healthy start in life. With something of the same sense of satisfaction an obstetrician must feel in ushering a sound, sturdy, appealing creation of another sort into the world, I slap it heartily on the backside of the cover and commend it to your careful attention.

BENJAMIN P. THOMAS

Contents

List of Illustrations

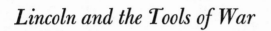

Lincoln and the Tools of War

CHAPTER 1

Captain Dahlgren

ON THE MORNING OF MARCH 4, 1861,
peril hung over the city of Washington. Though civil war had not
yet begun, it was plainly near, and its first shock was expected to
tumble Virginia and Maryland into the new Confederacy; caught
between them, the national capital would be cracked like a thin-
shelled nut. The city's pro-Southern majority longed for the event
and seemed disposed to hasten it. For weeks secessionists had been
whispering on street corners and plotting in taverns; and on this
day of transition menace more than ever filled the air.

President-elect Abraham Lincoln, his rawboned features newly
softened by a growth of black beard, sat waiting in Willard's
Hotel for his inaugural procession to form. The weather was fit
for the times, bleak and blustery, though the sun still shone. Outside on Pennsylvania Avenue, a March wind whipped through
bare ailanthus trees, rustling crinoline and imperiling plug hats
in the throng which pressed around the whitewashed tree boxes.
The broad avenue's ill-kept course of cobblestones had been dis-
interred for the occasion, but dust, whirling from unpaved side
streets, whitened lips and made eyes water. Southern sympathizers
glowered from windows and balconies overlooking the avenue.

As noon struck and militiamen with loaded rifles moved to their
posts on the housetops, gray-faced President James Buchanan
emerged with his lanky successor from a side door of the Willard.
A military band struck up "Hail to the Chief" with synthetic

3

sprightliness. Buchanan and Lincoln climbed into a waiting barouche, the driver seized the reins and the carriage began to jolt over the cobblestones, accompanied by a troop of restless cavalry. Wordlessly the two men rode toward the Capitol, where the travail of one would end and that of the other begin. Lincoln stared into the crowd that lined the avenue and from time to time lifted his glossy silk hat in greeting. The crowd stared back, impassive and inscrutable.

Among the onlookers stood Commander John A. Dahlgren, United States Navy, a slender man with piercing eyes narrowed beneath thin, straight brows. As is often the case with men of spare physique, his age was hard to judge, and some took him to be no more than forty. He was actually fifty-one, only nine months younger than the President-elect. At the moment foreboding lay heavy on him. As chief ordnance officer at the Washington Navy Yard, Dahlgren had already run up against the disloyalty which riddled the Federal Government; and unlike some of his colleagues, he loved the Union he served.

After the procession had clattered by, the crowd surged toward Capitol Hill to see the inaugural ceremony, and Dahlgren, his weather-beaten countenance still grim with apprehension, followed after them. Like the Union itself, the Capitol was in a state of upheaval. Its new, unfinished dome stood open to a turbulent sky, while scattered about the grounds lay marble blocks and scrolls, fragments of lumber and other debris. Dahlgren watched tensely as Lincoln stood tall on the platform and in a high-pitched, resonant voice delivered his inaugural address, a sincere and reasoned appeal to past ties and present sense. "We are not enemies, but friends," Lincoln told the South; "we must not be enemies." There was a burst of applause, and cadaverous Chief Justice Taney swore in the sixteenth President—and, for all he or anyone else could know, the last.

Suddenly the air shook with the prophetic thunder of guns, a salute from two batteries of light artillery which loyal, elderly General Winfield Scott had prudently posted near by. The spectators

dispersed, some relieved, others disappointed. Without violence—
or much enthusiasm—Abraham Lincoln had been installed as
President of the United States. Breathing more easily, Commander
Dahlgren returned to his duties at the Navy Yard.

Dahlgren's duties were to his taste. The taste may have been inherited: his American mother had a knack for designing, and the
family of his Swedish father had included several eminent physi-
cians and chemists. Young Dahlgren had joined the Navy as a
keen-eyed, ambitious boy of seventeen, at about the time Abe Lincoln had become a ferryman on an Indiana creek. But after Dahlgren
had put in a few years of sea duty, his heredity asserted itself, and
he turned to the study of weapons. An ambitious young officer could
scarcely have made a wiser move; for while a long peace was deny-
ing glory to sea-fighters, vast horizons were opening in the field of
ordnance. The new technology which had revolutionized industry
was about to transform the art of war. And Dahlgren was to have a
hand in the transformation.

It was in 1847, the year when Abraham Lincoln first came to
Washington as a freshman Congressman, that Lieutenant Dahlgren
arrived at the Washington Navy Yard to supervise the manufacture
of Hale's newfangled war rockets. Beginning with one end of a
timber shed as a workshop, Dahlgren took hold with characteristic
zeal. Within two months his duties spread to other ordnance activities. He set up foundries and machine shops, established the
waters off the yard as a firing range and carried on elaborate experiments. Within a few years the emphasis of the yard's work changed
from shipbuilding and fitting to ordnance, and the yard became in
fact what it now is in name also—the United States Naval Gun
Factory.

Meanwhile Dahlgren won an enviable reputation as a designer
of weapons. His contributions to naval armament included a bayonet
for Navy rifles and a light boat howitzer. When Commodore Perry
opened up Japan in 1854, he gave the Japanese a model of Dahl-

gren's howitzer, and those eager learners paid it the sincere compliment of wholesale imitation.

Dahlgren's proudest achievement in those years was his cannon, which for years after the Civil War was to remain the principal armament of the United States Navy. Sweeping aside convention and founding his design on reason and experiment, Dahlgren systematically fitted strength to strain at all points. In so doing, he shifted the weight of metal back from the forward part to the breech and created, as a result, a cannon with a slim chase flowing smoothly out of a bulbous breech, a gun that drew on itself the nickname of "soda-water bottle." This frivolity grated on the inventor, who was always quick to see an affront to his dignity.

Then came secession.

Dahlgren was a Philadelphian by birth, but most other officers at the Washington Navy Yard were Southerners. As the lower South fell away from the Union, Dahlgren's colleagues, in his words, "gradually receded from that frank communion which is apt to exist between officers of the same service." Even the commandant of the yard, a hawk-faced Marylander named Franklin Buchanan, made little effort to disguise his Southern sympathies; although when the naval officers of the capital, brightly decked out in gold lace and gilt buttons, paid their official respects to Lincoln shortly after the inauguration, Captain Buchanan assured the President unctuously that he could always depend on the Navy to support the honor and dignity of the flag. (A year or so later this patriot was to command the Confederate ironclad *Merrimac*.)

As chief of the yard's ordnance department during the secession crisis, Dahlgren held a crucial post. Though the stock of arms in his charge was not large, it was choice, and the placid-looking Maryland countryside a few hundred yards across the river swarmed with secessionists. The yard's defenses were meager. It was bounded on the south by the Anacostia River, a branch of the Potomac, on the north and east by a brick wall, and on the west, where precious artillery, rifles and powder were stored, by nothing more than a rickety wooden fence. Some weeks before the inauguration, being disposed for the moment to uphold his trust, Captain Buchanan had made the yard as ready for attack as circumstances allowed. For his part, Commander Dahlgren had hustled all the breech-loading rifles and light artillery into the most defensible building available, laid in a store of fuel and water, barred all but a few trusted men, secretly piled up the powder stores in the loft of a large ordnance workshop within range of his shellfire and braced himself for a siege.

Thus stood matters on Inauguration Day, and, knowing this, one can understand Dahlgren's forebodings as the reins of government passed from the limp hands of James Buchanan to the untried grasp of Abraham Lincoln.

As it turned out, neither inaugural violence nor a siege of the Navy Yard came to pass. But Dahlgren's readiness had its reward. The resolute loyalty he had demonstrated and his high professional standing marked him as a coming man in the Union Navy, especially when his Southern colleagues began leaving. So it happened that a famous war correspondent, William H. Russell of the *London Times*, drove down to the Navy Yard that March to view and interview the rising ordnance officer.

At the yard's massive stone gate, the portly, soft-spoken visitor encountered two sentries carrying brightly polished arms and dressed smartly in dark-blue tunics with yellow facings and eagle buttons, white Berlin gloves, and caps—"all very clean and creditable," he thought. Inside the yard Russell was impressed by the "air of agreeable freshness" about its red-brick buildings, picked out with white stone, and its two or three green grassplots, fenced in with pillars and chains and bordered by trees. Down by the river stood the great covered shipways, a huge barnlike structure with a gaping mouth big enough to swallow a ship whole. Indeed, the ribs of one ship rested there at that moment, as if in the process of being digested. Dark plumes of smoke trailed over the yard from two big stacks, and the noise of steam and machinery was everywhere.

Russell found his man in a modest office, surrounded by books, papers, drawings and models, shell and shot and racks of arms. The two men talked for a couple of hours and were mutually impressed. Russell reflected that "all inventors . . . must be earnest self-reliant persons, full of confidence, and, above all, impressive, or they will make little way in the conservative, *status-quo*-loving world," and he justly assigned Dahlgren to that formidable category.

But Russell's account, perhaps unwittingly, played an unflattering light on Dahlgren's high-strung temper. "He has to fight," Russell told the world, "with his navy department, with the army, with boards and with commissioners—in fact with all sorts of obstructors." However true this may have been, however real the "parsimony of the department" which Dahlgren was quoted as deploring, such criticism by Dahlgren of his colleagues and superiors looked a little peevish, not to say indiscreet, in cold print; and Dahlgren was understandably annoyed with the clever Mr. Russell when it came out. "How is Dahlgren?" wrote Russell penitently a few months later to a mutual friend. "I hope the dear old man's dander has gone down now—& that he will go on making his guns in peace & quietness."

March passed, and still Commander Dahlgren had seen the President only from a distance—not that Dahlgren suffered from diffidence, but that, in his own words, "the throng that gathered about the President was impenetrable." It was Lincoln who made the first move toward a meeting, and a surprise move at that.

Perhaps Lincoln was concerned for the safety of the Washington Navy Yard under pro-Southern Franklin Buchanan; perhaps curiosity alone drew him. Whatever the reason, Navy Yard officers were astonished, one gray, gusty day about a month after the inauguration, to see Lincoln and his family drive up to the great stone gate and into the yard. Despite a hubbub of impromptu ceremony and a twenty-one-gun salute, Lincoln drove straight to Dahlgren's office and asked for that spirited supporter of the Union. Dahlgren happened to be away just then. It was Captain Buchanan, therefore, who took the callers on a two-hour tour of the establishment.

There was much for Lincoln to see: heavy steam hammers for

forging anchors; a blast furnace and steam hammer for working up scrap iron; the chain-cable shop with its hydrostatic press for testing; the pyrotechnical laboratory; the rolling mill; the boilermaking shop; the machine shop; the foundries, brass and iron, where boat howitzers and fieldpieces were turned out; and an assortment of steam-driven machinery for boring, turning, planing and other operations. Lincoln was delighted with it all—not only with the ingenious machinery and the busy shops, but also with the cool, cavernous shipways and the general neatness of the yard. So, it may be supposed, were the Lincoln boys, Tad and Willie. How much of the first lady's rapture was real and how much merely polite is harder to gauge, and similarly unfathomable are the feelings of secessionist Franklin Buchanan as he escorted his Black Republican superior about the establishment.

Hoping, perhaps, to hold Buchanan's loyalty by a show of good will, the President had consented to give away the captain's daughter Nannie in marriage to a Marine Corps lieutenant at the commandant's quarters the next night. When the time came, Lincoln was late. The wedding itself, in fact, was over when the Presidential carriage drew up and its occupant alighted.

On that dark, chilly night, few guests could have lingered on the white-columned veranda that skirted the big brick residence, but inside, the spacious rooms were crowded with Washington society, gay in blue uniforms or fashionable evening dress. The mixed sentiments of the guests may have constrained talk of gathering war clouds, of Federal forts like Sumter and Pickens, holding out precariously along the coast of a new nation which called itself the Confederate States of America. Washington partygoers were schooled in glib self-possession, and they doubtless maintained the proper volume of innocuous chatter. But many eyes grave with fears and racking indecisions turned toward Lincoln as he walked in. Perhaps they found a moment's reassurance. Lincoln seemed to have left his cares at the great stone gate, and presently he was chatting and joking with the gaiety that could so astonishingly transfigure his deep-lined countenance.

Dahlgren was there, too, and doubtless holding his own. With all his usual austerity, the commander could be convivial enough when he chose. "In New York," one of his friends once wrote him, "I heard that you could not get a glass big enough to hold a bottle of beer, so I have ordered one cast for you the size of a fifteen-inch shell and sent for your own especial tippling." At any rate, if he nursed chagrin at having missed Lincoln the day before, Dahlgren's feelings were assuaged when someone brought him over to the President.

Lincoln took an immediate fancy to the man he saw standing before him, a man of earnest and thoughtful mien, utterly without self-consciousness, whose thin nostrils expanded with the intensity and enthusiasm of his speech. The President grasped Dahlgren's hand in both of his as if the two men had been friends for years; and an easy, offhand conversation ensued until interrupted by the claims of others. Lincoln had found his chief adviser on the tools of war.

As Dahlgren stood chatting with Lincoln that evening, he could not have realized how much they had in common. Like the rest of the world, Dahlgren accepted the rail-splitter image of Lincoln, so firmly established by the Presidential campaign of 1860. And well he might have, for there was much truth in it. Born in a log cabin, brought up on a farm, having struck out for himself in a prairie hamlet, Lincoln could scarcely have disguised the country flavor of his manners and speech had he tried; and he never tried. In his accent, in his homely turn of phrase, in his whole way with people, Lincoln was the complete Westerner, careless of ceremony and brimming with broad humor. His long limbs with their large-sized extremities; his farseeing gray eyes set deep in a lean, weatherbeaten, craggy face; his unruly, tousled hair; his firm but cautious stride —all suggested the American pioneer, not the engineer or scientist.

Yet, as Dahlgren soon discovered, there was a streak in Abraham Lincoln that reflected young America's delight in the Machine Age, a streak that had more in it of Eli Whitney than of Henry Thoreau.

Lincoln had witnessed and welcomed the coming of machines,

and he loved them, not only as an ex-rail-splitter might love a circular saw, but also as a mathematician loves a difficult equation neatly solved. Lincoln had the engineer's exact and tenacious mind, not quick and facile like that of his hero Henry Clay, but marked by deliberation and reflective analysis. "I am never easy when I am handling a thought," said he, "till I have bounded it north, bounded it south, bounded it east, and bounded it west."

To be sure, because he had lived most of his life in half-tamed wilderness or prairie town, Lincoln had missed personal contact with certain refinements of technological progress. The White House was only six years ahead for him when gas lights first flared through the darkness of Springfield's main square. On the circuit he went to a little show at a local academy and afterward rambled on by the fire about the electrical machine, the magic lantern and other scientific toys he had seen there. His fellow lawyers were not impressed. They had known about those things as schoolboys. "Yes," said Lincoln sadly, "I now have an advantage over you, for the first time in my life seeing those things which are, of course, common to those who had, what I did not, a chance at an education when they were young."

But no China Wall encircled Illinois. During the fifties, the Machine Age began to take hold in Springfield. Steam engines hissed and pounded in its mills, ready-made clothes piled up on its counters, reapers clattered over its tributary farms. As Lincoln walked along a Springfield street one day in 1856, he spied a self-raking reaper on exhibition, the first he had ever seen. Here was technology helping to feed the millions who tended its shops and mills. Fascinated, Lincoln stared long at the new device. His imagination carried it to an Illinois wheat field and set it going; his supple mind followed the complex evolutions of sickle, revolving rake and reels. Presently the little group of spectators around him listened with profit while the prairie lawyer explained, clearly and succinctly, the mechanical principles involved.

A few months later Lincoln stopped to watch a young telegrapher, Charles Tinker, at his work. The onlooker asked questions, and young Tinker explained the workings of the wonderful contraption: the key, the making and breaking of the circuit, the electromagnet. Tinker found Lincoln an apt and intelligent pupil, "already well furnished with knowledge of collateral facts and natural phenomena."

Lincoln had picked up some of those collateral facts from the *Annual of Scientific Discovery,* which he had come across in 1855 among the books of his law partner, Billy Herndon, and liked so well that he bought his own copy. Lincoln's judgment was sound. The *Annual,* edited by a youthful Yankee named David Wells (whom Lincoln was to meet and like during his Presidency), covered the year's progress in science and technology for both general readers and specialists. Its contributors were able men, including such savants as Louis Agassiz and Jeffries Wyman. To their efforts were added two or three hundred pages of scientific and technological news from books and magazines here and abroad. There was a classified list of new patents; and for those readers whose thirst for knowledge remained unslaked the *Annual* provided a bibliography of recent scientific publications. "I have wanted such a book for years," Lincoln told his partner, "because I sometimes make experiments and have thoughts about the physical world that I do not know to be true or false. I may, by this book, correct my errors and save time and expense."

By keeping his eyes open to the world around him, by asking shrewd questions and by reading intelligently, Lincoln learned much more about the new Machine Age than the world at large gave him credit for knowing.

And he was more than just an interested bystander.

When he was in his twenties, Lincoln worked for a few months as a surveyor, studying geometry and trigonometry, bounding farms and mapping towns with neat lines and clear, careful script, learning to respect the painstaking accuracy of engineering. Later, when he became a lawyer, patent cases were his meat, and in them his analytical mind and taste for mechanics served his clients well.

From Lincoln's legal work for railroads came his greatest successes as a lawyer, and with them a further insight into the impact of technology on human life. Through his connection with the Illinois Central, Lincoln met a compact, forceful, redheaded West Pointer and Mexican War veteran named George B. McClellan, who had become the road's chief engineer and vice-president in 1857. "More than once," McClellan recalled in later years, "I have been with him in out-of-the-way county-seats where some important case was being tried, and, in the lack of sleeping accommodations, have spent the night in front of a stove listening to the unceasing flow of anecdotes from his lips." In those nocturnal gab fests Lincoln had an opportunity to learn about the latest progress in weapons, for McClellan had just returned from a thorough study of European military technology, with special attention to developments in the Crimean theater of war.

By then Lincoln had come to feel that he had some special acquaintance with technology. He demonstrated his self-confidence when, venturing forth in 1858 for the first and only time as a popular lecturer, he chose "Discoveries and Inventions" as the subject of his talk.

The lecture evolved from a piece by George Bancroft which a colleague had read to Lincoln on the circuit. After mulling it over, Lincoln got up a similar talk, one which leaned heavily on the development of ancient technology as revealed in the Bible, and delivered it before the Young Men's Association at Bloomington, Illinois. When he made bold to repeat it for the Ladies' Library Association in the same town, the public rendered a harsh verdict. "I paid a quarter and went early to get a seat," wrote a young law student to his father some months later. "It was a beautiful evening, and the lecture had been well advertised but for some reason not explained, only about 40 persons were present, and Old Abe would not speak to such a small crowd, and they paid us back our quarters at the door."

Despite the lecture's cold reception, its subject stayed with Lincoln. He rewrote his talk completely at some time during the ensuing

year, leaving out most of his Biblical lore and bringing in the influence of patent laws and the printing press on the development of
technology. As an essay in technological history, the effort was weak;
Lincoln himself presented it more as a humorous piece with political
overtones, and even in that light its merit was uneven. Trying out
his second effort on another audience in January 1860, he made no
better impression than before.

Lincoln's failure as a lecturer on technological history hurt him.
He drew back, crestfallen. Asked to deliver a lecture at Galesburg,
he begged off on the ground that he "must stick to the courts
awhile," adding in deprecation of his previous effort, "I read a sort
of lecture to three different audiences during the last month and this;
but I did so under circumstances which made it a waste of no time
whatever." He expressed his mortification more directly when teased
by a friend about the episode. "Don't," he said good-naturedly;
"that plagues me."

Yet time healed the cut. A few weeks before his death, Lincoln
spoke of the "Discoveries" lecture in talking with Louis Agassiz.
"When I get out of this place," he told the scientist wistfully, "I'll
finish it up, perhaps, and get my friend [Noah Brooks] to print it
somewhere."

The lecture fiasco notwithstanding, those who knew Abraham
Lincoln at the closing of his prairie years acknowledged his knack
for mathematics and machinery. In 1859, a generation after his
junkets with compass and chain, Lincoln's opinion on a disputed
point was sought by a convention of surveyors who met in Springfield. And one of Lincoln's former law partners said of him in
1860: "Has an inventive faculty. . . . Is always studying into the
nature of things."

When Lincoln came to the White House, he felt himself competent to tackle problems of technology. If he had ever believed himself infallible in such things, his lecturing experience had taught
him proper humility; but he had also learned as a surveyor and
patent lawyer that he could study those matters out and see through
them, if need be. Certainly he showed as President the same zest for

Brigadier General James W. Ripley   Brigadier General George D. Ramsay

Rear Admiral John A. Dahlgren   Dr. Charles M. Wetherill

THREE ORDNANCE OFFICERS AND A SCIENTIST

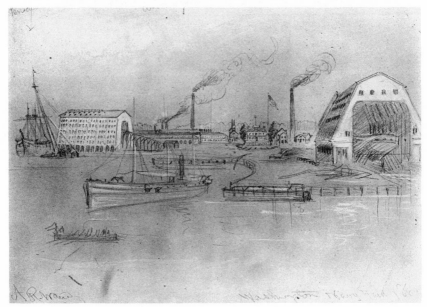

THE WASHINGTON NAVY YARD, 1861
A drawing by Alfred Waud.

A PARROTT RIFLED FIELD PIECE ON THE ROAD
A drawing by Edwin Forbes.

mechanical novelties he had manifested at the little show on the Illinois circuit.

Of this Presidential proclivity Commander Dahlgren was soon to be aware.

The friendship which had sprung up so quickly between Lincoln and Dahlgren took firm root and flourished. Events gave Dahlgren ample opportunity to cultivate it. On April 4, 1861, the day after Nannie Buchanan's nuptials, Dahlgren received a requisition for howitzers which cryptically referred him to the President for further details. He "posted to the White House." At first Lincoln himself was nonplussed, but it finally transpired that the guns were for an expedition to provision Fort Sumter. Civil war was at hand. At Lincoln's request, Dahlgren called again early the next day. He found the President "ill at ease, and not self-possessed."

Early on the morning of April 12 a Confederate signal shell burst over the dim outline of the fort in Charleston Harbor, and by nightfall both North and South blazed with war fervor. Five days later, as Northern men by the thousand answered Lincoln's call for volunteers, the state of Virginia seceded from the Union and left the capital of the United States wide open to capture by the Confederacy.

From his office window President Lincoln looked out over the Potomac to enemy territory on the west, while across the Anacostia River to the east the state of Maryland wavered on the brink of secession. Baltimore mobs attacked the 6th Massachusetts Regiment as it passed through the city to reinforce Washington. Maryland secessionists tore up railroad tracks and cut telegraph lines. Washington was cut off from the North and for a few days waited for some rebel blow as helplessly as a captive with his head on the block.

Seceding states drew their native sons with them, and the armed services of the Union lost many of their finest officers. In Washington Colonel Robert E. Lee and Brigadier General Joseph E. Johnston were among the leavetakers. Next door to the White House, at the little brick Navy Department building, disaffection rallied around the Chief of Navy Ordnance, Captain George A. Magruder, who resigned on April 22 and after a period of agonized indecision settled in Canada. When Magruder left, so did everyone connected with his bureau except the draftsman, the messenger and a Navy lieutenant named Henry Wise—of whom more will be heard later.

Magruder's successor as Chief of Navy Ordnance was Captain Andrew A. Harwood, an amiable officer of some ability but no technical training in the subject of his new command. The new chief confined himself to administering bureau affairs with the help of Lieutenant Wise. Even in this limited role he was unhappy. As for technical questions, in those Harwood gave carte blanche to the knowledgeable Dahlgren.

On the same day that Captain Magruder resigned, Captain Franklin Buchanan mistakenly concluded that his native state of Maryland was about to follow Virginia out of the Union. One of the steps he took in consequence was a letter to Dahlgren:

As I have this day resigned my Commission as a Captain in the Navy, and consider myself only temporarily in command here, you will . . . superintend the defence of the yard when necessary. I shall not take any part in the defence of this Yard from this date.

In this step, at least, Buchanan was in harmony with Secretary of the Navy Gideon Welles, who had already divined Buchanan's intentions and had told Dahlgren to take over. Undismayed by his elevation at so desperate a time, Dahlgren spent the rest of the momentous day arming and fitting some river steamboats, and worked far into the night posting his little force for defense.

At the close of his life Dahlgren underscored his service in that emergency as *"the best which I ever rendered to the country."* An exodus of rebel sympathizers left Dahlgren with only about a hundred and fifty men to defend the yard, while Confederate territory lapped at the city's western edge and threatened to ring it round. Dahlgren rose to the occasion. In the prophetic words of William H. Russell, he was "self-reliant . . . full of confidence, and, above all, impressive"—just the sort of man for the crisis. One of Lincoln's private secretaries encountered Dahlgren in those perilous days and was at once impressed by his "great coolness & power."

Lincoln saw the importance of Dahlgren's services and hinted to him of promotion "when the proper time arrived." After the arrival of Northern troops ended the crisis, certain Navy captains began vying for Commander Dahlgren's billet, since the law earmarked it for their rank. Lincoln declared: "The Yard shall not be taken from the Captain; he held it when no one else would, and now he shall keep it as long as he pleases." And for Dahlgren's benefit Congress amended the old law—an action which Dahlgren called "the best compliment I ever received."

By early May Washington had passed from under the shadow of rebel capture. In the Navy Yard, the 71st New York Regiment pitched its white tents, "adding not a little to the picturesque view from the entrance." When the regiment invited Lincoln to a concert by its fine band on the afternoon of May 9, he cheerfully accepted.

A thirty-four-gun salute proclaimed the arrival of Mr. and Mrs. Abraham Lincoln at the Navy Yard. The carriage rolled up to the concert hall, a big storeroom which had been festooned with banners for the occasion and which was now further ornamented with Cabinet members, Army and Navy officers and "a crowd of the *ton* of Washington" to the number of two or three hundred. The *ton* of Washington rose to its elegant feet and remained standing while the lanky President and his short, plump first lady walked down the aisle to their seats in the front row. Lincoln listened to a much applauded program of march tunes and sentimental ballads and asked at the end for the *"Marseillaise,"* which was vigorously rendered by one of the singers. (A Southern hymn tune had been rechristened "John Brown's Body" and was catching on among Union troops, but it still awaited lyrics that would equal this occasion.)

After the concert Lincoln asked to see the 11-inch smoothbore Dahlgren gun fired, so Dahlgren took the Presidential party aboard the *Pensacola* to watch the practice. The day had been nearly cloudless, and by the time the President and his friends boarded the vessel the last white streaks of cloud had drifted over the edge of the horizon before a fresh breeze from the northwest. The river sparkled in the sunlight of a springtime afternoon. On shore sat a gleaming new Dahlgren 11-incher. The gun crew performed their evolutions, the great gun boomed, and almost at once, as it seemed, the black shell could be seen hurtling through the air two thirds of the way to the wooden target in the river. The target was about as far from the gun as Fort Sumter had been from the nearest rebel battery, thirteen hundred yards. All the three rounds fired struck the target, one directly and two on ricochet from the water. Young John Hay, one of Lincoln's private secretaries, described the scene in his diary:

The splendid course of the 11 inch shell flying through 1300 yards of air, the lighting, the quick rebound, & flight through the target with wild skips, throwing up a 30 ft. column of spray at every jump, the decreasing leaps and the steady roll into the waves were scenes as novel and pleasant to me as to all the rest of the party. The Prest. was delighted.

Dahlgren, gay with gratified pride, took note of Lincoln's good spirits and wished that he, as commandant of the yard, could offer the President some hospitality. But he still had no other quarters than his office, so Lincoln just stood on the office piazza and reviewed the 71st Regiment on dress parade. Thus the pleasant afternoon ended. A salute was fired, the Marine Band struck up "Hail to the Chief," and the Presidential carriage rolled out through the great stone gate as the Stars and Stripes dropped from the flagstaff.

Lincoln was acquiring a taste for guns and for the company of the keen, earnest, loyal officer who knew so much about them. On May 24 the President was back again at the yard on a sad errand, that of viewing the remains of his young friend Colonel Elmer E. Ellsworth, who had been shot by a rebel innkeeper in Alexandria. On June 2 Lincoln brought along his Secretary of State, the bland, shrewd William H. Seward, and the eminent pair were saluted with twenty-one guns on leaving. Before long the President's visits were to become too frequent for such fanfare.

A great transformation was coming over Washington in those stirring days. Visitors who came in by train were warned of it by troop encampments on both sides, larger and closer together as the train neared the city. The fields around Washington resounded with shouts of command and the tramp of marching men and flashed with wheeling arms. Washington's magnificent distances turned out to be good for something. Parks of artillery studded the waste ground, and long trains of white-topped wagons filled up open spaces in the suburbs. Coming back to Washington that summer and driving up Pennsylvania Avenue, William H. Russell was astonished to find the drab thoroughfare he had last seen in March now "all red, white, and blue with flags, filled with dust from galloping chargers and commissariat carts; the side-walks thronged with people, of whom a large proportion carried sword or bayonet; shops full of life and activity." At the Navy Yard Dahlgren had gas fixtures put up, and he kept things humming day and night and Sundays. Working in shifts around the clock, the ordnance department at the yard was turning out two hundred shells, twenty-five thousand percussion caps, and thirty-five thousand Minié and musket balls every day, besides rifling cannon and casting, finishing and mounting howitzers.

Lincoln kept coming back to the Navy Yard, as if he drew fresh confidence from the grim efficiency he found there. Early in June Dahlgren was writing that "the President often comes to see the Yard, and treats me without reserve"; a few days later the commander recorded that he had dined at the White House. The journal entries indicate that the rail-splitter President was becoming a familiar figure in the shops and foundries of the Navy Yard.

In August, at Lincoln's prompting, the Navy Department offered Dahlgren command of the Bureau of Ordnance and Hydrography in place of Captain Harwood, a change which Harwood himself would have welcomed. Dahlgren chose to remain at the Navy Yard. "Washington," he reasoned, "had again become the center of great operations, and the importance conferred on the Yard made it equal to any naval trust that could be given." Besides, Dahlgren had no taste (and in the opinion of some officers, slight capacity) for administrative work. His heart was with the drawing board, the proving ground and the foundry.

Lincoln's visits to the yard continued. "The President came down in his usual off hand way," wrote Dahlgren on one occasion, "and sat some while in the office conversing with me on various matters." On fine days Lincoln and Dahlgren and sometimes Secretary Seward would go off on "a pleasant jaunt" down the river, but even the coming of cold weather did not keep Lincoln away from the yard. "Scarcely a day passes," Dahlgren noted, "but that I meet with our principal men, discussing our affairs, so that the company at Wash. never has been of like interest. The President everywhere—and always the same kind sagacious gentleman." Others at the yard shared Dahlgren's liking for their frequent visitor. As the President and "a part of his family" drove around the yard one day, "many of the worthy workmen expressed sentiments of high regard for the unostentatious and affable Chief Magistrate"—which was probably the *National Intelligencer's* sedate way of reporting a hearty cheer for Old Abe.

And yet Dahlgren could not escape occasional misgivings about his easy friendship with so high a personage as the President of the United States. One day in August 1861 Russell of the *Times* made one of his revealing visits to the Navy Yard and reported Dahlgren as being "rather inconvenienced by the perpetual visits of the President, who is animated by a most extraordinary curiosity about naval matters and machinery, so that he is continually running down 'to have a talk with Dahlgren.' " This deprecatory reference to Lincoln's visits must, on the face of it, have come from Dahlgren himself.

There was some reason for Dahlgren to shun the appearance of toadyism. Even the Secretary of the Navy, bewigged and bewhiskered Gideon Welles, whose patriarchal benignity led the President to nickname him "Father Neptune," suspected Dahlgren of being prone to that unattractive vice. Ever watchful of his authority, Mr. Welles further objected to the President's habit of passing him by and dealing directly with Dahlgren. While praising the "distinguished Commandant of the Washington Yard" to the skies in official reports, the Secretary relieved his feelings with some biting asides in his famous diary. There he characterized Dahlgren as "always attentive and much of a courtier." The deadly diarist gave the captain full credit for intelligence and ability and conceded that he would "gallantly sustain his chief anywhere," but added that "he is intensely ambitious, and, I fear, too selfish. . . . He shuns and evades responsibility."

There was much truth in Welles's estimate of Dahlgren, but whatever else he may have been, the captain was no hypocrite. His pleasure in the President's company was no less real because he displayed it to Lincoln himself; he confided it with equal or greater force to his own private journal.

And why did Lincoln, for his part, seek Dahlgren's company? Most of the reasons have already appeared: Dahlgren was a man of intelligence and vigor; he had proved his loyalty and earned the President's gratitude at a time when the fabric of government seemed to be dissolving; and his unsurpassed knowledge of ordnance made him useful, as will be seen, to a President as busy in such matters as was Abraham Lincoln.

Aside from Dahlgren's personal qualities, Lincoln found refuge and refreshment in the atmosphere and activity of the Navy Yard. This lure to yard excursions was clearly revealed by an episode in December 1861. When Lincoln came alone late that month and proposed a trip down the river, Dahlgren took him aboard the *Pensacola* to Craney Island and back again. "We had a quiet time," wrote Dahlgren of the trip. "The President looks grave and absorbed, and a little the worse for his cares." Lincoln rambled on about many things to Dahlgren, until at last the *Pensacola* anchored off Alexandria and the two men landed. "Well," said Lincoln gratefully as they stepped ashore, "*there* has been a pleasant day. Such a relief from politicians!"

CHAPTER 2

General Ripley

AT THE CORNER OF FOURTEENTH STREET and Pennsylvania Avenue, symbolically close to the Treasury Building, rose the six-story, quadrangular pile of Willard's Hotel, an establishment noted for its gargantuan meals and for the multitudes of place-seekers and place-bestowers who jammed its smoke-fogged corridors and lobbies. From this hive swarmed most of the petty politicians whose buzzings drove Lincoln to the Navy Yard; through its doors pushed men and women of many purposes, good, bad and inscrutable, as well as those who came merely to look on. One of the last-named category, Russell of the *Times,* estimated late in March 1861 that Willard's held "more scheming, plotting, planning heads, more aching and joyful hearts, than any building of the same size ever held in the world."

But the noise of Sumter startled the crowds, and the secession of Virginia sent them scurrying. Outside on the broad, ill-paved avenue, shops were shuttered, blinds pulled down, public buildings sandbagged and barricaded. Inside, an unwonted silence fell in the empty halls, broken by little more than the echoing footsteps of servants. The thousand guests had dwindled to fifty.

One of those nonconformists was a sharp-faced lieutenant colonel who had arrived in the capital on or about April 20, 1861, just as frightened crowds were jamming the last trains to Baltimore. It was not the first time in his forty-seven years of Army service that this West Pointer had swum against the current; he had done it often and seemed to find the exercise congenial. Despite his white hair and his sixty-six years, he had an air of soldierly vigor. His grave, regular features, his high forehead, even his rather formidably aquiline nose suited both his uniform and his stiffly formal bearing. To those despondent stragglers who passed him in Willard's desolate lobby, the old warrior must have been a bracing sight, a blue-clad incarnation of all the military virtues, an embodiment of the nation's proud past and a living reproach to its inglorious present.

His name was James Wolfe Ripley.

"There has been nothing remarkable in my life," Ripley insisted in his retirement, "nor do I intend to make it appear otherwise. I have simply endeavored to do a soldier's duty." And accordingly the aged veteran refused to furnish autobiographical information to those—chiefly editors of encyclopedias—who requested it. Largely because of old Ripley's inconvenient reticence, our view of young Ripley's first twenty-four years is confined to his birth in Connecticut in 1794, his entry into West Point in 1813, his commission as a second lieutenant of artillery in 1814 and his promotion to first lieutenant in 1818.

But an unguarded letter of reminiscence gives us a closer look at Lieutenant Ripley soon after his first promotion, and we see that by 1818 the twig had already bent precisely as the tree was to incline. Ripley wrote:

I have not forgotten that during the Creek War a requisition was made on a certain lieutenant of ordnance [meaning himself], stationed at the South, which he refused to comply with, on the ground that it had not reached him through the channel pointed out by the regulations. He soon after received a message from General [Andrew] Jackson, the substance of which was that if he did not make the issue immediately he would send a guard to arrest and bring him into camp, and there hang him on the first tree. The requisition was, of course, promptly complied with.

After his run-in with Old Hickory, Ripley served here and there on recruiting service. In 1823 he was back in Florida surveying

Indian tracts with Colonel James Gadsden (whose name was to be perpetuated thirty years later by the nation's final addition to its continental territory). In the following year Lieutenant Ripley married Sarah Denny, a Massachusetts girl, and presently began to dream of a more settled life than the Army offered. For some time he weighed his Army career against the possible charms of life as a Florida sugar planter. But he already had a decade and a half of military service to his credit; Colonel Gadsden warned him of the large capital he would need for the plantation and admonished him to "be not precipitate in resigning"; and it may be that Ripley's later repugnance to the idea of change had even then begun to stir. After a last trip to Florida in 1829 Ripley talked no more of leaving the Army.

By that time children were coming along, but of the nine born to James and Sarah Ripley, only three—all girls—lived to maturity. Ripley grieved for his children who died and gave his heart to those who lived. After little Roland died in 1838 at the age of four, the sorrowing father put his dead son's belongings in a small trunk and carried them about from post to post as long as he lived. In the early eighteen thirties he sent his small daughter Adie to the "model boarding school" of a shy, intense spinster named Dorothea Dix, who later became one of the great humanitarian reformers of the nineteenth century. "Mind that you do not spoil the idol," Miss Dix felt obliged to caution the captain; "she is very fond of indulgence."

After Andrew Jackson came to the White House, Ripley performed a service for his irascible commander that more than made up for the Seminole War blunder of a dozen years before. South Carolina presumed in 1832 to nullify the tariff of that year. Jackson, dead set on enforcing the law, strengthened the garrison of Fort Moultrie at Charleston. For a breathless moment civil war loomed. During those tense days at Fort Moultrie, Ripley, newly commissioned a captain, did well for himself and his country. That remarkable Charlestonian Joel Poinsett wrote President Jackson that Captain Ripley's "indefatigable exertions to prepare his post to resist the lawless attacks which threatened it, and his gentlemanly deportment have won the esteem and respect of the friends of the government in this city." And Major General Winfield Scott, who had been on the scene during the crisis, warmly commended Ripley to the Secretary of War:

He has no superior in the middle ranks of the Army, either in general intelligence, zeal or good conduct. . . . His arrangement for [Fort Moultrie's] defense was admirable. . . . No one left a higher reputation, either with our officers or the citizens of Charleston.

The years which did most to make James Ripley what he was in 1861 were those he spent as commanding officer of the national armory at Springfield, Massachusetts. Before Ripley came there in 1841, the armory had been more or less governed by a civil superintendent who could be removed by vote of the men and who was neither respected nor obeyed by them. Every day at eleven in the morning and four in the afternoon, the men would drop work, go down to the spring back of the shops and regale themselves with rum, cider brandy and impromptu wrestling matches. Ripley set out to restore military discipline and order to the establishment and immediately became the center of a storm that shook the town. When he shut down the plant for repairs and reopened it without hiring back his opponents among the workmen, fury burst on him; but he ignored it. He cut wages. He struck against a hostile newspaper by threatening to fire any armory workers who subscribed to it. There is evidence to suggest that he also used such threats to influence Springfield town meetings—and even to recruit converts to his own religious denomination, Episcopalianism. Three times during his superintendency the unmoved disciplinarian was hanged in effigy from the top of the armory flagpole.

Howl as they might against his methods, few denied that Ripley was improving the state of the armory. Amid a flurry of suits and countersuits he enlarged the grounds around the armory, graded them, landscaped them and began, after a while, to put up a heavy iron fence which still stands. He added new machinery, too, and during the last four years of his regime at Springfield more muskets were made every year than ever before, at a lower cost per arm.

The author Jacob Abbott paid a visit to the Springfield Armory in 1852, near the close of Ripley's superintendency, and was charmed by what he saw—the elegant buildings symmetrically arranged within a great square, the gardens and shrubbery, the broad, neat, tree-shaded walks. High on the brow of a hill stood Lieutenant Colonel Ripley's official residence, a new house of ample proportions, overlooking the town and the Connecticut Valley on one side and the armory grounds on the other. No rum-prompted roisterings broke the stillness of the scene, only the peaceful sounds of an occasional pedestrian or carriage, a distant train rumbling over a wooden viaduct or a dog barking somewhere in the town. In his article for *Harper's Monthly* Abbott paid admiring tribute to the "great resolution and energy" with which Ripley had brought about "the order, the system, the neatness, the almost military exactness and decorum which pervade every department of the works."

Thus pleasantly situated, Lieutenant Colonel Ripley must have felt a pang when his Springfield idyll came to an end in 1854. The *Springfield Republican,* just beginning its rise to national influence under Samuel Bowles, had supported Ripley vociferously; now it predicted that under Ripley's civilian successor, James Whitney, the armory would suffer from "just that system of political corruption which is and will ever be the great evil of the civil superintendence." There were, however, those who received the change philosophically, consoling themselves with a parade, a banquet and the firing of salutes. And as it happened, the *Springfield Republican's* prophecy was not fulfilled. Though Whitney, "a politician of considerable ability, and a gentleman of popular manners," might not have been able to bring order out of disorder as Ripley had done, he was able to maintain order once it was established. In his six years as superintendent the politician proved to be quite as efficient and successful as the soldier. What was more, Whitney avoided quarrels, while enlisting the support of the War Department, the politicians, the townspeople and Ripley himself. The armory had never been in better shape than it was in 1860, when the suave Whitney left to become Collector of the Port of Boston.

For a time after his departure from Springfield, Ripley traveled about inspecting arsenals; then Secretary of War Jefferson Davis sent him to California as Chief of Ordnance on the Pacific Coast. On June 23, 1860, the day Stephen Douglas was nominated for the Presidency by one fragment of the Democratic party, the pro-Southern Secretary of War, John B. Floyd, sent the redoubtable Yankee officer to Japan in charge of certain arms and military stores to be presented to the Shogun. Before returning, Ripley was supposed to "visit and examine professionally the most important arsenals and military manufactories in Europe and England." He never made the tour. When he heard of the Southern rebellion on his way back from the Japanese court, Ripley took the swiftest course for home. "Your country needs you," said a friend, as Ripley stepped from the gangplank of the *Persia*. "It can have me," he said, "and every drop of blood in me."

His entrance speech may have been a little florid, but his timing was perfect. Within a week after he checked in at Willard's, James Wolfe Ripley was Chief of Army Ordnance.

In retrospect it all seemed logical enough, even inevitable. The change, wrote an astute ordnance officer shortly afterward, was one "which I had expected as soon as I heard of Col. Ripley's return from abroad." And yet there was an element of chance in it, too.

In March 1861 Colonel Henry Knox Craig, Chief of Army Ordnance, was seventy years old. For thirty years he had served in the Ordnance Corps; for ten years he had been its head. He was honest, and he was loyal to the Union. But his age, his long years of peacetime service and the convenient proximity of an experienced assistant had all confirmed the colonel in habits of sloth and inefficiency. It was that fact which made his removal inevitable.

To understand why the change hung fire until Lieutenant Colonel Ripley was able to arrive on the scene, we must consider the new Secretary of War, Simon Cameron of Pennsylvania. Cameron was a tall, slender, thin-lipped man with a "marked Scotch face," keen gray eyes, a high forehead and luxuriant gray hair—a man of Senatorial mold, though affably democratic in manner. Indeed, he had been a Senator and was to be one again. Moreover, though he was no military man, he had been highly successful in business and so might have been expected to run his department competently. But Simon Cameron's political honors were tributes not to his statesmanship so much as to his skill in political bargaining, for he was a prime specimen of the nineteenth-century American political boss. And whatever the reason may have been, he showed no administrative talent in the War Department.

Throughout the unhappy negotiations which trapped Abraham Lincoln into giving Cameron the War Department, the aspirant seems to have regarded his objective less as an opportunity for patriotic service than as the deepest, fattest and fullest pork barrel within his reach at the time. Much of the new Secretary's attention during his first six weeks in office apparently went to rewarding past political services and making sure of future ones. His course, it must be said, had the incidental virtue of clearing out rebel sympathizers. So charitable was the Secretary to fellow Pennsylvanians that by mid-April the War Department had lost its traditional Southern character and resembled an outpost of Harrisburg. But the command of the Ordnance Bureau was not a matter of patronage; and though Cameron mended his political fences with admirable foresight, he had less thought for his duty to the nation.

At length, in the third week of April 1861, with Sumter fallen, Virginia out of the Union and most jobs disposed of, Simon Cameron's attention swung round to the two large facts that a Civil War had begun and that he was Secretary of War. On April 22 the comfort-loving functionaries of the War Department were startled and dismayed by an order from the Secretary: they were to keep the various bureaus open for business till five o'clock in the afternoon. This was war!

At that heroic moment the Secretary discovered that his Chief of Ordnance, having injudiciously yielded to a minor illness two or three days before, had left his duties to the temporary care of others.

Colonel Craig's absence at so trying a time annoyed Secretary Cameron exceedingly. He talked it over with General Winfield Scott, then commanding the Army, and the general agreed with him that Craig fell decidedly short of what the times demanded. Scott further pointed out that Lieutenant Colonel Ripley, next in seniority to Craig, was available at Willard's. Looking back to Ripley's competence and good judgment at Charleston some thirty years before, and perhaps also to his energy and firmness at Springfield, the general was moved to recommend him as a successor to Craig. And there may have been another recommendation. More than once in his career Ripley had shown a peevishness toward Democrats and an affinity for Whigs and Republicans which the politically minded Mr. Cameron must have thought eminently suitable, if he knew of it—as he probably did.

Thus originated Special Order Number 115, which appeared on April 23, 1861, and assigned James W. Ripley to the charge of the Army Ordnance Department "during the feeble health of its chief."

It was, perhaps, a measure of Craig's sluggish wit that he was surprised as well as aggrieved at being thus superseded. When he had recovered himself, he protested furiously; he believed the assigned reason for his removal to be "a pretense" shielding "the machinations and misrepresentations of unprincipled speculators and military officials." His view, incidentally, was shared by the Washington correspondent of the *New York Times*. The irate old soldier called upon the influence of his friend Postmaster General Montgomery Blair to win him reinstatement. In reply Craig was told by Cameron that "the exigency of the present crisis demands young, healthful, vigorous faculties, especially in your Department, & it is this necessity alone that makes the change, not my will." Craig kept fighting. He appeared before a board of officers, which generously pronounced him able to carry out the duties of Chief of Ordnance. Then he appealed to President Lincoln himself.

Craig wrote his note of protest to Lincoln just as the 7th New York Regiment reached Washington to break the spell of fatalistic despair which had settled like a choking fog over the city. Once the capital's fear of rebel capture had been dissipated, government activity quickened with fresh confidence. Beset by details, Lincoln had little leisure to investigate an old man's grievance. Indeed, there seemed no reason why he should; nor did there appear to be grounds for appointing anyone but Ripley as Craig's successor. The adjective "young" may have been somewhat strained as applied to a gentleman of sixty-six, but Ripley's faculties seemed to be "vigorous" as specified. And Craig could not qualify on either count.

To be sure, still younger and more vigorous men than Ripley were at hand, but seniority was not to be regarded lightly even by the President. Secretary Cameron's opposition gave Lincoln plenty of trouble a few weeks later when he ignored seniority in appointing an energetic and intelligent Quartermaster General. "Doubtless you begin to understand," wrote Lincoln to General Scott on that occasion, "how disagreeable it is to me to do a thing arbitrarily, when it is unsatisfactory to others associated with me." In rejecting Ripley as Chief of Ordnance, Lincoln would have run counter not only to Cameron, but to Scott also.

Lincoln therefore declared that he could not interfere with the arrangements which the War Department deemed essential for the efficiency of the service; his note passed from Cameron to Craig, and the old man temporarily subsided. Ripley, it seemed, was secure in his triumph.

Across Seventeenth Street from the small, brick War Department stood the "Northwest Executive" or Winder Building, where the Army Ordnance Department had its headquarters during the Civil War. The Winder Building (pronunciation as in "stem-winder") was a plain, boxlike, brick structure five stories high, with marble facing on the basement and a plaster coating over the remainder. In Lincoln's time the double doors of its main entrance opened onto the pavement—not, as now, onto a flight of stone steps—and there was an iron grillwork balcony along the second floor which made a convenient reviewing stand when soldiers of the Union paraded down the dusty street below. Otherwise the Winder Building stands today with much the same face it first presented to Washingtonians when Zachary Taylor lived in the White House across the street.

To find the Chief of Ordnance during the Civil War, a visitor climbed a wide, iron staircase to the second floor, where he found himself in a dark and dingy hallway—"a disgrace to any public office," wrote the Chief of Ordnance one day in 1864, shortly after President Lincoln had paid him a visit. In cloudy weather the hall was so murky that the office numbers were scarcely distinguishable, and if brighter weather revealed them it exposed also the places where paint had worn or peeled away from the grimy woodwork. Not until the last year of the war was the corridor brightened by fresh paint on the woodwork and frosted glass in the office doors. From the hallway the visitor entered a room with a cold, stone floor and an arched ceiling, a room crowded with desks and bookcases, gun models, ledgers and papers, clerks, officers and probably a disgruntled inventor or contractor. That was the office of the Chief of Ordnance.

And that was what James Ripley saw when on April 24, 1861, he pushed through the Winder Building's double doors, mounted its iron staircase and walked into his new office. The normal ruddiness of his stern face was perhaps somewhat heightened by triumph. If so, events would justify him. There he would rule through the climactic years of the Civil War, through First and Second Bull Run, through the Peninsula Campaign, through Shiloh and Fredericksburg, through Antietam and Chancellorsville, Vicksburg and Gettysburg. There he would stick while Scott gave way to McClellan, McClellan to Burnside, Burnside to Hooker and Hooker to Meade. And there, while thousands poured out their lives into the mud of Chantilly or Marye's Hill or the Chickahominy, the balance on which they had thrown such terrible weight would be tipped back by the scratch of an endorsement, the filing of a letter or the curt dismissal of an inventor.

Abraham Lincoln was to be protagonist and General Ripley

antagonist in the hidden struggle over new weapons which was played out in those fearful years and which is the principal subject of this book. In following the course of that struggle, we see the general in his least admirable role. What will be said of him in these pages will not be pleasant. Yet there was a great deal more to the arming of the Union than simply deciding which types of weapons were to be used; and since we are to haul James Ripley from the historical limbo in which he has been mercifully sheltered for ninety years, simple justice to the old man's memory calls for a few words about what he faced and what he did in those other respects.

All of Ripley's troubles were complicated by the peacetime office routine which he had inherited and which he was content to pass on intact to his successors. Perhaps this was because he also inherited Captain (later Colonel) William Maynadier, the grand vizier of the Ordnance Office, whose fifteen years of bureau experience made him indispensable to any chief with a decent respect for red tape. "From the time I took charge of the Ordnance Office till the day I left it," wrote Ripley later, "Colonel Maynadier occupied the same room and a desk beside me, and was cognizant of almost every business matter that occurred during that time." In spite of Maynadier—or because of him—the Ordnance Office fell behind in its paper work. Ripley was a year late in filing his monthly return for April 1861. Yet it did not occur to Ripley that procedure might be streamlined; he could think of no better remedy than frequent increases in the number of clerks.

Far worse than office inefficiency was the desperate shortage of trained ordnance officers which lasted all through the war and for which Ripley can scarcely be blamed. At the end of 1860 the Ordnance Corps had only fifty-nine officers, and many of the best dropped from the ranks when war came. Some joined the rebels; others, like Oliver O. Howard and Jesse Reno, took field commands in the Union Army. In the summer of 1861 an act of Congress permitted volunteer officers to perform field duties for the Ordnance Department. (The same act made Ripley a brigadier general.) In 1863 another act raised the corps's authorized officer strength to sixty-four. But sixty-four officers were far from enough to command all the arsenals, contract for arms, inspect arms, deliver arms, serve at the several field headquarters and at the same time consider the hundreds of new weapons urged on the Department.

The Northern state governors, especially Dennison of Ohio, Curtin of Pennsylvania and Morton of Indiana, joined in beating an epistolary tattoo on General Ripley's official skull. Governor Morton, for example, wrote the Secretary of War that he had "had embarrassment in transacting business with General Ripley from the beginning of the war." In the same letter, he denounced an offending officer as "superannuated, fretful, and slow, and not very much superior to General Ripley as a business man."

According to the governors, the troops of their respective states never had a fair share of arms, the arms they got were no good, and they did not get them soon enough. Not content with writing angry letters, the governors in the first few months of the war sent out state agents to compete with one another and with the Federal Ordnance Department in the purchase of arms. This drove prices sky-high. But the states were not dismayed, since the Federal Government was obliged to reimburse them for every cent expended.

As if the governors were not enough, the generals in the field gave a rousing performance of the "Anvil Chorus" with the Chief of Ordnance as the anvil. They clamored incessantly and often unreasonably for more and better arms. Some, like John C. Frémont and Benjamin Butler, took it on themselves to order arms directly, regulations notwithstanding. Perhaps Ripley derived some bleak consolation from the disclosure that General Frémont, the worst offender, had been royally swindled.

General Ripley might have made a stinging reply to some of those generals, but he forbore. Captain Kingsbury, Chief Ordnance Officer of the Army of the Potomac, was not so magnanimous. On one occasion he wrote caustically:

It may be observed that to a certain extent, the Ordnance Department has been compelled to supply both armies. Since the Army of the Potomac landed at Fort Monroe, fifty-three pieces of field artillery, with caissons, carriages, etc., and perhaps twenty-five thousand stands of small arms, have been transferred to the enemy, while a single 12 pdr. bronze howitzer, captured by General Butterfield, is the only field trophy yet rendered as an equivalent.

Antiquated routine, dearth of officers, carping governors, impatient generals, defeat in the field—troubles like these explain the short temper for which Ripley became notorious, and they make his achievements more notable. After all, however Union troops may have come out of battle, they seldom went in without a fair number of serviceable arms and a good supply of ammunition. After a spring and summer of heavy campaigning in 1862, for instance, the Chief of Artillery for the Army of the Potomac wrote:

The Ordnance Department in the main kept the supply constantly up to the demand, and by the cheerful and ready attention to complaints, and the prompt creation of the requisite means enabled me to withdraw inferior material, and substitute such as was found to be more reliable.

Full credit for this cannot be given to Ripley personally, but he deserves at least a share of it.

One more thing Ripley did which deserves a grateful remembrance: by his characteristically dogmatic insistence that all small arms be produced with interchangeable parts, he gave a powerful impetus to the American system of mass production.

These trials and achievements must all be weighed in Ripley's favor before judgment is delivered.

General Ripley did not have to seek out his President. Whenever possible, Abraham Lincoln preferred exercising his own legs to sending a messenger. Almost every day he could be seen strolling casually along the tree-shaded brick walk that ran from the White House to the War Department. What with his interest in weapons and the convenient proximity of the Winder Building, Lincoln became a frequent visitor in General Ripley's office. Once, for example, Lincoln got a letter from an eccentric Hoosier inventor and referred it to the War Department. There, a day or two later, Lincoln saw the same letter, now earmarked for General Ripley. So he took it along to the Ordnance Office, where an impressed clerk labeled it LEFT BY HIS EXCELLENCY THE PRESIDENT.

General Ripley was not a man to fawn on the great. He was always ready to point out bluntly to Lincoln wherein His Excellency erred—as in the case of Lieutenant Harris. Senator Ira Harris of New York was one of Lincoln's particular cronies. Early in September 1861 Lincoln gave the Senator's son an appointment away from the Ordnance Corps, to which the young West Pointer belonged. Ripley objected vigorously: the President's act was against regulations, worked "great injury to the operations of the Department" and deprived Lieutenant Harris of the professional experience he needed for future advancement in the Corps. Ripley could only explain Lincoln's aberration by supposing that these "serious objections . . . were probably not known or considered, when this paper was endorsed."

Ripley's readiness to take issue with Lincoln was not the work of a passing impulse. Later that month, a Maine man named Charles Weston asked to be made a military storekeeper in the Ordnance Department. Since Weston's brother George was an influential newspaper editor, Lincoln was inclined to listen sympathetically; he agreed to make the appointment if General Ripley would request it in writing. Weston, however, could get nothing more out of Ripley than a note conceding his probable competence for the job. This was not what Lincoln had wanted, but he wrote Secretary Cameron in support of Weston's appointment. Presently Weston came back to complain that someone else had got the job and to ask for some other appointment. Lincoln patiently wrote an account of the situation to George Weston, adding, "I went to Gen. Ripley, who told me plainly, he did *not* ask for his appointment, and could not be induced to ask for it. I have got the Sec. of War to promise to try to fix a place for him."

A place was duly fixed, and Weston became military storekeeper at the arsenal in Watertown, Massachusetts. There he vindicated Ripley's forebodings. Within a year Ripley had removed him for neglect of duty and disobedience to orders. Political wheels turned. Prodded by two Maine men, Vice-President Hamlin and Senator Lot Morrill, Lincoln looked into the case once more. The Assistant Secretary of War warmly assured the President that Weston's accounts were "not only in arrears, but in great confusion, demonstrating conclusively his unfitness for the office." After much delay, and probably with misgivings, Lincoln nevertheless reinstated Weston. "Through all these weary months," wrote the latter, "I never doubted, if you examined the case, you would do me justice." What General Ripley thought was not recorded, but then it scarcely needed to be.

Brother George Weston, having become editor of the *National Republican* in Washington, took up gun peddling on the side. In trying to palm off a lot of carbines on the Ordnance Office, Editor Weston became so "pertinaciously offensive" that he was "ejected, per nape of neck and *a posteriori*—hatless, breathless, and umbrella-less." Presently his editorials were thundering against Ripley's "disdainful refusal to examine and adopt the improvements in arms and *materiel* by which the superior civilization of the free States could have put down this semi-barbaric rebellion." But Ripley cared nothing for that. As early as the fall of 1861, Ripley had shown his determination to be cowed by no man, not even President Abraham Lincoln.

CHAPTER 3

Men Without Guns

THE NEWS OF FORT SUMTER'S FALL STRUCK
the North like a blow in the face of a sleeping giant. With a rush
men offered themselves to the Union. How many troops would
Ohio send? "The largest number you will receive," replied Governor Dennison. Iowa? "I am overwhelmed by applications," declared
Governor Kirkwood. Massachusetts? "How many regiments
will you take?" asked Governor Andrew. The response was magnificent, inspiring, a phenomenon. It was also embarrassing. "The
plain matter-of-fact is," confessed Lincoln, "our good people have
rushed to the rescue of the Government, faster than the government
can find arms to put into their hands."

When the war began, enough old-fashioned smoothbore muskets
were on hand to equip the army of two hundred and fifty thousand
then envisioned. The first task of the Chief of Ordnance was to get
those smoothbores into the hands of the troops who were pouring,
eager but unarmed, into Washington and into camps all over the
North. That job alone was formidable, what with the guns scattered
in arsenals from Maine to California and the railroads choked with
traffic, but it was only a start. For the day of the smoothbore gun
was past, and the day of the rifle had come.

Rifled guns had been born centuries before, when some gun-
maker discovered that an elongated projectile would hold straight
and true in flight if given a spin about its long axis. The spin could

37

be imparted by spiral grooves in the bore of the gun; and these grooves, as well as the process of making them, were called "rifling." Without that all-important spin, elongated projectiles would tumble and wobble through space, unpredictable in both course and impact. For that reason, most projectiles to that time had been made spherical. But the volume, and hence the weight, of a spherical projectile was limited by the diameter of the bore, whereas an elongated shot could be made much heavier, and therefore much more formidable in range, accuracy and penetration.

Until the middle of the nineteenth century, however, rifled small arms were loaded at the muzzle. The bullets had to fit tight enough to take the grooves, and ramming them home by main force was too conspicuous and protracted an operation to be feasible in open combat. But in 1855 the *Annual of Scientific Discovery* printed, to the edification of Abraham Lincoln among others, excerpts from the latest report of the Secretary of War*, which told of not just one but two promising answers to the problem of loading rifles. One solution had come with the recent development of efficient rifles which could be loaded at the breech. The other, favored by the Secretary, was a newfangled bullet with a concave base which expanded on firing, so as to take the rifle grooves. Using such bullets, especially one developed by Captain Minié of the French Army, the nations of the world began that year to adopt muzzle-loading rifles as their standard infantry arm, and one of those nations was the United States.

In 1861 smoothbore muskets, well polished, still looked smart enough on parade. They served as well as any other arm for practicing the drill manual. Some of them had value as historical curiosities. But when life itself depended on their performance, not even raw recruits would take them without protest, and the soldiers' complaints were backed by the home folks. "It is the opinion of all military men here," wrote Ripley's gadfly, Governor Morton of Indiana, "that it would be little better than murder to send troops

---

* None other than Jefferson Davis of Mississippi.

into battle with such arms as are a large majority of these [smooth-
bore] muskets altered from flint to percussion locks."

As a son of the frontier the President knew firsthand how much
better rifles were than smoothbores. When Lincoln's grandfather
was felled by an Indian bullet, he left behind him an "Old Smooth
bore" and two "Riffle" guns; if the grandson did not use those particular relics, he had ample opportunity to try others like them. A
knowledge of firearms came naturally with such a childhood as
Lincoln had known, in half-tamed country where game was both
plentiful and welcome. Seven-year-old Abraham Lincoln, armed
with a rifle that must have been longer than he was, fired through a
crack of his Indiana cabin and killed a wild turkey outside. He never
after pulled a trigger on any larger game, he said later; but that did
not necessarily mean that he ceased to use guns. In the days of
the Black Hawk War some sixteen years later, young Captain A.
Lincoln wrote that he had "Received, April 28, 1832, for the use of
the Sangamon County Company under my command, thirty muskets,
bayonets, screws and wipers, which I oblige myself to return upon
demand."

And Lincoln had some feeling for the beauty of a good weapon.
At his own expense during the Civil War, he once presented the
King of Denmark with a pair of Colt revolvers inlaid with gold in
"beautiful arabesque, with representations of the mechanic arts,
agriculture and commerce elegantly designed." When Seth Kinsman, the California hunter, visited the White House, an artist
sketched Lincoln holding the hunter's long rifle and regarding it
with evident pleasure. On the sketch is scribbled a note: *Titivate
Lincoln.*

As an inventor's agent once remarked, President Lincoln was
"not entirely a novice in such matters."

It seemed, however, that even as late as the spring of 1861 some
authorities did not see eye to eye with Lincoln on the subject of
rifles. "Colonel Ripley says, Mr. Lincoln," remarked a White House

secretary, "that men enough can be killed with the old smoothbore and the old cartridges, a ball and three buckshot."

"Just so," replied Lincoln. "But our folks are not getting near enough to the enemy to do any good with them just now. We've got to get guns that'll carry further."

Lincoln's views on this subject and his readiness to take a hand in weapons policy were brought home to Ripley a few days after that hot-tempered warrior took charge of the Ordnance Office.

Early in May 1861, the 1st Vermont Volunteer Regiment was alarmed by rumors that the Ordnance Department was about to foist a lot of worthless Belgian muskets on it, even though in New York, where the Regiment was due next day, a cargo of new Enfield rifles waited in the harbor. On the appeal of Governor Fairbanks, a Vermont-born Treasury official named Lucius Chittenden took up the cause of the Green Mountain boys.

War Department officials sent Chittenden to see the Chief of Ordnance. At the Winder Building, Chittenden found his quarry "hedged in by more successive guards than the Secretary of War." Vermont's champion plunged valiantly through the cordon and into the office of Ripley himself, "an elderly gentleman . . . with very white hair and a very red face." Cutting short Chittenden's apologies for the intrusion, Colonel Ripley asked the visitor what he wanted.

"An order from the War Department on the proper office in New York," Chittenden said, "to deliver one thousand Enfield rifles to the governor for the use of the First Vermont Regiment."

Ripley's face "deepened into crimson." "Such an application is unheard of!" he snapped. "Why was it not made regularly through the Secretary of War?" Before Chittenden could answer, Ripley continued fiercely: "It is too late. The guns for that regiment have been issued and the orders signed. They will not now be changed."

"I supposed the order had been issued," said Chittenden. "It is that order which I wish to have changed. I know that the Department has Enfield rifles; the Vermonters want them. . . . If I cannot get the order for them here or elsewhere, I must go to the President."

At this, Ripley was speechless. His face and hands turned to "a dark purple" as he struggled to express his feelings. He bounded from his chair with a rush which the startled Vermonter thought for a moment was aimed at him; but the impetus carried the colonel to a corner of the room where stood an old Springfield flintlock musket altered to the use of percussion caps. Except for its percussion lock, Chittenden noted, "it was the identical arm which frightened the crows from the cornfields in my boyhood."

The old man seized the gun in both hands, raised it above his head and shook it furiously. "These volunteers don't know what they want!" he roared when he had recovered his voice. "There is the best arm that was ever put into the hands of a raw volunteer! When he throws that away, as they generally do, he does not throw away twenty-five dollars' worth of government property!"

Retorting huffily that Vermonters had no use for guns to be thrown away, Chittenden quit the room. Back in the War Department he got the order for the rifles without further difficulty. "The fact that President Lincoln could be reached in this case was controlling," the triumphant civilian wrote in his recollections of the incident.

In this instance, Ripley was not as obtuse as he seemed. What the White House secretary had said about him was superficially true. So long as Ripley had to pass out smoothbores, he sang their praises. To an importunate general, for example, Ripley wrote: "Except for fighting at long distances I consider the smooth bore more efficient. It is equally as good with the bayonet, and is also suitable for use with ball and buckshot, which is not the case with rifled arms." But notice that he was writing only about action at close range. To suppose that Ripley recommended smoothbores as the basic infantry arm would be to do the old man an injustice. After all, the 1855 Springfield rifle, the first rifle adopted for the general use of United States troops, had been largely designed during Ripley's regime at the armory, and Ripley was intensely proud of it.

If the Chief of Ordnance seemed to entertain an archaic affection for smoothbores, it was because he had little else at the moment to give the troops. There were not enough Springfield rifles and rifle muskets on hand to arm one regiment in ten. In his heart Ripley knew as well as Lincoln that sooner or later all smoothbores would have to be replaced by rifles. What he did not know was where to get those rifles.

Government manufacture offered little immediate relief. In April 1861, after the fortunes of war had brought destruction on the United States Arsenal at Harper's Ferry, Virginia, only one important small-arms manufactory remained in government hands. This was Ripley's old demesne at Springfield, Massachusetts. Toward the end of April Lincoln ordered the building of a government small-arms factory at Rock Island, Illinois, but progress there was slow until 1863. During the arms shortage of 1861-1862, therefore, government-made rifles had to come from Springfield. And when war began, the armory's capacity was only twelve hundred rifles per month.

What about private manufacturers, then? After June 1861 a contract for small arms was handed to almost every firm that would accept one at fairly reasonable rates, and subcontracts for rifle parts were filled by firms that had heretofore made solar compasses, rules and levels, bells or sewing machines. "Every possible exertion is being made," insisted Ripley, "to obtain additional supplies by contract, by manufacture, and by purchase." But the special imported iron needed for gun barrels was scarce, as also skilled labor, and machine tools were at a premium. In laboring from June of 1861 through June of 1862, American manufacturers brought forth less than fifteen thousand rifles.

One other possibility remained: foreign arsenals. In the early weeks of the war Ripley proposed to buy a hundred thousand arms in Europe to supplement those on hand and being made. Confederate authorities had the same idea, and their overseas agents were already hard at work. But Secretary Cameron thought such measures extravagant and unnecessary. In his opinion, the Union had too many soldiers for its guns, rather than too few guns for its soldiers. As late as July he was saying, "We have already an army composed of more than 300,000 men, a number greater than we need for the actual crisis." As a loyal son of industrial Pennsylvania, moreover, Cameron insisted that all guns be bought at home.

The distractions of politics and patronage soon crowded Ripley's foreign-arms proposal out of Cameron's mind. Ripley spoke once more, scaling down his recommendation to fifty thousand arms, and then subsided helplessly. For more than three precious months Simon Cameron held in check the tremendous power of the United States Government to pre-empt the European arms market and forestall the arming of the Confederacy. That delay was one of the costliest blunders of the war—which is saying a great deal.

From the start Abraham Lincoln had a keener appreciation of the need for more rifles than did his Secretary of War. "While in the Ordnance Office," wrote Dahlgren in May, "the President came in with the Secretary of State, seemingly on ordnance matters. The President was exercised about communications by the Potomac, the quantity of arms, &c. I hinted deficiency of nitre and powder."

For a while, Lincoln left the purchasing of arms to Cameron and Ripley. But the *distribution* of arms, so long as all needs could not be satisfied, was a matter of high military and political policy, and Lincoln did not shrink from assuming his share of that burden. His policy was consistent: in the arms-distribution dilemma of 1861, President Lincoln stood forth as special pleader for the border states.

In this Lincoln took care not to seem dictatorial. He had already learned that Ripley could get his back up in a hurry if rubbed the wrong way; and with Ripley, all ways seemed wrong. So Lincoln sought Ripley's help as a friendly favor, rather than as obedience to a command. Early in May, for example, when Lincoln urged Ripley to send arms to the Kentucky borders of Indiana and Illinois, he added soothingly: "Of course you understand this subject better than I; and therefore this is to be taken as a general suggestion, and, in no sense as dictation." All the same, Lincoln was in earnest.

Lincoln's determination to arm the loyal men of the border states was consistent with his kindly nature. He knew that in those regions the crisis had visited neighborhoods and even families with an agony of internal suspicion and hate. He knew that brave men risked much for the Union in the midst of secessionist communities. And he never forgot that he himself was a son of that middle border. But another consideration guided him more strongly than sympathy. Lincoln realized that the states through which the great division ran were vital to the Union in the most severely practical sense, both politically and militarily.

Of all the border states, Kentucky was first in the delicacy of its balance between Union and Confederacy, and first also in Lincoln's heart. Through a pass in Muldraugh's Hill, a stern upthrusting of limestone some miles south of Louisville, ran a fast, clear stream called Knob Creek, and on that creek had been the farm that was Abraham Lincoln's first remembered home. Lincoln's childhood on Knob Creek had not been easy. His earliest memory was of a disastrous freshet that washed out his father's spring planting. The boy's food was coarse, his clothes homemade. Winter cold struck through cracks in the cabin walls. But Lincoln's Knob Creek years went by in the sparkling time of life when everything new was good and all was new—warm sunlight and cool earth, tumbling water and still cliff, green-sprouting corn and slow-falling leaves. His mother, who had been Nancy Hanks, was alive in those years. Though Lincoln left Kentucky when he was seven, Kentucky never left him; and his wife Mary in 1861 still called him "the tall Kentuckian."

The bitterness that split the nation in 1861 ran like a raw gash through the length of Kentucky. Muldraugh's Hill was secession country. Abraham Lincoln was hated and reviled along Knob Creek. This he well knew. In 1860 he had written a Kentuckian correspondent ironically: "You suggest that a visit to the place of my nativity might be pleasant to me. Indeed it would. But would it be safe? Would not the people lynch me?"

As war began Kentucky hung trembling in the balance, and many of her people hugged the vain hope of neutrality. But not all. There was danger and daring in that country. Once it had been the "Dark and Bloody Ground," and now it seemed on its way to being so again. From loyal citizens of Adair County came an appeal to Lincoln. "Being as we think in danger of our lives living in Secession neighborhood," they wrote, "we . . . call upon you to furnish us at least one good musket each for the purpose of defending the Union and you in your Constitutional rights." From Garrettsburg near the Tennessee line came a letter for Secretary Cameron. In that hotbed of secessionists was a secret company of Union men, "all excellent marksmen," who begged for a hundred good rifles. "We are now almost entirely unsuspected," they wrote, "and intend as soon as we receive them to seize by surprise the camp and stores of a party of about 75 Secessionists encamped near the borders of Tennessee."

Lincoln was already moving in the matter. Remembrance and compassion urged him on, but he had a larger motive still. "To lose Kentucky is nearly the same as to lose the whole game," he reasoned. "Kentucky gone, we can not hold Missouri, nor, as I think, Maryland. These all against us, and the job on our hands is too large for us. We would as well consent to separation at once, including the surrender of this capitol." On the fate of Kentucky hung the life of the nation.

The chief difficulty aside from getting the arms, as Lincoln saw it, was to see that they were "put in the hands of friends, and not of enemies." At first Lincoln depended for this on three trustworthy and loyal Kentuckians, one of them his old friend Joshua Speed of Louisville. Then early in May, he found his right-hand man in the Kentucky matter, a remarkable naval lieutenant named William Nelson.

Lieutenant Nelson was himself a tall Kentuckian, six feet four inches in height, weighing three hundred pounds, with a deeply tanned face and bushy black hair. For all his bulk he was active in both mind and body. He read widely and could repeat verbatim page after page of his favorite authors. He was also fluent in several languages, including the variety known as billingsgate, which at last cost him his life at the hands of an insulted Union general. Most important of all to Lincoln just then, the extraordinary Kentuckian was stanchly pro-Union. Russell of the *London Times* met him at dinner in Washington and thought him "the very largest naval officer I have seen in company. . . . He inveighed fiercely, and even coarsely, against the members of his profession who had thrown up their commissions. . . . Sumter and Pickens are to be reinforced [this was in March], Charleston is to be reduced to order, and all traitors hanged, or he will know the reason why; and, says he, 'I have some weight in the country.' "

Visiting Kentucky that spring, Nelson found disunionists holding most of the state's guns. He was not the sort to wring his hands and weep. Instead, as soon as he returned to Washington, he called on Lincoln to warn him that arms must be given to the Union men of Kentucky. Lincoln assented heartily, and then, pointing out the risks involved, asked expectantly where he could find the man for the job. "Cast your eyes," said the fierce lieutenant, "on a little man of my size." That was all Lincoln needed; he began at once to discuss the details of Nelson's mission.

Nelson's task was too delicate for written credentials. Kentucky secessionists might make too much capital from such orders if they got hold of them. So Lincoln gave Nelson a verbal message for Joshua Speed, and, as soon as the President had ordered five thousand muskets sent to Cincinnati, Nelson took the train to Louisville. There he convinced Speed of his genuineness, and by mid-May the guns were being quietly passed out where they would do the most good. Early in June, Lincoln sent five thousand more muskets to Nelson and another thousand to be distributed by ex-Congressman Emerson Etheridge of Tennessee. In July the Navy sent its burly alumnus three hundred Sharps breech-loading rifles and a Dahlgren howitzer.

Lincoln's gamble paid off handsomely and at once. Early in June he got a letter from his old acquaintance Brigadier General George B. McClellan, then commanding the Department of the Ohio: "The issue of the arms to Kentuckians is regarded by the staunch men as a masterpiece of policy on your part, & has—if I may be permitted to say so—very much strengthened your position among them." Lincoln's stratagem was not so abrupt as to nudge his native state off her fence and into the Confederacy. Yet Kentucky secessionists were wholesomely aware of what was going on; in fact, the disloyal element considerably overestimated the number of arms reaching loyal hands and were daunted in proportion.

In their anger and frustration disunionists cursed what they dubbed "Lincoln guns." Loyal Kentuckians caught up the name as readily as they had caught up the muskets and shouldered their "Lincoln guns" with confident pride. Joshua Speed wrote Lincoln jubilantly, "We are fast getting them on the hip." He went on to tell his old friend the merry story of how pro-Southern Governor Beriah Magoffin had paid sixty thousand dollars for arms to give secessionists, only to find that the guns had no touchholes, could not be fired and, worst of all, had been foisted on him by a sly Yankee.

Meanwhile, sharing Cameron's cheerful assumption that the war would be just a summer outing, the North clamored for an immediate advance into Virginia. The pressure proved irresistible, and on July 16 General Irvin McDowell led a gaily confident army out of Washington in the direction of Richmond. Sun glinted from the army's serried bayonets, but misgivings darkened its general's heart. His fears were realized: at the end of the road lay, not Richmond, victory and peace, but Bull Run, defeat and the real beginning of war.

July 21 was a fine, quiet Sunday. At about six in the evening Lincoln drove down to the Navy Yard for the ride and, as Dahlgren rode with him, remarked that the armies were hotly engaged and the other side getting the worst of it. When he got back to the White House, Lincoln found that Secretary Seward had been there, haggard and hoarse, with news that the battle was lost and the army in full retreat. Darkness came, and rain. Lincoln lay sleepless on a sofa. Midnight found him listening to stories of the disaster. By daybreak what had been the Union's hopeful army began streaming past, now only a rain-soaked mob.

Four days later Lincoln put George B. McClellan in command of the army. Lincoln's engineer friend of Illinois Central days had youth, vitality, brains, self-confidence and even some small victories to his credit. He was short, like Napoleon, but broad-shouldered and muscular; his eyes were light gray, his complexion ruddy, his chin firm and his auburn hair so thick it looked like a wig. No better choice could have been made for the emergency. McClellan was a born organizer, a meticulous planner, who could simultaneously command discipline and enthusiastic liking among his men. Later, when McClellan's excessive caution began playing into rebel hands, Lincoln spoke rather irritably of his engineer friend's "special talent for developing a stationary engine." But in the days after the rash and ill-prepared excursion to Bull Run, McClellan's tireless preoccupation with details met the nation's great need.

Among its other consequences, the defeat at First Bull Run brought about a salutary change in War Department thinking. Within the week Secretary Cameron was writing the chairman of the Senate Military Affairs Committee that "in order to supply arms to the five hundred thousand volunteers to be accepted by the President, a further appropriation of $10,000,000 will be needed immediately."

Government arms production was still meager. Despite Ripley's repeated urgings and advice, despite the doubling of the working force and an increase in the working day to eleven and a half hours, the output of the Springfield Armory during August was only four thousand rifles. In that month, through Ripley's influence, the civilian superintendent was replaced by an energetic ordnance officer named Major Alexander B. Dyer; and under Dyer production rose to ten thousand a month by January 1862. That was still not enough to equip an army of half a million men and keep it equipped through a number of difficult and mostly unsuccessful campaigns.

After Bull Run, therefore, Ripley returned to his initial views on foreign purchases, carrying Cameron with him. Lincoln moved even faster. Before July was over the President had dispatched Colonel George L. Schuyler to Europe as his special agent, with two million dollars for the purchase of arms.

By then most of the first-class arms had gone to the Confederacy or other buyers, and prices for the leavings had soared. Furthermore, Schuyler got little support from the War Department. Nevertheless, Lincoln's agent sent back about a hundred and twenty thousand rifles, mostly Austrian and Saxon, as well as thousands of sabers and revolvers and ten thousand cavalry carbines. Presently the War Department stirred itself, and by the summer of 1862 the United States Government had bought another six hundred thousand European arms.

A heavy price in lives and money had to be paid for Simon Cameron's wasted months. Before Bull Run the War Department had moved too slowly in ordering foreign arms. Afterward it moved too fast—or at any rate, too recklessly. Cameron trustingly referred contract hunters to his fellow Pennsylvanian, Assistant Secretary Thomas A. Scott, who fired off orders broadside. Though Cameron gave him standing instructions to consult Ripley on quality and price, Scott wrote off the Chief of Ordnance as a querulous old fogy, remarking that "if the gun business were left to General Ripley, the government would get no guns."

Notwithstanding Scott's mockery, Ripley himself was temporarily stampeded. He gave out contracts without advertising for bids or even requiring written proposals; and he let certain ordnance officers buy up all the arms they could find, without regard to price.

Easy profits found ready takers. Middlemen with no qualification but political influence gorged at the War Department trough. United States Senator James F. Simmons of Rhode Island charged one contractor a ten-thousand-dollar fee in return for wangling a rifle contract. Henry Wikoff, a debonair adventurer who had captivated Mrs. Lincoln with his flattery, complained to Cameron about

General Ripley's "obstinate imbecility" in refusing to give him a rifle contract. "Please order these contracts to be made forthwith," Wikoff demanded; and Cameron complied.

In New York men deserted the stock market and dropped all other business to get in on the arms-contract bonanza; and imported guns, or promises of them, were offered the government by "lawyers, brokers, hatters, and apothecaries." In Europe, reported the junketing politician Thurlow Weed, "the knowledge that our government needed arms has sharpened the cupidity and wits of all who deal in them." By early 1862 contracts had been given out for 1,903,000 rifles and muskets, more than half of which were never delivered, and charges of corruption and waste had swelled from a whisper to a general uproar.

Some of the foreign arms that were purchased turned out to be rank swindles, useless, if not positively dangerous to the men who carried them. Hard pressed by demands from the field, Ripley's undermanned Ordnance Department sometimes snapped up arms on hasty inspection, and far too many of those worthless guns found their way into the hands of troops. Lincoln himself heard about them from the colonel of the 101st Illinois Regiment, an outfit which included many personal friends of the President. "The Guns with which we are supplied are entirely useless," Colonel Fox wrote Lincoln. "They are what is termed the Austrian Rifle Musket, evidently from their Manifacture were intended for sale but not for use. We have 720 of them, and not more than one half of them can be discharged."

Yet these purchases of foreign arms, tragically belated as they were, marred as they were with corruption and recklessness, had been worth making.

More than half of the Union regiments that went into battle before the fall of 1862 were armed with foreign rifles and muskets. The 104th Pennsylvania, for example, got Austrian rifles early in 1862, found them "rough, but good and reliable," and carried them for the rest of their three years in service. The 23rd Pennsylvania started out with Harper's Ferry rifled muskets, "most miserable weapons, in bad condition and the hardest kind of kickers." They were overjoyed to exchange them for Austrian rifles. "Most efficient firearms" they were called by the regiment's historian, who recalled firing sixty rounds from his Austrian rifle at Malvern Hill without any trouble.

Thus European arms helped sustain the Union through its darkest hours.

For the most part Lincoln kept clear of the arms-contract mess; reading a parody of the Episcopal church service in which his name was invoked as the Lord's, Lincoln was amused most of all by the line, "The noble army of contractors, praise Him!" But there was heavy pressure on him. In the office of a White House secretary, for example, stood a musket rejected by the Austrian government. The gun was to be "a speculation for somebody," wrote the secretary, "if the agent who represents a shipload like it can induce the President to force an unwilling Ordnance Bureau to buy them."

In September 1861 came a letter from Herman Boker and Company of New York City offering a hundred thousand European rifled muskets, and on the letter Lincoln scribbled a note to Cameron: "I approve the carrying this through carefully, cautiously, and expeditiously." It was not Lincoln's fault that Cameron accepted the Boker offer without consulting Ripley and thus fell into the hands of sharpers.

Two days later Lincoln heard of an abortive scheme to buy European arms, inflate the price by thirty or forty per cent and sell them to the government. He listened to the two men who had planned to split the profits, and then he made a memo which set down the twists and turns of the affair with troubled particularity.

A different case was that of two New York contractors, Josiah Heddon and John Hoey, who had agreed to deliver fifty thousand Prussian arms by January 15, 1862. Twenty-eight thousand were delivered by that time, accepted and paid for; but the remainder, which arrived only ten days after the deadline, were refused by the Ordnance Department simply on the grounds of time. Presently the Ordnance Department repented its fit of punctilio, and an old friend of Lincoln's, Congressman George Ashmun of Massachusetts, asked the President to authorize receipt of the Heddon-Hoey guns. Lincoln never let red tape stand in the way of justice and the national interest. Carefully explaining the situation to the Secretary of War, he added: "If this statement be true, and these men acted in good faith, I think they should not be ruined by the transaction, but that the guns should be accepted & paid for." When the Secretary hesitated, Lincoln gave a flat order to receive the arms, and justice was done.

Nothing could have shown Lincoln the need for rifles more poignantly than the tragedy at Ball's Bluff in October 1861. There, a few miles up the Potomac from Washington, Union troops armed with smoothbores had been led across the river into foolhardy battle against heavy odds. There they had fallen and died under the deadly accurate fire of rebel rifles, some of which were breechloaders made in Massachusetts before the war. And there a rebel sharpshooter had sent his rifle bullet smashing into the brain of Lincoln's old friend Colonel Edward Baker, a friend so dear that his name had been given to Lincoln's second son. When the telegraph chattered news of Colonel Baker's death, tears ran down Lincoln's cheeks, and he stumbled as he left the room. This, he said long after, was the keenest blow of the war for him, smiting him "like a whirlwind from a desert." At Baker's funeral Lincoln saw his dead friend's bullet-torn uniform—pathetic evidence of what rifles could do.

Lincoln did more than grieve. On the day after the funeral he strode down the slope of lawn south of the White House and through an unkempt waste lot called the Treasury Park, stopping finally at the edge of an inlet where the abandoned city canal joined the Potomac. With him walked an inventor named W. B. Chace and the Secretary of the Interior, a smooth-shaven Hoosier politician named Caleb Smith. One of the three carried a smoothbore musket, the sort of weapon which had been of so little help to the men who had died upstream at Ball's Bluff and whose bodies were still being found within sight of the White House. Chace claimed to have a bullet that would make such smoothbores as good as rifles, and he probably spared Lincoln none of the details as the trio made their way toward the water. Once there, Chace began firing specimens of his bullet in alternation with regulation bullets. A chill wind blew acrid white smoke out over the Potomac. Standing near by, President Lincoln scanned the leaden river and calculated distances as bullets struck spurts of white from its cold, gray surface; it seemed plain enough to him that the new bullets outdid the old. As he walked back to the White House, a cautious hope rose in his heart.

The mere thought of General Ripley already seemed to paralyze inventors. "I am aware," wrote Chace to Lincoln three days later, "that I ought to make application to the Ordnance Bureau, but the stereotyped reply of the Chief of that Bureau, 'han't got time,' will be certain to be given to any request for a Board of Examination for any purpose." Lincoln probably read the letter with a smile, recognizing the accuracy of Chace's prediction. Without bothering to comment on the inventor's charge, Lincoln turned the letter over and wrote his own report on the back: "I saw the projectile mentioned within, fired alternately, with the ordinary round ball cartridges, from the same smooth-bore musket, at the same elevation, and the projectile carried a full third, or more, farther upon the water of the Potomac than the round ball. I therefore believe it is worthy of a regular test." And he sent the paper over to the War Department.

A clue to Ripley's reception of the document survives. All letters coming into the Ordnance Office were regularly summarized in ponderous registers. But the entry for Chace's letter contains only the date and sender, the beginning of a summary, and a penciled note: "Handed back to Gen Ripley without copying." To General Ripley's way of thinking, it seems, his commander in chief had tacitly endorsed a reflection on his competence, and the clerk's puzzled memorandum suggests a picture of the choleric veteran snatch-

ing away the letter before his ignominy could be spread on the
record.

Once Ripley had read that letter, Chace was not likely to win
favored treatment from the Ordnance Office. To be sure, the War
Department had given Ripley direct orders to test the bullet, as
recommended by Lincoln, and so that was done. But no report survives, and no Chace bullets were bought. Perhaps the Union suffered little loss thereby. In the ninety years since, no one has
achieved what Chace claimed; and in all likelihood, therefore,
neither had Chace.

In his quest for better small arms Lincoln wasted no time waiting
for a report on the Chace bullet. Before the week was out he had
turned his attention to an offer made by Solomon Dingee and Company of New York City to deliver fifty thousand Austrian rifles, supposed to be as good as English Enfields, at nineteen dollars apiece.
Of all contracts for European arms, this was the one that was to in-
volve Lincoln most deeply.

Lincoln was not alone in welcoming the Dingee offer. General
McClellan, insistent on the best in weapons as in everything else,
thought the offer a bargain, and both Lincoln and Cameron caught
his enthusiasm. An early obstacle arose, however, in the person of
the Ordnance Department's representative at New York City, Major
Philip V. Hagner, commandant of the New York Arsenal—"a
charming gentleman socially, and a cranky and perverse autocrat
officially." From the first Hagner seemed to detect a fishy odor
about the Dingee proposal. He hung back from making the order
until pressure from above became irresistible. And when the first
delivery fell short of contract specifications as to caliber, weight,
material and finish, Hagner cancelled the contract *in toto,* even
though most of the guns were serviceable.

Dingee and his allies were too much for the cranky major. General McClellan, for one, supported the contractor. "Entire regiments
and brigades of this army ought to be rearmed at once," the general
protested, "and all the available arms in the country should be sent

hither immediately." Lobbyists for the Dingee Company descended on Washington in force, and its business agent laid siege all day to the President's office. Finally Dingee engaged the services of Oliver S. Halsted, Jr., universally known as "Pet" Halsted, a fast-talking New Jersey lawyer who already had some influence with Abraham Lincoln; and Halsted put the case before the President.

According to Halsted, Lincoln expressed his "decided disapprobation" of Hagner's action and declared that he "wanted substantial justice done." At the lobbyist's suggestion, Lincoln ordered Major Hagner to accept all the Dingee arms that lived up to the letter of the contract, reject those that were actually unserviceable and buy the remainder at a reasonable valuation. Three days later Hagner and Dingee agreed on a schedule of prices for the last category.

When Hagner left to serve on a commission investigating arms contracts, a new complication arose. Hagner's place as autocrat of the New York arsenal was taken by Captain Silas Crispin, "a man of erratic temper, a consistent drinker, and a bachelor." Instead of adhering to Hagner's price schedule for substandard arms, Crispin insisted on appraising each shipment as it came in. Once more Dingee brought Pet Halsted's powers into play. Presently the lobbyist stalked into General Ripley's office flourishing Lincoln's written decision on the point at issue:

It is said that in the case of the contract of S. Dingee & Co. in relation to arms a dispute has arisen as to the proper construction of a clause in an order signed by me, which clause is in these words: 'and that all not conforming thereto' (the contract) 'be appraised by the ordnance officer at New York, and received at such price as he may determine.'

This order was prepared with reference to *a definite number* of arms expected to be delivered within a *definite time,* and not in reference to an *indefinite* number to be delivered in an *indefinite time.* I certainly did not expect that under the clause in question a lot of guns would be appraised at one price at one time, and another lot of precisely the same quality appraised at different prices at another time. I expected that when under the clause the price of a particular quality of gun was fixed it would stand throughout the transaction, neither going down or up. I still think this is the just construction.

That point was settled, but Crispin had another string to his bow. When some of the Dingee arms arrived after the delivery deadline, the crusty captain declined to receive them. Halsted promptly informed General Ripley that "this is one of that class of futile objections which *I do know* was intended to be forborne and overcome by the President as immaterial, unjust, and unbecoming [to the government]." After offering to deliver Enfields in lieu of the rejected arms, Halsted added, "Should it be deemed necessary to see the President again, I will cheerfully accompany the general, or get the President to make an appointment to see us together at an early day." The Enfields were accepted.

It would seem, however, that even with Pet Halsted's help, Dingee's enterprise was not a complete success. As late as December 1862, Halsted was still asking for an extension of delivery deadlines. And Ordnance Office records through 1867 show total payments to Dingee of only $385,947.37—which would account for less than half of the original contract.

Such was the course of Lincoln's sole essay at personally directing a transaction in foreign arms. Environed with difficulties, he had made no misstep. On the one hand, despite the outcries of McClellan and the blandishments of Dingee's business agent, Lincoln had refused to take unserviceable weapons; on the other, despite the hairsplitting protests of Hagner and Crispin, he had accepted serviceable arms at fair prices. He saw, in short, to the core of the question: what would best advance the cause of the Union.

Through the summer of 1861 Lincoln kept an eye on the arms situation in Kentucky. "The Union men of Kentucky are still *pleading* for arms with which to defend themselves," wrote Colonel Lovell H. Rousseau from a camp near Louisville on July 26. "The distribution already made has saved her from Secession. A further distribution will bring her with whatever power she has into the fight." Lincoln was ready to act. In early August, Tennessee secessionists were getting ready to invade southern Kentucky. When two delegates from the imperiled region got no satisfaction from their

Congressman or from Secretary of War Cameron, Lincoln ordered a thousand arms put at the disposal of each.

At the same time Lincoln kept his perspective. In September, for example, a wire came to him from Joshua Speed in Louisville: "Men plenty but no arms." On the same day came one from Governor Gamble of Missouri: "For God's sake get me arms for infantry and cavalry." And Lincoln gave priority to Missouri.

It was Governor Morton of Indiana who stung Lincoln into an explanation of the arms situation and his policy toward it. For weeks Lincoln had done what he could to pacify the excitable governor, who howled incessantly for arms for both his own state and neighboring Kentucky. "Morton is a good fellow," Lincoln remarked wryly, "but at times he is the skeeredest man I know of." At last, toward the end of September, Lincoln told the clamorous governor what was what:

I wish you to believe of us (as we certainly believe of you) that we are doing the very best we can. You do not receive arms from us as fast as you need them; but it is because we have not near enough to meet all the pressing demands; and we are obliged to share around what we have, sending the larger share to the points which appear to need them most. We have great hope that our own supply will be ample before long, so that you and all others can have as many as you need. . . . As to Kentucky, you do not estimate that state as more important than I do; but I am compelled to watch all points. While I write this I am, if not in *range,* at least in hearing of cannon-shot, from an army of enemies more than a hundred thousand strong. I do not expect them to capture this city; but I *know* they would, if I were to send the men and arms from here, to defend Louisville, of which there is not a single hostile armed soldier within forty miles, nor any force known to be moving upon it from any distance.

Lincoln's judgment proved sound. By the time of his wire to Morton twenty thousand arms had been shipped to Kentucky, and the crisis was just about over in that state. A few weeks later, in December, Joshua Speed was able to write home from Washington: "I have now ordered and on the way to Kentucky as many guns of good quality as we will need for some time to come." And five days before that Lincoln had told Congress: "Kentucky, too, for some time in doubt, is now decidedly, and I think, unchangeably, ranged on the side of the Union."

The game had not been lost.

CHAPTER 4

No Time for Novelties

THE GODS MAY HAVE BOUND PROMETHEUS, but they failed to confine his spirit. It walked in Lincoln's time as it has always walked. Then, as ever, men played with fire. "The question of ordnance," said the *New York Times* blandly in 1863, "is one for discussion in every drawing-room and in all polite circles." The *Times* might have added that the question was not restricted to drawing rooms. For in cellars and garrets, in barns and woodsheds all over the North, the disciples of Prometheus were laboring over diagrams and piecing together crude machines meant for the more efficient dealing of death. In this they saw good for their country and glory for themselves.

Most were pitifully deluded. But the smiles of the antiquarian who comes across their plans may well be tempered with another emotion than pity. For among those long-forgotten schemes one sees in silhouette almost all the feral implements of modern war: the machine guns, the rockets, the armored tanks, the submarines, the poison gases, the air-borne incendiaries—everything but the ultimate force of nuclear bombs. And even this last peerless goal was being groped toward by some in Lincoln's day. In the spring of 1862, as armies stirred in Virginia, young Professor James Clerk Maxwell of King's College, London, was turning his mind to the nature of energy and matter. At the same moment, and not far from Maxwell's garret laboratory, young Henry Adams, son of Lincoln's minister to England, played the uncanny light of his historical in-

59

tuition over the same tremendous theme. He wrote his brother in the Union Army:

I tell you these are great times. Man has mounted science, and is now run away with. I firmly believe that before many centuries more, science will be the master of man. The engines he will have invented will be beyond his strength to control. Some day science may have the existence of mankind in its power, and the human race commit suicide by blowing up the world.

If Lincoln, with his feeling for the course of history, shared the forebodings of Henry Adams, he left no record of it. But the prototypes of modern armament commanded his close attention, and he had a real if unstoried share in fixing their destiny. Of all that Lincoln had to do with the tools of war, his experiences with new weapons and his struggles to overcome the inertia of the bureaucrats are the most fascinating to modern eyes and perhaps the most meaningful to our times.

Lincoln's introduction to the world of the inventors came long before the outbreak of the Civil War. He was only a freshman Congressman from Illinois when, in the year 1848 or thereabouts, he walked with his small son Robert down a wheel-rutted earthen road, bordered by occasional clusters of low, wooden houses, which Washingtonians knew as F Street. Down the way stood the beginnings of the Treasury Building, a columned façade with nothing behind it. And at the intersection of Seventh and F Streets, the Post Office and the Patent Office faced each other "like white Greek temples in the abandoned gravel-pits of a deserted Syrian city."

The man and the boy were bound for the Patent Office, a massive structure, Greek in style, but built of Virginia freestone and Maryland marble. Its collection of models, not its architecture, made the Patent Office one of the great sights of Washington. Even the acidulous Charles Dickens, predisposed against most things American outside Boston, had seen in the Patent Office of the 1840s "an extraordinary example of American enterprise and ingenuity." Temple architecture suited the building, for it was the shrine of America's peculiar genius. Indeed, in his first report after Lincoln's arrival in Washington, the Commissioner of Patents slipped for a moment into the exalted language of a high priest:

While the steam engine, most potent of all the creations of genius, is daily coursing before our eyes, wafting as upon the wings of the wind its precious freight of human life, and its countless treasures of industry and commerce; while the mysterious telegraph speeds our thoughts with the swiftness of lightning which is its obedient and trusty messenger; while magnificent manufactories stud our land, stunning but delighting us with the never-ceasing movement of their wonder-working machinery, it seems unnecessary to remark upon the incalculable value of the labors of the inventor and his claims upon society for protection in the enjoyment of his just rights.

Some factory workers may have been more numbed than delighted by "the never-ceasing movement of their wonder-working machinery," but there were few others in the America of 1848 who would not have joined heartily in the Patent Commissioner's hymn of praise. And Congressman Lincoln emphatically concurred with the majority.

Up the temple's monumental steps and past great fluted Doric columns trudged the two visitors, stopping at last in one of the model rooms. In five years the "immense number of models" seen by Dickens had more than doubled; they were now a tax on available space about which the Patent Commissioner had complained five distinct times to Congress. Since cramped conditions prevented a systematic arrangement of the models, their total effect must have left Congressman Lincoln and his son slightly dizzy. Here and there they might have seen models of John Ericsson's screw propeller, Alfred Vail's printing telegraph, Jonas Chickering's grand piano with iron frame, Stephen Fitch's turret lathe, Elias Howe's sewing machine, or Richard Hoe's rotary printing press. Jumbled together with these were hopeful gadgets designed to expedite almost every conceivable object from the writing of letters to the propulsion of ships—there was even an "electrifying machine" and a device with the forbidding name of "sacrificator." The man and the boy, whom his father feared would be "one of the little rare-ripe sort that are smarter at about five than ever after," stared in amazement at the variety of offspring to which American ingenuity had already given birth; and Congressman Lincoln seriocomically agreed with his small son that nothing remained to be invented.

Lincoln himself was presently to refute that notion. In 1849, just after his single term in Congress, he patented an invention of his own for buoying vessels over shoals. On each side of the craft were to be great collapsible chambers which could be expanded by an ingenious system of ropes and pulleys and forced down into the river like a combination of water wings and stilts. Though Lincoln dreamed briefly of becoming the Fulton of the West, he did little or nothing to promote his invention; and so his little wooden model sat in its corner of a Patent Office showcase, stolid and unnoticed under the dust of the 1850s.

After Lincoln's election to the Presidency, his invention enjoyed a measure of belated notoriety. In December 1860, a few days before South Carolina left the Union, the *Scientific American* allotted nearly all of one column to the device, expressing the modest hope that the President-elect would have "better success in presiding as Chief Magistrate over the people of the entire Union than he has had . . . in introducing his invention." For a few days after the secession of Virginia in April 1861 it seemed likely that the *Scientific American's* hope would be blighted by rebel seizure of the capital, chief magistrate and all. But the arrival of Northern troops assured Lincoln of a fair chance to do better as President than he had as an inventor.

When the first Northern regiments came to deliver Washington from its peril in the spring of 1861, they found temporary shelter in public buildings. At the Capitol the 6th and 8th Massachusetts skylarked and staged mock debates with the 7th New York. The

5th Massachusetts set up housekeeping in the Treasury. The 1st Rhode Island happened to draw the Patent Office.

Since 1848, when Congressman Lincoln and his little son had visited the Patent Office, that establishment had spread hugely. Two more wings had sprouted from the Greek temple on F Street, leaving yet unrealized only one of the four wings originally planned. Nevertheless, the Patent Office proved to be cramped quarters for twelve hundred Rhode Islanders and their mass of baggage, which included two portable forges and three washerwomen. For two days and nights army wagons, backed up hub to hub, lined F Street for two blocks to unload the regiment's impedimenta. Bunks were set up on tessellated marble floors between glass cases in the three great model halls; in the central hall the cabinets were jammed together on one side to make room for dining tables. A civilian visitor had to move a couple of dozen muskets in order to see the model of a plow. In such conditions awkward incidents were inevitable. In their fortnight's occupancy of the Patent Office, with all it implies of horseplay, jostling, the setting up of bunks and the handling of muskets in close quarters, twelve hundred Rhode Islanders between them broke some four hundred panes of glass. A few models vanished—though no one with larcenous leanings noticed the model of a boat with the name of Abraham Lincoln inscribed on its prow— and one morning a pistol ball went crashing through two model cases. But on the whole the Yankees restrained themselves.

It behooved the Rhode Islanders to deal tenderly with the Patent Office. Its exhibits were gratifying and often lucrative testimonials to their own mechanical aptitude and that of their Yankee neighbors. The colonel of the regiment, genial Ambrose Burnside, was best known at that time for his patent breech-loading rifle, a model of which doubtless reposed behind glass somewhere in his regiment's quarters. (His rifle, however, did not stand up under combat conditions, and Burnside's name found its way into the dictionary on the strength of his whiskers rather than his weapons.) "Here," the regimental chaplain wrote, "were models of all kinds of ma-

chines, which our mechanics viewed with perpetual interest. . . .
Here a soldier would find the model of a machine which had been
invented by some member of his own family—perhaps by himself." Now and then the chaplain would see a man "intently studying some new arrangement of mechanical forces, which would be
suggestive of subsequent investigation." Perhaps some followed up
those suggestions after the war; others did not, among them Andrew White, Paul Downes and Albert Burdick, machinists, who
fell at Bull Run in July.

On the first of May Abraham Lincoln revisited the Patent Office
as President of the United States. The Rhode Islanders, looking fit
and businesslike in their simple, coarse uniforms of gray pants, dark-
blue flannel shirts and Army hats turned up at the side, were assembled under arms on F Street, facing the building. At noon Lincoln came out on the portico with members of his Cabinet and
hoisted a large American flag to the top of the staff, where the
breeze unfurled it amid the hurrahs of soldiers and spectators. Then
there were cheers for the President and Secretary Seward, a drill exhibition by the regiment and the presenting of arms. Next day the
regiment was formally mustered into United States service, and a
few days later it moved to a more conventional camp outside the city.

The cramped conditions under which the 1st Rhode Island had
sojourned in the Patent Office could not be laid wholly to the regiment's excess of baggage. Though the Patent Office's available space
had trebled since the Mexican War, it had not kept up with Yankee
fecundity in mechanical invention. About the time Lincoln patented
his device for getting vessels over shoals, the number of patented
mechanical inventions began to rise in an exponential curve which
did not pass its peak till the first quarter of the twentieth century.
Far from bearing out the jesting prophecy of Congressman Lincoln
that the great days of invention were over, the last of the fifties saw
applications flooding in on the Patent Office as never before. The
golden age of gadgetry had dawned.

Those were the days when a lone inventor could succeed without capital or formal training, so long as he had imagination, mechanical ingenuity and a few tools. Invention was a pastime still wide open to the general public. During the war years, for example, a family newspaper like the *Boston Transcript* made room in its four pages for a regular weekly list of patents granted to New Englanders, and a long list at that. In the nation at large Abraham Lincoln was not the only prominent nonprofessional to get his name on the lists of patents granted; so did such others as Eli Thayer, the abolitionist, and William Rosecrans, later to command the Army of the Cumberland.

Curiously enough, the number of patents granted by Union authority dropped sharply during the first eighteen months of the war. Those granted in the first ten months of 1862, for example, numbered less than half as many as in the corresponding months of 1860. The unexpected development was brought home to Lincoln by appeals from dismissed Patent Office employees. Patent Commissioner David P. Holloway laid off Edward W. Jones in August 1861 on the grounds of decreased business. Jones tried in vain to see the Secretary of the Interior, then called on Lincoln with a letter of recommendation written several months before by former Secretary of War Joseph Holt. "Mr. Jones," Lincoln said, "I have only your say so for it, but if Mr. Holt will express a wish that you shall be retained in office, I will direct you to be reinstated." In September Lincoln reviewed the case of J. E. Holmead, who had been dismissed as a patent examiner despite his ability, promptness and "unchanging suavity of manners"; but Commissioner Holloway insisted that business was too slack to warrant keeping him.

Lincoln's first annual message to Congress, in December 1861, blamed the decline in patents on a temporary business depression which had followed the outbreak of war. Commissioner Holloway suggested as an additional factor that "the great inventive mind of the country" had been "attracted in another direction by the startling scenes of rebellion"—by which he presumably meant that the Army and Navy had absorbed a lot of active or potential inventors. The *Scientific American* thought there must be more to it than that. "Where are the inventors?" asked the magazine, mindful perhaps of its heavy stake in the matter (it operated a flourishing patent agency on the side). "Certainly," it insisted, "half of them cannot have gone to the war."

Scientific American to the contrary, it often seemed that half of the nation's inventors had indeed "gone to the war." The 1st Rhode Island was not unique. As a preview of exploits to come, there had been the experience of Major General Benjamin F. Butler and his troops at Annapolis in April 1861. With the fate of the capital still uncertain, a dismantled locomotive in the Annapolis engine-house threatened to delay the Massachusetts troops in their race toward the city. Butler assembled his men and asked them if any of them could repair it. A stalwart Yankee stepped from the ranks. "Well, General," said he, "I rather think I can. I made that engine." In a few hours the locomotive was in order, men were found to run the engine, man the brakes, feed the fires and conduct the train; and the secessionist ears of Annapolis were serenaded by its triumphant whistle, dying away in the direction of Washington.

At the siege of Fort Pulaski a year later a mortar battery lay idle for want of fuse plugs for its shells. Suddenly the ordnance officer had a happy thought: "There was a Yankee regiment on the island; all Yankees are whittlers; if this regiment could be turned out to-night, they might whittle enough fuse-plugs before morning to fire a thousand rounds. So . . . the 6th Connecticut was ordered out to whittle, and did whittle to advantage, providing all the plugs that were used in Battery Totten on the two succeeding days."

Similar, if less dramatic, incidents were common throughout the war. Streams were spanned, canals cut, railroads built and rebuilt —all with skill drawn from the ranks. "Among the national peculiarities developed by the war," commented the *Scientific American,* "not the least striking is the versatility of our soldier mechanics." But convenient as the military may have found its reserves of skill to be, few patents proceeded therefrom.

Whether business depression or the demands of the military or both together caused the slackening in patent activity, it was no more than a temporary dip. The upturn had begun by the end of 1862. Meanwhile, Northerners needed only to look south to revive their spirits. In fertility of invention the Northern states, with their industries and diversified farming, had long surpassed the one-crop South with its unskilled slave labor. During the week in May 1849 when "A. Lincoln of Springfield, Ills." received his patent for an improved method of lifting vessels over shoals, nineteen other inventors were granted patents. Only two of them lived in slave states, and one of those two had patented an improved cotton gin. The sample was a fair one, and the pattern had not changed by 1861.

The Civil War forced the South to recognize and repent its dereliction in that respect. The Confederacy exempted its cobblers from military service, and still its troops went shoeless; while after a year of war, the North had the McKay sewing machine, which could sew a hundred pair of shoes for every pair sewed by hand. Lack of rails and rolling stock almost paralyzed Southern railroads; while the North set a new record for iron-rail production in every year of the war except the first. Much the same overwhelming disparity held true for almost every kind of industry.

Even if the South had been given the machines, it would have lacked the skill to maintain and run them. "The truth is *all* of the engine runners on our roads are Yankees," complained one Southerner to his wife just before First Bull Run, "and I hear in various quarters of the delay of troops attributed to them." In at least one case, the rumors were well founded. Thus the South which had lately scorned and repelled skilled workers as "mudsills" missed them badly in wartime.

And Southern inventiveness did not spring into action at the call of war. "There are at least forty inventions, each of them infallible, for totally demolishing the Yankee fleet and army," commented the *Richmond Enquirer* sarcastically. But the Confederate Patent Office issued only two hundred and sixty-six patents during the whole war, as against more than sixteen thousand granted by the Union.

The military implications of "Yankee ingenuity" were not lost on some Northern commentators, who cheerfully assumed that the weapon would be wielded promptly and energetically against the rebels. "Take our word for it," trumpeted the *Philadelphia Enquirer,* "these geniuses will yet produce some patent Secession-Excavator, some Traitor-Annihilator, some Rebel-Thrasher, some Confederate States Milling Machine, which will grind through, shell out, or slice up this war, as if it were a bushel of wheat or an ear of corn, or a big apple."

Even after a year of war had shown the Confederacy to be somewhat less digestible than a big apple, John Ericsson, the designer of the *Monitor,* wrote to Lincoln in the same vein:

The time has come, Mr. President, when our cause will have to be sustained, not by numbers, but by superior weapons. By a proper application of mechanical devises alone will you be able with absolute certainty to destroy the enemies of the Union. Such is the inferiority of the Southern States in a mechanical point of view, that it is susceptible of demonstration that, if you apply our mechanical resources to the fullest extent, you can destroy the enemy without enlisting another man.

In the last prewar Congress, Senator Jefferson Davis of Mississippi had managed to put through a law prohibiting the use of patented articles by the Army or Navy, ostensibly in the interests of economy; but after the desertion of its Southern members, Congress swept away the disability and overhauled the patent laws generally. After that, hopes ran high among those with ideas for new weapons. "The patentees of articles used in camps and by the army are reaping a rich harvest," reported the *Scientific American* in the first weeks of the war. "There is an enormous demand for improved firearms, cannon, shells, projectiles, explosive grenades and military accouterments of all kinds."

The *Scientific American* spoke too soon, hoping, perhaps, to drum up business for its patent department. Its alluring picture sprang not from fact but from assumption, and the assumption turned out to be unfounded. The *Scientific American* and its eager clientele had reckoned without the Chief of Army Ordnance.

It was on June 11, 1861, that Colonel James W. Ripley, Chief of Army Ordnance, drew up a memorandum which deserves to be recognized as one of the basic documents of the Civil War. Ripley's manifesto—for such it was—set forth his unalterable views on military inventions in general and newfangled small arms in particular. It reads as if its author had drawn a long breath and set out vigorously on a course from which he knew there could be no turning or retreat. And from the bitter determination with which he held to that course ever after, the impression would seem to be accurate.

The core of Ripley's declaration is in the following passage:

A great evil now specially prevalent in regard to arms for the military service is the vast variety of the new inventions, each having, of course, its advocates, insisting on the superiority of his favorite arm over all others and urging its adoption by the Government. The influence thus exercised has already introduced into the service many kinds and calibers of arms, some, in my opinion, unfit for use as military weapons, and none as good as the U. S. musket, producing confusion in the manufacture, the issue, and the use of ammunition, and very injurious to the efficiency of troops. This evil can only be stopped by positively refusing to answer any requisitions for or propositions to sell new and untried arms, and steadily adhering to the rule of uniformity of arms for all troops of the same kind, such as cavalry, artillery, infantry.

Ripley had good reasons for his stand. Certainly, any major

change in weapons, with its necessary disruption of production, would have been risky in the middle of a desperate war.

But if a new weapon promised to be valuable in battle and was not prohibitively expensive, the Chief of Ordnance, especially at the start of a war, should have racked his brains for ways to produce it outside the regular sources or to bring about a gradual change-over. Ripley did no such thing. Instead of seeking out better designs, he applied his ingenuity, which was considerable, to fighting them off. And on occasion he put that great object above truth, above honor, even above Army regulations.

In 1852 a War Department regulation had spelled out the policy which the Ordnance Department was expected to follow in dealing with that pestiferous creature, the civilian inventor. First, the inventor had to explain the nature and advantages of his device. Then, if the Ordnance Department thought it worth a test, the inventor had to furnish the test model. This helped to discourage the more grandiose paper projects. The regulation was printed in circular form, and Ripley occasionally sent it out to inventors when he thought it would silence them. But Ripley usually refused to make tests, whether a model was supplied or not, without a direct order from his superiors—which generally meant President Lincoln.

Ripley's customary excuse for such a refusal was lack of time. To do him justice, this was no imaginary obstacle. In the words of one prominent ordnance officer, "every officer had so much to do that he could not spend much time on inventions." Had it been otherwise, the corps might have come up with some good things itself; for it had many talented officers and at least one, Major Thomas J. Rodman, who approached genius. But Rodman testified that what little time he and his colleagues could spare for research and experiment had been used for "testing and considering the plans proposed by inexperienced persons."

To plead the pressure of business may have been valid within limits. But Ripley's tone with applicants suggested that if that excuse had not existed, he would have invented it. Ripley seemed to regard the chastening of inventors as an act of virtue in itself. Inventors who made the futile pilgrimage to the Winder Building were received with undisguised contempt. The clerk in charge of Ordnance Office correspondence once appeared before a court of inquiry. "Has it been the custom," he was asked, "to enter into scientific and theoretical discussions with inventors when they presented their inventions to the department?" "Oh, no!" replied the astonished witness.

The fog of mutual detestation that rose between Ripley and the inventors soon became thick beyond dispelling. In an editorial entitled "Impertinence of the Ordnance Department toward Inventors" the *Scientific American* charged Ripley with "rudeness and circumlocution of the rankest kind." Against such treatment the periodical waged a determined campaign—which probably did more to widen the breach than to close it. "Things have reached such a pass," the magazine complained presently, "that inventors are shy of presenting plans that have to be experimented upon by Government before acceptance, and the consequence is that the country suffers."

Inventors fared somewhat better at the hands of the Navy Ordnance Bureau. That bureau's problems and responsibilities never rose to the proportions that overwhelmed its Army counterpart, and so its officials had more time for the exercise of tact and patience. Their rules for dealing with civilian inventors were essentially those of the Army Ordnance Department: tests would be made by the government if models were furnished, and if successful would lead to trial in service. It was the Navy Department's attitude from the top down that made the difference. Secretary Welles himself, impressed by the flood of inventors' proposals pouring in on the Department, asked Congress in March 1862 for $100,000 to be used in experiments and in trials of proposed inventions. He did not get the money, but he made the gesture, which was more than Secretary Cameron or his successor thought of doing.

Nevertheless, the Navy Ordnance Bureau's kindliness gave small comfort to most applicants. Its spirit was willing, but the Navy had too few ordnance officers, and these had too little time to hear out all comers. Besides, there were many types of weapons, such as small arms, which the Navy was not likely to want in quantity, however ingenious and effective they might be. And so, gruffly dismissed by Ripley and suavely put off by Dahlgren, the resourceful inventor looked elsewhere for help.

One possibility was an appeal to a general in the field. Despite regulations, military commanders often bought arms without consulting the Ordnance Department, and often enough the War Department honored their vouchers. If the generals had scruples against breaking Army regulations, they could still pester General Ripley with requisitions for particular kinds of arms, standard or otherwise. In both these lines of approach, Frémont and McClellan were, to General Ripley's mind, maddeningly active.

Still more often generals were persuaded to give inventors testimonials and letters of recommendation; but no such letter, however warm, ever melted General Ripley's heart.

By all odds the most gadget-minded of the generals and therefore the sharpest thorn in Ripley's side was Benjamin F. Butler, Major General of Volunteers. Butler was a "political general," appointed not for his military experience or talent— he had none— but for his utility as a powerful Massachusetts Democrat who might carry along some of his party in support of the war. He was a strong, heavy man in his early forties, quick in wit and manner, with shrewd, fleshy features, thinning hair and heavy eyelids, one of which drooped oddly, as if to suggest the moral obliquity of which he was so persistently accused. The South execrated him, calling him "Beast Butler," while the North half admired him for his blunt insensitivity and sly opportunism. Butler rushed in where angels feared to tread, but he was no fool, for all that. "A vivacious, prying man, this Butler," said Russell of the *London Times,* "full of bustling life, self-esteem, revelling in the exercise of power."

Historians have often pointed out how fertile the mind of Benjamin Butler was in unorthodox political and legal expedients; none, not even Butler himself, seem to have realized how strikingly this same bold originality characterized his approach to military technology. Few if any new devices appeared during the war of which Butler was not either the first or a very early champion. In the summer of 1861 he became the first American general to employ aerial reconnaissance. "It is greatly to his credit," says the leading historian of Civil War balloon activities, "that he encouraged a branch of military science then in its infancy in this country, where his administrative superiors failed or refused to recognize its possibilities." Butler heartily endorsed the use of wire entanglements in the static warfare along his front at Bermuda Hundred in 1864. During that same period he devised a kite which was sent over the Confederate lines with a bundle of Lincoln's amnesty proclamations to be released by a string and showered upon the rebel troops. A submarine was built for him, and what appears to have been a steam-driven helicopter had been nearly completed, with encouraging results, when construction was halted by his final departure from the Army.

If Ben Butler and his fellow generals remained cold, the hopeful inventor could invoke civilian influence, Congressional or otherwise.

The *Scientific American* cynically advised a correspondent that "your only chance of making anything by your invention is to get some person of capital and influence interested with you by giving him a good share." It is to be hoped that solicitude for constituents moved them, rather than vile avarice; but in any case, some Congressmen came to know the dusky second-floor hallway of the Winder Building as well as they knew the Capitol Rotunda. A law requiring the Chief of Ordnance to publicize lobbying done by Congressmen was finally passed; but at least once the chief had to be reminded rather sharply that the law did not apply merely to proposals *initiated* by Congressmen.

Men in almost every walk of public life transmitted inventors' requests and applications to the Ordnance Office. Vice-President Hannibal Hamlin put in a word for a fellow townsman in Bangor, Maine, who had a steel point for slugs. Secretary of the Interior Caleb Smith took an interest in a patent shell. Spencer F. Baird, noted geologist and Assistant Secretary of the Smithsonian Institution, paused in the labors of pure science to notify the Office that his brother Thomas, a Pennsylvania iron founder, wanted an order. The President's private secretary, John Hay, asked a hearing for one Adalbert Parsch, who had an explosive bullet. On the stationery of the New York Customs House, Collector Hiram Barney invited General Ripley's attention to the bearer, Mr. William Page, "the distinguished artist & author, who has made an invention in fire arms which he wishes to place at the disposal of the Government." H. F. Mann, a Pittsburgh inventor, wanted a job as assistant inspector in conducting trials of his own breech-loading cannon, and in this ambition he was sustained by Schuyler Colfax, Speaker of the House of Representatives. The Chief of Ordnance respectfully dissented. "It would scarcely be proper," he explained to the affable politician, "to employ Mr. Mann to test his own invention." The point seems well taken.

The inventor in search of a government order thus had more than one string to his bow. But in spite of everything, in spite of their appeals to the Army Ordnance Department, to the Navy Ordnance Bureau, to the generals and to the politicians, somehow inventors found themselves unable to "grind through, shell out, or slice up this war" as so many had hoped they would. And so they turned to the one man in the United States Government who had both the will and, they supposed, the power to push the development of new weapons.

That man was President Abraham Lincoln.

CHAPTER 5

Inventors in
the White House

SCARCELY HAD PARADE TORCHES GUTTERED
out, campaign songs died away and votes been counted in the election which made Abraham Lincoln sixteenth President of the United States, when inventors began writing the successful candidate. Three weeks after the election a newspaperman at Lincoln's Springfield headquarters observed that inventors were "exceedingly liberal with circulars and samples." One man wrote: "It looks like war. I have invented a machine which will fire 400 bullets simultaneously; write me if you wish me to explain it to you." Across the letter Lincoln jotted down a note for his secretary, the serious, methodical young John Nicolay: "Need not answer this."

Nicolay must have welcomed such instructions, for the inventors who wrote Lincoln had plenty of competition from constituents with other interests. From the time of his election until he died, Lincoln never lacked for unsolicited advice of all sorts on all subjects and from all quarters. Millions who never laid eyes on him somehow felt that he was a reasonable man, and tens of thousands were encouraged by that feeling to enlighten him by mail. Every weekday morning during the Civil War a perspiring messenger with a mail sack mounted the stairs to the second floor of the White House and spread the writing public's offerings before the President's three private secretaries.

Besides Nicolay, Lincoln had brought along the brilliant, flip-

pant, slightly snobbish John Hay, an Illinoisan two years out of
Brown University; and early in April 1861 the two were joined
by a young ex-newspaperman named William O. Stoddard. Stoddard screened the incoming correspondence, depositing a good
part of it in two big wicker wastebaskets on either side of his desk.
Most of the rest was referred to appropriate departments by one
or another of the secretaries without troubling the President. The
remainder—only one in fifty of the total received, according to
Hay's casual recollection—went to Lincoln, to be referred elsewhere by him or to be answered and then filed in pigeonholes of a
tall desk in his office.

Surviving records indicate that the secretaries gave Lincoln at
least three times as large a proportion of inventors' letters as they
did of other kinds. The secretaries' partiality no doubt stemmed
mostly from their awareness of Lincoln's special interest in new
weapons, but their own bias may have had something to do with
it. Nicolay, Hay and Stoddard were all in their twenties and
therefore, presumably, receptive to novelties. The later writings of
Hay and Stoddard, moreover, show that both felt an amused
affection for the inventors. And, subject to some adjustments with
one Columbus Johnson of Pike County, Missouri, Nicolay himself was the proud inventor of a shot charger, on which he patented
improvements during the war.

Why did the inventors write Lincoln instead of the ordnance
bureaus? Looking at some of the scrawled, blotted, misspelled
scraps that reached him, one suspects that the unsophisticated
writers simply did not know of anyone else to address. The same
difficulty probably applied to foreign inventors. Lincoln received
letters about new weapons from Germany, Italy, Spain and Mexico;
and nearly a score came from England and France. (The French
took the numerical lead and also the prize for the most unlikely
proposal, one from St. Sulpice which promised to combine, in some
unspecified and inconceivable fashion, the destructive elements of
incendiary and plague.)

But ignorance could account for only a small fraction of inventors' letters to Lincoln. Some were inspired by regard for and trust in the President personally. An Illinoisan confided in him because he had seen and heard him debate with Douglas. "From the estimate I then formed of your character," the inventor wrote, "I believe you would despise the being who would *fear* to address you on a subject of importance to our common country, & of vital interest to his very, very, needy family." Soldier-inventors, who increased in number as battle experience gave them ideas, shared the regard of their comrades for the commander in chief. *"You* are the only man with whom I will trust the secret," wrote one veteran with a projectile to offer. And from Auburn, New York, Secretary Seward's home town, a disabled veteran explained: "I take the liberty of addressing you with no other excuse than that I knew you to be the friend of the Soldier even though he be a *Private."* He had written the Ordnance Department, said the invalid, but had got no answer. (This time the Ordnance Office did answer—and promptly.)

Others turned to Lincoln as a last resort. "I have tried every means a poor man could, to get a hearing by the Government, without success," a New Yorker wrote; "I now appeal to you." Some echoed an inventor who wrote Lincoln in June 1861: "I applied at first to the Ordnance office and was there told, that, Government would be at no expense, that my modell was too small for a satisfactory experiment, and that I must construct and bring here, a large gun, at my own expense, which I am unable to do." A Michigan experimenter had written a letter to Secretary of War Stanton, but suspecting that the Secretary "threw it into the fire and called it a thing," he appealed to Lincoln. (His guess as to Stanton's disposition of his missive was a shrewd one; just a month before, Stanton had said of another inventor's letter: "It might as well be put in the fire.") An East Tennesseean wrote Lincoln from New York because White House ushers had barred him from a personal interview with the President; all he asked was "a friendly note of recommendation" to manufacturers so that he might get backing for a trial gun.

Young and old alike sent ideas to the President. A Brooklyn teen-ager named James Littlefield wrote to offer the plan of "a Air gun, made in a different way from any gun that I ever saw" for a modest compensation of "not lest than $800, per year during life," with the reasonable proviso that "if the gun proves unsuccessful say nough about it." A venerable Bostonian named William Foster wrote Congressman Samuel Hooper to outline a plan for twenty small boats, each with a gun, all fixed together in an arc and so arranged as to discharge all guns at once at the same point. As an engineer on the defenses of Boston Harbor in 1812, he had made the same suggestion without avail; but he was not easily discouraged. "If what has been said do not find ears," he wrote, "I am willing to live ninety more years for a trial. . . . Will you please to hand this to the President after giving two reading, if you have time?" (Hooper sent the letter to Nicolay, suggesting a "complimentary acknowledgement . . . signed by the President.")

Ideas and suggestions for new weapons came to Lincoln from unexpected quarters. An Ohioan wrote the President in Quaker style "to send thee a diagram of an improved shell." In the humanitarian tradition of Dr. Guillotin, the medical profession was also represented. Dr. McCabe of Auburn, Iowa, offered Lincoln a gun that would bombard Norfolk from Fortress Monroe; Dr. Wallace of Buffalo, New York, offered the President a projectile; and from Dr. Richardson of Matherton, Michigan, Lincoln received a proposal for an incendiary shell.

The record for impudence was probably achieved by a Philadelphia lawyer named A. M. Densmore, representing a cannon inventor named William Beschke, who claimed to have been a tutor in the family of Secretary Seward. Without even describing Beschke's cannon, Densmore asked the President for money or influence or both. When Assistant Secretary Watson asked him for more details about the gun, Densmore did not reply. Instead he wrote Lincoln again and insisted that mere drawings or descriptions could not do justice to the cannon's ineffable merits. But a model might, so would the President kindly contribute $500 toward one? Densmore exhorted the President on his duty to the nation in a matter of such "extreme importance," but both his screeds wound up unanswered in the Ordnance Office's files.

Not all inventors were like Densmore and Beschke. A Kentuckian wrote Stanton in May 1862: "I sent a moddle of this invention to the President last summer, about the last of July, with a request that he would have it used against the rebles. I would have taken out a Patent, but I was fearful that in that way the rebels would get hold of it. I am very poor, and love profit; but I love my country more." It would be pleasant to learn that Lincoln saw that letter, but the evidence is against it.

Inventors usually had better luck with Lincoln when they met him face to face. It was not as hard then as it is now to see the President—not nearly hard enough, thought Lincoln's secretaries. All through Lincoln's Presidency, Hay, Nicolay and Stoddard strove to erect barriers against the constant interruptions that wasted the President's time and sapped his strength. Lincoln himself was always the first to break the barriers down. "You will wear yourself out," remonstrated Senator Wilson of Massachusetts. With a sad smile Lincoln replied, "They don't want much; they get but little, and I must see them."

Most inventors took their chances with the crowds who hung about in the corridors and anterooms from morning till night. While waiting for others to be done, those in the President's own office had plenty of time to study its simple furnishings: the upright desk with its well-filled pigeonholes, a big cloth-covered oak table at which the Cabinet met on Tuesdays and Fridays, a marble fireplace with brass fender and irons, a few straight-backed chairs and two sofas, glass-globed gas jets and, on the walls, military maps, an old engraving of Andrew Jackson and a photograph of John Bright, the English liberal leader. Two tall windows looked south over the White House lawn and the unkempt White Lot, past a brackish canal grandly designated the Tiber, across an expanse of churned-up mud and grass on which hundreds of cattle grazed, to the squat marble stump of the unfinished Washington monument and the dusky-red towers of the Smithsonian Institution, built in a style which the British visitor Trollope pungently labeled "bastard Gothic." Beyond lay the broad Potomac and the Virginia shore. In an armchair flanked by the windows and with a table before him, President Lincoln sat listening to his callers. The inventors might scan his leathery, deep-marked, wise, sad face, but they could not see the "tired spot" far within him which no rest or laughter could reach, which grew with the slow passage of every war-racked day.

Lincoln was resourceful in handling the touchy and unpredictable inventors. Once, for example, three men, backers of some war-like device, crowded petulantly before the President. "Now," said their spokesman. "We have been here to see you time and again; you have referred us to the Secretary of War, to the Chief of Ordnance, and the General of the Army, and they give us no satisfaction. We have been kept here waiting, till money and patience are exhausted, and we now come to demand of you a final reply to our application."

At this impertinence another man might have stood stiffly on his Presidential dignity or even burst into a tirade. Lincoln merely listened quietly until the men had finished what they had to say, and then he smiled. "You three gentlemen remind me of a story I once heard," he said. A little boy, he related, had been doing well in Sunday school until the teacher came to the trials of Shadrach, Meshach and Abednego in the fiery furnace. That was too big a dose. The boy could neither spell, pronounce nor remember those three outlandish names. He was given another chance, but when the next lesson came around, he was still stumped. The teacher gave him one last chance. "Now," he said sternly when the time arrived, "tell me the names of the men in the fiery furnace." "Oh," the boy said, "here come those three infernal bores! I wish the devil had them!"

The "three infernal bores" got the point and departed, red-faced and silent.

On another occasion, Lincoln found himself harassed by a Western farmer who wanted the government to adopt his repeating carbine. The President had more important business to conduct with another visitor, yet he was too kindhearted to dismiss the inventor abruptly. Just then Adjutant General E. D. Townsend came in on business, and Lincoln saw a way out of his dilemma. Townsend was greeted cheerily with the remark that he had come just in time to examine a new carbine and advise its inventor better than the President could as to what should be done with it. Townsend had nothing to do with ordnance, but he was rather flattered at Lincoln's confidence in his judgment. The inventor in his turn was encouraged by the newcomer's military rank. So Lincoln and his other visitor were left to talk in peace while Townsend and the ingenious farmer contentedly discussed the carbine. Finally Townsend delivered the hopeful inventor to the not-so-tender mercies of General Ripley. (The gun was not adopted.)

Whatever else might be said about the inventors, they were not dull. John Hay remembered them as "more a source of amusement than annoyance." Lincoln had always enjoyed meeting odd specimens of the human race, and the inventors were usually, in Hay's words, "men of some originality of character, not infrequently carried to eccentricity." Furthermore, the devices they lugged in with them appealed to Lincoln's zest for things mechanical. "Specimens of new rifles and cannon came to him by the dozen," Stoddard wrote somewhat hyperbolically, "with a large variety of new shell, pistols, torpedoes, and gunboats." Stoddard's office in particular became a sort of executive arsenal. "Newly-invented guns, and specimens of all manner of old-time weapons offered for sale to the Government, stood leaning against the wall in corners, or lumbered the desks and tables."

Lincoln's indulgence toward inventors did not proceed merely from caprice or a desire for amusement. He fully appreciated the weight of weapons in the scales of war; and he soon came to realize that if he did not encourage the development and use of better weapons, no one would. Lincoln's concern for the tools of war was a distinct phase of his role as commander in chief.

Lincoln got no thanks from the ordnance bureaus for his pains. "What does Lincoln know about a gun?" one functionary growled. "We're bothered to death with these inventors running here all the time." To the bureaucratic way of thinking, Lincoln should have left such matters strictly to their proper arbiters: the chiefs of the two ordnance bureaus. But Lincoln was no respecter of red tape. "He did despise forms and almost hated those that loved them," wrote his former law partner Herndon.

Lincoln knew his own technical limitations. He also knew that Captain Harwood of the Navy Ordnance Bureau was a stopgap administrator, not an ordnance expert. And General Ripley was undoubtedly correct in taking Lincoln's endorsement on W. B. Chace's letter as an expression of no confidence. So Lincoln put no trust in either Harwood or Ripley and looked about him instead for men who had technical training and yet were not dismayed by new ideas.

For a while during the winter of 1861-1862, he turned to Brigadier General Joseph G. Totten, Chief of the Army Engineer Corps. Like Ripley, General Totten was an old Connecticut Yankee, born at New Haven the year his state ratified the Constitution. During the War of 1812 Totten had been chief engineer of the army on the Niagara frontier and had won a brevet lieutenant-colonelcy for gallantry. He had served with distinction under Scott at Vera Cruz in 1847. Though he was fifty-six years out of West Point when the Civil War began, the vigor of his mind belied his age.

As will be seen, Lincoln called on General Totten several times in the first winter of the war for advice about proposed new weapons. Presently, however, Totten betrayed some distaste for his new role. "I give my opinion at your command," he wrote Lincoln on one occasion, "but with distrust of my ability to decide on matters as to which I have general knowledge only—having had therein no technical experience." And when Totten began to show delicacy about treading on the ground of his fellow officer in the Ordnance Department, Lincoln gave up the experiment.

Totten was only one of the experts to whom Lincoln turned for help in judging the tools of war. Now and then the President left his office to cross the Mall and visit the Smithsonian Institution, which in those days came near to being the lengthened shadow of its secretary, Joseph Henry. In Henry, Lincoln found not only a good companion, but also an able guide through some of the technological tangles which confronted him.

Born in 1797 at Albany, New York, Joseph Henry had grown up to become the greatest American scientist since Benjamin Franklin. Like Franklin, he was best-known for his contributions in electricity; but, also like Franklin, he was active in many other scientific fields. He had genius of a technological as well as of a purely scientific sort; six years before Morse's experiments, Henry had not only discovered and stated a basic principle of the telegraph, but had also made and demonstrated a working instrument. In 1846 this remarkable man made a hard decision. It was to give up full-time research for an administrative post as secretary of the new Smithsonian Institution. Now and then he felt the weight of the sacrifice. "Of all places in the country, Washington is, I think, the worst in which to pursue scientific investigations," he wrote dispiritedly in July 1861. "The constant drudgery and anxiety of an office unfits a man for profound and continuous thought; and as he is under the restraint of the sentiment of the dominant party, he finally loses his manly independence and that love of truth which constitutes an honest man." But despite his moments of regret, Henry's thirty years as head of the Smithsonian were in themselves a magnificent contribution to the advancement of science.

Among the annoyances Henry had to endure when civil war came were the suspicions that dogged him for his prewar Southern sympathies. Fearful of a misstep, he insisted that nonscientific lecturers using the Smithsonian hall make a set announcement disclaiming Smithsonian responsibility for the lecture. One night when Horace Greeley came to speak, the chairman set the audience chuckling over a burlesque disclaimer of responsibility for the sentiments expressed by the Smithsonian Institution. Lincoln was there, and afterward he dropped in on Henry's quarters in the east wing and teased the scientist. "The laugh was rather on you, Henry," said the President with a smile.

Lincoln and Henry were bound to meet. As official head of the Smithsonian, the President was expected to attend the regular meeting held every spring. Once in a while Lincoln passed on to Henry some communication he had received as titular head of the institution. A few days after the outbreak of war, a letter from Henry had informed Lincoln that the latest volume of the *Smithsonian Contributions* had been sent by messenger for the White House library. The weight of war was settling on Lincoln, and so he merely glanced through the volume. But he kept in touch with Henry. "I had the impression the Smithsonian was printing a great amount of useless information," Lincoln later remarked. "Professor Henry has convinced me of my error. It must be a grand school if it produces such thinkers as he is. He is one of the pleasantest men I have ever met; so unassuming, simple, and sincere. I wish we had a few thousand more such men." Henry, in his turn, was won over completely by Lincoln's transparent honesty and surprised by the President's grasp of scientific matters.

More than once Lincoln drew on Henry's knowledge and wisdom in matters not usually within the Smithsonian's range. Henry steered Lincoln right on the alleged coal deposits in a proposed freedmen's colony in Central America, and the scientist also helped expose a fake spiritualist who had preyed on Mrs. Lincoln's grief for the Lincolns' dead son Willie. Lincoln looked to Joseph Henry for advice on military technology also.

One such episode had an unexpected sequel. Lincoln, Henry and some others stationed themselves in a tower of the Soldiers' Home outside Washington one gentle summer evening to watch an experiment with night signals. A calcium light in the tower was equipped with a screen that permitted the light to be blinked in

Morse code. From across the darkened capital an answering light flashed from the tower of the Smithsonian. Lincoln enjoyed the demonstration and predicted that the system would be of great use to both Army and Navy.

A few evenings later, while Lincoln chatted with a couple of friends, an agitated citizen was ushered in to see the President with a tale of treasonable signals from the Smithsonian—everyone knew that Professor Henry had secesh leanings. After the story was told, Lincoln turned and said solemnly, "This is Professor Henry; perhaps he will be able to answer for himself." Then he burst out laughing. But the President took pains also to thank his abashed informant for his patriotic vigilance.

In the first summer of the war, Lincoln and Henry between them ushered into being the first successful military air force in American history. Balloons, of course, were nothing new in warfare. As a means of reconnaissance they dated back to the Battle of Fleurus in 1794. The dean of American aeronauts, John Wise, had offered to drop bombs on an enemy citadel in the Mexican War. Something about aeronautics, however, fascinated men less steady and sensible than John Wise, and Lincoln's favor was wooed by balloon inventors whose claims were more apt to be inflated than their gasbags.

Lincoln never assumed that an idea must be mad because madmen pursued it. When Joseph Henry came to the White House one June evening in 1861 with a young balloonist resoundingly named Thaddeus Sobieski Constantine Lowe, Lincoln listened attentively.

Lowe, a twenty-eight-year-old New Hampshire man, dreamed of a transatlantic flight with the aid of prevailing winds, but on Henry's advice he had first tried his theories with a jaunt from Cincinnati to South Carolina. The sky-borne Yankee had triumphantly landed in South Carolina about a week after Sumter was attacked and had become (he later asserted) "the first prisoner of the Civil War." Now, as Lincoln listened, he enthusiastically sketched the possibilities of military balloon reconnaissance, even including a plan for telegraphic air-ground communication. Lincoln fell in with the notion, and the War Department furnished funds for tests and demonstrations.

Only a week after the interview, Lincoln received what he labeled the "First Balloon Dispatch":

To President United States

This point of observation commands an area near fifty miles in diameter—The city with its girdle of encampments presents a superb scene—I have pleasure in sending you this first dispatch ever telegraphed from an aerial station and in acknowledging indebtedness to your encouragement for the opportunity of demonstrating the availability of the science of aeronautics in the military service of the country.

T. S. C. LOWE

Lowe's captive balloon hovered for a while over the armory between Sixth and Seventh streets with Lowe's friend Henry watching from the crowd. After the demonstration, the *Enterprise* was hauled down and towed along Pennsylvania Avenue to the White House, its gaseous dome bobbing above the rooftops as if the Capitol had broken loose and was moving on Lincoln's works. Lincoln watched from an upper window while the outlandish contrivance was moored for the night on the White House lawn. Next day, June 19, several ascents were made, and the captivated correspondent of the *Boston Transcript* wrote:

A balloon is now floating nearly over the President's house. The plan of sending telegraphic messages is found to work admirably. A bugler was just sent up and the strains of the bugle grew clearer and more distinct as he mounted.

Armed with a letter of introduction from Lincoln, Lowe called on General Scott, but found that the old commander of the army was "very infirm, pompous, and with many of the affectations that sometimes go with extreme age, and it was extremely difficult to engage his attention. His mind was centered on the make-up of an army as he had always known it, and he did not care for innovations. It was evident that the General of the Army had no interest in a balloon corps."

A month slipped by and First Bull Run was history when Lowe saw Lincoln again. The President wondered why Lowe had not gone ahead with his plans. "Professor," Lincoln said, "I wish you would go and confer with General Scott again." He wrote out another note:

Will Lieut. Gen. Scott please see Professor Lowe once more about his balloon?

July 25, 1861   A. LINCOLN

In the morning Lowe went to Scott's headquarters in the Winder Building and sent in Lincoln's card. An orderly reported that the general was busy. A couple of hours later Scott was still busy, then eating lunch, finally sound asleep and not to be disturbed. Fuming inwardly, Lowe strode back to the White House and told Lincoln how he had been put off. Lincoln looked at him sharply, then laughed and rose to his angular height of just under six feet four inches. "Come on," he said, clapping on his fuzzy, old stovepipe hat.

The two men marched through the White House grounds, across Seventeenth Street and into the Winder Building. Sentries snapped to attention. The courtly old general gave respectful ear to Lowe's story and promised immediate action. He kept his word. Lowe's services were accepted, and in his Army balloon the young man made frequent and valuable ascensions through the fall of 1861. By 1862 his air corps included seven balloons and a Navy vessel on the Potomac—the nation's first official aircraft carrier. Some of Lowe's telegraphic reports, especially those at Fair Oaks and Gaines's Mill in 1862, were of inestimable value to the Union Army.

In the public mind Lincoln long remained associated with balloon warfare, but in fact his active part in promoting Lowe's military fortunes ended with his walk to the Winder Building. This was unfortunate, for despite his spectacular successes Lowe never managed to find a niche in Army organization. His corps remained a waif of the services, tossed from one jurisdiction to another, always unwanted. Without an Army commission Lowe was at the mercy of every bewildered lieutenant or captain who found himself in temporary charge of the aggregation. Shortly after Gettysburg Lowe blamed his troubles on "first, the very limited means allowed, secondly, want of authority to properly organize a Corps, and thirdly, the very few persons experienced with glasses to take observations from the Balloons." About that time he quit, and thereafter the corps declined rapidly until it was abandoned; the Confederates never understood why, but were thankful nonetheless.

In such matters as night signaling and aerial reconnaissance, to which good sense and general scientific knowledge were sufficient keys, Joseph Henry was the man to see, and Lincoln consulted him on occasion almost to the end of the war. But hard facts remained: that Henry was not a specialist in ordnance; that Totten, though experienced and able, hated to tread on Ripley's toes; that Harwood was inexpert; and that Ripley was fiercely and unalterably opposed to any change in weapons.

In the end Lincoln turned to Captain Dahlgren as the only man he knew who combined the requisites of intelligence, special training, a forward outlook and willingness to be adviser to the President.

CHAPTER 6

Ramsay and the Arsenal

ABRAHAM LINCOLN ALWAYS LIKED TO SEE
things for himself. And in 1861 especially he indulged that fancy
to a degree which some found slightly ludicrous. "This poor President!" wrote Russell of the *Times* that October. "He is to be pitied;
surrounded by such scenes, and trying with all his might to understand strategy, naval warfare, big guns, the movements of troops,
military maps, reconnaissances, occupations, interior and exterior
lines, and all the technical details of the art of slaying. He runs
from one house to another, armed with plans, papers, reports, recommendations, sometimes good-humored, never angry, occasionally dejected, and always a little fussy."

Lincoln saw a lot of weapons trials, most of them held at his instance. Some Ordnance Bureau people regarded these trials with
annoyance and contempt, feeling that they were rigged to impress
the President, rather than to test the weapons. Since ordnance officers ran the tests, such misgivings might seem a little illogical, not
to say disloyal to the corps. But the misgivings existed, nevertheless. "That kind of experiments did not have much weight with the
bureau," testified one Ordnance Office factotum. "They were what
we usually denominated *champagne* experiments."

Many of the "champagne experiments" which Lincoln attended
were conducted by Captain Dahlgren or his subordinates at the
Navy Yard. Most of the others took place at the Washington Ar-

senal, located south of the White House on Greenleaf's Point, where the Anacostia joined the Potomac.

Greenleaf's Point was split by a sluggish rivulet called James Creek, and the arsenal stood on the tongue of land to the Potomac side of the creek. On both sides of the mile-long peninsula low tide uncovered noisome mud flats, reminiscent of the point's original name, "Turkey Buzzard." Aside from that regrettable untidiness of Nature, the grounds were carefully kept. Hundreds of guns in neat ranks and thousands of projectiles in symmetrical piles lined the sea walls and blighted the grass between the arsenal's numerous trees. Had ordnance been removed and grass permitted to flourish in the yellowed squares where shot piles had been, the arsenal, with its weathered brick buildings ranged in hollow-square formation about a verdant, tree-shaded lawn, would have looked very much like the campus of some quiet university.

Two wharfs jutted into the Potomac from the arsenal grounds, and sometimes Lincoln used them in making his river junkets. More often his presence at the arsenal betokened the firing of some new weapon. From the middle of the river rose five posts or piles, about ten feet apart and about fourteen hundred yards from the gun. By the position of the waterspout in relation to the posts, the projectile's line of flight was roughly determined. The approximate range was found by plane-tables: one in a summerhouse near the commandant's quarters, one behind the gun and one down at the dock. Because the spout disappeared so fast that it was hard to spot accurately, regular targets were erected in the fall of 1864. All the trials that Lincoln saw, however, were made with the posts as aiming points.

At the tip of the little peninsula was the old arsenal property, where most of the buildings were. Halfway up, the tongue of land was cut across by the United States Penitentiary. And from there northward to the city proper ran a tract of land called the Extension, which had by way of improvements little more than a railway track and half a mile of rough, muddy road. Midway through the war Lincoln had Secretary of the Interior Smith move the prisoners out of the penitentiary and transfer the building to the War Department for arsenal purposes. In a matter of weeks, according to the *Washington Star,* the building and its grounds were "filled with formidable weapons of war."

The use to which the old prison was put typified the function of the arsenal as a whole. The Washington Arsenal was not a manufacturing establishment like the nearby Navy Yard. Rather, it was a depot for the storage and distribution of arms. But the tremendous war which it fed taxed its capacity even in that limited role. The arsenal buildings were crammed with guns and ammunition in bewildering variety and profusion. Temporary buildings were thrown up, and those too were quickly filled. In the stormy month of January 1862 an observer saw great stores of valuable equipment left out in rain and snow because available cover was needed for still more valuable matériel. The rumble of Army wagons, an unceasing obbligato to life everywhere in wartime Washington, rose to a crescendo at the arsenal. In February 1862 it was estimated that five hundred wagons per day were jolting in and out of the arsenal grounds, rutting the dirt roads and scraping bark from the shade trees.

Storage and distribution, though the arsenal's chief functions, were not its only ones. Troops in the field soon made the happy discovery that when their muskets and rifles got fouled, rusted or caked with mud, the weapons could sometimes be turned in as unserviceable. Clean ones would be issued in exchange, and the dirty work would be passed on to the Washington arsenal. So the arsenal's overworked force spent a great deal of time on routine upkeep that should have been done in the field.

Furthermore, though the arsenal buildings were small and too closely spaced to be enlarged, the peacetime manufacture of small-arms ammunition was continued through the war. A visitor in June 1861 found one building occupied by over two hundred boys, from twelve to sixteen years of age, preparing about a hundred and thirty thousand cartridges a day. Each boy earned from sixty to eighty cents a day, "thus enabling them to render important assistance to—in many cases—their widowed mothers."

Men and women were also employed in such work. And under the pressure of war, their operations sometimes led to the creation as well as the support of widows. One afternoon, for example, a workman used a cold chisel to cut a defective fuse out of a spherical case shot. A spark from the chisel ignited the fuse, the shell exploded, seven or eight other shells—some in the hands of workmen—were detonated, and deadly fragments of iron flew in all directions. Surprisingly, only one man was killed outright, though three were terribly mangled. The explosion lifted the ceiling, blew out doors, buckled walls and set ammunition boxes ablaze. In the smoke-filled building were more than thirty-six thousand artillery shells and nearly seven million rounds of small-arms ammunition. But for the cool courage of the arsenal commandant, who came at once and supervised emergency measures till the fires were out, a fearful disaster might have struck Washington.

Despite wartime exigencies, the setup at Storehouse Two did not reflect credit on the commandant's judgment. But in that emergency, Colonel George Douglas Ramsay's pluck and luck made up for what he had lacked in foresight and intellect. It is perhaps not too farfetched to see in that incident a key to Ramsay's remarkable career.

Son of a Scottish-born merchant of Alexandria, Virginia, young Ramsay grew up in the capital. After graduating from West Point in 1820, he served in the light artillery and then in the Ordnance Corps. In 1835 he became a captain, and a captain he remained for twenty-five years, though his gallantry at Monterey earned him the brevet rank of major. At last, on April 22, 1861, the day before Ripley's appointment as Chief of Ordnance, Ramsay became a full-fledged major.

Twenty-five years a captain! Something was surely lacking in George Ramsay, and, studying his photograph alone, one might be tempted to guess what it was. His bland, unfurrowed features, though not without their solid dignity, suggest an American counterpart of the proverbial British colonel, heroic under stress, but handicapped by an unimaginative and somewhat sluggish mind. There is some corroboration for such an estimate. A quick-witted Creole named Lieutenant Stephen V. Benét served under Brevet Major Ramsay at the St. Louis Arsenal before the war. "When orders come," Benét wrote rather smugly at the time, "I am cool and collected for the work, because I have all along anticipated it. The Major thinks it the most extraordinary circumstances and hands them over to me." And another long-time intimate of Ramsay testified as to his technical aptitude and knowledge: "I cannot say that his opinion had very great weight with me."

Yet it was of this man that Abraham Lincoln's close friend Joshua Speed wrote in October 1861: "He is rendering great service & has been sadly neglected. I know Lincoln's appreciation of him to be very high."

Abraham Lincoln's faith in George Ramsay was not misplaced. True, Ramsay could be flustered by surprises, and many things surprised him. Professionally, moreover, he was no Thomas Rodman or John Dahlgren. But he was a hard and conscientious worker. In September 1861 General McClellan found him "untiring in energetically pushing forward the work in hand." Four months later, the Secretary of War sent Miles Greenwood, a Cincinnati industrialist, to report on affairs at the arsenal. Greenwood gave Ramsay "great praise for the performance of his arduous duties with such inadequate means." And in September 1862 General McClellan's chief of artillery paid warm tribute to Ramsay's "promptness, industry and active general co-operation."

More than that, Ramsay was a man of rare personal qualities. If wit and learning were not among them, neither were certain other common ingredients of success, such as cold ambition, guile, egotism and readiness to barter self-respect for advancement. On the contrary, Ramsay displayed a trustful naïveté that charmed even those who used it for a steppingstone.

Like most genuinely courageous men, Ramsay had an even temper. His quiet affability and unstudied courtesy won the instant liking of those who met him. In the spring of 1861 a Pennsylvania newspaper correspondent came to the arsenal and called on Ramsay, "who (though intently engaged in writing and receiving requisitions from the War Department, and issuing orders) very politely requested us to be seated. . . . He insisted on our remaining and accompanying us to see everything of interest, with which we were both surprised and delighted beyond measure, and which was greatly enhanced by the *manner* in which it was done. . . . After visiting Major Ramsay's residence, located immediately on the bank of the Potomac and in the midst of a beautifully shaded and extensive grove, and satisfying the inner man, we took our leave." The friendship of a man like Ramsay is the kind cherished by kings —and presidents.

Lincoln's "champagne experiments" would have brought him often into Ramsay's company, whatever the personal relations of the two might have been. But beyond their official or quasi-official encounters Lincoln and Ramsay were good friends personally. One tangible sign of this is the tone of their correspondence. "Mr. Lincoln was kindly disposed towards me," Ramsay said after the war. "He wrote me the most familiar notes." Such a note survives, dated October 17, 1861: "The lady—bearer of this—says she has two sons who want to work. Set them at it if possible. Wanting to work is so rare a want, that it should be encouraged." Lincoln wasted no such wry humor on General Ripley. But with his knack for divining character the President detected in Ramsay a distinct sense of humor beneath the accumulated starch of forty years in the Regular Army. Ordnance Office records are no mine of witticisms; yet even here Ramsay's endorsements now and then betray a lively sense of the ridiculous, as in the following:

Respectfully returned. On an exhibition of the carbine, by the person referred to within, to dispel my doubts as to its safety—the cartridge exploded and I barely escaped accident. And as I do not believe it would be safe to introduce such an arm into the service, I declined giving it further trial.

General Ripley's horror of new ideas has robbed history of much information about Lincoln's "champagne experiments" at the arsenal. Presumably because of Ripley's attitude, Lincoln often had Ramsay test inventions without formal orders, and for that reason no records were kept or reports made. Nevertheless, such trials are mentioned in certain little-known correspondence of the period, and in terms that suggest their extensiveness. There was, for instance, the case of Chaplain Jones's gun carriage.

In October 1861, the month when he so astonished Dr. Russell with his multifarious activities, Lincoln found time to listen to the Reverend Paul Franklin Jones, chaplain of the 1st New York Volunteers. Jones delighted the President with an ingenious plan for a coastal gun mount with a worm-gear elevating mechanism and a rack and pinion arrangement for traversing. Lincoln did more than merely praise the chaplain's scheme. To begin with he sent a note to the Patent Commissioner: "The Invention of P. Franklin Jones being deemed of practical importance to the Government it is desirable that it should be taken up and passed upon at once." What he did thereafter was summed up later by Jones himself:

In perfecting of this plan, the President has rendered me every means at his command and given me the encouragement of his personal presence wherever and whenever it would tend to facilitate the object. . . . The invention has been thoroughly tested in the presence of the President, who expressed his decided approval of its great merits.

Although in the Jones case, as in others, no official record was made of any arsenal tests during 1861, surviving correspondence refers to the exhibition of a full-scale model at the arsenal for several months. And the words of Chaplain Jones, fortunately preserved, are enough to fill in the picture. Reading them, we can see Lincoln escorting Chaplain Jones to the War Department, as he had done with Professor Lowe, the aeronaut. We can picture the President putting in one or more appearances at the arsenal to arrange with Ramsay for the setting up of the Jones gun carriage. We can picture Lincoln on the tree-shaded riverbank, inspecting the completed model and delightedly twirling the crank which moved a ponderous gun so easily. (The scene recalls that of Lawyer Lincoln entranced by his first sight of a self-raking reaper.)

To make the Jones gun carriage standard equipment in Union fortifications would have taken a lot of money and a lot of work, and Lincoln wanted reassurance from the experts before proceeding. The reassurance did not come. Lincoln first asked General Totten for his opinion of the device, "whether the government should have it, and on what terms." Totten took his assignment seriously (unless a seven-page report can be called frivolous). Cannily he pointed out to Lincoln that the mechanisms were too much exposed and too delicate to stand up long under fire; that, despite Jones's claims, just as many men would be needed to operate the new carriage as the old; and that the cost of installing the device along the Atlantic Coast alone would be nearly a million dollars. Totten conceded what Lincoln had already discovered—that Jones's carriage made elevation and traversing easy and quick; but the general took the pains to present a better way of achieving the same ends. When Jones complained that Totten was unfair, the patient President had Major James G. Benton of the Ordnance Department submit a separate report. Benton's report read like an echo of Totten's.

The reports of Totten and Benton were enough for Lincoln. Some months later Lincoln's good friend Senator Orville Browning of Illinois saw the Jones gun mount at the arsenal and took a fancy to it. "Seems to me a great invention," he noted in his diary. He and Mrs. Browning called at the White House with Chaplain Jones to argue the case. But no Jones gun mounts were ever ordered.

Not all the trials ordered by Lincoln were conducted under his own eye. As the war continued, more and more were carried out at West Point, or at the Parrott gun foundry in near-by Cold Spring,

New York, by a slender, quiet ordnance officer named Benét, who sympathized heartily with what the President was trying to do.

Captain Stephen Vincent Benét was to be the grandfather and namesake of the author who won a Pulitzer Prize in 1929 for his epic poem on the Civil War, *John Brown's Body*. Dignified and serious as a rule, with a resolute gleam in his keen, dark eyes, the captain could nevertheless relax into pleasant geniality among friends. Born in Florida of Spanish stock, as a boy he had planned to be a lawyer, and, by his father's order, had got through Blackstone's *Commentaries* before he was twelve. Though West Point diverted him from the law, Benét found scope for his legal talents in his *Military Law and the Practice of Court-Martial*, which went through several editions in the 1860s. He wrote also on military subjects, translated such classic military authors as Jomini and, while stationed in St. Louis before the Civil War, wrote newspaper articles under various pseudonyms. In his private letters occur foretastes of his grandson's talent for imagery.

Though Southern-born and married to a Kentucky girl, Benét put the Union first when the test came. He spent most of the war stationed at West Point or, as the Ordnance Department's representative, at Robert P. Parrott's Cold Spring Foundry. The comparative calm of those posts may explain why the Ordnance Department so often chose him to try out Lincoln's pet inventions. Or the choice of Benét may have been Lincoln's idea. In Captain Benét, Lincoln clearly found a kindred soul. Benét's attitude toward new weapons presented a striking contrast to that of General Ripley. Benét looked for the good points of inventions. He seemed to feel that a new weapon should not be scorned unless its worthlessness was either self-evident or proved by a fair trial. Ripley searched for the flaws in any proposal. To him, a new weapon must be assumed worthless unless proved otherwise—and he was not prepared to do any of the proving.

Whether or not Lincoln's "champagne experiments" had practical effects on ordnance, the President drew strength from them.

Whether in the company of Dahlgren, the keen, wiry, nervous climber, or Ramsay, the earnest, brave, trustful, good-humored plodder, Lincoln enjoyed a respite from politicians. In each of the two men, Lincoln saw the substantial good and winked at the inconsequential bad; in him, each of them found a warm and kind friend.

Perhaps whoever coined the phrase "champagne experiments" spoke more aptly than he knew. The weary leader's excursions to the arsenal and the Navy Yard did indeed serve as a tonic and stimulant. In the absorbing novelty of some warlike device, in the sharpening of logic and wit as he sought to master its intricacies and expose its flaws, in the wind, air, sun and sound of the proving grounds, in the sober, precise talk of technical experts, Lincoln found refreshment of mind and renewed steadiness for the grinding days ahead.

CHAPTER 7

Bureaucrats and Breechloaders

ONE CLEAR, STILL MORNING IN THE EARLY summer of 1861 Abraham Lincoln set out across the south lawn of the White House with his young secretary William O. Stoddard. Lincoln carried a repeating rifle (probably a Henry) and Stoddard a Springfield rifle which had been converted into a breechloader. The nine pounds of wood and metal in Lincoln's hand offered a key to victory, and Lincoln was beginning to sense the fact. It was the grim question of muzzle-loaders *versus* breechloaders, and not the beauty of the morning, that absorbed the two men as they strolled across the grass.

Lincoln and Stoddard were well acquainted with the tedious process a soldier had to go through to load and fire the regulation Springfield muzzle-loading rifle. Reaching into his cartridge pouch, the soldier took out a paper cartridge containing the powder charge and the bullet. Holding this between his thumb and forefinger, he tore it open with his teeth. Next he emptied the powder into the barrel and disengaged the bullet with his right hand and the thumb and two fingers of the left. Inserting the ball point up into the bore, he pressed it down with his right thumb. Then he drew his ramrod, which meant pulling it halfway out, steadying it, grasping it again and clearing it. He rammed the ball halfway down, took hold of the ramrod again, and drove the ball home. He then drew the ramrod out and returned it to its tube, each movement again in two stages. Next he primed the piece by raising it, half cocking it, taking off the old cap, taking a new one out of the pouch and pressing it down on the nipple. At last he cocked the gun, aimed it and fired. And if he had a particular target in mind, which was unlikely in all the excitement, he probably missed it clean.

An experienced man with steady nerves could fire three rounds per minute at the most. Choked by fear and battle smoke, unnerved by the shrieking of shells and the whining of bullets, rattled by the screams of dying men and the wolfish yipping of the charging enemy, not many soldiers did so well. And entirely aside from speed, a lot could go wrong if a man got overexcited. He might ram the bullet into the barrel before he poured in the powder. He might leave the ramrod in the barrel and then fire it off, past retrieving. He might load the cartridge, paper and all, without breaking it open.

If he made any of those easy mistakes, his gun was useless, probably for the rest of the battle. On the field of Gettysburg more than twenty-four thousand loaded muskets and rifles were found. Six thousand of them had one load apiece, twelve thousand had two loads each and six thousand had from three to ten loads. One famous specimen had twenty-three loads rammed down in regular order.

The obvious solution was a gun which could be loaded at the breech. At a stroke, almost all the pitfalls and complexities of loading would be eliminated. The soldier with a breechloader could not, even if he tried, put in more than one load at a time. He would not have to worry about a ramrod in loading. He could lie prone and load just as rapidly and easily as when he was standing. Not only would loading be gloriously simple, but breech-loading rifles would be better than muzzle-loaders in range and accuracy also, since tighter-fitting bullets could be used. And with such advantages would come the priceless asset of confidence, especially in the face of an enemy armed only with muzzle-loaders.

In retrospect, the dependence of the Union Army on muzzle-loaders seems inexcusable.

Breechloaders had been known for centuries. Two made during the reign of Henry VIII were exhibited in London during the 1860s and found to be remarkably like the contemporary Snider rifle. The breech-loading rifle of a British officer named Patrick Ferguson was used to good effect at Brandywine in 1777. An American named John Hall patented a breech-loading rifle in 1811, and in 1825 two companies at Fortress Monroe were armed with it and liked it.

But before whole armies could be given breechloaders, new machine tools and techniques had to be developed. Only then could breech mechanisms be made cheap, efficient and safe. Only by precision manufacture could the breech be tightly sealed against the escape of gas. Some types of breechloaders were tried by the Army before this stage had been reached; and so, by the early 1840s, older officers had acquired a stubborn prejudice against all such arms. Just before the Mexican War, therefore, the Ordnance Department abandoned the manufacture of breechloaders.

Within two or three years Christian Sharps had patented his single-shot breechloader, and the breech-loading rifle began to meet the requirements of a good military weapon. Other good breechloaders followed in close order. During the fifties Secretaries of War Jefferson Davis and John B. Floyd had some tried, with excellent results both on the proving ground and in the field. "Some of these arms," reported Floyd in 1857, "combine, in a very high degree, celerity and accuracy of fire, with great force, at long range." In 1860 Floyd discarded all reservations and wrote:

The long habit of using muzzle-loading arms will resist what seems to be so great an innovation, and ignorance may condemn; but as certainly as the percussion cap has superseded the flint and steel, so surely will the breech-loading gun drive out of use those that load at the muzzle.

It was a truer prophecy than most made by that unlucky Virginian.

If by 1860 Davis and Floyd had carried their point, if they had adopted a regulation breechloader and had begun converting the

Springfield Armory to its production, how different the course of history would have been! An able and intelligent Confederate general who encountered Yankee breechloaders during the war later maintained that the Confederacy would have gone down within a year had Federal infantry been thus armed at the start. Conversion begun as late as 1860 may not, probably would not, have been complete when war came. But if a large part of the Union Army had been given breechloaders by late 1862, Gettysburg would certainly have ended the war. More likely, Chancellorsville or even Fredericksburg would have done it, and history would record no Gettysburg Address, no President Grant, perhaps no carpetbag reconstruction or Solid South. Instead, it might have had the memoirs of ex-President Lincoln, perhaps written in retirement during the administration of President Burnside or Hooker.

But it did not happen that way. The Chief of Ordnance, Colonel Henry Knox Craig, was preoccupied with artillery and paid no heed to new small arms. Army officers remembered only the unhappy experience of the forties. The War Department, dazzled by the variety of good breechloaders and the rapidity of improvements, sat back and twiddled its thumbs, waiting for the perfect weapon.

And the war came.

So matters stood when Lincoln and Stoddard took their morning stroll south of the White House. At the end of the lawn was a low retaining wall, and beyond it lay a tract of land known then as the Treasury Park and later as the White Lot. This was their destination.

The Treasury Park was a humpy stretch of weeds, grass and gravel, surrounded by a wooden fence about shoulder high. At each end of the north side stood a cluster of wooden sheds and stables, and close to the fence along the other three sides ran a fringe of trees. The center of the lot was bare, except for one or two small huts, a big woodpile and a half-mile race track.

At the far end of the Treasury Park was a little estuary into

which the abandoned city canal emptied before joining the Potomac, and beyond that lay the marshy grounds about the Washington Monument. Over these grounds, called the Mall, ranged scores
of cattle, pastured there by the Army and moving obliviously about
a macabre reminder of their purpose in life—a government slaughterhouse close by the unfinished monument. The Mall was not a
lovely sight, and other senses than the visual were assaulted by the
slaughterhouse, the muddy field and the stagnant canal, which was
essentially an open sewer. Worse still, those were the days before
window screens, and so White House occupants resigned themselves to regular visitations of "the ague." "A more unfit position
for the Executive Mansion could not well be imagined," scolded
the *Washington Star*.

The Treasury Park, not much prettier, at least had pleasant
uses. One day, for example, the Maryland Club of Baltimore
played baseball there with the National Club of Washington,
Baltimore winning thirty-three to thirty-one. On another summer's
day, a soulless policeman surprised a pair of star-crossed lovers in
their Treasury Park tryst. The gentleman ungallantly "skedad-
dled," but his Juliet, less fleet of foot, was nabbed and sent to the
workhouse. And midway through the war, Company K of the
150th Pennsylvania—the "Bucktails"—pitched camp there for
the duration.

Most notably of all, the lot served as President Lincoln's personal rifle range and weapons proving ground, and more than one
passing citizen stopped to watch the tall Kentuckian fire at a target pinned to the woodpile.* Lincoln's usual companion on these
shooting expeditions was Nathan Mullikin, an ex-soldier from
Maryland, who had since 1836 been a messenger at the Ordnance
Office. But in the morning, before Mullikin came to work, and in
the evening, after he had left, Lincoln had to look for other com-

---

* At nine o'clock one night in November 1862 a musket ball from the Treasury
Park went through the side of Mrs. Grady's house on Fifteenth Street and lodged
in the opposite wall, near a startled young lady. But this can doubtless be laid to
an exuberant member of the newly arrived Bucktails.

pany. Thus William Stoddard enjoyed the honor on this morning of breechloader competition.

Both men favored breechloaders, and the only difference between them on this occasion was over the relative merits of repeaters and single-shot rifles. Lincoln took the more conservative view. To him the single-shot rifle seemed the weapon of the future. Yet even on this point, he told his young companion, "the Bureau officials" were against him.

Down at the Treasury Park, Lincoln and Stoddard commenced to bang away at a board leaning against the big woodpile. Gunfire had been banned in the capital, and a detail of men presently charged up, led by a noncom who shouted, between curses, "Stop that firing! Stop that firing!" When the unmistakable eminence of President Lincoln loomed up through the drifting smoke, the astounded guardians of public tranquillity beat a hasty retreat. "Well," said Lincoln, looking after them, "they might have stayed and seen the shooting."

Few Civil War battles were so epochal in their consequences as the battle over breechloaders. And since few have received so little notice from historians, we might do well at this point to review the pros and cons.

Those who opposed the breech-loading rifle talked about "its complication of mechanism and the danger of its being disabled by accident in hurried loading." Even if this had been true, the experience of Gettysburg would suggest that muzzle-loaders were no better. But it was not true. Breechloaders proved themselves reliable and durable in many a Civil War action. On one occasion, to be sure, some Sharps rifles became "so choked with dirt and dust, and so heated with the rapid and continuous firing, as to be almost unserviceable." But that was after two hundred rounds apiece, a record no muzzle-loader was likely to equal.

The old guard claimed, somewhat inconsistently, that men with breechloaders used up ammunition too fast and recklessly. It was true that toward the end of the war troops with repeaters carried a hundred rounds instead of the usual forty. The added weight made itself felt on a long march, and in one such regiment "sometimes the bundles of cartridges were surreptitiously lightened." But greater fire power was to be welcomed, not avoided. If ammunition ran short, the real problem was how to get more, not how to use less. And as for the charge of reckless waste, troops with breech-loaders soon learned to husband their ammunition. In three days of fighting at Gettysburg, with twenty per cent casualties, one experienced outfit armed with breechloaders fired an average of only thirty-two rounds per man. Moreover, even when ammunition did run out, the confidence engendered by breechloaders seemed to persist. At Wapping Heights troops with breechloaders drove the enemy back a mile. While waiting for more ammunition, they stayed put and nonchalantly picked blackberries.

Men with muzzle-loaders were notoriously apt to fire wildly. Were men who used breechloaders likely to be even more careless in aiming, as the old guard claimed? Consider a letter written to the *Army and Navy Journal* in 1864 by one who signed himself "SOLDIER":

Let them come to the front armed with one Springfield musket, and oppose themselves to an equal number of Rebs armed with repeaters or breech-loaders. If they can stand that, let them go to the picket line, and while fumbling for a cap and trying to get it on the cone one of these cold days, offer themselves as a target to some fellow on the other side who has nothing to do but cock his piece and blaze away. If they don't throw down their bungling, slow-shooting gun in disgust, they may be excused for indulging in remarks not complimentary to those who compel them to the unequal contest. The objection has been urged that we fire too many shots with our present muzzle-loaders, and consequently it would be folly to add to the waste of ammunition by affording us greater ease or facility in loading. Do our good friends ever reflect that the loss of time in loading is the great *cause* of haste, and consequent inaccuracy in firing? . . .

More plausible was Ripley's argument that ammunition must be standardized. At Malvern Hill one regiment had to leave the fight because no more Sharps cartridges could be obtained. At Second Bull Run the chief ordnance officer requisitioned eleven different kinds and calibers of small-arms ammunition, of which five were for breechloaders. Ripley was obsessed by the problem, and he seemed to blame it all on breechloaders. In the summer of 1861, for example, he warned Massachusetts that if she gave her men breechloaders they had better bring their own ammunition.

One easy answer to this argument was the existence of good breechloaders which used the regulation muzzle-loader paper cartridge. But there was more to it than that. Breechloaders could use metallic cartridges, which were much better than the paper kind. If these had been adopted, the South, which could not turn out metallic cartridges in quantity, would have been unable to use the captured arms on which it counted for survival. Of course, if muzzle-loaders had still been used along with the breechloaders, at least two types of ammunition would have been needed. But in actuality, breechloaders or no breechloaders, Civil War ammunition from first to last never got even that close to standardization.

Ripley's strongest argument was that breechloaders could not be turned out in time to do any good. Large-scale production of muzzle-loaders by American manufacturers was a year in getting under way. Breechloader production would have been slower still. And until the war was half over, Ripley shared the common belief that it could, and probably would, end at any moment. In the circumstances, it is easy to understand Ripley's opposition to the ordering of expensive "fancy arms" which might never be used. Furthermore, Ripley maintained, to set factories to work on breechloaders would reduce the supply of desperately needed muzzleloaders.

Yet Captain Harwood of the Navy Ordnance Bureau saw a way out of the dilemma. He wrote Secretary Welles in May 1861:

The Bureau has reason to believe that facilities can be found abroad—especially in the great manufacturing towns of Belgium— where, should a competent agent be sent with the pattern of a [breech-loading] fire arm which has been proved to combine essential elements of success, the arms could be fabricated more speedily and economically than in the United States.

In January 1862 the War Department officially forswore the purchase of any more European arms. Evidently the Union was prepared to supply its own muzzle-loaders thereafter. It follows that if a good breechloader had then been ordered from European arms makers, nothing would have been risked but expense; and by the middle of 1863 at the latest much of the Union Army might have been armed with breechloaders.

But if General Ripley ever heard of Harwood's proposal, he ignored it.

The gun that William Stoddard fired in his shooting match with Lincoln was probably the one invented by a Washington man named Samuel Wilmer Marsh. The Marsh gun was a converted Springfield rifle with a plug or bolt hinged to the upper part of the breech. When the trigger was pressed forward, the plug was thrown up so that the cartridge could be inserted into the breech. A blow of the hand brought back the breech plug, which was held in place by a steel pin. A double ring of steel, expanded by a steel cone, served as a gas check.

To Lincoln, the Marsh gun seemed to forestall all objections. Most good breechloaders cost at least thirty-six dollars (as compared to nineteen or twenty for muzzle-loaders) but Marsh offered his for just under thirty. Marsh's gun used the regulation .58-caliber paper cartridge. As for the bugaboo of fragility, if anything actually did go wrong with the Marsh gun as a breechloader, it could be converted back into a muzzle-loader on the field with one swift and easy operation.

So pleased was Lincoln with the Marsh gun that he had Lieutenant Benét try it at West Point that summer. Marsh lent Benét the only gun he had. It was old and obviously worn. Yet escape of gas was no problem, and Benét's moistened finger easily cleaned off such fouling as occurred in the gas check and breech. In the course of the trial Benét got off ten rounds in less than two minutes. After firing 121 rounds, Benét reported the gun to be simple, strong and not easily deranged. It had "great merit," he told Lincoln.

Marsh and his partner, a shrewd Virginian named Robert Gallaher, did not rely on Benét's praise alone. They showed the gun to two influential Tennesseeans, Senator Andrew Johnson and ex-Congressman Emerson Etheridge, and the latter cannily advised them to sell Lincoln the idea of arming Kentucky with Marsh breechloaders. Marsh and Gallaher also hired an old friend of Lincoln, a stogy-puffing Indiana politician named Richard W. Thompson, to lobby for them, and Thompson pleaded their case with both Lincoln and Secretary Cameron. "If all fails," Cameron assured his Hoosier friend, "I will attend to your interests."

General Ripley seemed to be the only obstacle to an order. He delayed and delayed and at last spurned the Marsh-Gallaher proposition entirely. "We do not want such arms as you offer," he told the two men.

It was at this point that Lincoln stepped in and overruled his Chief of Ordnance. On October 14, 1861, at Lincoln's direction, Ripley reluctantly ordered twenty-five thousand Marsh breechloaders, three thousand to be delivered in four months and a thousand a month thereafter.* In a last fling Ripley slipped in the unusual stipulation that a single late delivery would cancel the entire contract. He was overruled on that point also, and at least twenty-five thousand Union soldiers were assured freedom from the nightmare of loading muzzle-loaders.

Or so it seemed.

While Marsh and Gallaher were still seeking their order, Lincoln struck another blow for breechloaders with the help of Colonel Hiram Berdan.

Progress often has strange allies. Some people liked Hiram Berdan. Others decidedly did not. Old General Winfield Scott was

---

* This was destined to be the largest single order for breech-loading rifles given during the Civil War.

"very favorably impressed" with the man, but an associate of Berdan called him "most unscrupulous" and "totally unfit for a command." Major Dyer of the Springfield Armory considered Berdan "thoroughly unscrupulous and unreliable." "I accept everything that Berdan tells me *cum grano salis*," declared Dyer shortly after the war.

The subject of these remarks was an aggressive man in his middle thirties with a receding hairline and a drooping mustache. By profession a trained mechanical engineer with offices in New York City, he was better known in 1861 for his avocation, which was rifle marksmanship. In a list of the nation's best rifle shots for fifteen years previous, Berdan's name stood first. Not only could Berdan draw a sure bead on his target, but he also had a keen eye for the main chance. His first reaction to the outbreak of war was to offer Ripley a patented musket ball. As if sensing the futility of this, he next called, via the newspapers, for "the best marksmen in the country, to form a corps of skirmishers" under his command. By mid-June General Scott had approved the plan. Lincoln persuaded Governor Morgan of New York to equip a company in the Berdan outfit, and other states followed suit.

The success of the Sharpshooters depended on their weapons. Berdan knew this, and therefore, when he started recruiting, he promised breechloaders, with hair triggers and telescopic sights, to those who did not bring their own target rifles. But Berdan also shrewdly suspected that the good will of General Ripley was worth cultivating. "If I could not secure your able assistance in the matter," he wrote Ripley ingratiatingly, "I should have but little hope of success." So when Ripley insisted that the Sharpshooters should have Springfield muzzle-loaders, Berdan gave in.

Recruiting was brisk, and by early September the first few companies were arriving in Washington. Meanwhile, something—perhaps the attitude of his men—changed Berdan's mind and he began once more to ask for breechloaders. To Ripley, this was basest perfidy; from then on he and Berdan were enemies.

The United States Sharpshooters were scarcely settled in camp when tales of their marksmanship began appearing in the newspapers. The oufit became a favorite with the swarms of sight-seers who toured the capital's encircling camps. One sultry afternoon in late September President Lincoln appeared at the Berdan camp, accompanied by three Cabinet members, the Prince de Joinville with his son and nephews, and a constellation of generals, including McClellan, McDowell and Mansfield.

After Lincoln had reviewed the troops, Berdan invited the party to the rifle pits where a hundred Sharpshooters were engaged in target practice with their own rifles. Two life-size canvas Zouaves at six hundred thirty yards were subjected to some four hundred shots, of which about a hundred took effect. McClellan and others tried their skill with borrowed rifles, and Lincoln himself fired three good shots. The President handled his borrowed weapon "like a veteran marksman," to the crowd's delight. Resting the gun (it weighed thirty-five pounds) on what he called a sapling, he remarked, "Boys, this reminds me of old-time shooting." A cheer went up from his audience.

Assistant Secretary of War Tom Scott, who disliked the pushing colonel, asked Berdan sneeringly what he knew about guns and war, that he should set himself up against all these officials. This, it would seem, was an oblique reference to Berdan's fight for breechloaders. When Berdan refused to rise to the bait, Scott challenged him to try his own skill, hoping, presumably, that Berdan would either back down or bungle his shot from nervousness. Nerve was Hiram Berdan's long suit, as Scott should have known. Berdan took up the challenge, and a target was set up at six hundred yards.

The target was a man's figure, labeled JEFF DAVIS. Berdan expressed some delicacy about perforating one chief executive in the presence of another, but Lincoln reassured him good-naturedly. "Oh, Colonel," he said, "if you make a good shot it will serve him right."

Berdan borrowed his sergeant major's rifle. "Now," said Scott, "you must fire standing, for officers should not dirty their uniforms by getting into rifle pits."

"You are right, Colonel Scott," Berdan said coolly, "I always fire from the shoulder." He stepped forward and raised the ponderous gun.

"What point are you going to fire at?" Scott asked.

"The head," Berdan replied, taking aim.

"Fire at the right eye!" the Assistant Secretary shouted desperately. And Berdan fired.

When the target was brought in, Lincoln burst out laughing: Berdan's bullet had cut out the pupil of "Jeff Davis's" right eye. At six hundred yards, as Lincoln well knew, this was sheer coincidence, but he was tickled to see Scott's ill-humored taunts boomerang so neatly. Besides, we may reasonably surmise, the incident gave Lincoln an excuse he had been waiting for.

Still laughing, the President climbed into his carriage, settled himself and then called back, "Colonel, come down tomorrow, and I will give you the order for the breechloaders."

The publicity value of Sharpshooter patronage was already evident. From all over the North and even from Europe arms makers and inventors flocked to Berdan's camp. After a course in the anatomy of small arms such as fell to no other outfit, the Sharpshooters gave their vote to the 1859 Sharps, a single-shot breech-loading rifle.

The Sharps's action was simple: a vertically sliding breech block, worked by a lever under the gun. Like most other breechloaders which used paper cartridges, its earlier models had given trouble with escape of gas from the breech; but the 1859 Sharps had a new and effective gas check. To load the gun, one simply pulled down the lever, inserted a paper cartridge (.54 caliber, not the regulation .58) and pushed the lever up again. Special primers were provided, little round, flat copper discs which were inserted below the hammer, but in action troops found them undependable and preferred to use the regular Army or "hat" cap. The Sharps could be fired eight or ten times a minute—half again as fast as the Marsh gun and three times as fast as a muzzle-loader.

To General Ripley, all breechloaders were "newfangled gim-cracks"; but the Sharps, at least, were scarcely "newfangled." Already these guns had behind them a dozen years of honorable history. In the struggle for Kansas, Sharps rifles had won nationwide fame as "Beecher's Bibles," after Henry Ward Beecher had professed to see "more moral power in one of those instruments so far as the slave-holders were concerned than in a hundred Bibles." As early as 1850 an Army Ordnance Board had tried and highly praised the gun; as recently as January 1861 a captain of the 1st United States Dragoons had informed the Ordnance Office that after some years' service in the West, Sharps carbines (using the same action as the rifles) were "considered exceedingly efficient."

All this was of no more concern to General Ripley than were the wishes of Colonel Berdan, the Sharpshooters and President Lincoln himself. With Assistant Secretary Scott backing him up, Ripley flatly refused to order the Sharps. In November General McClellan asked Ripley to order a thousand Colt revolving rifles, breechloaders made on the principle of the famous revolver; although the Colt firm was one of Ripley's special pets, Ripley scorned the compromise. And since the Chief of Ordnance answered directly to the War Department, not to the commanding general, McClellan could do no more.

Company A of the Sharpshooters appealed to their Congressmen for help, promising to pay the difference between Sharps and Springfields out of their own pockets. Assistant Secretary Scott coldly endorsed their petition: "They will be provided with first class Harpers Ferry rifles—& new pattern Springfield Rifles."

By mid-December Berdan's men were turning ugly. Snuffing trouble, a *New York Post* correspondent drove out to their camp, past sodden, brown fields and forlorn trees. After his gloomy drive, he welcomed the sight of the Sharpshooters' hilltop camp in a grove of cedars. On the way up, he passed groups of men around campfires, over which cooked great joints of meat and cauldrons of coffee. It was sunset, and bugles were calling. "The sky was flushed all over with rosy crimson, and below a silver mist was rising

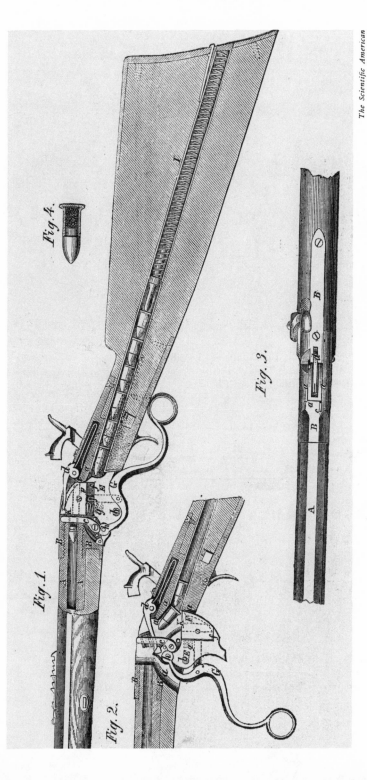

THE MECHANISM OF THE SPENCER REPEATING RIFLE

LINCOLN SEES A RIFLE

A drawing by Alfred Waud. The occasion was a presentation of an elkhorn chair to
Lincoln by Seth Kinsman, the California hunter.

A ROCKET THREATENS THE EXISTENCE OF THE UNITED STATES

Lincoln's brush with death, unmentioned by several diarists present, is here revealed.
This loose memo was tucked into a naval ledger and remained hidden for ninety years.

through," he noted, "while from our high position the city and the great white Capitol looked pale and shadowy as the city of a mirage." The men themselves, in their dark-green uniforms, gray overcoats trimmed with green, and fur-covered knapsacks, "had a decidedly sylvan appearance, suggestive of Robin Hood and his merry men."

Sylvan the men may have been, and there was a certain aptness in comparing their commander to Robin Hood, but they were far from merry. Some had their own target rifles, and fifty muskets had been issued them for guard duty. Yet, as they stared out over dreary fields at their shadowy Capitol, most of Berdan's men, two thousand strong, were disagreeably conscious of being marksmen without guns. The *Post* man remarked ominously:

It is a wonder that the men retain their spirits under such long delay, and it speaks well for their officers that they are not discouraged. Sharps rifles were promised them by the President and ordered by General McClellan, but some trouble in the War Department has thus far prevented their getting them. Let us hope they will soon have the weapon they are so competent to wield.

While Colonel Berdan wrestled with his problems, Lincoln was coming to the rescue of still another champion of breechloaders, young Christopher Spencer.

Like General Ripley, Christopher Spencer was a Connecticut Yankee. Other similarities between the two are hard to find. Elderly General Ripley abhorred new ideas; the twenty-seven-year-old Spencer spawned them. At thirteen, Spencer cut down his grandfather's Revolutionary musket to carbine size, using a homemade hack saw. At fifteen he built a working model of a steam engine from information in an old volume of *Comstock's Philosophy*. By his late twenties he was driving to work in a steam automobile of his own design. And, as evidence that youth did not make the difference, Spencer at the age of eighty-seven was to take up aviation as a hobby. When Mark Twain wrote *A Connecticut Yankee in King Arthur's Court*, he may well have modeled the hero on

Christopher Spencer, who had by then lived seventeen years in or near Mark Twain's Hartford.

Like Twain's Yankee, Spencer became a machinist and worked in the great Colt works at Hartford. After three years there he shifted to the Cheney Brothers' silk factory near Hartford, where he invented an automatic silk-winding machine that revolutionized the thread industry. In March 1860 Spencer patented his ingenious repeating rifle, the fruit of three years' experimentation. A loading tube containing seven rim-fire metallic cartridges, end to end, was inserted into the stock, after which the gun chamber was loaded simply by working a lever.

Since Secretary Welles was a Hartford man himself and a close friend of the Cheneys, Spencer had no difficulty in getting the Navy to try his gun in June 1861. But Dahlgren's enthusiasm for the weapon sprang from more than political pressure. Of five hundred cartridges tried, only one misfired, and that because of defective fulminate. After seven shots were fired in ten seconds, the barrel grew ominously hot. But a sustained rate of fourteen rounds per minute gave no trouble at all. Without cleaning, the gun worked as well at the end of the trial as at the start. Moved by Dahlgren's delight, Harwood promptly ordered seven hundred Spencers for the Navy.

Lincoln came down to the Navy Yard next day, and it was probably then that he was introduced to this latest marvel of Yankee ingenuity. Whether he first handled the Spencer then or at a slightly later time, he was soon familiar with it, in both its rifle and its carbine form.

One afternoon, feeling that the Spencer carbine-sight could be bettered, Lincoln took a stick of pine and whittled his idea into shape. Then he walked over to the Winder Building in search of Nathan Mullikin, the Ordnance Office messenger. The building's corridors were darker than ever, for evening was coming on. Up and down the murky hallway paced Abraham Lincoln with his Spencer carbine. In deserted offices, the pens were stilled and the ledgers put up. "I do wonder," he murmured to himself, "if they have gone already and left the building all alone."

At last, from a doorway down the hall, a late-working Navy Department clerk appeared. "Good evening," Lincoln said, "I was just looking for that man who goes shooting with me sometimes."

Mullikin had left, but the clerk offered himself as a substitute, and the pair strolled down to the Treasury Park in the early twilight. Fixing a sheet of white Congressional stationery to the woodpile (it would be interesting to know who had written the letter) Lincoln turned, paced off a few score feet, faced the target, and raised his carbine. Seven shots in quick succession struck in or around the target. "I believe I can make this gun shoot better," remarked Lincoln, extracting his whittled sight from a vest pocket and fitting it on the gun. He emptied the magazine, reloaded and emptied it again. Of the fourteen shots, nearly a dozen hit the paper.

The record of the Lincoln gunsight, if it can be given so formal a name, ends there. But the Spencer rifle went on to fresh conquests. At Fortress Monroe in August, Captain Alexander Dyer (not yet promoted to the Springfield Armory) fired a Spencer rifle some eighty times. In the course of the trial, it was buried in sand, but no clogging or other ill effect resulted. The breech mechanism was soaked in salt water and exposed for twenty-four hours. The gun continued to work easily. And though it was not cleaned during the tests, it worked as well at the end as at the beginning, which was very well indeed. The only improvement Dyer could suggest was to make the extracting ratchet of tempered steel to reduce wear. "I regard it," he said, "as one of the very best breech-loading arms I have seen."

General McClellan shared the views of Dahlgren and Dyer. A three-man board set up by him to consider such weapons had some minor suggestions—a chain to prevent loss of the loading tube and some spare springs for the magazine—but otherwise saw no flaws in the Spencer rifle. Finding it compact, durable and "very accurate," the board recommended that it be adopted generally, if a limited trial in the field proved successful.

Again it was General Ripley who struck the jarring note. The Spencer rifle, he reported, was too heavy and too expensive. It required special ammunition. Arms should be standardized. And anyway, orders had been given for "nearly 73,000 breech-loading rifles and carbines." The last remark demonstrated Ripley's squidlike capacity for clouding the issue. To be sure, twenty-five thousand Marsh breech-loading rifles had been ordered, thanks to Lincoln. But almost all the other breechloaders were carbines, which were cavalry arms, whereas the question was one of arming infantry.*

Blocked by Ripley, Christopher Spencer appealed to the President. And again, Lincoln helped to make ordnance history. On December 26, 1861, by Lincoln's direction, General Ripley ordered ten thousand Spencer repeating rifles.

Lincoln intended to give Berdan's Sharpshooters a share of Spencer's wonderful rifles. One of them was sent to Berdan for trial. On Christmas Day, while Berdan was firing the gun, a cartridge burst prematurely, blowing powder through a slot and temporarily blinding Berdan's right eye. But Berdan was magnanimous about the incident, merely suggesting from his sickbed that the Spencer Company do something "to guard against similar accidents with the new guns." Although he could not bring himself to recommend the gun, he refrained from condemning it. The order was permitted to stand, and on the last day of 1861 the Spencer Company accepted it.

As 1861 ended, the Union Army seemed about to settle the rivalry between breechloaders and muzzle-loaders. Berdan's men suspected otherwise, but Abraham Lincoln's promise should have

---

* Not even Ripley had the face to insist that mounted men carry muzzle-loaders, and so breech-loading carbines were ordered in considerable quantity from the first. Their effectiveness, however, failed to attract much notice till after Gettysburg; and, in any case, few people seemed to realize that infantry might profit from the experience of cavalry. Indeed, we shall later see how Ripley used the need for breech-loading *carbines* to discourage orders for breech-loading *rifles*.

stilled their doubts. Thirty-seven thousand breech-loading rifles, both single-shot and repeating, using both paper and metallic cartridges, had been ordered or were soon to be ordered, all of them by Lincoln's direction and on his responsibility.

Lincoln could not wisely have done more. Committing the Army to breechloaders without an extensive field trial would have been betting the nation's life against the opinion of most experts. But if breechloaders were really superior, thirty-seven thousand men should be able to prove it, and prove it soon.

CHAPTER 8

The Coffee-mill Gun

EARLY IN JUNE 1861 THREE MEN OF
Gotham signed the register at Willard's.

One of them was Simeon Draper, a small-fry New York politician with a loud voice, a large, long nose and a well-developed potbelly. (He was once compared to a good-natured pelican digesting a surfeit of sprats.) Although his reputation was not spotless, he stood well with Secretary Seward, and that still counted for something in Washington. Another was Orison Blunt, for thirty years a New York arms maker and importer. He contributed quiet respectability to the little group. No less a nabob than John Jacob Astor II vouched for him as "a perfectly honest & reliable man." Blunt was a patriot, too, already hard at work procuring arms for the Ordnance Department and for New York's Union Defence Committee without profit for himself.

The third man, as was his custom, signed himself merely "J. D. MILLS." The antecedents of a New Yorker so reticent about his given names must remain obscure, which is a pity. For whatever he had been, J. D. Mills was soon to become the world's first successful machine-gun salesman.

No one had yet coined the phrase "machine gun." Mills called his curious device "the Union Repeating Gun . . . An Army in six feet square." Just who had invented it is hard to say. Two New Yorkers named Edward Nugent and William Palmer battled over patent rights from the summer of 1861 to the fall of 1863, but there is no record of the outcome. Mills seems to have represented the Nugent faction.

If Draper and Blunt came along to open the way for Mills, they did their work well and speedily. Before the week was out, Mills, Blunt and Abraham Lincoln were climbing the stairs to the loft of Hall's carriage shop across from the Willard. There in the loft Lincoln had his first look at the fascinating contraption. Mounted on a two-wheeled light artillery carriage, the Union Repeating Gun consisted of a single rifle barrel with an ingenious breech mechanism. On top was a hopper which Mills had filled with steel cartridge cases, designed to hold regular .58-caliber paper cartridges. Lincoln turned a crank on the side of the gun and delightedly watched the cartridge cases drop one by one into the grooves of a revolving cylinder, while the mechanism automatically tripped the firing pin, extracted the cylinders and dropped them into a receptacle for reloading. Seeing the level of the cases sink lower in the hopper while others were spewed into the receiving tray, Lincoln drew on his knack for homely imagery to dub the device a "Coffee Mill Gun." The name stuck to it for the rest of the war.

It was a peculiarly Yankee notion, this substitution of cogs, cams and linkages for human brain and muscle. As Elias Howe's sewing machine had outmoded the sore eyes and stiff fingers of Thomas Hood's seamstress, so now William Palmer (or Edward Nugent) had, it seemed, made obsolete the panic and careless haste which rendered thousands of muskets useless in every great battle.

A day or two later Simeon Draper badgered General Ripley into having the gun fired on the Washington Arsenal grounds before an audience which included five generals, three Cabinet members, the governor of Connecticut and President Lincoln. All were impressed. Gray-bearded, soldierly General Joseph K. F. Mansfield, who commanded Washington's defenses, promptly asked Secretary Cameron to get a number of coffee-mill guns for the city's fortifications. "I think it an excellent rampart gun," he wrote, "a good field gun against cavalry & horse Artillery, an excellent gun to defend the passage of the bridge and should be thoroughly tested in the field at once."

Lincoln sought Dahlgren's advice. "You have seen Mr. Blunt's new gun," he wrote the captain on June 10. "What think you of it? Would the government do well to purchase some of them? Should they be of the size of the one exhibited or of different sizes?" Dahlgren was all in favor of buying some, although he felt that "for the present emergency, it would be well to adhere to the dimension now constructed."

And to General Ripley, Lincoln wrote: "I saw this gun myself, and witnessed some experiments with it; and I really think it worth the attention of the Government."

After this splendid beginning, the coffee-mill trio returned to New York in the naïve belief that an order was assured. Presently Mills began to have qualms. Toward the end of June he wrote Lincoln, asking him to give the matter his "personal and early consideration." "One word from your Excellency would suffice," pleaded the salesman, "and subsequent events would prove to you its momentous consequences." One of Lincoln's secretaries apparently sent the letter on to the Ordnance Department without comment. To another letter Ripley replied that he could give no opinion on the gun without far more extensive trials, and he gave no indication that he would order any such trials.

When the news of Bull Run reached New York late in July, Mills wrote Lincoln again, more urgently:

I am reliably informed that General Ripley thinks very favorably of [the gun], but does not wish to take the responsibility of ordering anything new in arms. If no one else is willing to "take the responsibility," will not the President take it?

That letter, too, went to the Ordnance Office without comment.

Blunt and Draper seemed to feel that they had done their share. Draper's next letter to General Ripley was in behalf of a "balloon shell" (along the lines of those used by the Japanese against the

United States in World War II). Ripley, of course, scoffed at the idea.

Early in July Orison Blunt introduced Lincoln to another machine-gun inventor, a Newark mining engineer named Edward B. Wilder, who fired his "rifle battery" for the President. In those days, a "rifle battery" usually consisted of a row of rifle barrels fixed side by side and fired in volleys. But Wilder's claim that his gun could fire eight thousand regulation Minié balls an hour suggests that it was more like the coffee-mill gun. Wilder's fortunes suffered a turn for the worse in September, when he was thrown into Fort Lafayette on the charge of offering his invention to the rebels. Lincoln accepted his denials at face value and had him released in October. But by then Wilder had given up his machine gun as a dead loss, since he lacked "the influence necessary to obtain an order from the War Department to have a few constructed." In 1863 the Newark directory still listed him as a mining engineer.

In September, S. D. Newbro of Lansing, Michigan, offered Lincoln a crank-operated, hopper-fed, multibarrel machine gun which he claimed could fire three or four hundred shots a minute and could be made for $200. But one of the White House secretaries intercepted Newbro's letter and sent it to General Ripley, who ignored it.

Forsaken by Blunt and Draper, J. D. Mills meanwhile had found a new ally: benign, white-bearded old Peter Cooper, pioneer of railroading, partner with Cyrus Field in the Atlantic Cable project and founder of Cooper Institute, where Lincoln had made the speech that won him recognition in the East. Like Blunt and Draper, Cooper had no personal stake in the matter, but he wrote Lincoln enthusiastically in September. A few weeks later the old philanthropist went to work on Secretary Cameron: "Half a dozen men with one of these guns can do the work of a thousand. . . . It is an immense saving to the country in equipment and rations alone. . . . Beside which, you risk the lives of but half a dozen men in place of a regiment."

Late in October J. D. Mills turned up again in Washington, this time with ten of his coffee-mill guns; and he found that Lincoln had not forgotten him. The President sent a note to McClellan: "A battery of repeating guns, on wheels, can be seen at the Arsenal any hour to-day. Could you, without inconvenience see them at 3. or 4. oclock—please answer." The dashing young general had made a previous engagement to review troops, but Lincoln drove down to the arsenal anyway; and before the day was over, he had, on his own responsibility, bought all ten of the guns at $1300 apiece—although Dahlgren had estimated the cost of manufacture at $615 each.

This was the first recorded sale of machine guns in history.

That evening Lincoln and young John Hay walked across Pennsylvania Avenue to McClellan's headquarters. Lincoln was elated with his purchase. When the general came in, Lincoln greeted him with a spirited account of his "wonderful new repeating battery of rifled guns, shooting fifty balls a minute." He urged McClellan to go down and see the guns, and, if proper, detail a corps of men to work them. Then the two men discussed the rising clamor for an immediate advance against the South. "I have a notion to go out with you and stand or fall with the battle," Lincoln exclaimed buoyantly.

An incident presently occurred in Boston that might have dampened Lincoln's elation, had he known of it. Lincoln had authorized Major General Ben Butler to raise troops in New England and arm them "with such serviceable arms as he may deem fit." That gadget-minded general took full advantage of the latter dispensation. Among the several military novelties he purchased on the strength of it were two coffee-mill guns, which arrived in Boston toward the end of November.

No headquarters exhibitionist could resist cranking an unguarded coffee-mill gun, the nearest military equivalent to a big, brazen, ratchet-type noisemaker. As someone gratified that compulsion, the racket suddenly ended with a dull twang; the mainspring, which forced the hammer against the cap, had flown into pieces.

"If the guns are going to act in that way," Butler's adjutant wrote to Woodward and Cox, the manufacturers, "we shall at least require some spare parts immediately. . . . Please send them." There survives, as evidence that the adjutant's prognosis was sound, a subsequent bill of $172.91 for repairs to one of the guns. At Butler's headquarters, at least, it began to appear that Woodward and Cox had not given the customers their thirteen hundred dollars' worth.

In Washington the cloud was still invisible. McClellan caught some of Lincoln's enthusiasm for the new weapons, and at his request Mills made a written offer to furnish them in quantity at $1200 each. The price gave McClellan pause, and he asked Secretary Cameron whether or not fifty should be bought on those terms. This McClellanesque wavering led Lincoln to insist that the commanding general support him unequivocally. "He knows whether the guns will be serviceable," Lincoln told Mills. "I do not. It avails nothing for him to intimate that he has no *objection* to my purchasing them." At last McClellan agreed to the purchase of fifty coffee-mill guns at cost plus twenty per cent (which finally worked out to $735 each). On December 19, 1861, Lincoln gave the order.

The end of 1861 thus brought the machine gun, like the breech-loading rifle, close to its first great battle test. And like the breech-loader, the machine gun owed its first chance to a man who could "take the responsibility" when others flinched.

CHAPTER 9

Lincoln's Field Artillery

IF GENERAL RIPLEY'S PASSION FOR STAND-
ardizing arms had its tragic consequences, it had also its merits,
especially in field artillery. A requisition for field-artillery ammunition during the Civil War was apt to be an exercise in permuta-
tions and combinations. Cannon might be rifled or smoothbore,
bronze, steel or iron. They might be Parrott, Napoleon, Wiard,
Whitworth, Woodruff or Ellsworth guns, mountain or prairie howitzers, mortars or coehorns. They came in nine common calibers,
fired solid shot, grape shot, canister, case and seven principal types
of shells—Dyer, Parrott, James, Shenkl, Dimmick, Hotchkiss and
Whitworth. The varieties of ammunition were not infinite, but by
late 1862 they had passed the six-hundred mark.

The resulting confusion may have been slightly comical, but its
effect was not. At the most critical moments in more than one
battle, guns fell silent for lack of some freakish type of shot or
shell, though great stores of standard ammunition were on hand.

Backed by such commanders as U. S. Grant, Ripley worked
heroically to standardize field artillery. He found a zealous ally in
McClellan's chief of artillery, Brigadier General William F. Barry,
a shrewd veteran and "a most companionable gentleman of the old
school." By October 1861, reported Russell of the *London Times,*
Barry had "done wonders" in reducing the numbers of calibers. In
the following summer, at Ripley's urgent request, Barry was made
"Inspector General of Artillery" with the special duty of standard-

izing field guns; and by the time of Gettysburg, only a hundred and forty kinds of ammunition were in use. The increase in efficiency was unmistakable.

The circumstances explain, and perhaps excuse, Ripley's undisguised annoyance whenever President Lincoln introduced a new kind of field artillery. A case in point was that of the Woodruff guns.

James Woodruff, a keen-faced, sharp-minded Connecticut man, migrated to Quincy, Illinois, in 1842 at the age of twenty-one, and became a pillar of Quincy society, as well as a good friend of Lincoln's crony, Orville Browning. Woodruff and Browning were both conspicuous in the "Great Union Meeting" held outside the Quincy courthouse one warm moonlight night just after war began. As his mite toward the cause, Woodruff designed a little 3-pounder wrought-iron fieldpiece to be used by the 6th Illinois Cavalry in Mississippi Valley campaigning. His gun was a muzzle-loading smoothbore, three feet long, weighing about two hundred and fifty pounds, and having a $2\frac{1}{8}$-inch bore. It could throw round shot about a mile and a quarter, and was effective at seven hundred yards with a canister shell containing seven 1-ounce lead balls.

Ripley was not impressed by the gun or by the recommendations Woodruff carried from prominent Illinois politicians. If the 6th Illinois Cavalry had to have light guns, he pointed out, they could use mountain or prairie howitzers.

Early in November 1861 the peppery Chief of Ordnance was brought up short by a note from the President:

Please see Gov. Wood and Mr. Woodruff, bearers of this, and make the arrangements for arms which they desire if you possibly can. Do not turn them away lightly; but either provide for their getting the arms, or write me a clear reason why you can not.

Not caring for either alternative, Ripley tried one of his subterfuges: he had his right-hand man, Lieutenant Colonel Maynadier, refuse Woodruff's proposition. This availed him nothing. Lincoln promptly put his foot down and ordered thirty Woodruff guns at $285 each.

Except for his muzzle-loading Woodruffs, the light fieldpieces favored by Lincoln were all breechloaders. In this partiality, the President stood almost alone. Ripley, Ramsay, Barry and Dahlgren were all opposed to breech-loading cannon. Even the newspapers and magazines, though quick to support breech-loading small arms, doubted that the principle could be applied to cannon. In the first place, it was argued, a breech mechanism adequate for the tremendous shock and pressure of cannon charges would be prohibitively expensive and unwieldy. In the second place, rapidity of fire in a cannon was not worth much, since the heavy smoke of Civil War black powder had to clear away before the next shot could be aimed. (The latter argument, of course, reflects contemporary reliance on aimed shots as opposed to saturation tactics.)

In spite of these plausible arguments Lincoln stood ready to give breech-loading cannon a fair chance.

In June 1861 a Cincinnati lawyer named Walter G. Sherwin wrote the Ordnance Office in behalf of his "Cincinnati Breech-loading Cannon," invented in collaboration with two local mechanics. Ripley's reply was not cordial. But Sherwin's gun had interested Captain Charles P. Kingsbury, chief ordnance officer for McClellan's Department of the Ohio, with headquarters at Cincinnati. So when Kingsbury came to Washington with his high-flying commander just after Bull Run, Sherwin tagged along.

A week or so after McClellan's elevation to command of the Army of the Potomac, Sherwin set a model of his invention on a cloth-covered table in the White House and proceeded to instruct President Lincoln and his Cabinet in the workings of the device.

The breech mechanism, he explained, worked something like a spigot. A movable cylinder passed through the breech from one side to the other. The cylinder contained a chamber, into which the cartridge was lowered through a hole in the top of the breech. By means of a crank the cylinder was then given a quarter turn, which brought the cartridge chamber into line with the bore. (Automatic alignment and a tight seal were insured by making the cylinder eccentric.) The gun was discharged by means of a percussion cap. In muzzle-loaders, Sherwin pointed out, the vent of the gun had to be stopped by hand; and if the gunner carelessly took his thumb off the vent, the gun was apt to take an arm off the man who was loading. In the Cincinnati Breech-loading Cannon, the vent was automatically cut off until the gun was ready to fire.

The gun looked good to Lincoln, and he wrote Ripley:

I have seen a model of a breech loading cannon exhibited by Mr. Sherwin of Ohio and would be glad for the Ordnance Department to assist Mr. Sherwin in making an experiment with a six-pounder of the same patern, provided it can be done at reasonable cost, and without injurious interference with the business of the Department.

Lincoln left too many loopholes. "The mechanical ingenuity exhibited by the model you presented," Ripley informed Sherwin with a hint of irony, "has favorably impressed the President, as indeed it is well calculated to do, and that ingenuity is acknowledged as creditable to you." But he concluded by saying that such a gun would be too heavy to handle or sight, that present guns were good enough and that the Department was too busy to be bothered.

Sherwin stuck to his gun. He appealed to Secretary of the Treasury Salmon P. Chase, a Cincinnati man. He sent testimonials. If the President would only give him a token order on which to raise capital, he wrote, he would give a money-back guarantee on the guns. "Gen. Ripley will do nothing, if he can avoid it," Sherwin informed Lincoln, who does not seem to have been much surprised.

Sherwin's fatal mistake, it appears, lay in his impugning of Ripley's loyalty in a letter to Secretary Cameron:

As Genl. Ripley is, in my opinion, tinctured with extreme Southern proclivities, and therefore obnoxious to me personally, privately, and publicly, I cannot hope to get an order from *him*. I can only get it through the President and Cabinet.

Ripley's nephew, Roswell Ripley, was in fact a Confederate general and was said to be "a red-hot and indefatigable Rebel." But so was Lincoln's brother-in-law. Cameron's opinion of the charge may be guessed from the fact that he sent the letter to Ripley himself for disposal.

Finally Sherwin tried to raise and command an artillery regiment —to be equipped, of course, with the Cincinnati Breech-loading Cannon. Unfortunately, Governor William Dennison of Ohio did not admire the voluble lawyer. "Is it possible," he asked Cameron, "that you have authorized W. G. Sherwin to organize a regiment of artillery? If so, for God's sake withdraw the authority. Such commission will make a farce of the public service." Dennison prevailed. The career of the Cincinnati Breech-loading Cannon was not yet over, nor was Lincoln's interest in it; but W. G. Sherwin's name appears no more in its history.

"A living steam engine," one of his fellow Congressmen once called Eli Thayer of Worcester, Massachusetts, "a man of eccentric humor and of wonderful and advanced thought, mixed with practical sense." At various times Thayer was an inventor, an educator and a politician; in the character of abolitionist he founded the New England Emigrant Aid Society, which sent free-soilers and Sharps rifles into Kansas during the middle fifties.

Having bought manufacturing rights to B. F. Joslyn's new breech-loading rifle, the imaginative Yankee applied the same design to a little breech-loading fieldpiece and sent a dozen specimens out to chastise the Kansas "border ruffians." In April 1861, when the conflict flared up again on a continental scale, Thayer sold two of his little cannon to the Union Defense Committee of New York, for the use of Elmer Ellsworth's Zouave regiment. Thereafter he called his cannon the "Ellsworth Gun."

This curious hybrid, somewhere between a Brobdingnagian rifle and a Lilliputian cannon, fell under Lincoln's interested scrutiny in September 1861. The gun Lincoln saw was four feet long, had a 1½-inch bore and weighed about three hundred pounds without its carriage. Like the Joslyn rifle, its breech mechanism consisted of a cone and expanding rings, held in place by a tapered steel key which passed through the shank of the breech and was operated by a compound lever. A handle opened the breech piece. The conical chilled-iron ball, wound with tallow-soaked cord, fitted into a cup at the end of a brass cartridge; and the 3-ounce charge was ignited through perforations near the other end. Instead of a limber, the carriage had a drag rope attached for hauling by manpower.

Thayer made much of the gun's maneuverability, cheapness and rapidity of fire; and Lincoln at last consented to order twenty guns at $350 each, subject to the inspection of McClellan's chief ordnance officer (who had now become *Colonel* Kingsbury). When the guns arrived late in November, Kingsbury pronounced them "in many respects superior" to the original model, and they were duly paid for.

Lincoln took pride in his purchase. "Col. Ramsey," he wrote on one occasion, "please see Mr. Hegon, and show him one of the little breech-loading cannons I got of Hon. Eli Thayer." At the arsenal where they were stored, however, the guns were regarded with tolerant skepticism. "I never supposed the gun would be introduced into the service," Ramsay confessed later, "and I gave little or no attention to it." As we shall see, Ramsay was mistaken.

Before the year was out, one other small breech-loading fieldpiece captured Lincoln's interest.

One day in November 1861 John H. Gage of Nashua, New Hampshire, came into Lincoln's office and spread out the plans of a gun invented by George A. Rollins, the young proprietor of a Nashua machine-tool factory. The gun was a breech-loading iron fieldpiece, about four and a half feet long, and having a 2-inch bore. Five ounces of powder, Gage told Lincoln, could send the gun's 4-pounder ball as far as two and a half miles. Moreover, the Rollins gun was phenomenally rapid in operation. One had been fired a hundred times in six minutes without overheating. Lincoln was a busy man. But by now, after his examination of the Cincinnati Cannon and the Ellsworth gun, he was decidedly interested in breech-loading cannon; and so he spent three quarters of an hour poring over the plans and discussing them with Gage. Before Gage left, the President had promised to order a test of the gun, if only Governor Berry of New Hampshire would see one fired and write a letter approving the results.

A few days later the governor wrote a letter that was all Lincoln could have asked. Lincoln endorsed it and sent it on:

I believe my promise is one that upon the writing of this letter by the Gov. of New Hampshire, the gun mentioned should be examined and reported upon by a competent officer—I therefore will thank the Secretary of War to send a competent officer to Nashua, N. H. to test and report upon the gun.

Months before, Ripley had received a letter about the Rollins gun and had refused the gun, sight unseen. Lincoln's interest in the weapon left the general unmoved now. When the War Department ordered him to send an officer to Nashua, if possible "in the present state of the service," Ripley promptly replied that the state of the service did not permit it. As the spring of 1862 began, something, presumably an order from Lincoln, made Ripley change his mind. But he was equal to the emergency. The officer's report was neither filed nor recorded; Lincoln had weightier matters pressing on him. No Rollins guns were ever ordered.

In his fight against breech-loading artillery General Ripley thus far had more reason to congratulate himself than in the case of machine guns and breech-loading rifles. President Lincoln had, to be sure, forced him to order the Woodruff and the Ellsworth guns. But the former were conventional in all but their dimensions, and both had been ordered in small quantity. Against these minor setbacks, Ripley could pride himself on having withstood the Cincinnati Cannon and stifled the Rollins gun.

And yet, the old soldier's mind could not have been very easy. His adversary was, after all, commander in chief; and who could tell what newfangled gimcracks might presently seize the man's fancy?

CHAPTER 10

Patent Nonsense

BEFORE PASSING FROM THE HOPES OF 1861
to the realities of 1862, we must add one more element to complete
the group portrait of the inventors who pressed their ideas on Lincoln and Ripley. Without that addition we could not fully appreciate Lincoln's patience. Nor could we fully understand Ripley's
chronic rage. This is the category of cranks and dreamers.

Because he was President, and because he was known as a sympathetic listener, Lincoln drew more than his fair share of such
originals. "Lunatics and visionaries are here so frequently," John
Nicolay wrote to his fiancée, "that they cease to be strange phenomena to us, and I find the best way to dispose of them is to discuss and decide their mad projects as deliberately and seriously as
any other matter of business."

The President's secretary used his technique skillfully in dealing
with Edward Tippett, a mad machinist who boarded in Georgetown during the war. One of his letters to Lincoln ran:

I have told you that this war is of God to liberate the Slaves, but
that you must have my balloon to put down all foreign foes. I
again warn you against secret enemies. Watch well, and you will
find the golden wedge, and the acon too [evidently referring to
Joshua, VII; 21]. I say, you cannot conquer without my navigating
balloon. Have it examined speedily, and do your duty to God; for
1864 is drawing nigh.

As the years passed, Tippett's mind drifted further and further from reality. One of his last letters was four pages of nonsense in beautiful handwriting, offering among other things a machine to run "by gravity" which had appeared to him in a vision in 1816, along with a preview of the Civil War. One passage in the letter, however, suggests the ingenious defense Nicolay had evolved by then. Nicolay had assured him, wrote Tippett to Lincoln, "that the problem is correct; and that if the mechanical actions can be effected, it is a discovery of great magnitude to the world." Very neat, but Lincoln's analysis of the proposition was neater. He simply labeled the letter: *Tippett. Crazy-man.*

Some self-styled inventors suffered from what in Lincoln's time was called "monomania." They were men who appeared—indeed, who were—highly intelligent and eminently reasonable on almost every subject, who carried on businesses, followed careers, mingled in society, all with scarcely a sign of aberration. But they had somehow got their lives entangled with a single wrong idea, and some subtle weakness kept them from casting it off. When that fixed delusion came into question, their narrow madness showed itself.

Such a man was Peter Yates of Milwaukee, Wisconsin. In 1879, when he died at Grand Rapids, Michigan, Yates was appreciatively recalled in the sober *Collections* of the Wisconsin State Historical Society as "a prominent and able lawyer . . . a man of much pluck, zeal, and pertinacity, both in his profession and in political contests"; nothing in his long letters to Lincoln impugns that estimate. Yates's letters have eloquence, persuasiveness, cogency and charm. Rarest attribute of all among inventors gone astray, they show a lively sense of humor which did not spare their writer's own crosses and crotchets. In asking for an interview Yates once asserted:

Mr. President, I may write like a crazy man—in truth, my parents while living, my sisters & brothers & many of my friends and clients, have all accused me to my face of being a monomaniac upon this subject, & this for the last 15 years—but I am *not* crazy in the knowledge & practice of the law, as all admit, & as the Law Reports of our state will attest. . . . and I assure you, that however crazy I will not *bite.*

"More than twenty-five years since," wrote Yates, "my attention was directed to an improvement in the Steam Engine." His "improvement" apparently consisted of a device to eliminate a supposed (but actually nonexistent) loss of power incurred in using a crank mechanism with a reciprocating engine. "I have spent some ten years of time in building models & making experiments, and about fourteen thousand dollars in money upon it," Yates continued. "Mr. President," he insisted, "my invention is the greatest of the age, & worth more than twenty Millions of Dollars, and I not only believe, but *know* it." He wanted to build a river boat on the Mississippi, using his invention, and he asked Lincoln to appoint him postmaster of Milwaukee "as a means to this End."

One evidence of Yates's shrewdness was his effort to draw parallels between himself and Lincoln. In one letter, for example, he referred to himself as "a lawyer of 32 years practice, a man of your own age, and who never voted a Democratic ticket in his life." He wrote further: "It is said that your Excellency has likewise been an inventor & the recipient of a Patent therefor. It is this circumstance that emboldens me to make the request of assistance I now ask." And in an earlier letter Yates had written: "Your Excellency can fully appreciate the motives, or rather heart yearnings, of the inventor who for more than a quarter of a century has given his time, his money and his health to the perfection of what he esteems, if he can but find the means and theatre for its display, an Enduring monument of his fame."

In 1862 Joshua Speed talked with Lincoln about the forthcoming Emancipation Proclamation. "In that conversation," Speed recalled, "he alluded to an incident in his life, long passed, when he was so much depressed that he almost contemplated suicide. At the time of his deep depression he said to me that he 'had done nothing to make any human being remember that he lived,' and that to connect his name with the events transpiring in his day and generation, and so impress himself upon them as to link his name with something that would redound to the interest of his fellow man, was what he desired to live for."

It would not be surprising if Lincoln, reading the letters of Peter Yates, a middle-aged Midwestern lawyer who sought remembrance through an invention for the improvement of steam vessels, saw himself, save for certain elements of power and stability, as the author of just such heartsick appeals. Certainly Yates's anxiety for "an enduring monument" bore an uncanny resemblance to Lincoln's own melancholy longings of fifteen or twenty years before. But Milwaukee already had a postmaster, and when the city's collectorship fell vacant, it was humanity's good fortune that Lincoln gave it to a newspaper editor named Christopher Sholes, thus affording that gentleman enough leisure to invent the typewriter. So Peter Yates moved on into eternity, via Grand Rapids, with no "enduring monument" to mark his passage through life.

Other devices were presented to Lincoln for which "mad" would be too strong a word, devices which worked but had no practical value. There were, for example, the water walkers.

One crisp, clear day late in December 1861 Lincoln drove down to the Anacostia River to see the Army engineers build a pontoon bridge. Attorney General Bates, Jesse Dubois of Illinois and Congressman Schuyler Colfax of Indiana rode with him in his carriage. The engineers bridged the icy river with speed and efficiency; the Presidential party crossed over and were followed by a battery of artillery. While they were there, the party watched a man "walk the water" with each foot in a little watertight canoe and with a slender paddle in his hands, apparently for both propulsion and balance.

Water walking was a minor fad at the time. At Vincennes, France, it was said, troops had done it with two-layer, one-piece boots and trousers, in which the space between inner and outer layers was inflated. According to the reports, the French soldiers had sunk only two feet into the water and had moved along rapidly, loading and firing their muskets as they went. Whether or not there was any affiliation between French and American water-walking interests, President Lincoln was not convinced by the Anacostia exhibition that the scheme would be useful. Water walkers bobbed up again in the pages of the *Scientific American* for 1863, but not in the Union armies.

Another passing vogue was that of body armor. The well-dressed but slightly apprehensive recruit of 1861 often wore such garb as the divided breastplate made from thin spring steel by J. S. Smith of New York. The Smith vest lay unobtrusively (its wearer hoped) between the cloth and lining of a military vest, with the two leaves lapping over where the vest was buttoned. Weighing three and a half pounds, it was supposed to resist bayonet or sword thrusts.

Body armor continued to receive serious attention through the spring of 1862. "A suit of steel armor" was tested at the Washington Arsenal in January, and in March the *Scientific American* reported experiments at Hartford with "a steel vest fastened to a tree." The Hartford armor was dented by an Enfield rifle, and a Colt rifle penetrated it at fifty yards.

Such armor was reported to have served its purpose in the early battles of 1862. Hood's jewelry store on Pennsylvania Avenue exhibited a steel vest, about an eighth of an inch thick, taken from the body of a Confederate captain at Williamsburg early in May. A glancing ball had dented it slightly; a Minié ball had made a deep indentation, but had not penetrated; a grapeshot had made "an ugly looking breach, the ball evidently carrying with it a portion of the plate." At Fair Oaks on June 25 two balls struck a Union lieutenant squarely on his steel vest, neither penetrating. "He frankly confesses," wrote a correspondent, "that when he discovered the first ball did not hurt him, he 'was ten times as brave' as he had been."

Steel-vest inventors made their way into the White House in the early months of the war; Stoddard's office exhibited a "pretty blue shell of polished steel" among other models whose makers aspired to Presidential support. Lincoln reportedly disposed of steel-vest inventors by offering to let the inventor wear his own device in a test.

The same anecdote was told of Secretary Stanton, with more convincing detail; and for that matter, it was also attributed to the Duke of Wellington before the war ended.

Whatever value such apparel had in battle, no steel vest ever managed to turn aside the barbs flung at it by the unshielded comrades of its wearer. After the owner had been labeled a coward and reminded to wear his "cuirass" behind in battle, the heavy encumbrance usually ended its military service derelict on a Southern roadside. On the morning of October 24, 1862, for example, the newly organized 14th New Hampshire Regiment began a movement westward from its camp on Capitol Hill to its first military assignment. The regimental historian recorded the march:

The first halt was made in front of the White House, and at least one-third of the battalion took a vigorous account of stock. The men with bullet-proof vests—their hope and pride—in Concord— vowed that they would prefer to risk Rebel bullets rather than carry so much old iron any farther. Steel breast-plates sufficient to coat a small gunboat were hurled into the gutter in front of Father Abraham's marble cottage.

Though body armor was rarely heard of after 1862, there were exceptions. A Wisconsin inventor of German origin offered Lincoln a coat of mail or "Panzerhemd" as late as July 1864. And in that same month L. E. Chittenden, the Treasury official who had once stimulated such remarkable changes in the complexion of General Ripley, rode out to Fort Stevens in the outskirts of Washington to watch the attack of the Confederate General Jubal Early. Near a large fallen tree he saw the body of a Confederate officer with a rifle in his hand. Placing his hand on the officer's chest to see if life remained, Chittenden felt a metallic substance. It turned out to be a shield of boiler iron molded to fit the man's body and fastened in back by straps and buckles. Trusting to that protection, the officer had gone out that morning to gun for Yankees. But directly over his heart, through the shield and through his body, was a hole "large enough to permit the escape of a score of human lives." Chittenden was reminded of a quaint epitaph in his native Vermont over one who had died from vaccination:

> The means employed his life to save,
> Hurried him headlong to the grave!

Proposals came to Lincoln for more cumbersome battlefield armor. A Wisconsin man wrote the President about his individual handbarrow-type portable breastworks; while a Connecticut Yankee who would have been well received in King Arthur's Court suggested iron shields for the front ranks. From Massachusetts and Kansas came other proposals for portable breastworks. A horse-drawn affair was suggested independently by a New Yorker and a Londoner. T. G. Boetig of Cincinnati boasted that his iron field casemates could be assembled in five seconds and wanted to show them to the President; but, perhaps not having five seconds to spare, Lincoln sent Boetig's letter over to the War Department next door.

From Pawnee City, Nebraska, came a letter advocating an iron-clad battery propelled by an armored locomotive; but the Nebraskan was late, for such precursors of the armored tank had already been used in battle and would be used again before the war ended —one of them by Ben Butler. As for armored vehicles intended to move freely on the battlefield, several inventors put forward suggestions—one even included the Gatling machine gun as armament. But a practical armored tank had to wait on the invention of the caterpillar tread.

Some curious substitutes for conventional artillery were brought to Lincoln's attention. One was the Perkins steam gun.

Old Jacob Perkins, an American who had died in England a dozen years before the Civil War, left many useful inventions behind him; but his steam gun, which applied steam pressure directly to the missile, could hardly be classed among them. Confronted with the old Yankee's inspiration, the Duke of Wellington was said to have remarked, "Well, if steam guns had been invented first, what a capital improvement gunpowder would have been."

Early in September 1861 Senator Henry Wilson of Massachusetts commended the Perkins steam gun to General Ripley's attention, remarking, "It seems to me there is something in it." Ripley was less witty than the Iron Duke, but quite as final. The Messrs. Perkins had stated that their steam 12-pounder gun would discharge ten balls per minute with an initial velocity of five thousand feet per second, using steam at a pressure of fifteen hundred pounds per square inch. Ripley declined to comment on the feasibility of using steam at that pressure, but he pointed out that in a conventional 42-pounder gun the maximum pressure was forty-five thousand pounds per square inch, declining to forty-five hundred pounds per square inch as the ball left the muzzle; yet even with such vastly greater pressures than the Perkinses commanded, the initial velocity was only twelve hundred feet per second. He drew the inescapable conclusion that the Perkins claims were unworthy of credence.

Wilson thereupon sent President Lincoln a petition in behalf of the Perkins gun, a petition which bore such distinguished names as Peter Cooper, William Cullen Bryant, George P. Putnam, Parke Godwin, Edwin D. Morgan and J. W. Harper. Whatever Lincoln thought of the gun, he could scarcely ignore the eminent persons who were so unaccountably enamored of it. So he asked Benjamin F. Isherwood, the brilliant Engineer in Chief of the Navy, to examine the documents in the case and give "an opinion as to the reasonableness and plausibility of their statements." In reply Isherwood declared his disbelief that "any steam gun can be made to compare in effect with the powder gun." On that note of agreement with the Iron Duke, the Perkins affair ended.

Whereas the Perkins gun brought steam to bear directly on the projectile, a type of gadget which in May 1861 seemed to be "the rage among inventors" used steam power indirectly. This was the centrifugal type of gun, of which the most publicized specimen was one captured by Butler's troops near Baltimore. Ross Winans, a fiery, pro-Southern Maryland millionaire, was popularly supposed to be that gun's inventor and manufacturer. Actually it was made in Boston under the direction of the true inventor, Charles Dickinson.

In principle, the Dickinson centrifugal gun added little to the slingshot of David. In elaborating on that principle, however, the gun became a mechanical Goliath of formidable appearance, served by a crew of four men, a team of horses, and a steam engine. Balls were poured from a hopper into the center of a horizontal wheel or drum, which was driven at high speed by the engine. A mechanism permitted the balls to fly out on reaching the proper point for discharge at the enemy. The four-man crew worked and fed the gun, the horses drew it, and an iron shield supposedly protected the ensemble from enemy fire.

Dickinson labored under a misconception common to inventors of that time, who seem to have supposed that a battlefield, like a pool table or a bowling alley, presented the objects of attack in a single convenient plane, to be cut down from front ranks to stragglers in one bloody swoop. "For use on the battle field," Dickinson wrote of his gun, "the musket caliber engine would mow down opposing troops as the scythe mows standing grain." In August 1862, a year after one of his guns was captured by Butler, he wrote Lincoln to explain that the southward journeying of his dizzy device had been the work of secessionist thieves; he offered to construct another for $10,000. His offer was not accepted.

Lincoln took more notice of Dickinson's rival, Robert McCarty. Perhaps the word "rival" is a misnomer; "predecessor" might be more just. How long Dickinson worked at developing his centrifugal gun does not appear; but when the Civil War broke out, McCarty had spent some ten years on his device. The *New York Herald* called the McCarty gun "one of the most singular implements of war that has ever been exhibited to the American people" and believed that it placed Dickinson's gun "entirely in the shade." On June 20, 1861, a hand-cranked model of the McCarty gun—in-

tended, according to the inventor, merely to demonstrate the principle—was exhibited at the foot of Thirty-third Street in New
York. Two men cranked the apparatus. Geared to the crank at a
ratio of sixty-four to one, curved tubes revolved inside an iron drum
about three feet across. Four-ounce balls were fed into an upright
hopper at the center of the drum and were sent flying through an
external barrel toward a wooden target at the edge of the North
River, a hundred yards away. Except for the clanking of the balls
as they dropped into the drum, the contraption sounded much like
a threshing machine. About a hundred balls struck the target; most
fell into the water about a hundred yards offshore.

There is some evidence that it was Senator Henry Wilson, a
fancier of steam guns, who introduced McCarty to Lincoln. At any
rate, the inventor and his gun appeared at the arsenal one day with
a note from the President. Ramsay's opinion of the McCarty weapon must have been exceedingly low. With none of his usual urban-
ity the colonel complained that he had no time to waste on the gun
and no place to put it, but he supposed the President's order must
be carried out. When Lincoln came down with John Hay, Ramsay
tried to lure them away from the trial to watch some troops drill,
and failing that, he harassed the inventor with "constant objections
and remarks." Such guns, Ramsay pointedly insisted, were an old
and rather funny story; he had seen one tried and found wanting
twenty years before. When McCarty undertook to point out the dif-
ferences between the two machines, Ramsay snapped, "Oh, well,
it is the same thing, same thing." According to one of the inventor's friends, the crusty colonel was "a perfect thorn all the time,
hurrying and making remarks, making McCarty feel very uncomfortable."

Because of all this, McCarty claimed later, he failed to adjust
the barrel properly, and it "threw the shot down, striking the upper
part of it." When Lincoln cranked the drum, the balls rattled off
the near-by target and came bounding back among the shins of the
bystanders. This sent Lincoln into what John Hay described as
"peals of Homeric laughter." It also ended Lincoln's active interest

in the device, although the same gun later redeemed itself by sending a ball across the Potomac which "struck a mule in the hip and wounded him so that he was brought over to Washington."

Oddly enough, Captain Dahlgren took the McCarty gun seriously, tried it at the Navy Yard and persuaded his department to finance the building of a steam-driven 12-pounder. When finished, this fired (or flung) fifteen shots in sixteen seconds, with a range of a mile and a half at 15° elevation. But the gun was fearfully inaccurate and almost shook to pieces the building which housed it.

McCarty continued to lobby for his gun all through the war, and in 1864 he managed to get it tried again at the arsenal before a board of three Army officers. But it was never adopted, and the sole casualty of centrifugal gunfire during the Civil War seems to have been one ill-starred Army mule.

Of all the weird notions predicated on a level battlefield and a co-operative enemy, the most widespread and persistent was that of forked cannon firing chain shot. From two diverging cannon, joined at the breech, were to be fired two projectiles linked by a chain. As the two shot spread apart, the chain between them was supposed to snap taut and cut a terrible swath through rebel ranks. Letter after letter came to the Ordnance Office with that suggestion—from England, from Mexico, from a teen-age prodigy in Rochester, New York—who offered also an incendiary shell—and from almost every state in what remained of the nation.

Every writer was certain that his idea was a new thing in the world. A disgruntled Hoosier maintained that the model he had sent Lincoln must have been intercepted, for he had read of just such a gun being made in Connecticut. Yet the model of such a contraption glowered schizophrenically from a Patent Office showcase at that moment, and had since 1859; at the same time the *Scientific American* was being serenaded with innumerable variations on the same theme—"all impracticable," it sourly declared.

The "inventors" of double cannon did not spare Lincoln. Two days after Sumter was fired on, a correspondent who signed himself "Citizen of Rhode Island" sounded the opening blast. It was echoed from San Francisco, and presently Upper Savoy in France brightly contributed the suggestion of "Boulets à Chaînes." Most persistent of all was one Charles Raymond of Norwalk, Connecticut, who wrote Lincoln five long letters on the subject.

The Confederates built a double chain-shot cannon, but bad luck attended it. When the guns failed to fire simultaneously, the chain swept back and killed most of the crew. The gun was never fired again, though it survives to this day in Athens, Georgia. In the North, twin cannon were fired without such mishaps, one at Rochester, New York, and another near Boston. The Ordnance Department finally tested one. "One difficulty," it reported, "seemed to be to give both projectiles the same initial velocity, without which they do not spread out effectually; but the chain, if it does not break, moves in an oblique direction without covering much space in front of the enemy."

As the gun crew of the Confederate double cannon found out too late, there was physical danger in trying some new weapons. Abraham Lincoln exposed himself to that risk in his "champagne experiments," and more than once narrowly escaped accidental death. Furthermore, his risk was double, for death or injury might have come to him not only by accident, but also by design.

Consider how easily an assassin reckless of his own life might have entered Lincoln's office with a repeating rifle or a bomb. Many men did just that, although none, luckily, with murder in their hearts. "On my arrival at the White House," one inventor remarked matter-of-factly, "I was ushered immediately into the reception room, with my repeating rifle in my hand, and there I found the President alone."

Another instance is that of Joshua Stoddard of Worcester, Massachusetts. Stoddard's best-known invention was not a weapon—though the *London Athenaeum* thought it "richly calculated to excruciate all who come within its sphere." It was the steam calliope, now so mellowed by associations. The war turned Stoddard from the peaceful arts (if the phrase is applicable to the steam calliope) and brought him into Lincoln's office with a model of his "novel construction of Gunboats, with a new method of opperating the *Guns.*" Perhaps this "new method" involved some sort of rocket. At least, when Stoddard struck a match and applied the flame to his model, Lincoln prudently took shelter down behind a desk. "Mr. Lincoln," Stoddard said, "you make a better President, I guess, than you would a soldier." After seeing how Stoddard's device worked, Lincoln said he was much pleased with it, and told the inventor he could go and practice on the rebels all he wanted to.

A Massachusetts man once notified Lincoln of his intention to call with a bomb disguised as a shoeblacking box, his scheme being to enter rebel vessels as a seaman and then jump ship, leaving his infernal machine behind. That the Yankee got his interview is uncertain, but not unlikely.

An assassin who had a little acting ability—a man, for example, like John Wilkes Booth—might easily have passed for such a well-meaning inventor. Or the President could equally well have died at the hand of some crank inventor, maddened by some fancied or real rebuff. Such things could be. In 1863 a Bay State inventor who had quarreled with his agent sent him a box through the mail. Doubting that affection had inspired the present, the agent put it into the hands of a detective. The gift was placed between two rock ledges and opened with a long rope. Fifteen pounds of gunpowder went off with a roar heard for miles.

In spite of Lincoln's incredible accessibility to armed inventors, events seemed to justify his fatalism. Hannibal Hamlin served out his term as Vice-President; and when Andrew Johnson acceded to the Presidency, he owed his elevation not to a deranged inventor or a proving-ground mishap, but to the little Derringer pistol of a warped tragedian.

By midsummer of 1861 the wild schemes offered to Lincoln had become a Washington byword, and so had Lincoln's readiness to give them a hearing. The satirist Orpheus C. Kerr found rich comedy in the "champagne experiments." "I visited the Navy Yard yesterday, and witnessed the trials of some newly-invented rifle cannon," began one Kerr skit. "The trial was of short duration, and the jury brought in a verdict of 'innocent of any intent to kill.' " Kerr went on about the "double back-action revolving cannon for ferry-boats" to be delivered "in time for the next war," and a scheme for taking privateers with a pair of huge clamps which would hoist them up and into the Federal hatches. "The President's gothic features lighted up beautifully at the words of the great inventor," Kerr wrote, "but in a moment they assumed an expression of doubt," and Lincoln was supposed to have disconcerted the inventor by asking what would happen if the enemy fired meanwhile.

Even when he was the subject, Lincoln liked the solemn nonsense and ludicrous truth of Orpheus C. Kerr, often reading selections to his friends and laughing with them. If he read the aforementioned sketch, his "gothic features" probably lighted up with a smile. Lincoln was not afraid of laughter. Inventors still came to him, and, ridicule notwithstanding, the President listened.

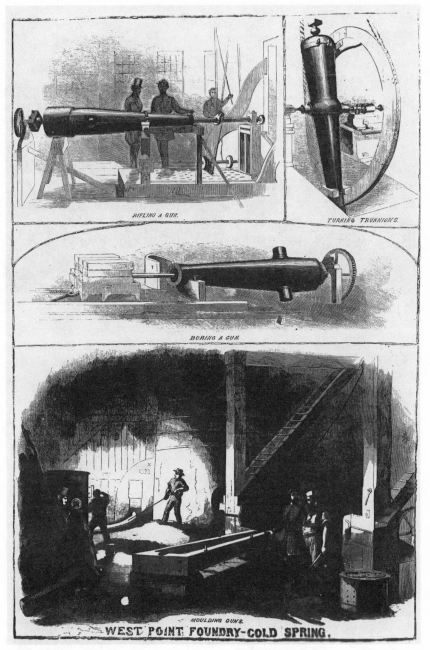

RIFLING A GUN.

TURNING TRUNNIONS.

BORING A GUN.

MOULDING GUNS.

WEST POINT FOUNDRY—COLD SPRING.

Harper's Weekly

WHAT LINCOLN SAW ON JUNE 24, 1862

A WIARD STEEL CANNON AT THE WASHINGTON ARSENAL,
DECEMBER 1861

Brigadier General Daniel Sickles is standing by the gun, and the Potomac River is in the background.

AN INVENTION WHICH INTERESTED LINCOLN

An artist's conception of Obadiah Hopkins' cannon mount. There is no evidence that a full-scale model was ever built.

CHAPTER 11

The Trent Affair

EIGHTEEN SIXTY-ONE ENDED DRAMATIC-
ally, but with the spotlight on London, not Richmond. Early in
November Captain Charles Wilkes of the United States man-of-
war *San Jacinto* stopped the British mail steamer *Trent* in the Ba-
hama Channel and removed two Confederate diplomats bound for
Europe. England roared with anger at the Yankee impudence.
"This nation means to make war," Henry Adams wrote from London. Yet the Northern public cheered as wildly as the British
raged. Lincoln faced a dilemma: to hold Mason and Slidell would
mean war with England; to release them might mean political defeat at home. In either case, the final result might be the death of
the Union.

For a century Lincoln's handling of the affair has been left, not
unreasonably, to the analysis of specialists in diplomatic history.
But while ably canvassing the points of international law involved,
these historians have said little or nothing about certain other factors in Lincoln's calculations. The omission is understandable.
Those factors were not such as come readily to the mind of the political or diplomatic historian, and indeed it has not heretofore been
known that Lincoln himself was aware of them.

Nevertheless, Lincoln and his Cabinet based their decision at
least in part on two considerations: rifled cannon and niter.

When Roger Bacon and his Oriental predecessors first mixed

potassium nitrate (known to commerce as niter or saltpeter) with equal parts of sulphur and charcoal and touched the mixture with fire, they did not understand that the charcoal and sulphur explosively robbed the niter of its oxygen. But men, though long in learning the theory, were quick to learn the unholy uses of that chemical commotion. And as they gained experience in the new art of making black powder, they used a larger and larger proportion of niter, until by the eighteenth century it accounted for seventy-five per cent of gunpowder by weight. "This villanous saltpetre," as Shakespeare called it, had become one of the prime essentials of warfare.

By the middle of the nineteenth century the world was getting most of its niter from India, a British possession; niter had therefore become a potent instrument of British diplomacy. For years, Lincoln's friend Joseph Henry had seen the danger in this, and in 1857 he had urged Secretary of War Jefferson Davis to finance a search for some other source of niter or its equivalent. Davis supported the idea, but he was soon out of office, and his successor did nothing. In 1860 Lieutenant Henry Wise went on a good-will mission to Japan and, at Dahlgren's instance, investigated that nation's possibilities as a niter source. He made little headway with the Shogunate.

When the war began in 1861, the Army had three million pounds of niter on hand. This it proposed to hold in reserve against the possibility of "a maritime war," leaving gunpowder contractors to find their own. Ripley, expecting a short war, felt that this was enough. The Navy was more conscious of British naval power. Early in May Commander Harwood was disturbed to learn from the president of the Du Pont Company that only six months' supply of niter was in the country, en route or being loaded, and that speculators were busily striving to corner the market. Dahlgren "hinted deficiency of nitre and powder" to Lincoln and Seward a few days later. But Ripley insisted all was well, and so Harwood stopped worrying.

By fall niter stocks were dwindling rapidly, imports were falling off and prices were rising. On behalf of the Navy, Lammot Du Pont hastened to England and quietly but swiftly bought up all available niter—about four and a half million pounds. Before loading of the niter had been completed, word of the *Trent* incident reached England, and the British slapped a ban on niter exports.

Lincoln's government took immediate alarm at the British action. In Paris, Thurlow Weed held a worried conference with the American ministers to France and Belgium about chances of buying niter elsewhere. Uneasiness became manifest at home, and to allay it the government planted a reassuring article in the *New York Evening Post* which declared niter stocks to be "sufficient for all emergencies." Privately, Lincoln and Seward were not so cheerful.

The North was not unanimous in defying Great Britain. In the coastal cities there was a good deal of peace sentiment. These cities had nothing to fear from the rebels, but the British Navy was something else again. New York businessmen feared a sneak attack like the one by which the British had destroyed much of Copenhagen during the Napoleonic Wars. What made such an attack seem most dangerous was the fact that England had recently begun armoring her vessels. In the late fall of 1861 every coastal gun in the North was a smoothbore; and smoothbore guns were already beginning to be obsolete.

During the fifties artillery had followed small arms in adopting rifling. Like other weapons, rifled cannon had to breach thick walls of tradition. "I can't say I think much of the new guns," a British artillery commander remarked in 1860. "We won Waterloo without them, and what do we want with them after that." But they made their way, nevertheless. Ripley's predecessor, Colonel Craig, had an open mind on the subject of artillery, and, when the Civil War began, the Ordnance Department had already made some experiments with rifled guns. One of Craig's last acts as Chief of Ordnance was to send an officer to Cold Spring, New York, to see Robert Parrott's new rifled 10-pounder, reinforced by a wrought-iron band shrunk over the breech; on the strength of Captain Benton's report, a number were ordered. When Ripley took over a few days later, he promised to take all the guns Parrott could make in the next year.

Ripley's defenders made much of his early support of rifled cannon. "This is one instance, at least," commented a Washington newspaper, "in which he has encouraged and aided a new idea, and not only a new one, but a good one." Yet even here, Ripley had his reservations. The round shot fired by smoothbores could skip and ricochet, whereas rifled projectiles burrowed into the ground. For this reason, perhaps, Ripley expressed his opinion early in June that "with our present knowledge" rifled batteries would be found less efficient than smoothbores. And a year later he still insisted that in small calibers smoothbores were better.

From the start Lincoln liked rifled cannon. As early as April he helped the James T. Ames Company of Chicopee, Massachusetts, get a large order for rifled cannon, probably of the type patented by Charles T. James of Rhode Island. In June he met with Cameron and Ripley at the Washington Arsenal, where they watched "some interesting experiments with the new rifled cannon now being brought into use." It may have been Lincoln's influence, as well as the success of the trial, that led Ripley shortly after to give rifled cannon more support.

By July public opinion had set strongly in favor of Lincoln's views. "Experiments in our army, as well as in all others," the *Scientific American* commented, "are rapidly convincing military men that the day for smooth-bored cannon has gone by, and that all artillery must henceforth be rifled." People were becoming aware that only the power and penetration of rifle projectiles offered an answer to the new ironclad warships of the British. And so, when the *Trent* crisis came, seaboard towns clamored for heavy rifled Parrotts.

As British warships were being conditioned for sea and British bands were practicing "Dixie," General McClellan, always methodical, set up a Military Armament Board to decide on the number and kind of guns needed for field batteries and permanent fortifications.

Six more distinguished authorities on the design and use of cannon could scarcely have been assembled. Old General Totten, Chief of Engineers, presided; his corps was further represented by the Army of the Potomac's chief engineer, John G. Barnard, a sharp-eyed, long-faced West Pointer who had just published two books on coastal defense. The Ordnance Corps provided its cranky chief, General Ripley, and its most brilliant officer, Captain Thomas Rodman. For the Artillery appeared General Barry, noble of nose and square of jaw, whose Burnsides, verging on Dundrearies, gave him the look of a stage milord; and also McClellan's aide, Colonel Henry Hunt, an able and vigorous West Pointer from Michigan. Dahlgren was there for the Navy, but soon went off in a sulk when he was outvoted six to one on the question of harmonizing Army and Navy calibers.

Lincoln kept in close touch with the board. Early in its proceedings Lincoln submitted a letter from the designer of a new steel cannon. General Ripley promptly had the letter tabled. A few days later Lincoln sent along Obadiah Hopkins, inventor of a new coastal gun carriage. The Hopkins device was a sort of seesaw, carrying a gun at each end, mounted on a revolving platform. The idea was to load one gun below the barbette of the fort while the other was raised for firing.

In the circumstances the board had to listen to Hopkins, but it made short work of his models and drawings. "While the inventor has displayed much ingenuity," it reported politely, "the Board cannot recommend his arrangement for adoption." Two days later, the President himself escorted Obadiah Hopkins into the room where the august six were deliberating on the coastal defenses of Massachusetts. Lincoln and the board looked on solemnly while Hopkins put his model through its paces—firing real charges from two small brass guns by way of artistic verisimilitude. Despite the fireworks display, the board would retreat only to the extent of admitting itself unqualified, in Dahlgren's absence, to pass on the *naval* value of the device.

The next day General Totten sent Lincoln an indignant letter marked *"Not official."* Hopkins, it seemed, had approached Totten that morning in a confidential way and offered the old soldier a half interest in the gun carriage. "The least I could do, I did," wrote Totten, "which was to order him out of the room." In writing his letter, of course, Totten did one thing more: he ended Hopkins's chances with Abraham Lincoln.

But Lincoln's meetings with the Military Armament Board were not wasted. Coastal armament was the chief subject of those meetings; and if Lincoln had not known before of the North's vulnerability to British ironclads, he learned of it then.

On Christmas Day, 1861, less than two weeks after the Hopkins affair, Lincoln met with his Cabinet to discuss the British ultimatum in the *Trent* case. Thanks to the Military Armament Board, Lincoln came in the knowledge that not one gun in Northern ports could stop even the most lightly armored British warship. Secretary Seward, who shared Lincoln's conciliatory views, had kept himself fully informed of the niter situation through Lammot Du Pont and Captain Dahlgren, and he brought with him reports from both those watchdogs of the niter supply. No transcript was made of Cabinet proceedings that day, but if one existed it would surely have recorded warnings from Lincoln and Seward that a war with Great Britain would mean the unhindered bombardment of Northern ports and the swift onset of gunpowder starvation. The Cabinet dispersed not yet convinced, but a night's rumination permitted them to digest the unpalatable truth. Next day Seward dispatched a note to the British announcing that Mason and Slidell would be released.

As if by reflex action, the end of the crisis cut short the sessions of the Military Armament Board, and only the emergence of a rebel ironclad revived interest in rifled coastal guns. Meanwhile the British lifted their niter embargo, and Du Pont's purchases arrived to swell Army and Navy stock piles.

But the future of Anglo-American relations remained clouded for nearly two years more, and Lincoln did not forget the lessons of 1861.

CHAPTER 12

Winter of Discontent

THE NEW YEAR BEGAN FOR LINCOLN WITH the ordeal of handshaking which an admiring republic then inflicted annually on its chief executive. Wearied by that and by the mounting cares of his office, he fled next day to the Navy Yard, accompanied by his Assistant Secretary of the Navy, a rotund, affable, full-bearded Yankee named Gustavus Vasa Fox. Although Fox was the picture of easygoing joviality, he could perform incredible feats of labor, and his encyclopedic mind held about all there was to know of things naval. "A live man," Lincoln had called him, "whose services we cannot well dispense with."

After watching a rifled cannon plunge its 150-pounder missiles into far reaches of the Anacostia, Fox and Lincoln went with Dahlgren to his quarters, the big brick house where Lincoln had been so cheerful at the wedding of Nannie Buchanan. A change had been wrought by the energetic new commandant since those anxious days. Grading and graveling, for instance, had made the approaches to the wharves and slips permanently hard and dry, and the mudhole on the west side of the yard was now a fine avenue of gravel and cinders leading to the ordnance department.

But national affairs were not so tidily in hand, and Lincoln was gloomily aware of the fact. The "On to Richmond!" clamor had risen to a new crescendo now that McClellan, the cocky, redheaded "Little Napoleon," had shaped a splendid army from beaten recruits. The press and the politicians longed to avenge Bull Run and

Ball's Bluff, or rather to have them avenged; but week after week slipped by with nothing but more drilling, more inspections, more requisitions for more arms. Symptoms of what Lincoln would come to call "the slows" already showed themselves in the young general. And the same complaint seemed to afflict General Henry Halleck in the West, where destiny had not yet made alliance with a stumpy, dogged fighter named U. S. Grant. An expedition was on the verge of departing for the North Carolina coast. It had been on the verge for some time now. The subject came up as Lincoln sat talking despondently with Dahlgren. "No one is ready!" said Lincoln with feeling.

The weather, to which Lincoln's moods had always been sensitive, stayed mostly clear that afternoon. The next day, however, a light hail fell from dark skies, the prelude to what one old Washingtonian called "just the d——ndest weather that ever was sent to poor afflicted warriors. First it rains a few days, & then it snows, & then it hails and then it drizzles, & then they all come together, & then the snow gets about six inches deep, and then comes *one day* of sunshine, & the roads are rivers of slosh & mud, and then it freezes, & then it rains again & snows again & so on—and our armies are stuck in the mud and there is no *forward*—it is all *up and down* like a cow's tail!" On the sixth of January Congressman Henry L. Dawes of Massachusetts stared moodily at the snow falling past his hotel window and then resumed a half-finished letter to his wife:

The times are exceedingly dark and gloomy—I have never seen a time when they were so much so. Confidence in everybody is shaken to the very foundation. The credit of the Country is ruined—its arms impotent, its Cabinet incompetent, its servants rotten, its ruin inevitable. . . . The Govt. can't survive sixty days of such a life as it is now living.

Lincoln, who bore the responsibility, could not sit back and let the Union go to smash, but he must have felt as if he were neck deep in January molasses. "Have arms gone forward for East-Tennessee?" he asked General Buell. They had not. "Delay is ruining us, and it is indispensable for me to have something definite," he wired General Halleck. Halleck wired back: "I have no arms." That evening at a White House reception, Lincoln seemed "a little careworn" to the *Washington Star* man.

On the tenth of January Lincoln awoke to find a cold fog pressing against his windows. During the day he sent Secretary Cameron a copy of the latest from Halleck. "It is exceedingly discouraging," Lincoln commented. "As everywhere else, nothing can be done." Wandering restlessly through the fog, Lincoln found his way to Quartermaster General Meigs's new office in the Winder Building. He took a chair in front of the open fire and stared bleakly into the flames. "General," he asked, "what shall I do? The people are impatient; Chase has no money and he tells me he can raise no more; the General of the Army has typhoid fever. The bottom is out of the tub. What shall I do?"

In Cabinet meeting that day, Attorney General Bates urged Lincoln "to take and act out the powers of his place, to command the commanders." Lincoln was about to do just that. And he began next day, by accepting Simon Cameron's resignation.

By mid-January of 1862 Simon Cameron had given offense in too many ways to be longer tolerated as Secretary of War. He had been careless and profligate in awarding contracts. He had brazenly sought, in defiance of the President, to capture abolitionist support by inserting a plea for immediate emancipation into his annual report to Congress. So when the conveniently distant post of Minister to Russia fell vacant, Lincoln gave it to Cameron, willy-nilly. Into Cameron's old place came his former adviser and the sometime Attorney General in Buchanan's Cabinet, Edwin M. Stanton.

In naming Stanton, Lincoln ignored a rude snub administered to him by that Pittsburgh lawyer half a dozen years before; and if he knew of them, he also ignored the slurs and epithets still flung at him behind his back by the same stubby, whiskered, ill-tempered conniver. For all his churlish outbursts and bullyings, his lies, his ready tears, Stanton offered the nation a combination of energy, loyalty and official integrity that was hard to match. He wasted no time in digging his spurs into the War Department. "As soon as I can get the machinery of the office working, the rats cleared out, and the rat holes stopped, we shall *move*," he wrote a New York newspaperman.

A few days after Stanton's appointment, Joshua Speed came to the War Department in search of more guns for Kentucky. Instead of "that loose shackeling way of doing business" he had seen so much of before, he now found "order, regularity and precision." Speed told Stanton what he wanted; Stanton asked to have it in writing; Speed wrote out the request, and Stanton immediately endorsed it: "To the Chief of Ordnance—fill the order at once, if not in whole as much as could be done at once." And this was done. "I shall be much mistaken," wrote Speed, "if he does not infuse into the whole army an energy & activity which we have not seen heretofore."

Unknown to Berdan's Sharpshooters, as they fretted still unarmed on their hilltop outside Washington, their fortunes were involved with those of Simon Cameron. One of Cameron's last acts as Secretary of War on January 13 had been to order the signing of a contract for two thousand Sharps rifles for the Sharpshooters. (One senses in this sudden move the hand of Abraham Lincoln, who was now beginning to "command the commanders.") But Cameron's resignation transpired on the very day Ripley received the order, and so Ripley felt safe in delaying. A few days later, he persuaded Stanton that he should suspend the order "until further direction."

When word of this leaked out, the Colt Company offered a thousand of their revolving rifles for immediate delivery. Ripley was no fool. With Lincoln's impatience growing more and more evident, the Chief of Ordnance prudently contented himself with a partial victory: better a thousand Colts than two thousand Sharps. Colonel Post of the 2nd Sharpshooter Regiment thought well of the Colts; and so, although with misgivings, Colonel Berdan went along with the compromise.

Then came unexpected drama. Colonel Post had misjudged his men. The Colts were breechloaders, all right, and very pretty to look at; but they were also inaccurate, unreliable, prone to get out of order and even dangerous to the users. The men of the 2nd Regiment, seven hundred strong, were fed up with the delay and outraged by what seemed a betrayal of the President's promise. Rather than take the Colts, or indeed anything else but the Sharps, the regiment threatened to mutiny. The crisis was kept out of the newspapers, but it was real nonetheless. Determined to keep order, Berdan armed a hundred reliable men and, in his own words, "was about to use force." For a while it looked as though a bloody skirmish between Union troops might erupt within sight of the Capitol itself.

An Army mutiny at that moment, however small in scale, simply could not be permitted to happen. The Union still floundered in a slough of despond. Stanton's appointment had brought hope, but it seemed to admit past failure. The new Secretary meant the emphasis of his administration to be on organizing victory, not suppressing mutiny.

The authorities therefore hastened to placate the grumblers. Colonel Post conferred earnestly with his men and at last persuaded them to take the Colts if Secretary Stanton would promise solemnly to substitute Sharps as soon as they could be procured. McClellan supported Post's action, and Stanton made the desired promise with almost unseemly speed. "In the meantime," the new Secretary wrote, "it is hoped the patriotic feeling of the troops and their sense of duty will prevent their doing anything to the prejudice of their good character and military discipline." And Ripley wired the Sharps Company for a thousand of their rifles with accoutrements and ammunition *"as soon as possible."*

A few days later, the *New York Tribune* referred vaguely to "the difficulties in Col. Berdan's Regiment," but the whole truth was never publicly revealed. Among the few who knew it, more spectacular events crowded it into forgetfulness. Many years later, a historian of the Sharpshooters alluded mysteriously to "demoralization . . . in an alarming form." The other and better known chronicler of the corps said even less about the affair.

When the Sharpshooters got their marching orders some weeks after the near mutiny, their Sharps had still not arrived, and there were mutterings. But the military situation had improved, and Hiram Berdan was not the man to let mutiny become a habit. "I armed the most of my men with such arms as I could get," he wrote a few months later, "and those that refused I had court martialed and they are now cracking stone at the Rip Raps." The delay, after all, was only temporary. In a month or two all the Sharpshooters were proudly carrying (and formidably using) their long-awaited breechloaders.

During that season of mud and melancholy in which Stanton took over the War Department, a storm blew up which, to those who figured in it, came to be known as "the mortar business."

The idea sprang from the fertile brain of Gustavus Fox. In the summer of 1861 the Assistant Secretary of the Navy foresaw that warfare in the West would follow the rivers—the Tennessee, the Cumberland, the Mississippi—which ran through the heart of the Confederacy and had long served that region in lieu of roads and railways. Fox also perceived that in those campaigns the Navy would face an unaccustomed assignment: siege warfare at close quarters.

On land such operations were so old a story that special artillery had long since been designed for them. These were the mortars. Squat, wide-mouthed and uptilted, like the utensils from which they took their name, the mortars sent heavy shells roaring into the blue, to drop at a steep angle inside forts and entrenchments. The Navy had had little use for them before. Now, with a river war in prospect, Fox suggested building a number of solid little craft, each to carry a mortar, which would present smaller targets than full-sized ships, could be deployed more flexibly and could take cover more easily.

In July Fox's scheme won the support of General Frémont, who had charge of operations on the Mississippi. The War Department contracted with Knap, Rudd and Company of Pittsburgh for thirty ponderous thirteen-inch mortars, the largest size; and Frémont ordered the construction of thirty-eight small mortar boats.

On the Upper Ferry at St. Louis, a curious little fleet presently began to take shape. Its components were "nothing more than rafts or floating platforms for one large mortar each, with iron parapets or rifle screens, and an awning overhead." Solid layers of timber formed the basis for the craft. In the timbers were openings for eight magazine pits thirty inches deep and about five feet square. Armored oak bulwarks rose up about twenty inches along the edges, and above those stood rifle screens of boiler plate three-eighths of an inch thick and six or seven feet high, sloping in and pierced with loopholes. Each boat was shaped like a rectangle, twenty yards by eight yards, with the four corners cut off to sharpen the bow and stern. Its draft was three feet when loaded, and it was worked by oars or sweeps or was towed by one of eight steam tugs which Frémont ordered for the purpose.

Complications began in November, when General McClellan for some reason requisitioned fifteen of the mortars then being made for Frémont. Complications increased five days later, when Commander David D. Porter, vigorous, enterprising and well endowed with the gift of gab, came to town with a plan for taking New Orleans. The leading element of Porter's plan was a forty-eight hour bombardment of the city's defenses by thirteen-inch mortars, each mounted in a small, specially reinforced schooner.

It seems to have been Porter who first aroused Lincoln's interest in mortar boats. And the commander's eloquence prevailed with Secretary Welles and General McClellan, as well as with the President. McClellan's fifteen requisitioned mortars were turned over to the Navy, and Porter set briskly to work on his flotilla at the Brooklyn Navy Yard. At first Porter planned to build fifteen vessels, one for each mortar. In the end he had twenty-one schooners, ranging from one hundred sixty to two hundred fifty tons, each one filled in almost solidly with heavy timber to strengthen the deck against the tremendous concussion, and each carrying a crew of about forty. Porter's zeal burned high. When his flotilla was completed, he promised McClellan, it would be "the terror of the secessionists" and the "most formidable arm of offense yet put afloat," ready, with the aid of the other vessels' Dahlgren 11-inchers, to "destroy every fortification it can get within reach of."

The Navy had ordered twenty-one mortars from Knap, Rudd and Company. Porter bombarded the company with telegrams and letters until it agreed to fill this order with the mortars originally made for Frémont's flotilla. By January 1862 the giant mortars were arriving in New York.

Mortar beds presented a problem. Such beds had to be more than the single-piece cast-iron affairs used in the past. The huge new thirteen-inch mortars required a ton and a half of wrought iron and woodwork, with roller rings, recoil buffer, slide frame and other pieces. Fortunately for his plans, Porter had an energetic ally in Lieutenant Henry Augustus Wise of the Navy Ordnance Bureau.

"I am no politician," Wise wrote, "but I listen to what people say." In his forty-two years of life, the listener had already heard and seen much. When he was five, his father, a Navy captain, died; and the boy was reared in his grandfather's house on Craney Island near Norfolk, Virginia. During the Mexican War, Wise's dark complexion and linguistic facility helped him in carrying important dispatches through the enemy lines. His cousin and one-time guardian was Henry Alexander Wise, the fire-eating Governor of Virginia who let John Brown hang in 1859; the lieutenant met his cousin at a railroad junction, "just from the scene of the Brown exploits," and heard about "the whole matter from beginning to end." In 1860 Wise toured the Orient aboard the U.S.S. *Niagara* with a lively company which included Lieutenant Colonel James W. Ripley.

Unfortunately for his reputation as a serious ordnance officer, Wise was a born wit and raconteur, who wrote books on his travels in both hemispheres; and so the world came to regard Harry Wise affectionately as "a smart young fellow, with no particular fondness for his profession." He enjoyed life and its pleasures, including those of the hop and the grape. "The fact is you don't drink enough," he wrote his grim Virginian cousin, "a little old brandy is better than pills." Later, another convivial traveler and observer, Russell of the *London Times,* was much taken with the "lively, pleasant, and amusing little sailor," and the two became boon companions and fellow tipplers.

Wise's first wartime job was to burn the Norfolk Navy Yard, near his boyhood home. It came hard, but he did it—"as effectually," he cheerfully related, "as if I had been a professional arsonist." In the spring days of Washington's peril he was the only officer in the Navy Ordnance Bureau to remain loyal. "I made up my mind," he wrote his father-in-law, Edward Everett, just afterward, "to stand by the flag so long as there is a stripe in it."

Wise, in short, was not the lightweight so many thought him to be; and he proved it again when David Porter called on him to help outfit the mortar flotilla. "Never during the existence of the Ordnance Department," Porter wrote years later, "was there more zeal or ability displayed in collecting the material of an expedition." "We are at it here night and day in getting off the mortar fleet, and then, stand from under," Wise himself wrote late in December. Cooper, Hewitt and Company of Trenton, New Jersey, outdid themselves in making the mortar beds; Abram Hewitt subcontracted for parts with three other establishments and saw to it that the Navy was not overcharged. By early February the last of the mortar schooners had been fitted out. "Day by day they quietly slip their anchors," reported the *National Intelligencer,* "and depart for their rendezvous, nobody knows where."

While Porter and Wise hustled their enterprise to its climax, Lincoln waited eagerly for news of the flotilla at St. Louis. On those mortar boats, he felt more and more certain, depended the success of the coming expedition through Kentucky and into Tennessee, via the Tennessee River. And by that venture he set great store. New Orleans would be a grand prize, surely; but to Lincoln, the Tennessee expedition counted for more, both strategically and sentimentally. It came as a stinging blow to him, therefore, when he learned early in January 1862 that Frémont's mortar boat project had in effect been abandoned, and that the mortar boats themselves, like so many expensive toys, were swinging idly from their moorings at St. Louis.

What was the reason for this? Primarily one which has delayed the success of many a new weapon: lack of faith on the part of the commanders in the field.

Fox, who first proposed the fleet, had switched his enthusiasm to Porter's flotilla, a Navy rather than an Army project. Frémont himself had been superseded by Major General Henry W. Halleck in November 1861; and Halleck, unaware of Lincoln's enthusiasm for the mortar boats, had regarded them as merely one of Frémont's numerous follies.

Captain Andrew H. Foote, a pious old sailor who preferred preaching to rum and a good fight to either, commanded the naval arm of the Tennessee expedition. Although not against mortar boats as a general proposition, he scorned the contraptions at St. Louis. He had tried to have an army officer sent there to have mortar beds made; but Halleck had been unwilling, and so Foote shrugged off responsibility. To Wise he wrote:

We have palmed upon us some 30 Mortar Boats of logs banded together, without a Navy or Army officer having had anything to do with them. Rodgers & I told Genl. Fremont we didnt like them. A Board is appointed to inspect them, & I guess "entre nous" will condemn them.

No wonder Halleck and Foote sat back complacently while Porter bagged all available mortars and mortar beds.

By the tenth of January, that foggy day when he sat before General Meigs's fire, Lincoln had begun to realize the state of affairs. In Cabinet meeting that day he spoke bitterly of the negligence, the indifference, the lack of forethought all around him; and his bitterness was greatest on the subject of the mortar boats. They had been moved to Cairo, Illinois; but, noted Attorney General Bates in his diary, they were "not ready—not manned—Indeed we do not *know* that the mortars have reached there . . . no one knows any thing about them."

Lincoln began to act. On that very day he had Fox wire Foote at Cairo for a full report on the mortar flotilla's status, progress and probable time of completion. Feeling the direction of the wind, Foote commenced to veer with it. To Lincoln he replied querulously and at length, but without reporting the number of mortars on hand. Meanwhile he fired off frantic telegrams to St. Louis and to the Allegheny Arsenal at Pittsburgh, where some mortar beds were being made.

Lincoln directed another searching inquiry at General Ripley, to which the Chief of Ordnance replied that he had sent everything Foote had asked for except some cannon powder which would soon be on its way.

Ripley might have added that the Navy had assumed responsibility for supplying Foote with at least twenty-one of the thirty-eight mortars, in place of the ones sent to Porter. There was, however, enough ignominy to go around. It turned out that not a single mortar had actually been made for the mortar boats at Cairo, let alone shipped there.

Foote, prompted by McClellan, suggested that it did not matter, that "we can get along without the mortar boats." Lincoln ignored this cry of "sour grapes." Taking the mortar business out of the hands of Foote and Halleck, he stalked into the Navy Bureau of Ordnance and told Lieutenant Harry Wise to "put it through." "Now," said Lincoln grimly, "I am going to devote a part of every day to these mortars and I won't leave off until it fairly rains bombs."

Next day Wise notified Foote of the new aspect of affairs and instructed the captain to wire the President every day "showing the progress, or lack of progress in this matter." "Oh, that this telegram had come two months ago," mourned Foote, "but I will now go ahead and obey orders."

Wise's conduct of the mortar business raised him high in Lincoln's esteem. The President, Wise recalled later, "was perplexed to know how to get matters straight, but when he put me on the track I made it clear to him."

Not only were mortars lacking, but it also turned out that only two mortar beds had been made. Lincoln wired the Allegheny Arsenal to give top priority to Foote over both the New Orleans and the Carolina expeditions, and by early February nine beds had been finished and shipped out. Thirty-eight were needed in all. Wise came up with the solution: Cooper and Hewitt. According to Hewitt, Lincoln wired him personally and appealed to him to save the Tennessee River campaign. Hewitt surpassed his performance for the Navy a month before, subcontracting for parts, cajoling, threatening, organizing. When Hewitt promised to have the beds ready by March 9, General Ripley was incredulous. Yet even this did not satisfy Lincoln, who wanted the delivery date advanced to February 15. Hewitt agreed; and Hewitt was better than his word, for all thirty beds were finished by February 14. On the cars that carried them west, Hewitt had painted in glaring black and white the legend: U. S. GRANT, CAIRO. NOT TO BE SWITCHED UNDER PENALTY OF DEATH.

Seizing his chance to strike a blow for Ohio as well as for the Union, Secretary Chase brought E. M. Shield of Cincinnati to see Lincoln and Stanton about a mortar-bed contract. "Mr. Shield," said Stanton, "the President, yourself, and I are Western men, and the West shall be attended to." A model bed was rushed to Cincinnati, and Shield pitched in with a zeal that rivaled Hewitt's. "The honor of our Cincinnati mechanics is in some sort pledged, and I want it redeemed," Chase admonished. Redeemed it was. On February 15 Shield wired: "Mortar carriages ready"; and Chase sent the wire to Lincoln with the triumphant endorsement: *"Cincinnati Mechanics up to time!"*

Day and night Lincoln kept in touch with progress in the production, shipment and mounting of the mortars themselves. As late as January 22 not one had been earmarked for shipment to Cairo. Within three days Colonel Symington of the Allegheny Arsenal had rounded up ten of the huge guns and dispatched them—probably drawing on those made at Pittsburgh for the other two expeditions. Secretary Stanton deputed a Pittsburgh industrialist to check on Symington's progress, and, trusting nobody, sent Assistant Secretary Tom Scott for the same purpose. Both had only praise for the colonel's work.

Despite the heat generated elsewhere, Foote remained lukewarm toward the mortar business. At the end of January, he reported in some perplexity that more than eleven thousand mortar shells had been ordered to Cairo, whereas he wanted no more than three thousand. Wise wrote promptly:

The President remarked that he thought it would be expedient to receive all the mortars and shells sent to Cairo, so as to be able to meet any probable amount of work that may be demanded; that he wished you to be sure, when you opened fire . . . "to rain the rebels out," as he desired to "treat them to a refreshing shower of sulphur and brimstone."

And Wise added significantly that Lincoln "is evidently a practical man, understands precisely what he wants, and is not turned aside by any one when he has his work before him."

Foote, of course, had seen the mortar boats, and Lincoln had not. Anthony Trollope, the rambling British novelist, passed disdainfully through Cairo early in February and heard about the new idea in river warfare. "The grandeur of the idea is almost sublime," he thought. "Could any city be safe when such implements of war were about on the waters?" After a look at the sublime implements, Trollope changed his tune. Their magazines leaked. They were roughhewn and ungainly. One was towed out into the river, but could scarcely be moved against the current, even with two tugboats pulling it. Trollope wrote:

When we saw them, many of the rivets were already gone. The small boats had been stolen from some of them, and the ropes and oars from others. There they lay, thirty-eight in number, up against the mud-banks of the Ohio, under the boughs of the half-clad, melancholy forest trees, as sad a spectacle of reckless prodigality as the eye ever beheld.

On February 2 without waiting for the mortars to be installed in the sad flotilla, Foote took three wooden gunboats and four ironclads up the Tennessee; and on February 6 Fort Henry fell before his bombardment. "We all went wild over your success," wrote Wise. "Uncle Abe was joyful, and said everything of the navy boys and spoke of you—in his plain, sensible appreciation of merit and skill." Brigadier General Ulysses Grant's army had landed at Fort Henry. Now it marched eastward across country to Fort Donelson on the Cumberland, which ran parallel to the Tennessee. Foote's flotilla steamed confidently down the Tennessee, along the Ohio, and up the Cumberland to support Grant—still without the mortar boats.

The omission was unfortunate. The first trial of a mortar boat had been made on February 9 and had vindicated Lincoln's faith. Tying the boat to the Mississippi shore, the crew aimed their massive gun down a broad stretch of water toward Columbus, Kentucky. A correspondent of the *Missouri Democrat* described the scene with verve and fidelity: "Ready! fire! A deafening concussion, and in an instant the huge shell was seen mounting in the air with a magnificent curve, and its terrible roar gradually diminishing, as its distance from us rapidly increased. It may have risen to the height of half a mile, and was almost lost to view before it began to make its descending curve. . . . It was wonderful to wait so long, the seconds lengthening out, as it seemed, to minutes. The suspense was relieved by the sudden shooting up, from the water's line, of a white column of spray, far down the Mississippi, and, as it was estimated, two miles and a half away from us. The mortar-boat was scarcely moved by the explosion, and the mortar-carriage recoiled but two or three inches."

Five sand-filled shells, each weighing two hundred and thirty pounds, were fired with charges up to twenty-three pounds of powder. Fears that the tremendous reaction would push the little boat under proved to be groundless. Some defects were discovered: the iron bulwarks made the concussion worse, and the bow and stern needed altering for easier towing. But these were easily attended to. Despite their unpromising appearance, the boats were well adapted to their function, which was simply to provide floating platforms for the great mortars.

Foote had reason to wish he had brought the boats along. At Fort Donelson, his flotilla ran into a murderous fire which its conventional guns could not silence. Shell and solid shot ripped through the gunboats, driving needlelike splinters and fragments of iron into the men, carrying away flagstaffs and smokestacks and small boats, disabling steering gear, tearing off side armor as lightning strips bark from trees. "Before the decks were well sanded," related the captain of the *Carondelet,* "there was so much blood on them that our men could not work the guns without slipping." Foote himself was wounded. And when Donelson fell, it fell before the land attack of Grant's men.

Day after day, night after night, through the news of Henry and Donelson, Lincoln read telegrams from Cairo on progress in the mounting of the mortars. At last, early in March, word came from Foote that the boats were ready and would be used on the Mississippi in an attack on Island Number Ten. On the morning of March 20 Lincoln read a telegram from the scene of action: "The mortar shells have done fine execution; one shell was fairly landed on [the enemy's] Floating Battery and cleared the concern in short metre."

A *Chicago Tribune* man was enraptured by the performance. "The firing of a mortar is the very poetry of a battle," he wrote. "A bag of powder weighing from 18 to 20 pounds is dropped into the bore of the huge monster. The derrick drops the shell in; the angle is calculated; a long cord is attached to the primer; the gunner steps out upon the platform, and the balance of the crew upon the shore.

The captain gives the word, the gunner gives his cord a sudden jerk, a crash like a thousand thunders follows, a tongue of flame leaps from the mouth of the mortar, and a column of smoke rolls up in beautiful fleecy spirals, developing into rings of exquisite proportions. One can see the shell as it leaves the mortar flying through the air, apparently no larger than a marble. The next you see of the shell, a beautiful cloud of smoke bursts into sight, caused by the explosion."

At night, the show was equally spectacular. The burning fuse had "the appearance of a star, which appears and disappears as the shell rolls through the air, very like the twinkling of the celestial orbs. The explosion of the shell at night is a magnificent and fearful sight, sending a glow of surpassing brightness around it as though some world of combustible light had burst."

Island Number Ten surrendered on April 8, and Federal troops and gunboats knifed deeper into the Confederacy's vitals. Before the month was out, Porter's mortar flotilla, which had been waiting off Mobile, was dropping nearly seventeen thousand thirteen-inch shells into Forts Jackson and St. Philip, the chief barriers before New Orleans. Porter's "chowder-pots," as the big guns were called, had much to do with the fall of those forts and of New Orleans.

Gustavus Fox's idea had been gloriously proved, and Lincoln's support of it gloriously vindicated.

Repercussions of the "mortar business" were felt elsewhere than New Orleans and Island Number Ten. Bureaucrats quaked behind more than one Washington desk. Someone had blundered. Who would be blamed?

Looking back after ninety years, we can see that no one involved was wholly guiltless, and no one solely responsible. The basic difficulty, in fact, seems to have been that lack of clearly assigned responsibility, a fact recognized in Lincoln's Cabinet meeting of January tenth. "Strange enough," Attorney General Bates wrote in his diary record of the discussion, "the boats are under the *War* Dept., and yet are commanded by *naval* officers. Of course, they are neglected."

If individual scapegoats are demanded, Halleck and Foote would seem to be logical candidates. Yet Halleck rode serenely above the storm, by his very indifference to the affair seeming to dissociate himself from it. And Foote had a powerful friend at court in the person of Lieutenant Harry Wise, who saw Lincoln every day and grew in his favor. "Be certain," Wise assured Foote, "that I shall do all I can for you, come fair weather or foul, and I make no doubt, nor ever have, but that the whole thing will redound to your reputation and honor"—as, indeed, it did.

The Navy Department had been remiss in not replacing the mortars it commandeered for Porter, and Gustavus Fox's New England conscience seemed to recognize this. "It is impossible," Fox wrote uneasily, "for us to shake off from our Department some little blame with regard to these mortars, for people will never care to investigate the whole facts." Nevertheless, Fox tried, rather ignobly, to shift the blame to Foote, who took this as "the unkindest cut I ever have had."

But the Navy soon became thankfully aware that Lincoln's wrath had fallen on General Ripley.

The President made no secret of his feelings. "President sent for Gus," noted Mrs. Fox in her diary. "*Mad about mortars.* . . . The President says 'he believes he must take these army matters into his own hands. The Navy have built their ships & mortars for N. O. & are ready to go. Gen. McC. & Ripley & all are to blame.' " Fox himself shed crocodile tears for the Army. "I doubt," he wrote next day, "if the history of any war ever furnished such an exposure. . . . The President has determined to remove Ripley from the ordnance, and it has shaken his confidence in many others. . . . Our twenty mortar vessels . . . will shame the Army people for their great crime in neglecting these boats."

It was true. Ripley was marked at last for dismissal. On January 24, 1862, Lincoln formally authorized Stanton to make "some changes" in the Ordnance Office for "the success of military operations and the safety of the country." Next day, that pugnacious, redheaded Virginian, Major Alexander Dyer, arrived in Washington after a hurried trip from the Springfield Armory, got a room at the Columbian Hotel, and reported in obedience to orders. Major Dyer, as the newspapers at once proclaimed, was slated to be Ripley's successor as Chief of Ordnance.

Ripley's official neck was saved by his own protégé from Springfield. To the surprise and confusion of Lincoln and Stanton, Major Dyer declined the honor tendered him. Perhaps he was grateful for Ripley's part in his earlier promotion. He based his refusal, however, on the ground that he could be of far greater service at Springfield, where he was in the midst of organizing large-scale rifle production. Dyer assured Lincoln that he would, of course, obey any order given; but Lincoln did not want a Chief of Ordnance who served only under compulsion.

No other likely candidate could be found. Colonel Craig suffered from the progressive and incurable disability of old age. Colonel Maynadier, that master of red tape, kept his desk, but was out of the question as chief. The only other ordnance officer not impossibly low in seniority was the brilliant Major Rodman, then commanding the Watertown Arsenal; but his administrative ability was questionable, and he drew royalties from an important cannon patent—which disqualified him as a maker of contracts.

Stanton kept searching for a replacement until mid-March, when he offered Ripley's post to ailing Brigadier General Ethan Allen Hitchcock. The old man declined, as soon as he had recovered from the shock. Stanton and Lincoln, who held Hitchcock in high regard, kept him on as a sort of military adviser. One of Hitchcock's first pieces of advice was against a change in the Ordnance Department, on the ground that if the Corps believed in its chief's competence, it made no difference whether that belief was true or not. "If this belief be shaken," urged Hitchcock, "the operation of the whole system is endangered." The notion seems a little tenuous, but it appears to have persuaded Stanton. "I concluded not to make any change just at that time," recalled the Secretary, "and not until I had become further acquainted with the business of the office."

Ripley survived, but his status had changed. Lincoln and Stanton took care to give him a prop in the person of Peter H. Watson, a chunky, red-bearded Scot, who had been banished from British soil for his part in the Canadian Rebellion of 1837. By January 1862, when Lincoln nominated him for Assistant Secretary of War, Watson was being acclaimed as "probably the first patent lawyer in the United States; a business man of great industry, clear head, and sterling integrity." He was also one of Stanton's few close friends. Since Watson had learned a good deal about weapons as a patent attorney, Stanton put him in charge of the Ordnance Office and made no move in that regard thereafter without Watson's advice and concurrence. Ripley, in turn, had "very little direct communication with the Secretary of War."

Ripley did not pine for Stanton's company. With Adjutant General Lorenzo Thomas, he was a favorite butt of the Secretary's bullyings. On one occasion Stanton peremptorily summoned Ripley to his office, where Stanton was just then receiving the public. After threading his way through the press of supplicants, Ripley found his chief standing by the window with a contractor and looking over a musket with a new type of lock. On Stanton's demand Ripley reported the number of such locks he had ordered. "Now," said Stanton fiercely, "if you dare to adopt another musket of this kind, I'll dismiss you from the service."

"But Mr. Secretary," stammered Ripley.

"Not another word," snapped Stanton, "you can return to your Bureau." Flushed and shaking as if struck with palsy, the white-haired veteran passed silently through a gaping crowd.

Donn Piatt, who knew Stanton well, once wrote: "He was approached by all about him in fear and trembling. And the same ugliness seemed to be contagious. The officer coming from his presence, wounded to the quick, gave to others under him the same treatment."

The mortar business had one other notable by-product. On January 26, 1862, Lincoln, "mad about mortars," told Fox that he believed he must "take these army matters into his own hands." One day later the generals were astonished and the public heartened to read the President's "General War Order Number One," which decreed a general movement on February 22 of all land and naval forces of the United States against the insurgents. On January 31 came his "Special War Order Number One," ordering an advance by the Army of the Potomac directly on Richmond by way of Manassas, this advance to begin by February 22.

The orders were not carried out literally. McClellan submitted a long letter explaining why they could not be, and Lincoln consented to waive them. Washington's Birthday passed quietly by without an advance, and it was not until late in March that McClellan shifted his army to Fortress Monroe, whence it was to move on Richmond via the York Peninsula.

Nevertheless, the orders had been worth making. They roused the North from its cynical lethargy until the news of Henry and Donelson could fire its spirit; and they gave McClellan a healthy jolt. In December McClellan had hastily penciled his replies to Lincoln's careful inquiries about the coming campaign. In his elaborate communication of February 3 the young Napoleon betrayed a new awareness that Lincoln was, after all, his commander in chief. "From that time," wrote John Hay, "[the President] influenced actively the operations of the campaign. He stopped going to McClellan's and sent for the general to come to him. Everything grew busy and animated after that order." And Stanton remarked after the war that if Lincoln had not issued those orders, "the Armies would have remained in front of Washington to this present."

However that might be, Dahlgren was able to write in March:

The move for the Peninsula is now fairly afoot—the Potomac is crowded with every description of vessel carrying troops, horses, field guns—stores of all kinds—the President is constantly on the move, looking with deepest interest at the proceedings.

The winter of the Union's discontent had given way to a hopeful spring.

CHAPTER 13

An Encounter at Hampton Roads

MEANWHILE, THE CONFEDERATES HAD NOT been idle. At the Navy Yard near Norfolk, burned by Lieutenant Wise nearly a year before, but now partially restored, they were preparing what they hoped would be a shattering surprise for their enemies: the hulk of the steam frigate *Merrimac,* raised from the mud of Norfolk Harbor, patched up and transformed into an ironclad warship. The secret did not keep long after Norfolk sightseers began paying calls at the construction site. Lincoln heard vague reports about the project almost from the first, and he was in a position to guess the details.

Ironclad warships were an old story to Abraham Lincoln. More than a dozen years before, during his term in Congress, Lincoln had taken up the cause of an inventor named Uriah Brown, who had plans for a vessel much like the future *Merrimac*—an armored steam warship with sloping sides to deflect shot. Since 1814 Brown had been seeking support for his proposed ironclad and the steam-powered flame thrower he planned to use with it. Encouraged by the outbreak of war with Mexico, he persuaded Congressman Lincoln to sponsor his petition to Congress for an experimental grant.

Before Brown's petition had been acted on, the Mexican War ended, and with it ended Uriah Brown's last chance at fame. Nevertheless, the idea of armored warships remained very much alive. William O. Stoddard encountered it in a White House anteroom early in the summer of 1861 and wrote:

The broad-shouldered, plain-looking fellow sitting there seems to have his lap full of joiner-work, painted black. It reminds one of the Noah's arks he used to get at Christmas, only that it is very low and wide, and has no procession of wooden animals. There are toy cannon, too, looking out of the windows, instead of giraffes. That man was in to see the President yesterday, and they sat down together and discussed Western steamboats and flatboats and gunboats, and they turned that thing inside out. It has been here a good while, sitting on the mantel. It is the first model of a "tin-clad" gunboat, for use upon the shallow waters of the West, and the President has had more to do than most men are aware of with the beginnings of the Mississippi flotilla.

Perhaps Stoddard exaggerated Lincoln's role in the building of the Western ironclads. Yet the great engineer James B. Eads once sent Lincoln a photograph of the *St. Louis,* later the *De Kalb,* "the first iron-clad built in America . . . the first armored vessel against which the fire of a hostile battery was directed on this continent; and so far as I can ascertain . . . the first ironclad that ever engaged a naval force in the world." In the course of his letter Eads referred to Lincoln's "identification with the interesting incidents of her history"; and Eads should have known, for he built her.

Certainly Lincoln's enthusiasm for ironclads began early and lasted through the war. When C. S. Bushnell of Hartford, "a massive, vigorous, fine-looking man," came to him in 1861 with John Ericsson's plan for the *Monitor,* Lincoln at once promised his support. Next morning Lincoln joined a naval board which had met to consider the plan. Opinions differed; but as the session closed, Lincoln remarked: "All I have to say is what the girl said when she put her foot into the stocking, 'It strikes me there's something in it.' "

Whatever weight Lincoln's approval carried, the plan was eventually adopted; and Ericsson set to work, racing against the time when the rebels would finish armoring the raised *Merrimac.* On March 4, 1862, Assistant Secretary Fox was able to notify Lincoln that the *Monitor* was "now on her way to Hampton Roads."

Before Ericsson's "cheesebox on a raft" reached her destination, the *Merrimac* appeared at Hampton Roads and, impervious to broadsides, disposed of five stately wooden frigates. The rebel ironclad was commanded by Dahlgren's former superior, Franklin Buchanan. Dahlgren first heard the epoch-making news from Lincoln himself, who drove down to the Navy Yard about ten o'clock Sunday morning and brought Dahlgren back with him to the White House. There in the Cabinet room were gathered Secretaries Seward, Welles and Stanton, with Generals McClellan and Meigs. Later Dahlgren wrote:

We only knew of the disasters of Saturday and deliberated on the best way of meeting the consequences, little dreaming that at the very time the Monitor was settling the question by hard knocks. The President was not in the least alarmed, but maintained his usual pleasant & suggestive mood. Generals McClellan, Meigs, & myself were assigned the planning of some measures, and when I left it was with no despair of the Republic, though all of us were thoughtful enough. It was a serious business, and if the Merrimac were successful no one could anticipate the consequences to our side.

Word came that evening that after the *Monitor's* "hard knocks" —delivered by two Dahlgren 11-inchers—her opponent had labored back to Norfolk. This, while not a clear-cut victory, sufficed. The *Merrimac* no longer menaced the Union fleet, and McClellan's shift to the Peninsula could proceed unhindered.

Although ironclads made Eads and Ericsson famous, they brought only tragedy to one of Lincoln's old friends.

George C. Bestor, a native of Washington, D. C., moved to Peoria, Illinois, at twenty-four and rose swiftly in the esteem of his new neighbors, who chose him three times as their mayor. Like Lincoln, Bestor had been an earnest Whig, and more than that, a personal friend of Lincoln's political hero, Henry Clay. Not only was Bestor a "first-rate businessman" but he was also known as one of the "best tacticians" in the Illinois state senate. Widely popular, he possessed what the *Springfield Journal* called "a fund of anecdotes which he relates with inimitable grace." "He is fond of his home and its surroundings," remarked the *Journal,* "and his hand and heart are open to his friends." Altogether, Bestor was a man after Lincoln's own heart.

In April 1861, the day after his fiftieth birthday, Bestor offered Lincoln a volunteer company of middle-aged men for the protection of Washington. For some reason, the company never marched. Instead, Bestor came to Washington that fall with "an ingenious model of an ironclad steam gun boat" and a letter of introduction from Captain Foote to Captain Dahlgren.

During December, Lincoln wrote a note in which he referred to Bestor as "my intimate personal friend." It was not until March 15, 1862, however, a few days after the epochal events at Hampton Roads, that Lincoln sent Bestor to General Meigs with a note asking the general to "look at his model of Boat, before letting boat-contracts." Even this was not enough. Before he could get a contract, Bestor had to invoke Senator Orville Browning's influence with Lincoln. It was common talk at Washington that Bestor "had a host of friends who would insist on his having a contract for gun boats." At last, in May, the Navy yielded.

Bestor's triumph turned out to be a snare. Having sunk almost all his fortune into building the gunboats, Bestor found that some technicality stood in the way of his getting paid for them. He took his claim to Congress and became a pathetic frequenter of the Capitol. Years passed. The war ended; Lincoln died; and Congress after Congress assembled and adjourned while the heartsick petitioner waited in vain for his claim to be settled. Bestor's health gave way. In May 1872, ten years to the day from the signing of his gunboat contract, the man who was so "fond of his home and its surroundings" died at the National Hotel in Washington.

The *Monitor-Merrimac* fight opened a new field to weapons inventors. "Since the naval fight in Hampton Roads," the *Washington Star* observed early in April, "some 1,500 different schemes for sinking or otherwise disposing of the Merrimac, have been offered to the Navy Department by Yankee inventors." Lincoln and his young secretary, John Hay, laughed together over a New Yorker's suggestion that the rebel ironclad be bombarded with red pepper. Hay wrote:

Respectfully referred by the President to the earnest consideration of Mr. Wise. This kind of "Peppercaster" is a novelty in furniture. How do you think Comr. Buchanan would like this style of condiments on the halfshell? The music of the Muse's shell would be nothing to the strains of this man's "Piper." A classical joke—very chaste. Yours for Abraham, John Hay.

Lieutenant Wise was capable of returning pun for pun, but mercifully forbore.

Other inventors turned their attention to armor, trying all kinds of material from rubber to compressed hog bristles. In May Lincoln went down to the Navy Yard and watched guns pound away at a target sheathed in the armor adopted by the Navy. The trial resulted in a verdict for the defense.

Early in the war Benjamin Severson, a self-made engineer and architect specializing in iron frameworks and trusses, submitted a projectile with a hard, sharp tip of chilled "Franklinite, the hardest and best iron." Secretaries Chase and Welles were on his side, but General Ripley had no officer to spare for "investigations and trials of new discoveries and inventions." After the affair at Hampton Roads Severson tried his luck with Lincoln, bragging that his projectile could sink the *Monitor* in fifteen minutes and the *Merrimac* in ten. Lincoln consulted Totten, who told him that Severson's claims were "so superlative, and at the same time, so unsupported, that I can only avow myself unable to credit them."

Lincoln paid no more heed to Severson's projectile. But the inventor had fallen on hard times; and, touched by his story, Lincoln found him a job as a clerk in the War Department clothing depot. Two years later, when Lincoln was up for re-election and his prospects seemed dark, another clerk wrote the President that Severson was "operating against you with all his power and influence, pronouncing you a man wholly unfit for the Office you hold, a traitor on your own party, a man in whose hands the reigns of Government were intirely misplaced." Lincoln submitted the letter to Stanton, and the next Washington directory listed Severson as an inspector of the Washington aqueduct.

As soon as ships began to be clothed in armor down to the water line and below, inventors resorted to the obvious countermove of striking them from beneath. Thus it happened that Abraham Lincoln encountered the feeble progenitors of the lean gray sea wolves that were to terrorize the North Atlantic half a century later.

In September 1861 Lincoln read a long letter from M. Brutus de Villeroi, late of Nantes, France.* At the Philadelphia Navy Yard the Frenchman had a veritable submarine, an iron cylinder about thirty-three feet long and four feet wide at its greatest diameter, propelled by means of a screw in its stern. De Villeroi provided "an artificial atmosphere" by "a chemical process" which he kept secret. His outlandish vessel could submerge, crew and all, for as long as three hours without communicating with the surface, could rise again at will, and would allow crew members to enter and leave underwater by means of an air lock.

De Villeroi pointed out to Lincoln how easy it would be for the submarine to "reconnaissance the enemy's coast, to land men, ammunition, etc., at any given point, to enter harbors, to keep up intelligence, and to carry explosive bombs under the very keels of vessels and that without being seen. With a few such boats, maneuvered each one by about a dozen men, the most formidable fleet can be annihilated in a short time."

Impressed by these arguments, as well he might have been, Lincoln sent De Villeroi's letter to the Navy Department with an endorsement in his own hand. After seeing the craft in operation,

---

* At Nantes in 1835, when De Villeroi and a companion submerged for two hours in a ten-foot submarine, there lived a seven-year-old boy named Jules Verne. For years after, De Villeroi's submarine experiments were carried on at young Verne's home town. Thus, besides having met the probable inspiration for Mark Twain's Connecticut Yankee, Lincoln encountered the prototype of Captain Nemo.

Navy officials ordered a larger one early in November. Had it not been for a squabble between De Villeroi and the contractor over installation of the breathing equipment, the *Alligator,* as it came to be called, might have beaten the *Monitor* to Hampton Roads, and the history of naval warfare might have been somewhat different. That unfortunate quarrel delayed the launching of the *Alligator* till the end of April, deprived it of its breathing apparatus and led to the substitution of a bank of oars on the duck-foot principle for the proposed screw propeller. De Villeroi thereupon washed his hands of the affair and left for parts unknown.

The *Alligator* was towed down to Hampton Roads and crawled about on the inhospitable bottom of the James River for a while in June 1862. But without De Villeroi's secret breathing apparatus, the *Alligator* was helpless. After a series of vicissitudes, it ran into a heavy gale while being towed off Cape Hatteras in April 1863 and was cut loose to save the tow ship.

The *Alligator* was not the only submarine to interest Lincoln. He also recommended that the proposed submarine of one Oliver B. Pierce be considered by Navy experts. Early in May 1862 Secretary Welles sent Lincoln the report of Rear Admiral Joseph Smith, who vetoed Pierce's proposal. Smith's chief objections to the Pierce plan were the lack of sufficient air for the crew and the probable speed of the craft, which Smith doubted could exceed one knot.

A year later Lincoln asked Assistant Secretary Watson to "please see the bearer, who is the man of whom I spoke in reference to a diving invention." But that invention may not have been a submarine.

Four days after the *Monitor* worsted the *Merrimac,* a Washingtonian named Pascal Plant was ushered into Lincoln's office bearing a small wooden model of a submarine gunboat "to be propelled by gun powder fired from revolving vertical cylinders at either end" and having "similar cylinders for hostile purposes at the sides"—in other words, a rocket-driven submarine. Lincoln was interested. Sending Plant to the Navy Ordnance Bureau, he asked Lieutenant

Wise to have ordnance officers look the model over. Presently word came to Lincoln from the Navy's Board of Examiners that Plant's vessel was "altogether speculative, and his explanations are not such as to induce the Board to recommend it for adoption or even for trial."

Plant lowered his sights. When next he appeared, it was with a more modest device: a rocket-driven submarine torpedo. In October 1862 Assistant Secretary Fox (probably at Lincoln's request) had Dahlgren make up two or three specimens. That December, Fox and Secretary Welles watched two of the torpedoes fired from a scow, lying about forty feet offshore from the Navy Yard. The first rocket plunged into the mud and exploded with "quite a shock." The second veered off suddenly at a sixty-degree angle and struck the *Diana*, an unoffending little schooner anchored near by, blowing up her bow and sinking her—fortunately, with no casualties. "The destructive properties of the rocket were certainly proven," the *Washington Star* commented. So they were. And they came near to being proven still more spectacularly, for had not the *Diana* intervened, Plant's rocket would have run into the "large and splendid steamer *State of Georgia*." As it was, Plant's submarine rocket had become (so far as is known) the first self-propelled torpedo to sink a ship.

A month later another Plant rocket torpedo was fired with results less disastrous but nearly as picturesque. The thing darted from the water like a flying fish about five feet from the boat, touched the surface briefly about twenty feet out, soared into the air, and finally plunged into the Anacostia about a hundred yards away, leaving some bubbles and "a slight smoke." The Navy's interest in Pascal Plant vanished like that smoke, and so, presumably, did Abraham Lincoln's.

CHAPTER 14

The President Perseveres

THROUGH IT ALL, THROUGH THE JANUARY
fogs and the mortar business, the *Merrimac* scare and the trouble
over Ripley, through all the whirring, darting distractions so neatly
pinned down and ticketed by his biographers, Lincoln held to his
resolve that the inventors should have from him what Ripley denied them: a fair hearing and a chance to prove their claims.

The nearest he came to wavering was early in January 1862, on
one of those days of deepest frustration, when a pair of New York
Congressmen ushered Levi Short of Buffalo into the White House
and introduced him to Lincoln as the inventor of an incendiary
mixture called "Greek Fire." For once, Lincoln lost his temper
with an inventor. Less than three weeks before, Obadiah Hopkins
had tried to hoodwink him by bribing General Totten. Just a day
or two ago, a Federal gunboat had bombarded a rebel battery at
Cockpit Point with shells containing "a peculiar combustible material"—which must have been more peculiar than combustible, for
it had no visible effect. After letting Congressmen Fenton and
Spaulding unburden their minds, Lincoln turned to Levi Short and
remarked witheringly that all the charlatans came to him with their
worthless inventions because they knew he could be easily imposed
on. "Judge you," Short wrote later, "whether I winced under the
lash."

That was all. Lincoln recovered himself immediately, and as if conscience-stricken at his outburst, gave Short a note to Dahlgren, asking that the inventor be given a chance to demonstrate his shell.

Incendiary weapons, of course, were not new to the world, nor to Lincoln. The very name of Short's material, "Greek Fire," came from the stuff Byzantine warriors had hurled at enemy ships hundreds of years before. The year after Tom Lincoln married Nancy Hanks, the British burned much of Copenhagen with incendiary rockets; and in the Crimean War of the mid-fifties, as Lincoln must have read in Wells's *Annual of Scientific Discovery,* the Russians used incendiary projectiles against the French. As early as 1814, Uriah Brown of Baltimore had successfully demonstrated his flame thrower, which projected a stream of burning liquid from a nozzle, before a "vast concourse" of citizens; he gave another spectacular demonstration in the Treasury Park in 1847; and as we have noted, Lincoln himself introduced Brown's last petition into the House of Representatives in 1848.*

In 1861, to be sure, General McClellan remarked that "such means of destruction are hardly within the category of those recognized in civilized warfare," but no one else on either side seems to have shared his scruples at that time. When Ripley turned down an offer of incendiary shells in May 1861, he did so not out of humanitarianism but because the arsenals were too crowded.

Even before he met Levi Short, Lincoln had helped another incendiary inventor, an old New Yorker named Robert L. Fleming, who styled himself "General" and had long acted as agent on the Pennsylvania lands of a wealthy New York businessman, William E. Dodge of Phelps, Dodge and Company. In the spring of 1861 Fleming had come to Washington with letters of recommendation from his influential employer, as well as from sundry politicians. Nothing availed until he met Lincoln, who, in Fleming's words, "granted me all the facilities I asked for the accomplishment of my

---

* At about that time, or shortly after, Levi Short worked on incendiary rockets with one "Professor Brown of Cincinnati," who may or may not have been Uriah Brown.

object, which was to perfect my incendiary shell." A note survives
from Lincoln to Ramsay in October 1861:

The bearer of this, well recommended to me, wishes you to furnish him a few shells, and give him some assistance in filling them
according to his direction. He thinks he can make a very destructive
missile, and, if not too much trouble to you, I shall be obliged, if
you can accommodate him.

As for Short, Dahlgren did not obey Lincoln's note in the spirit
intended: the only gun he could or would spare was too small. So
on January 14, 1862, Lincoln arranged for a public demonstration
of Short's Greek Fire in the Treasury Park, "understanding that it
is the wish of several military gentlemen to witness a formal test
. . . and further understanding that it will not incur either expense
or inconvenience to the War Department."

In the Washington papers Short announced his device as "the
most perfect and terrible invention for destructive warfare known
to man," and promised that the shell would blanket the ground
over a radius of a hundred and fifty feet with fire which would
burn intensely for ten or twenty minutes. This sounded to Washingtonians like a great show; and when the time arrived, thousands
of them waited on the snow-covered White House lawn. Lincoln
probably watched from a White House window. The air was cold
and still, and the night sky crystal clear.

Unfortunately, a shipment of Greek Fire had been delayed
somewhere along the road from Buffalo. Short went ahead with
what he had. But although his shell "scattered fire which burned
upon the snow and ice several minutes," the shivering crowd was
not impressed.

A few days later, after the delayed shipment had arrived, Short
gave a second exhibition. This time a thick curtain of clouds
blacked out the stars. Again Lincoln watched, while two thirteen-
inch shells were exploded, each tossing fire forty or fifty feet in the
air and carpeting the ground over a fifty-foot radius with a blaze
that lasted ten minutes. The crowd was delighted. Next day, sec-

onded by the two Senators from Kansas, Short offered Ripley two thousand shells at $12 each, for use in plains warfare. But to the great loss of today's technicolor Western movies, Ripley turned the offer down, and Lincoln did not choose to overrule his irascible Chief of Ordnance. On Ben Butler's invitation, Short headed for New England, where he spread the light of progress over Boston Common and sold the general a hundred of his shells for the New Orleans expedition.

Lincoln's other incendiary protégé, "General" Fleming, had meanwhile struck an alliance with a Washingtonian who called himself Dr. J. Rutherford Worster.

"Dr." Worster had given "Electrical Baths" to rundown Congressmen until his rooms in the Capitol basement were taken over in 1861 for use as Army bakeries. Undaunted, he set up shop at his home on Tenth Street nearly opposite Ford's new theater, and began treating all known diseases with his "Electro-Magnetic Insulators, Rejuvenating Elixir, Cough Syrups, Stomachic-Vegetable Electric, and many other things, preventive and preservative." Whatever the virtues of his elixirs, Worster himself was a likable man, highly spoken of by Western Congressmen especially, who may conceivably have profited from his nineteenth-century version of the shock treatment. To his contemporaries the pious old fraud was "a highly respectable citizen" and "the worthy Dr. J. R. Worster."

The "worthy Doctor" even claimed acquaintance with Abraham Lincoln. If he did know Lincoln, it was probably not through "Electrical Baths," but through Worster's son James, who moved to Bloomington, Illinois, a year or two before the war. In the fall of 1860 Worster wrote Lincoln a couple of letters on trends in capital politics. "I have nothing to ask at your hands," Worster assured the Republican candidate. "I am perfectly unharnessed & independent if not a 'railsplitter.' I am a very hardworking man, & drink no whiskey." (He said nothing of Rejuvenating Elixir, or other things preventive and preservative.)

By the winter of 1861-1862 Worster had become Robert Fleming's manager, ghost writer and press agent. His ornate style —he called falling leaves "autumnal defoliation"—flavored the advertisements which announced a Treasury Park demonstration on March 13 of "Gen. Fleming's wonderfully destructive Shell, and its tremendous power, one of the most remarkable discoveries of the age." Lincoln and his Cabinet, as well as Congressmen, Senators, the press and "a little million of good Union ladies," were all expected to be on hand.

Curiously, in view of the advance publicity, not a word of the exhibition appeared afterward.

While Dr. Worster bustled about his business, the war claimed his son James. After enlisting as a private in the 3rd Illinois Cavalry, young Worster, praised by his colonel as "active, intelligent, obedient and untiring," had risen rapidly to become regimental sergeant major. At Pea Ridge, Arkansas, on March 7 Sergeant Worster, then acting as a courier, saw a caisson about to be abandoned. He sprang from his horse, ran forward and was struggling to get the caisson away when the rebels overran the position and put a bullet through his head. He left a wife and son in Bloomington.

Young Worster's death brought about his father's meeting with Lincoln. Only two weeks before young Worster died, Lincoln had lost his own son Willie. It had been a fearful blow to his spirit. When the sorrowing Dr. Worster asked for a pass through the lines so that he might recover his son's body, Lincoln gave him a note: "I shall be pleased for the Military authorities to give Dr. Worster, any facilities they consistently can, in furtherence of his object expressed within." And the authorities complied, of course, with Lincoln's request, although the outcome of the doctor's search is not recorded.

By then, another breech-loading cannon had captured Lincoln's interest.

This one, invented by William F. Goodwin of Powhattan, Ohio, had its breech piece hitched to the gun by two arms, like the shafts of a wagon. When swung up to close the breech, the concave inner surface fitted snugly against the butt end of the gun. In the breech piece was a firing pin which, when released by a trigger, detonated a percussion cap on the end of the cartridge.

Coming to Washington in March 1862, Goodwin found that he could not get his gun looked at, let alone tested. He hunted up Senator "Bluff Ben" Wade of Ohio, and matters began to move. Wade pressed Stanton, Stanton gave orders to Ripley, and the gun was promptly inspected. According to the *National Intelligencer,* moreover, it was examined and fired "by President Lincoln, officers of the ordnance department and others, and very uniformly pronounced a simple, efficient, and entirely successful breech-loader." The specimen Lincoln fired was tricked out with a shield to protect the gunners and "turn back minie bullets upon the infantry sending them," as well as "a system of sword bayonets further to protect gunners against a charge of infantry." Goodwin claimed his gun could fire twenty-five times a minute; but with such accessories, this would seem superfluous.

Toward the end of April, Lincoln and Wade jointly requested quick action on Goodwin's patent application; and the patent was issued in May. It seems, however, that Goodwin owed his rapid progress to Lincoln's influence, for when that pressure relaxed, Goodwin's gun was forgotten. Late in the war, Goodwin was still trying vainly to sell the government a battery of four 10-pounders.

Even before Goodwin's patent came out, the Cincinnati Breech-loading Cannon was back in Washington. This time its sponsor was not the eccentric lawyer Walter Sherwin, but a Cincinnati go-getter named James C. C. Holenshade.

Born of Scotch-Irish parents, Holenshade had gone to work at the age of seven, educated himself by a course of reading, made his fortune in the hardware business and retired to his fruit farm in 1860, aged thirty-two. The war lured him away from the fruits of his toil. When the first call for army wagons came, Holenshade bid for and won the contract, quite undeterred by his total ignorance of wagon making. Presently he had several hundred men turning out wagons at the rate of two an hour, and his new business flourished through the war. Although draft-exempt on physical grounds, Holenshade furnished four substitutes. This seems a fair equivalent, for besides his other interests he was active in the Odd Fellows, the Masons, the Presbyterian church and the Cincinnati Fire Department. He was also a prime mover in Cincinnati's great Sanitary Fair. And at some point in the winter of 1861-1862, he took over the promotion of the Cincinnati Breech-loading Cannon.

When Holenshade arrived in Washington, he brought no mere model, but a full-sized bronze 6-pounder; and Lincoln promptly arranged for a trial at the Navy Yard on May 3. It turned out to be a fine spring Saturday, mild and clear, which may explain why a sizable crowd, including Senators and Representatives, showed up at the yard. What with the crinoline hoop skirts, the parasols, the Senatorial watch chains and string ties, the antics of the small boys who were doubtless on hand and the tall figure of President Lincoln, the event must have had a holiday air.

But the day brought little joy to Holenshade. To begin with, the primers were too tight, and so Holenshade had to enlarge the vent. Because of the tight primers, he had spent two minutes firing the first ten shots, which were supposed to demonstrate the gun's rapidity. Given another chance, he fired ten blank cartridges in one minute—but two primers failed, and a premature turn of the cylinder sliced one cartridge in half. Two rounds were then fired with solid shot. On the next round, the cartridge was again cut in two, and the upper half got stuck in the breech opening. The gun's breech mechanism seemed to be acting more like a meat grinder than a spigot. Red-faced, Holenshade shoved the half cartridge down into the chamber, and loaded another cartridge. When that heavy charge went off, the crowd was startled to see the trail leap from its rest.

Now the gun had to be got back into place. One can imagine the restless crowd, the quizzical President and the sweating proprietor struggling to make his gun behave. Despite Holenshade's efforts, affairs grew worse and worse. Bits of the chewed-up cartridges began working round in back of the cylinder and jamming the mechanism. It took Holenshade a minute and a half to fire the next five rounds, and the fifth cartridge was cut in half. Then the gun refused to work at all. Feverishly, Holenshade took the gun apart and put it together again, while the crowd murmured and the President cooled his heels.

The rest of the trial was supposed to prove Holenshade's claim that he had "the only gun in the world as yet revealed that can be limbered up & fired upon retreat"—certainly an appropriate moment for the demonstration. Horses were hitched up to the balky gun and started off at a funereal walk while five rounds of blanks were fired. At the third round, two men were needed to move the cylinder.

Perhaps Lincoln, who knew his *Hamlet* well, found the dismal cortége wryly suggestive of that tragedy's closing:

> Go, bid the soldiers shoot. [*A dead march. Exeunt, bearing off the bodies; after which a peal of ordnance is shot off.*]

If the trial of May 3, 1862, did little to sustain Lincoln's faith in breech-loading cannon, at least he knew by then that he had been right about rifled cannon.

Fort Pulaski, the chief defense of Savannah, Georgia, had been a huge brick pentagon, casemated on all sides with walls seven and a half feet thick, squatting grimly on the flat marsh of Cockspur Island, surrounded by broad, deep channels, and at least a mile from the nearest firm ground. Said General Totten: "the work could not be reduced in a month's firing with any number of guns of manageable calibers."

Union troops under the direction of Colonel Quincy Adams Gillmore, a brash Buckeye with no respect for his elder's opinion, set up some Parrott and James rifles on Tybee Island, and the impregnable walls of Fort Pulaski were presently dissolving in puffs

of yellow dust. When the rebel colors fluttered down on the afternoon of April 11, 1862, the fort looked like a sand castle kicked by
a passing giant.

After that, no one doubted the power of rifled cannon, or their
superiority over smoothbores for long range bombardment.

Scores of inventors now busied themselves with variations on the
rifling of cannon. One of them was John B. Atwater, a theater
manager from Ripon, Wisconsin, who, in the month Fort Pulaski
fell, interested Lincoln in his system. In rifling, the ridges separat-
ing the grooves are called "lands." Atwater's idea was to cut some
of these lands short before they reached the muzzle, on the theory
that after a certain point they cost more by friction than they contributed to spinning the shell. Lincoln ordered a trial of Atwater's
system at the Washington Arsenal in comparison with a conventionally rifled gun. The comparison was not made, and there is no
written evidence that Lincoln did any more for Atwater. Yet the
inventor was treated with unusual consideration by both ordnance
bureaus for many months thereafter. In the end, his idea came to
nothing.

Their success at Fort Pulaski had insured the fame of Robert P.
Parrott's rifled cannon; and on June 24, 1862, after a conference
with General Winfield Scott at West Point, New York, Lincoln
paid a visit to Parrott's Cold Spring Foundry, three miles away.
Rain fell in torrents that summer afternoon, and West Point wal-
lowed in mud; but Lincoln was always ready to look at guns and the
making of guns. He saw plenty at Cold Spring. A few days later,
a visitor wrote:

The Foundry is in full blast with everything in the ordnance
line. One can hardly worm his way through the piles of shot and
shell for rifles; and the machine shop, foundry, and boring mill
contain nothing but rifled Parrotts of all sizes. Wonderful place.

At the proving grounds, Lincoln watched 100-pounder and 200-
pounder Parrott rifles hurl their heavy shells thousands of yards
through a gap in the highlands to the precipitous banks of "Crows

Nest," while the deep clamor of gunfire echoed back from the hills like the roar of a great battle. Afterward, he tramped delightedly about the plant, regardless of mud and rain. Raised a few inches from the ground on sleepers were bars of iron four inches square and sixty feet long, ready to be heated red-hot and coiled around mandrels by machinery. Near by, Lincoln saw these coiled bars welded by a great trip hammer, turned down, reheated and shrunk onto guns—forming the bands which were the trademark of the Parrotts. His face felt the heat and dazzle of the foundry where the guns were cast. He looked on as they were bored, rifled, turned and polished. And in still another building he watched workmen turn out Parrott shells, distinguished by the brass expanding ring for taking the rifle grooves. Before Lincoln left Cold Spring, he had seen about all there was to see in the making of rifled cannon.

That night he took the train for Washington, and three days later Parrott shipped the proved guns to McClellan's army as it fought bloodily near Richmond.

In his twenty-five years as a small-town lawyer, not to mention his fourteen months thus far as President, Abraham Lincoln had encountered some unsavory individuals (we have already mentioned Obadiah Hopkins, the would-be briber; Benjamin Severson, the ingrate; and Edward Wilder, the suspected traitor). Few, however, could have surpassed the inventor who showed Lincoln a breech-loading carbine on May 5, 1862, two days after the Holenshade trial.

His name was Strong, and so was his personality. The latter, in fact, once inspired a government blacksmith to a flight of genuine eloquence. "I have looked for a similar character among living men," declaimed the smith, "but have found none—in the history of the dead, but found none. I believe there was but one such made, and that he is entirely original. . . . Sixteen months acquaintance with Samuel Strong has failed to present to my mind anything lovely, anything reverential, anything worthy of imitation, save his perseverance." General Montgomery Meigs later put the case more delicately when he remarked: "It has happened to me never to hear him well spoken of."

Samuel Strong had been a contractor and petty Whig politician who for thirty years had developed and refined his rascality in public construction for New York State. When the death of Zachary Taylor made Millard Fillmore President in 1851, Fillmore appointed his fellow New Yorker superintendent of work on the new Capitol extension. Here was a happy hunting ground. Several months later, a special committee of the Senate, braving the thugs Strong hired to assault its members, reported that Strong, literally under the eyes of Congress, had pocketed between a third and a half of the million dollars spent on the building. Yet Strong somehow escaped punishment. Not only that, but by hastily resigning, he even robbed Congress of the power to dismiss him.

Perseverance is a mighty virtue, and Samuel Strong prospered. By 1861, after a stay in California, where he mined the state treasury in preference to the Sierras, he was back in Washington and getting chatty letters from Horace Greeley. In the capital he was still "a well-known citizen," but not universally beloved—or so we may presume from the fact that "two Irishmen," one with a knife, attacked him on Capitol Hill in January 1862. We may also deduce something about Strong's temperament from the fact that he beat them off, despite his age.* Still more suggestive is an item in the *Star* some months later. As Strong walked home after dark, "he was suddenly attacked by two stout young men, who seized him by the throat and tried to rob him. Mr. Strong was armed with a light walking stick, and with it he defended himself as he best could, and finally managed to rid himself of his villainous enemies; not, however, until he was badly bruised about his body and head. The robbers tried to jerk his watch from his pocket; but the breaking of the chain disappointed them, and they failed to get in his pockets, although they several times made the attempt."

This was the doughty rapscallion who presented his breech-loading carbine to Lincoln's attention that May. Whatever might

---

* He must have been well past sixty.

be said about the man, his gun was not bad. Lincoln looked it over carefully. A lever at the side pulled back the movable chamber, which ended in a thin steel cylinder, intended as a gas check. A cam action brought the chamber into position to receive a .54-caliber paper cartridge. The lever then restored the chamber to firing position.

"This," Lincoln wrote to Ripley, "will introduce to you Mr. Strong who has what appears to me an ingenious and useful carbine. Will you be good enough to examine it and give an opinion as to its serviceability."

Ripley replied that two of his officers had already looked at the gun and, while admitting it to be "novel and ingenious," had concluded that it was no better than other breechloaders. "I avail myself of this opportunity," the Chief of Ordnance added waspishly, "to inform your Excellency that there are several kinds of breech-loading arms, at present, used in the service; and in consequence of the confusion and inconvenience arising therefrom, particularly in supplying ammunition, I do not deem it advisable to increase their number."

Disregarding this latest homily, Lincoln had Captain Crispin try Strong's carbine at New York. Early in June, Crispin reported that on the ninth round of rapid firing, a cartridge had exploded prematurely. Furthermore, escape of gas from the breech was visible immediately. Crispin admitted that the gun's mechanism was simple and had not fouled during the eighty rounds fired. But he feared that rust, especially, would be apt to disable the gun in the field.

Strong, persevering as ever, buckled down to work and a year later came up with a new breechloader, using .58-caliber copper cartridges and specially designed to meet Crispin's objections. Ramsay tried it out at the arsenal and gave it lukewarm approval. But it was not adopted.

The Commissioner of Public Buildings, a stout, bustling, side-whiskered Washingtonian named Benjamin B. French, had many friends in the capital, including "honest old Abe, who calls me 'French' and always tells me a story when I go to talk with him." He also knew a New Yorker named Samuel Gardiner, Jr., whose current pursuit, by our lights, was not so amiable. Gardiner had invented a time-fused explosive bullet.

"Rifle shells," as they were sometimes called, were nothing new. The British used them to explode ammunition wagons during the Indian Mutiny of 1857, and a textbook used at West Point during the Civil War gave directions for making "percussion bullets" intended to "blow up caissons, and boxes containing ammunition, at very long distances." Private letters and postwar reminiscences, which could not have been meant for propaganda, describe encounters with rebel explosive bullets in most of the major battles during and after 1862. Jefferson Davis and his Chief of Ordnance furiously denied in later years that their government had ever made, bought, or issued explosive bullets; but they were careful not to speak for the state governments of the Confederacy, all of which provided arms for their troops at one time or another.

Davis's vehemence is understandable. It was all very well to talk of blowing up ammunition wagons, but such bullets were bound to lodge in human flesh now and then, by accident or intent; and when they did, the results were horrible. "To my dying day," wrote a *New York Tribune* correspondent on the last day of May 1862, "I shall have in my ears the wailing shrieks of a private of the 1st Long Island, shot dead beside my horse with a percussion musket-ball, whose explosion within its wound I distinctly heard."

Three days after that incident, French and his friend Gardiner called on Lincoln with a sample bullet and fragments of exploded ones. Lincoln scrutinized the Gardiner "musket shell" with care. Inside, there was a copper chamber filled with fulminate. From the chamber a time fuse ran out through a tube in the base of the shell. Externally, except for the short projecting tube, the bullet looked much like the Minié ball. The time fuse could be fixed to run from one to three seconds after firing. Gardiner's purpose in using that, rather than a percussion fuse, was to make transport safer and to permit the bullet to penetrate deep within a caisson or ammunition chest before exploding.

According to French, Lincoln seemed to think the bullets "were an improvement on solid shot." He gave the two men a note: "Will Gen. Ripley please consider whether this Musket-shell, would be a valuable missile in battle?"

Through French's influence with Assistant Secretary Watson, the bullet had already been tested by Captain Benét at West Point. Benét had made no generalizations, but his report showed that the bullets tended to burst open in one piece, rather than shatter into fragments. After getting Lincoln's note, Ripley now asked Benét to give his over-all judgment of the bullet. Pointing out that a fixed time fuse was impracticable with varying ranges, and that a Minié bullet would put a man out of action just as surely and less brutally, the captain declared emphatically that the shell had "no merit as a service projectile."

That report ended Lincoln's part in the affair, but, as we shall see, not the story of the Gardiner shell.

Looking back over the first six months of 1862, we become aware that the pattern of 1861 had changed. In Lincoln's dealings with inventors we still see the same lively interest in new weapons —Severson's, Plant's, Pierce's, Gardiner's—and the same "champagne experiments," such as those for Short, Fleming, Goodwin, Holenshade, Atwater, Strong. But we encounter no such cases as those of the Marsh and the Spencer breechloaders, the Woodruff and Ellsworth cannon, or the coffee-mill machine guns, in which Lincoln, on his own responsibility, ordered the actual purchase of new weapons.

Why was this? So far as we know, Lincoln never set forth his reasons for the change. We may therefore only speculate. It was not that he saw no weapon worth ordering; the Goodwin cannon seemed to please everyone but Ripley. Nor had he suddenly grown apprehensive of charlatans, despite his remark to Levi Short in January, for he listened willingly enough to J. Rutherford Worster and Samuel Strong. If he already thought the war too far advanced for conversion to new weapons, he would have abandoned his "champagne experiments"; but he did not do so. We are left with the theory that before ordering any more new weapons, Lincoln wanted to see what would come of those he had already bought.

If this was so, he had not long to wait.

CHAPTER 15

Trial by Combat

WHEN 1862 BEGAN, A GRIM-FACED, INDOMI-
table Pennsylvanian named John W. Geary had already been the
first American commander of the City of Mexico under General
Scott, the first mayor of San Francisco, and the governor of Kansas
Territory. Before he died, he would become military governor of
Savannah, Georgia, and the twice-elected governor of Pennsylvania.
To this unparalleled catalogue of distinctions, he was now about to
add that of commanding the first regiment ever to fire machine guns
in action. For it was on January 2, 1862, that Colonel Geary received
two "Union Repeating Guns" from Paymaster Stebbins of the
Washington Arsenal.

There is no mystery about the choice of Colonel Geary and his
28th Pennsylvania Volunteer Regiment for the job of trying out
Lincoln's coffee-mill guns. Geary and his men were guarding a
twenty-four mile stretch of the Potomac River; and although the re-
frain "All quiet along the Potomac" was becoming a byword and a
mockery in the impatient North, frequent skirmishes occurred to
enliven the Pennsylvanians' tour of duty. In one of these brushes,
presumably, some rebel soldier shortly became the first machine-gun
casualty of all time. Since the coffee-mill guns fired regulation Minié
balls, the Confederate thus honored was unaware of his distinction;
and so his name is lost to history. Perhaps the place was Harper's

Ferry; for when McClellan's Army of the Potomac crossed into Virginia at that point in February, Geary's 28th took the lead, holding the town and the bridgehead.

As spring gentled the Virginia landscape, Geary and his men pushed cautiously westward with their machine guns toward the Shenandoah Valley, beautiful as its name. On March 29 they reached the outskirts of Middleburg, a quiet town containing three churches, seven stores, an academy, a tobacco factory and a few score houses. On that spring day Middleburg also harbored Confederate cavalry and infantry. An uproar of musketry broke in on the town's somnolence; the rebel pickets fell back; and there was fighting in the streets. Covered by their cavalry, the Confederate forces began pulling out of the town. "The enemy made a halt in a hollow beyond the town," reported a *Washington Star* correspondent. "Companies of the 28th now opened on them from behind stone fences with their rifles, when the cavalry dashed off precipitately." So much for the Battle of Middleburg.

And what did the *Star* man say of machine guns in this, their first pitched battle? Not a word, for the same reason that no press reports went out from Hodgenville, Kentucky, on February 12, 1809. It was a historic event which no one present recognized. All we have by which to identify the modern machine gun's baptism of fire with fair certainty is a chance remark dropped by one Captain Bartlett during a discussion at Cooper Institute in New York about four weeks later. "One of these guns," he said, referring to the coffee mills, "was brought to bear on a squadron of cavalry at 800 yards, and it cut them to pieces terribly, quickly forcing them to fly." Only the action at Middleburg fits this picture; and it was the only pitched battle fought by Geary's men while they had the guns.

Now the anticlimax. On April 23 Colonel Geary shipped his two machine guns back to Washington, tersely reporting that after "repeated trials" they had been found "inefficient, and unsafe to the operators." Geary's guns were from the first lot of ten bought by Lincoln; and since these had been made by Woodward and Cox, we may guess at shoddy workmanship. General Ripley did not choose to ask for more particulars, not being the man to look a gift horse in the mouth.

Ripley presently found a use for Colonel Geary's report.

Abolitionist pressure had forced Lincoln to give General Frémont a new command: the Mountain Department, embracing western Virginia. Three days after Geary's report, an exchange of telegrams occurred between Frémont and Ripley that must have unsettled Ripley's disposition for the rest of the day.

Frémont to Ripley:

Our experiments here with the Union repeating gun are satisfactory. Can you spare and will you send immediately sixteen (16) with equipments & full supply of ammunition for this Dep't by way of Pittsburg . . . Will send copy of report.

Ripley to Frémont:

Telegram received—Have no Union repeating guns on hand, and am not aware that any have been ordered.

Frémont to Ripley:

Upon the nineteenth of December on recommendation of Genl McClellan the President ordered fifty of the Coffee Mill or Union guns. Was there not some error of name in my dispatch.

There was, of course, no error in the dispatch received at the Ordnance Office; Ripley had simply lied and been caught at it. Neither was an answer possible to Frémont's second wire; and Ripley made none. After a few days, realizing that he would get nowhere with the Chief of Ordnance, Frémont took the matter up with Lincoln himself. On May 15 Lincoln sent to Ripley for "Gen. Frémont's original requisition for 'Coffee Mill Guns.' "

This put Ripley in a corner, but the old man worked out of it neatly if not altogether honorably.

At the moment, Stonewall Jackson was giving Frémont all the

trouble he could handle and a good deal more besides. This gave Ripley a free hand. Apparently he took his cue from Lincoln's failure to ask for Frémont's report along with Frémont's requisition. Ripley therefore withheld Frémont's report and substituted Geary's. More than that, the fact that an unrelated document of that period was given the file number originally assigned to Frémont's report, and the fact that the latter is no longer to be found in Ordnance Office files, inspire the ugly suspicion that Ripley removed the Frémont report permanently from the files.

After Jackson finished with Frémont in June, the beaten Pathfinder on his own responsibility ordered two coffee-mill guns from Woodward and Cox at the steep price of $1500 each. He never had a chance to use them; for a few days later, he was placed under the upstart John Pope, and, piqued by the slight, he quit the Army.

So far as the records show, Frémont never got the sixteen machine guns he had requisitioned in April. Yet, we may wonder. For at Harper's Ferry in September, from troops which had been part of Frémont's command, Stonewall Jackson captured what the *Richmond Enquirer* described as "17 revolving guns."

The same Harper's Ferry surrender that gave Stonewall Jackson his "17 revolving guns" gives us a clue to the fate of the Ellsworth guns, those "little breech-loading cannons" Lincoln had "got of Hon. Eli Thayer."

To the surprise of Colonel Ramsay, General Frémont asked for the Ellsworth guns in the spring of 1862; and all twenty of them, gleaming with oil and varnish, were accordingly sent off to the Shenandoah Valley. As already noted, they failed to stop Stonewall Jackson. During Jackson's siege of the Harper's Ferry garrison, Captain Acorn of the 12th New York militia took "a detachment of Frémont's, more familiarly known as 'jackass' guns," to Maryland Heights, where they rendered "valuable assistance." From "Ellsworth" to "jackass" is quite a comedown; but the *New York Times* listed the guns as twelve two-inch rifles, close enough to suggest their identity. Whatever they were, the rebels had them now.

Somewhere in the service were two other Ellsworth guns, bought by General Butler in January. But they made no name for themselves. By 1863 all the Ellsworth guns had vanished into limbo or Dixie.

Frémont must have got his first lone coffee-mill gun from J. D. Mills, that merchant of death with the impenetrable initials—else how could the general have known so much about Lincoln's ordnance transactions? At any rate, Mills remained active in promoting the coffee-mill guns.

After the mainspring broke in General Butler's coffee-mill gun, Mills dropped Woodward and Cox as manufacturers. Instead, he and his associates organized the American Arms Company of New York City, a joint-stock association of which Lewis Carr was president, Mills secretary and Frederick Avery treasurer. By April 1862 the company was well along on Lincoln's second order, the one for fifty guns.

McClellan had at last transferred the Army of the Potomac by water to Fortress Monroe, whence he was to make a lumbering drive up the Peninsula toward Richmond. Colonel Charles H. Van Wyck's 56th New York Volunteers were on the point of sailing for the Peninsula; and when Van Wyck heard about the marvelous new weapons being turned out at 498 Broadway, he applied direct to Avery for one. The transaction was an irregular one. If General Ripley should happen to have the final say, the company would be left to whistle for its money. But Van Wyck was a Congressman and a frequent visitor to the White House, and if the gun pleased Van Wyck, the President would very likely hear about it. Avery decided to take the chance and give Van Wyck his gun.

Meanwhile, McClellan had unhappily discovered that the Warwick River ran squarely athwart his line of march, instead of down the Peninsula as shown on the maps. Being McClellan, he halted his splendid army and settled down to a leisurely siege. The theatrics of "Prince John" Magruder and a handful of defenders in Yorktown kept the Army of the Potomac fussily immobile for a month. Van Wyck's regiment arrived with its coffee-mill gun in plenty of time to take its place on the left flank of the siege line, in the vicinity of Warwick Court House, which consisted of a one-story courthouse, a one-room jail and three houses.

The regiment was still there four days later on April 21, fretting in the marshes, when a correspondent of the *New York Evening Post* toured its lines and came away to write the earliest known eyewitness account of a machine gun in action. "At this time," the *Post* man reported, "a novel kind of weapon was brought into service. It consists of a large-sized rifle with a hopper and machinery at the breach, which loads and fires by turning a crank one hundred and seventy times in a few seconds. In fact, it is one continuous discharge. The balls flew thick and fast, and the Yankee invention must have astonished the other side. There are some half-dozen of these guns in the division on trial, and if we may believe our eyes while watching the effect, they are entitled to consideration."

The air grew heavy with the smell of spring in a wet country, and one day early in May the army realized that the rebels had abandoned Yorktown. Up and after them it rumbled, and Van Wyck's regiment with it. But not the coffee-mill gun. For some unknown reason, that stayed behind, to be incorporated into the Federal defenses of Yorktown.

Others came to take its place in the field, twenty of them altogether by late May. Not all were from Lincoln's two orders. Governor Andrew Curtin of Pennsylvania, whose zeal for new weapons approached Lincoln's, had already begun to supply the guns to the troops from his state. "I understand that every Pennsylvania regiment in the service is to have them," a private of the 83rd wrote to his sister on June 10. "All the Pennsylvania regiments near here have them." Of all the artillery on either side, he thought his regiment's coffee-mill gun "the greatest one yet. . . . It is a curious Yankee contrivance. It makes a noise like the dogs of war let loose. Don't you think one of those coffee mills would 'weed out' a secesh regiment about as quickly as any tools they have?"

In a brisk action at Golding's Farm on the morning of June 28, "our coffee mill guns did good work," wrote the historian of the 49th Pennsylvania. "George Wills, of Company D, was hurt in the thigh with one of these guns, but the old mule brought the gun and Wills out." His thigh wound made George Wills the first identifiable machine gunner.

Thus far the coffee-mill guns had pleased the press, the politicians and the privates (if we attribute George Wills's wound to enemy action and not to an accident with his gun). Unfortunately, there was dissent from the upper ranks. Colonel C. E. Pratt of the 31st New York had a coffee-mill gun in his regiment and found the weapon "very defective in several particulars." Colonel Kingsbury, the chief ordnance officer of the army, thought the guns' performance "not equal to the results obtained at the Washington Arsenal." Both shared Colonel Geary's tantalizing stinginess with particulars. A test of the gun at the Washington Navy Yard some months later, however, showed excessive escape of gas from the breech and an occasional failure to feed cartridges. There also seem to have been some fears, happily never realized, that a backfire from the breech would set off the cartridges in the hopper.

As for the causes of the trouble, Colonel Kingsbury blamed "inferior workmanship," and Frederick Avery charged "improper usage & neglect." General Ripley did not trouble to speculate— enough for him that the guns had gone wrong.

When McClellan's Richmond campaign reached its bitter end early in July, the American Arms Company had delivered the last of Lincoln's fifty-gun order; and despite Ripley's opposition, Lincoln ordered their bill to be paid.

Lincoln did not forget the fiery trials of January. Early in April he wired McClellan: "If you wish anything from Mr. Short in the way of fire shells or the like, telegraph to the Department or to me designating what it is." McClellan put aside his earlier qualms about the morality of fire shells; and by the end of the month at least thirty-three 100-pounder shells had arrived at the dépôt near

Yorktown. But for unspecified reasons most were turned back unused to the arsenal at Fortress Monroe.

That same month, Lincoln had Captain Benét try Fleming's incendiary compound at West Point. Benét reported vividly and at length, recommending that Fleming's shells be tried in the field. On the strength of this, Lincoln authorized Fleming and Worster to test their wares on Lee's army and saw to it, in spite of Ripley, that the War Department paid for the materials.

When Fleming and his crony debarked at Fortress Monroe with ten barrels of incendiary fluid, it was late June, and McClellan's Richmond campaign was entering its bloody climax in the Battles of the Seven Days. Sped by the blows of Lee and Jackson, McClellan had resolved on a massive change of base from the Pamunkey to the James. Fleming and Worster arrived at the doomed base to find it "in a state of unprecedented excitement—everything in confusion. . . . Immense quantities of goods were prepared in ponderous piles for the flames on the first approach of the enemy, momentarily expected." The two elderly eccentrics wandered through scenes of gargantuan destruction, dazedly trying to sell incendiary fluid while fire raged on every hand. At last, after being shunted from one harassed officer to another, Fleming retreated sick and disconsolate to New York, while his partner resumed the peddling of panaceas in Washington.

Fleming's ten barrels of incendiary fluid remained at the Fortress Monroe Arsenal until the officer in charge, conscious of the hazard, complained to General Ripley, who then had them decently buried.

Meanwhile, with characteristic resilience, James Holenshade returned to the attack. After tinkering with his Cincinnati Breechloading Cannon until its flaws had been corrected, he saw Lincoln again, and through him was given another trial in June at the Navy Yard. This time, things went more smoothly, and Lincoln had still another trial made at the arsenal. Now it was only the weight of the gun to which the Army and Navy objected.

At this point Lincoln decided on a move he had not made since

1861. Ripley flatly refused to take the responsibility for ordering breech-loading cannon into the Army, but Lincoln stood ready to assume it himself. More than that, he set no limit on the size of the order. All he required was a formal request from Major General John Pope, the bombastic Westerner to whom he had given command of the Army of Virginia, and who had already spoken in favor of the Cincinnati Breech-loading Cannon. The Union Army came this near to the general adoption of breech-loading cannon.

Pope promised to give the matter attention, but he never got around to it. Robert E. Lee kept him too busy. Late in August the disaster at Second Bull Run swept John Pope into the discard and Holenshade's chances with him. For Lincoln did not repeat his offer, and Holenshade was left to the mercy of General Ripley.

And what of the breech-loading rifles—the Marsh guns, the Spencers, the Sharps?

Marsh and Gallaher began their enterprises with no plant, no capital, nothing but Marsh's worn old prototype of a breech-loading rifle and President Lincoln's order for twenty-five thousand new rifles on that model. They nearly succeeded. Waving Lincoln's order as bait for investors, they organized the "Union Firearms Company" and managed to get some favorable newspaper publicity.

Then Stanton took over the War Department, full of righteous anger at his predecessor's laxity. Two hours after the close of business one day in late January, a Treasury official found Stanton "buried in accumulated heaps of requisitions . . . He would not approve the formal requisitions, which were unquestionably just, out of their regular order. He would do nothing but take up each account in its order, and either approve it or reject it, as the facts seemed to warrant." All this showed the right spirit, but it meant delay; and delay was fatal to the delicate operations of Marsh and Gallaher. Financial backing fell away from their Union Firearms Company, and its operations came to a standstill, while delivery after delivery fell due and was accordingly canceled.

The *coup de grâce* was a notice of patent infringement served on Marsh and Gallaher by the Joslyn Arms Company, which hired the fearsome Thaddeus Stevens as its counsel in the matter. Gallaher kept up a game pretense of activity. In August he wired Ripley: "Your dispatch just received. We have no guns yet. Working night and day to deliver as soon as possible." But 1862 ended without a single Marsh breechloader delivered.

Christopher Spencer and his backers avoided the reef which wrecked the Union Firearms Company. Up in Boston, with the fat purses of Beacon and State Streets to draw on, they organized the Spencer Repeating Rifle Company and rented part of the Chickering Piano Company building on Tremont Street for their factory. Spencer himself became superintendent of the works; and Warren Fisher, Jr., a Boston financier, was made treasurer.*

After Stanton took office Fisher, like most arms contractors, grew nervous. Assistant Secretary Watson reassured him: the gun was a good one and was needed for Berdan's men (the Sharpshooter mutiny had just come to a head). More good news came that same day: the *Scientific American* had given up two-thirds of its front page to "Spencer's famous breech-loading rifle, about which so much has been said." Spencer and Fisher had no trouble raising capital; and by the end of May they had sunk more than $130,000 into what Fisher called "the most extensive and completely fitted armory in the country" next to the Colt Works and the Springfield Armory.

The Spencer Company's troubles were of a different sort from those of Marsh and Gallaher. Like all arms firms at that time, it had difficulty getting machine tools and skilled labor. And Fisher soon began to see his mistake in making the inventor of the gun responsible for its manufacture. Spencer counted time, money and delivery deadlines as nothing compared to the further refinement of his rifle. While he patented an improved .50-caliber model and

---

* In later years Fisher became the addressee of the famous "Mulligan letters" which cost James G. Blaine the Presidency.

labored on the design of machine tools, deliveries began to fall due and be canceled. In June, after three deliveries had been forfeited, a commission set up by Stanton to re-examine arms contracts reduced the Spencer order from ten thousand to seventy-five hundred rifles, deliveries of a thousand a month to begin falling due in July.

Even these could not be met, and it was not until the last day of 1862 that the Spencer Company began to deliver rifles.

The Sharps alone, of all Lincoln's breech-loading rifles, took the field in 1862; and there were less than two thousand of them. That was still enough to transform warfare on land as the *Monitor* had done on the sea.

In the June sunlight of Mechanicsville the gray mass of A. P. Hill's division blundered on a small force of Berdan's men and shuddered with the sudden knowledge that this fly had a new kind of sting. Bullets flew at them as if three invisible helpers were serving up loaded muskets to every tangible green-clad Yank. The sight was to become discouragingly familiar during the succeeding Seven Days' Battles.

In the lush woods at Gaines Mill on June 27 the Sharpshooters discovered the marvelous comfort of loading while prone without the contortions which made wounds of the right hand and arm so common among less favored troops. Two days later, at Bottom's Bridge over the sluggish Chickahominy, two companies of Sharpshooters peppered the attacking rebels with lead until McClellan's army, on its way to the James, could cross without a stand. "So rapidly did our boys fire into them," a Sharpshooter wrote, "they were completely discomfited and forced to retire from the work."

Deploying through the woods at Glendale on June 30, a squad of Sharpshooters fired off their guns fast and often enough to make some near-by infantry officers stare in wonder. The next afternoon, Company F, 1st Sharpshooter Regiment, waiting in a ravine at Malvern Hill, peered through waving wheat and saw a heavy line of rebel skirmishers burst out of the forest at a run. F Company's bugler blared "commence firing," and a horizontal rain of lead whipped through the grain and sent the rebels racing for the woods "in great confusion and with serious loss." A heavier line of rebels pushed out, and a force of enemy skirmishers flanked the ravine from a hedge-covered roadway. Company F cheerfully yielded the ravine, re-formed in the open, and still kept the rebels down under cover "with the advantage of greater rapidity given by breech-loaders over muzzle-loaders."

Colonel Kingsbury wrote to General Ripley after the campaign:

Berdan's Sharp Shooters have demonstrated the value of breech-loading arms in the hands of skillful troops. If the organization of new regiments is to be continued, it is suggested that one of the three battalions in each regiment be composed of picked men, that this battalion be exercised almost exclusively as skirmishers [with breech-loading rifles].

Ripley already detested Kingsbury, who had been a supporter of Colonel Craig back in April 1861. This suggestion did nothing to endear Kingsbury to the Chief of Ordnance. Presently Kingsbury was relieved for reasons of "health," demoted to major and exiled to the Indian country.

Now came McClellan's eclipse, the rise of the gasconading Pope and the midsummer madness of Second Bull Run, when Washington shook with fear and not-so-distant gunfire, and the editor of the *Star* smelled black powder on the south wind. Pope went west by himself, like Kingsbury, and with him went the dream of James C. C. Holenshade. Lee went north with his army, and with McClellan back in the ring against him. McClellan won the decision at Antietam in mid-September, where Berdan's men, lying prone in open ground, did more damage to the enemy than any brigade in the neighborhood. (The opposing regiment lost more than half its strength, by its own admission.) After "skirmishes, battles, and other hard service," Berdan's Sharpshooters were "universally appreciated," Lincoln wrote the next day. A few days later Lincoln visited the Sharpshooters in the field, "which event, while it afforded them much pleasure, would have been more gratifying had they not been roasted for three hours by the hot sun."

Not long after, Colonel Berdan returned the call at the White House: he wanted his Sharpshooters to be made a separate corps, not a pool of skirmishers to be dribbled here and there throughout the Army, and he wanted them armed with Spencer rifles. "I will send for the Secretary and have the matter settled today, that you may get off at once," Lincoln said. "You don't look well."

Stanton came bristling in under the impression that Berdan wanted to make trouble, and a stormy scene ensued. While Lincoln listened uneasily, Stanton berated the colonel about the near mutiny of January, insinuating that Berdan was cooking up another serving of the same. Berdan left with nothing accomplished. He wrote Lincoln in November, again pleading for Spencers and again without avail.

There were mysteries in the battle record of Lincoln's new weapons during 1862. Why were Short's incendiary shells not used? Why did Van Wyck's regiment leave its coffee-mill gun at Yorktown? Just what was wrong with Colonel Pratt's coffee-mill gun? Were the Ellsworth guns captured at Harper's Ferry, and if not, what became of them?

But there was no longer any mystery about the value of breechloaders. Even old Army officers who remembered the breechloader mishaps of twenty years before were wavering in their allegiance to General Ripley's views. "The opinion is becoming very general among army officers," a speaker at Cooper Institute that December said, "that the power to load very quickly is of the very highest value." History is often made when the world accepts the obvious.

CHAPTER 16

Admiral Dahlgren

BY THE SUMMER OF 1862 WASHINGTON had ceased to be "the center of great operations," and Captain Dahlgren knew it. Baffled ambition fixed his thin mouth in grimmer lines. Only in Lincoln's feeling toward him did the captain see a straw of hope. Early in June the President had written Stanton: "I need not tell you how much I would like to oblige Capt. Dahlgren"; and through Lincoln's intercession, Dahlgren's brilliant young son Ulric had been made a captain of volunteers. Now, in July, Dahlgren wrote Lincoln recalling his own past services and pressing for the tour of sea duty in which he saw his only chance at glory and promotion to admiral.

Secretary Gideon Welles had other plans. For Dahlgren to forsake ordnance work, Welles thought, would be "wrong to the service, and a great wrong to the country. . . . He is not conscious of it, but he has Dahlgren more than the service in view."

Back in January, when Lincoln was stirring up the Army Ordnance Department, Lincoln had asked Dahlgren's views on the organization of the Navy Bureau of Ordnance. Dahlgren had told Lincoln that instead of being a "purely administrative" officer, the chief "should himself participate in the various operations," and should have an assistant to handle office affairs. These were tacitly understood as Dahlgren's conditions for accepting the post of chief, with Harry Wise as his assistant. And now the President had just signed into law a bill embodying them. Dahlgren's reluctance to leave his command of the Navy Yard could therefore come only from personal ambition—not a motive that Gideon Welles could respect. A week after Dahlgren's letter to Lincoln, the Secretary peremptorily made Dahlgren Chief of the Navy Ordnance Bureau.

It was "a change by no means acceptable to me," wrote the recipient of the honor, "but I had no choice." To his credit, Dahlgren pitched into his new job with vigor, aided by his assistant chief, Lieutenant Wise. Not only that, but he also kept on with his old job, staying at his Ordnance Bureau desk till noon every day and then going down to his old headquarters at the yard to conduct the "practical matters" so dear to his heart. "Uncle Sam," he wrote proudly, "could not complain of not getting the worth of what he paid me."

Since his new office was but a short stroll from the White House, Dahlgren became even more readily available to Lincoln than before. "He is a favorite with the President and knows it," wrote Secretary Welles somewhat testily that fall.

Early in June Lincoln met a French inventor named Rafael; his first name is uncertain, but he may have been the "George Raphael" of New York City who had been selling revolvers and swords to the Ordnance Department. In any case, Rafael brought with him a warm letter of introduction from Governor Morgan of New York. The Governor wrote:

Mr. Raphael has introduced a machine which is as remarkable for its effective simplicity, as it is for its novel mechanical adjustments; and while under trial before me exhibited none of the ordinary objections to similar inventions.

After talking with the man, Lincoln dashed off a note: "Captain Dahlgren, will be interested to accompany the bearer of this to see a new patern of gun."

The "new patern of gun" was a machine gun, mounted on a light artillery carriage and firing regulation rifle bullets. Its paper

Falls Village (Conn.) Savings Bank

LINCOLN'S MOST EXPENSIVE WEAPON

Horatio Ames (in silk hat) and his wrought-iron rifled cannon, of which Lincoln purchased thirteen at more than $16,000 each.

George H. Ferriss

James C. C. Holenshade

Isaac R. Diller

James Woodruff

FOUR INVENTORS WHOM LINCOLN HELPED

cartridges, however, carried a charge about two-thirds greater than the normal; and unlike the coffee-mill gun, it needed neither a hopper nor separate cartridge chambers. Unfortunately, the rest of its "novel mechanical adjustments" are obscure, except for what may be deduced from a letter by John Ericsson:

By a simple application of transverse reciprocating movements, exact and definite, the cartridge chamber is brought in line with the barrel, a perfectly tight joint being formed without any sliding movement across the joint of junction. Abrasion and wear are thereby prevented. The mode of filling and applying the sliding cartridge chamber is certain and free from all danger.

Dahlgren ran the Rafael gun through a series of tests at the Navy Yard, and the results were splendid. Even taking the heavy charge into account, the gun's range and accuracy were remarkable. At eighteen hundred yards—more than a mile—the lateral deviation was "very slight." Of sixteen shots fired at a wooden target six hundred yards away, "nearly all" were direct hits. Tested for rapidity, the gun fired forty shots in twenty seconds. "During the entire firing," said one of the reports, "the gun was easily worked. No part of the machinery became deranged or in any way out of order." Here indeed was a marvelous weapon; and one can understand John Ericsson's conviction that it formed "one of the many strides which mechanical science is now making to render war too destructive, long to continue the disgrace of civilization."

"One regiment of intelligent men provided with one hundred of these effective weapons can most assuredly defeat and destroy a four-fold number of enemies," Ericsson wrote to Lincoln early in August. Perhaps his letter was conveyed by a committee of citizens who called on Lincoln a few days later and invited him to see the Rafael Repeater demonstrated at the Navy Yard.

On that sweltering August afternoon not much persuasion was needed. Lured by the thought of Navy Yard breezes, Secretary Seward joined the party, and even the incorruptible Stanton tagged along. Dahlgren met them at the yard and had the Rafael Repeater hauled into position. For two hours Lincoln watched the new machine gun hammer away at targets in the river. According to a correspondent of the *New York Tribune,* the experiments were "in every way successful"; and if they approached the results of the previous trials, Lincoln must have been profoundly impressed.

Afterward, at Dahlgren's suggestion, the visitors trooped aboard a steamer at the wharf, to rest and enjoy the breeze. Talk ranged freely. Much was said about the new machine gun, especially about its freedom from escape of gas at the breech. "Well," said Lincoln, perhaps with a mischievous glance at the *Tribune* man, "I believe this really does what it is represented to do. Now have any of you heard of any machine, or invention, for preventing the escape of 'gas' from newspaper establishments?"

As a sort of grand finale to the afternoon's diversion, Dahlgren had one of his big eleven-inch guns fired. The concussions died away, and the party rose to leave. Spying an ax hanging outside the cabin, Lincoln took it down and remarked: "Gentlemen, you may talk about your 'Raphael Repeaters' and 'eleven-inch Dahlgrens'; but *here* is an institution which I guess I understand better than either." And he held the ax out at arm's length by the end of its handle. Most of the party tried, but none could duplicate the feat. With that they dispersed, and Lincoln drove Dahlgren home in his carriage.

Two days later, Lincoln wrote Stanton a letter:

I have examined, and seen tried, the "Raphael Repeater" and consider it a decided improvement upon what was called the "Coffee Mill gun" in these particulars, that it dispenses with the great cost, and liability to loss, of the steel cartridges, and that it is better arranged to prevent the escape of gas—Other advantages are claimed for it upon which I can not so well speak. While I do not order it into the service, I think it well worthy the attention of the Ordnance Bureaus, and should be rather pleased, if it should be decided to put it into the service.

In the face of so strong a letter from the President, General

Ripley could scarcely avoid having the gun tested; but when he read Major Laidley's glowing report from Frankford Arsenal, Ripley must have regretted his concession.

The gun's penetration, reported Laidley, was twice as great as that of the rifled musket. Sixteen shots were fired in five seconds, forty shots in eighteen seconds. After more than five hundred rounds were fired, the gun worked as well as when it started. The board which tested the gun thought it would be "most valuable" for defending river passages, bridges and similar key points; and recommended that a number of the guns be issued to each infantry regiment.

But when the proprietors of the gun offered five hundred of them at $850 each, the proposition was ignored. A few weeks later, through the good offices of Thurlow Weed, Rafael's partner and co-inventor (a New Yorker named James Haskell) secured an interview with Lincoln. Whatever may have been said, neither Ripley nor the War Department expressed the slightest interest in buying Rafael Repeaters.

To certain influential members of the British government the Union defeats of that summer suggested the advisability of recognizing the Confederacy. Lincoln knew, if the British did not, that such a step would mean war between Great Britain and the United States; and with the experience of the Trent crisis behind them, he and Dahlgren took thought of the niter supply. No sooner had Dahlgren become Chief of Navy Ordnance than he fired a buckshot blast at the problem: sent a naval vessel to Yokohama to look into the Japanese supply, advertised for domestic niter contracts and arranged with the Du Ponts for the unobtrusive purchase of British stocks.

Joseph Henry's suggestion of the late fifties, that a substitute for niter be developed, did not interest Dahlgren, probably because of the protracted research implied. But a few days after the Rafael Repeater trial, that avenue seemed to open wide before Lincoln when a solemn-eyed friend from Springfield paid him a call.

Captain Isaac Roland Diller, a bushy-haired, black-bearded son of Pennsylvania, had won his military title with Scott's army in Mexico. After that war he moved to Springfield, Illinois, where his brother kept a drugstore. There he prospered as a real estate agent, building an elegant home on what Springfield people called "Aristocracy Hill" and dabbling with fair success in Democratic politics. In 1857 Buchanan made him United States consul at Bremen; but the election of his old friend Abraham Lincoln to the Presidency cut short Diller's career as a diplomat and gave his place to a proper Republican.

In Germany Diller had met Samuel Ricker, the American consul at Frankfurt am Main, who described himself as "a Southern Democrat, sound on the slavery question, but as true a Union man as can be found in either of the great parties." Ricker, too, was turned out of office; but unlike Diller, he stayed on in Germany as the agent of a chemist named Hochstätter, who had developed a gunpowder using a chlorate in place of niter. In return for a third interest in the powder Diller agreed to plead its cause in the United States; and it was this that brought him to the White House in August 1862.

Chlorates were plentiful in the United States. In Diller's new powder Lincoln saw a chance to break the British niter monopoly, and he wasted no time in exploring it. Not wanting to commit himself and the government by accepting Hochstätter's secret, Lincoln arranged for Diller to confide it only to the government chemist who would be needed to make up a sample. Lincoln had no difficulty choosing the chemist on whose skill so great an issue might depend; for the first man ever to hold such a job had just started work at the new Department of Agriculture. He was Dr. Charles M. Wetherill, a big, gentle, pensive man in his late thirties, a Philadelphian turned Hoosier, who had studied in Germany under the great Liebig.

Poring over the crabbed script of Samuel Ricker, whom he nicknamed "Old Chinese," Wetherill deciphered enough to make up a small batch of powder. This proved to be stronger than Du Pont powder, less noisy, less smoky and not so quick to foul the test rifle. Dahlgren, who was keeping an interested watch over the project, agreed with Diller to have a large batch made at Philadelphia, a safer place for secrets than Washington. So Diller asked the President for more money and the continued services of Dr. Wetherill.

Since 1861 Lincoln had grown more cautious about sinking government money into new weapons; and the launching of a secret project, independent of both Army and Navy Ordnance Bureaus, was no light matter. The project hung fire for several weeks.

"I saw the President yesterday," a White House visitor wrote on December 11, 1862. "He is haggard & care-worn. The loss of the [Congressional] elections and the fact that his friends attribute it to his [emancipation] proclamation troubles him. He expressed great impatience with Rosecrans." Dark days had come to Lincoln, and darker ones were in store. Yet he had not forgotten Isaac Diller and the new powder. Four days later, after much discussion, long deliberation and a conference with Dahlgren, Diller, Wetherill and Assistant Secretary Watson, Lincoln struck a shrewd bargain with his Springfield friend.

Lincoln agreed to buy at least a thousand pounds of experimental powder at the cost of manufacture *or* $2 a pound *or* $5,000— whichever was least. In other words, Diller could lose money on the deal, but could not possibly make any. If the claims for the powder were met (and Lincoln specified them in writing), the government was to pay Diller $150,000 for exclusive rights in the United States—provided no important fault appeared in the powder. And Lincoln was careful to state further: "I can only promise to advise the payment, because I have not the money at my control which I could, by law, absolutely promise to pay."

If Simon Cameron's contracts had all been so canny, there would have been no arms scandals in 1861.

A week later Lincoln sent for Dahlgren, who found him discussing the recent terrible defeat at Fredericksburg with a visitor. Relaxing into his usual humor, Lincoln sat down and said: "Well, Captain, here's a letter about a new powder." He had burned a sample and thought it left too much residuum. "Now, I'll show you," he said. Shaking some powder onto a sheet of paper, Lincoln strode over to the open fire and picked up a live coal with the tongs. He peered down through his spectacles, pursed his mobile lips and blew the coal bright. (Watching him, Dahlgren marveled at his seeming ability to put aside thoughts of the war. The captain failed to see that trying out a pinch of powder was as much a part of the war for Lincoln as trying out a new general.) When Lincoln clapped the glowing coal to the powder, it flashed into a puff of smoke. "There is too much left there," he remarked triumphantly and handed Dahlgren a packet to try. Then his talk turned back to politics and battles.

Dahlgren, unlike Ripley, was an inventor in his own right and had some fellow feeling for others of the tribe. He had been fair with them, more than fair, he thought. In August he wrote:

Sixty-two inventions have been examined in the last six months, with much cost to the United States, and labor in the office. Of course, it is impossible that every invention could be successful—but I believe that no one person in the United States or abroad has been instrumental in introducing to public use so many inventions of others as myself.

But like the inventors themselves, Dahlgren was touchy and quick to take offense; and when certain unsuccessful inventors blamed their troubles on him, he brooded over it. Late in June, for example, a clerk had told Dahlgren that a disgruntled inventor had been grubbing for "means to assail" the captain, and that there was "a secret organization which would raise a fund to the end of removing" him. "This" raged Dahlgren in his diary, "is a sample of the unscrupulous scoundrels that infest the government, whose sole aim is to rob the United States."

Scarcely a month after he had become Chief of Ordnance, Dahlgren was asking Secretary Welles to give someone else "the duty of examining Inventions in Ordnance." The captain concluded: "I shall part with pleasure from a duty which has been onerous in the highest degree, and in spite of all efforts so illy requited." Although nothing came of this outburst, Dahlgren's discontent made him work all the harder for a command afloat; and by October Lincoln was freely informing Dahlgren and Welles that the former would have the highest grade if Welles would only write the President a letter requesting the promotion. "I am compelled," Welles wrote, "to stand between the President and Dahlgren's promotion, in order to maintain the service in proper condition."

Lincoln's feeling that he would sooner or later lose Dahlgren as his adviser on weapons may have inspired the curious episode of Herman Haupt's questionnaire later that month.

Herman Haupt, a turbulent and somewhat saturnine West Point graduate, class of 1835, had put his free education to immediate use as a civil engineer on the Pennsylvania state railroad. After that job of pioneering he became a professor of mathematics and engineering at a small college in Gettysburg, Pennsylvania, a peaceful little town then and later (except for three days in July 1863). There he wrote his *General Theory of Bridge Construction,* a landmark in structural theory. He was drilling the famous Hoosac Tunnel in Massachusetts when the Civil War called him to service as the Union Army's chief of military railroads.

Lincoln first took the measure of Herman Haupt in May 1862. "I have seen the most remarkable structure that human eyes ever rested upon," exclaimed the President. "That man, Haupt, has built a bridge across Potomac Creek, about four hundred feet long and nearly a hundred feet high, over which loaded trains are running every hour, and upon my word . . . there is nothing in it but beanpoles and cornstalks." Haupt, who relished a quarrel, engaged in one with General Pope and quit in June, only to return after the War Department wired: "Come back immediately; cannot get along without you; not a wheel moving on any of the roads." ("Be as patient as possible with the generals," Assistant Secretary Watson counseled him somewhat later, "some of them will trouble you more than they do the enemy.") During the debacle of Second Bull Run, which blasted so many shiny reputations, Haupt won Lincoln completely. Lincoln, noted John Hay, was "struck with the business-like character of his despatch, telling in the fewest words the information most sought for, which contrasted so strongly with the weak, whiney, vague, and incorrect despatches of the whilom General-in-Chief." In everything Haupt undertook he seemed "thoroughly to reflect and satisfy" Lincoln.

There is no mystery, therefore, about why Lincoln chose Herman Haupt as his new adviser on the mobilization of technology.

The episode began when someone (identity uncertain) proposed that President Lincoln call together a council of engineers and naval constructors so that he might learn and collate "the practical results of experience and observation"—a sort of National Defense Research Council with the President in the chair. The suggestion, according to Haupt, was founded on "the belief that it was only necessary to convince President Lincoln that any course was right, to insure its immediate adoption." It was finally decided, however, that a written questionnaire would be more useful for future reference and more convenient for those questioned.

Whoever may have originated the project, it was Haupt who took charge of it. On October 28, 1862, he sent out a searching questionnaire, mostly on naval technology, which got into the newspapers as well as the mails. Its preamble was scarcely calculated to mollify the department under scrutiny. "SIR," it blared. "Many experienced naval constructors, engineers, and practical men appear to think that our American Navy does not keep pace with the improvements of the age in any of the essential requisites of modern vessels of war, and that our chief cities and harbors are without suitable protection against maritime attacks."

Then followed more than fifty questions, many calling for long and detailed answers. They fell into three groups: those intended to sound out the addressee's experience; those aimed at comparing the cost, efficiency and effectiveness of private as against government construction methods; and those seeking information on the best and most recent developments in military and naval technology generally.

The rest is silence.

There survives no evidence that anything came of the experiment, not even a filled-in questionnaire. What happened to the project is a mystery; unless one theorizes that the questionnaire's tone toward the Navy Department frightened off those who looked to the Department for contracts. Haupt's detailed reminiscences of his Civil War career say not a word about the affair. Did he or his associates have some ulterior motive? Why did this questionnaire, drawn up by an Army man, focus on naval technology? Why did not Dahlgren figure in the affair at some point, and why does his journal say nothing of it?

The only hint we have of what lay behind the Haupt questionnaire is in a diary entry by Secretary Welles on January 18, 1864:

A batch of letters has been sent us from the provost marshal, disclosing a mass of fraud and intrigue on the part of a set of assuming men that is as amusing as reckless. General Haupt, Naval Constructor Griffiths, Gwyn [?] of the Treasury, Hamilton Norris, and others figure in the affair. About a year since General H. published a series of questions for the improvement and progress of the Navy Department, which he and his associates appeared inclined to take into their keeping. This correspondence brings to light the secret intrigues of these scoundrels.

Even this is not much help. The files of the Navy Department for the period disclose no such "batch of letters."

Dahlgren kept his place as Lincoln's technical adviser. A few days after the Haupt questionnaire went into the mails, a new war rocket gave the captain further cause to wish himself rid of the job.

As far back as the Napoleonic Wars, Sir William Congreve, who had seen rockets used by native troops in India, had equipped the rockets with explosive war heads, cast-iron tubes, and wooden tails (for truer flight) and used them effectively against the French.

They offered tempting advantages over field pieces. Rockets had no recoil. Their launching tubes or gutters were vastly lighter and easier to handle than equivalent artillery pieces. Even their fiery trails unnerved the enemy (although at Fort McHenry in 1814, they rather inspired than discouraged an observer named Francis Scott Key).

A few years later, William Hale of England dispensed with the wooden tail of Congreve's rockets and substituted tangential vents near the head, which gave the rocket the steadying spin of a rifled projectile. During the Mexican War, Hale's agent, a Connecticut man named Joshua B. Hyde, sold the rights to Hale's rockets for $20,000 to the United States government. It was to supervise the manufacture of the rockets that Dahlgren first came to the Navy Yard. The rockets were used by Winfield Scott's army all the way from Vera Cruz to Chapultepec.

When the Civil War broke out, Hale's offer to come over and make rockets for the Union was refused; but his rockets were used. Two "Rocket Troops" were organized in the fall, and next spring they were issued thirteen hundred rockets near Yorktown. Falling into rebel hands in the Peninsula, the Union rocket battery turned up to annoy Union troops that December in southeastern Virginia. "Its shells would come fizzing through the air without having given any warning report," wrote a Pennsylvanian soldier, "and our boys christened it the 'Slider battery.'" Annoyed beyond endurance, the 11th Pennsylvania Cavalry charged and captured the "slider battery." Thereafter, the rocket battery's trail is lost, save for a report nearly a year later that six hundred rockets were on hand at Fortress Monroe.

The great fault of the rockets was their wild inaccuracy. If something deflected them in flight—a tree branch, a gust of wind—they would shoot straight along in the new direction. They might even come back on the men who had fired them. In April 1862 a new rocket was tried on Capitol Hill, but performed with "the greatest inaccuracy." "Cannot the ingenuity of the country overcome the difficulty?" asked the *Washington Star* wistfully. If only rockets could be given the accuracy of rifled guns, it predicted, "a revolution in land service would follow their introduction, like that which has followed the introduction of iron rams and batteries in the sea service."

The same thought may well have occurred to Lincoln when Joshua Hyde, Hale's former agent, came to him with an improved version of the Hale rocket. Hyde's rocket carried a war head with an adjustable time fuse, instead of the fixed and inaccessible fuse of the Hale rocket; and its tangential vents were at the center of gravity, rather than the head.

On November 15, 1862, Lincoln drove down to the Navy Yard with Secretary of State Seward and Secretary of the Treasury Chase, picking up Dahlgren at his office in the yard. Their destination was a trial of the Hyde rocket. Down by the river, the eminent visitors gathered around the perforated iron-cylinder launching tube at which Lieutenant Commander Mitchell was setting up the test. When the rocket was ready, the onlookers stepped back a few paces, out of the way of the rocket trail, prepared to see the new weapon zoom up over the river and burst, pocking the water's surface with the fragments of its case.

Instead came a blast and a puff of fire—the rocket had exploded in its stand!

When the smoke drifted away, Dahlgren, who must have been white with horror, saw that a miracle had spared President Lincoln and the two ranking members of his Cabinet. Through the captain's mind may have flashed the terrifying recollection that back in 1844 the explosion of an experimental cannon had killed two members of President Tyler's Cabinet not many miles from that spot. Some historians believe the Civil War might have been avoided, save for the effects of that disaster. Who can say what the world would now be like if such a catastrophe had killed Abraham Lincoln, William Seward and Salmon Chase, between the rout of Second Bull Run and the futile slaughter of Fredericksburg?

But the unthinkable had not happened, and the shaken Captain Dahlgren returned thankfully with the party.

Two days later another trial was given Hyde's rocket, this time without such eminent observers. Just after the rocket left the stand, it "ascended into the air, whirling at the same time, took a direction nearly at right angles to the line of fire, and fell upon the roof of the Blacksmith Shop, and thence to the ground." Hyde himself admitted that to continue the experiment would be too dangerous, and so it was suspended. The next time Hyde's name appeared in Ordnance Office records, it was as the inventor of a musket.

By the end of 1862 Lincoln was growing impatient with ordnance experts as a class, and the case of Peter Peckham gave him a chance to say so.

One evening back in March, Senator Orville Browning had escorted Peter Peckham of Bloomington, Illinois, and Thomas Taylor of Roxbury, Massachusetts, into the White House and introduced them to Lincoln. Peckham, an uncommonly bumptious and assertive individual, proceeded to initiate the President into the fine points of Taylor's new fuse; and he was still at it when Browning left. For more than three months thereafter, Dahlgren, with unprecedented generosity, let Taylor use Navy Yard facilities to perfect his fuse and even paid him wages, terminating the arrangement finally on the ground that Taylor had not been able "to make a single fuse explode at all, except in the gun."

If he could win so much favor for a client, Peckham may have reasoned, what could he not do for himself? He was presently back to urge an invention of his own on the President, a rifle cartridge intended to make ramrods unnecessary in loading by the muzzle.

Basically, Peckham explained, his cartridge simply fitted the standard rifle so loosely that it dropped right to the bottom without assistance. What held it in place, then? Why, the cartridge was arranged so as to release a few grains of powder in loading, the grains then wedging the cartridge case firmly against the bottom of the bore. Being made of perforated metal or wire gauze, the cartridge case permitted ignition of the powder without having to be broken open. The bullet itself was much like the Minié ball, except that it had a deeper hollow in its base, since it had to expand more in firing.

Captain Benét tried the Peckham cartridge at West Point in May, somewhat disgruntled at having been given only four specimens by the inventor. The first two, as advertised, dropped clear to the bottom of the bore, the only catch being that they failed to take the grooves and therefore completely missed a four-foot target forty-three yards away. The bore now being slightly fouled, the next two got stuck part way down and had to be sent home with a ramrod. One missed the target, the other hit it with no more penetration than a regular bullet would have had at six hundred yards.

Peckham tinkered with his design and in November secured a trial at the Navy Yard—perhaps through Lincoln's influence, for the President was there that day. All the experiment showed was the weakness of the cartridge, even with an excessive powder charge. Worse still, Peckham was caught in some clumsy sleight of hand. The specimens he showed around had been altered to make them safer to transport; the ones he presented for firing were different, and more dangerous.

Unabashed, Peckham brought up more artillery. His biggest gun was Lincoln's old and close friend Supreme Court Justice David Davis, a fellow townsman of Peckham. He knew Peckham "very well," Davis wrote Lincoln, and at his home in Bloomington had seen five Peckham cartridges do well in competition with regulation cartridges. "It does seem to me," the Judge wrote, "that there is something in his invention."

So Lincoln asked Assistant Secretary Watson to take up the case; and after two weeks of badgering by Peckham, Watson ordered ten thousand cartridges. But he refused to pay for the machinery in addition, as demanded by Peckham.

The resourceful inventor got the ear of Major General Silas Casey, who had the cartridge tried by Captain Moses Gist of the 4th Delaware Infantry. Captain Gist fired eight Peckham cartridges and twenty-three of the regular type at a target made of twelve layers of one-inch boards, and his report meticulously listed the penetration and accuracy of each of the thirty-one shots. This time, Peckham's cartridges behaved themselves. "The result of the experiment," endorsed one Colonel Grimshaw, "has impressed us favorably with the ideas of the inventor."

Captain Gist's report, bearing the usual marks of its journey through channels, reached President Lincoln on December 12, 1862.

The Army of the Potomac, bereaved of its idolized McClellan and commanded by moon-faced Ambrose Burnside (who was the first to admit his own incapacity), waited numbly at Fredericksburg for the order which was to send it next day into foredoomed defeat. Marye's Heights, rising beyond an open plain, made as fine a defensive position as any soldier could wish; and on it, Lee's men longed for a Yankee attack. Lincoln feared the worst; but Burnside was a military expert, and perhaps the experts knew better than the President.

While Lincoln brooded in the shadow of that tremendous uncertainty, someone handed him Captain Gist's table of thirty-one rifle shots. Lincoln scanned it for some evidence of an Ordnance Office or War Department decision or even recommendation. All he saw was Colonel Grimshaw's tepid commentary. His patience suddenly ended. He wrote across the back of the report :

In this, as in other cases, I am disgusted with the character of this report made by a supposed expert. An opinion whether the cartridge should be introduced into the service, and not how many pine boards it penetrated at the 1st & 2nd & 3rd shot, is what is wanted. Does Gen. Casey say the cartridge should be introduced? That is the question. Will he please answer?

Not even this could extract a plain answer from General Casey. The general merely pointed out that if a soldier was never *certain* that the Peckham cartridge was all the way down—and evidently he could not be—he would use his ramrod every time anyway.

Casey also ventured the opinion that rapidity of fire was "not always a desideratum," against which Major General David Hunter set his conviction that it was "often very desirable."

This was not enough to silence Peckham. Backed by Judge Davis and Senators Lane and Pomeroy, he got another Navy test, with no better results than before. And still Peckham persisted. In May he sent Lincoln a seventeen page essay on his cartridge, on which Lincoln wrote desperately: "Will Mr. Watson please act upon this case as soon as possible."

Watson left it up to General Ripley, and that did it. No more was heard from Peter Peckham.

Others echoed Lincoln's opinion of the "experts." The *Scientific American* observed, "The only successes which we have yet achieved have been due to our superiority in the mechanic arts. With sadness, however, which we cannot express, we fear that the skill of our mechanics, the self-sacrifice of our people, and the devoted heroism of our troops in their efforts to save the country, will all be rendered futile by the utter incompetency which controls the war and navy departments of the Government."

What was wrong? A New Yorker named Benjamin Bates saw two difficulties, and so informed Secretary Welles: first, the experts were overwhelmed by "a great number of impracticable inventions," more than they had time to sift through; and second, they regarded outside suggestions as "intrusive and impertinent" anyway.

Bates may have been right, but there was more to it. The basic trouble lay in combining responsibility for production with responsibility for research. The two functions were incompatible—as the experience of the Spencer Repeating Rifle Company showed. The proving ground's peach was the assembly line's poison; and General Ripley, for one, believed with all his soul that production came first.

The only solution was to divorce the incompatible functions: to make the ordnance bureaus responsible for procurement, and to make some independent agency responsible for research. The idea was put forward by the *Scientific American* as early as May 4, 1861, and at intervals thereafter. Ordnance officers, including the eminent Major Rodman, were all for it; and even General Ripley thought such a board "very desirable." "But," Ripley added, missing the point, "it cannot be done now for the want of officers to form the Board."

The Navy came closest to trying the idea. Early in 1862 Secretary Welles appointed a three-man board to consider inventions, and in September he set up another. In February 1863, the so-called "Permanent Commission" was organized, on the suggestion of Rear Admiral Charles H. Davis, Chief of the Bureau of Navigation, seconded heartily by Joseph Henry. The three members, Davis, Henry and Alexander D. Bache of the Coast Survey, were to deal with "questions of science and art upon which the Department may require information." The Commission, although unpaid, "was constantly in session," wrote Davis's son; and fat volumes of minutes and reports survive to bear out his statement.

Inspired by the Permanent Commission, Congress soon after set up the National Academy of Sciences to advise the government in scientific and technical matters. Unfortunately, the Academy failed to capture popular favor. "Suddenly and unheralded," commented the *New York Times*, "it sprang up before the world full-grown and full-panoplied, with the authority of the nation on its brow, but enveloped in almost impenetrable clouds." Secretary Welles shared these doubts and refused to transfer either duties or funds from his Department to the Academy.

The role of the Permanent Commission and its counterparts during the Civil War was mainly negative. They saved bureau officials the trouble of saying no to inventors; among others, the Permanent Commission turned down Peter Yates, Benjamin Severson and Peter Peckham. But they had no funds to institute a research and development program of their own. That idea had to wait for its fulfillment until the Second World War—when it developed the atomic bomb.

During the Civil War, the nearest thing to a research and development agency was the President himself.

In January 1863 President Lincoln came down in person to prod the Navy Ordnance Bureau into preparing for the coming trials of Captain Diller's powder. He seemed to be the project's only advocate in high office. Secretary Welles had no sympathy with it, condemning it as "well-intentioned but irregular." "Something was said to me some days since in regard to the great secret of this man Dillon [sic]," he wrote querulously, "but I gave it no attention, did not like the manner, etc. So it was, I apprehend, with the War Department." To get Diller an advance from the Navy for machinery and materials, Lincoln had to write out a personal order to the grumpy Secretary.

The Navy decided that the project was too dangerous to be carried on at the Philadelphia Navy Yard, and so the captain had to buttonhole reluctant property owners until he managed to rent a big, ramshackle frame building—"a mere shell"—on Timber Creek in New Jersey, about six miles from Philadelphia. While Diller gathered machinery together, Lincoln sent down Dr. Wetherill and an Agriculture Department clerk named Francis Murray. These three, with a Negro helper named George, constituted the entire force of the Lincolnian equivalent of Oak Ridge.

The solemn quartet took an oath of secrecy and set to the President's work. The work went hard. Sickness caused delays—Timber Creek was "a most unhealthy location"—and the machinery broke down more or less regularly. At last, in April, the Timber Creek project began turning out powder, and by June twenty-five hundred pounds were ready. Sharing Diller's zeal, Dr. Wetherill had done his best to perfect the powder; and both men were hopeful of success.

Three days of testing in mid-June of 1863 gave marvelous results. Lieutenant Commander Jeffers wrote to Commander Wise:

So, the Bureau ignores Mr. Diller and his powder according

to the letter I received this morning. You had better get that $150,000 ready as soon as possible for it has proved a decided success, and everything now looks as if we shall have to make a report that will astonish everybody. . . . The powder as now made is two thirds dust as they had no machinery for graining . . . If it preserves its properties after graining it is everything that is to be desired, and will probably supersede common nitre powder.

In that happy hour, Lincoln's secret project seemed about to make ordnance history—and diplomatic history as well.

Going into the climactic year of 1863, Abraham Lincoln still, somehow, found time to think about new weapons. There was a clear cold day in early February, for example, when the White House grounds lay white with new snow and veined by the blue twisted shadows of tree branches. About noon Lincoln sent for Dahlgren. Governor Curtin of Pennsylvania had seen "some wonder in gunnery." The wiry, gaunt-faced Chief of Navy Ordnance stepped briskly up the White House stairs, sat with the President half an hour, and went back to work.

A few days later—the day after Lincoln's fifty-fourth birthday—Brigadier General Barnard invited the President to a demonstration of George W. Beardslee's electric detonating system, about which Dahlgren was enthusiastic. Lincoln and Stanton drove over to Fort DeKalb across the Potomac and joined the crowd of spectators. "There was a great explosion immediately in our front," wrote a Washington reporter. "The earth opened and vomited forth stones, shot and shell, vertically, horizontally, and, in fact, in all directions." Once more the winter earth heaved, "and the air was again filled with earth and smoke, stones and exploding shells; some of the latter falling in uncomfortable proximity to our person." After a third mine went up, soldiers pushed back the crowd. "Taking up our position close to the President," reported the *Chronicle* man, "we heard a heavy explosion, as if some of the internal fires of the globe were escaping, and the earth belched forth a volcano of smoke, stones and exploding shells even more fearful than before. It rained stones for acres around and in front of us."

Lincoln emerged unscathed. As for Beardslee's blasting apparatus, it had certainly proved its efficacy. Presumably it had its chance in combat: a complete set was sent to Admiral David Porter's Mississippi squadron early that summer.

All this annoyed Secretary Welles. When the Diller affair came to his notice, he cautioned Dahlgren, as he had often done before, "against encouraging the President in these well-intentioned but irregular proceedings." Welles noted in his diary:

He assures me that he does restrain the President as far as respect will permit, but his "restraints" are impotent, valueless. He is no check on the President, who has a propensity to engage in matters of this kind, and is liable to be constantly imposed upon by sharpers and adventurers. Finding the heads of Departments opposed to these schemes, the President goes often behind them, as in this instance; and subordinates, flattered by his notice, encourage him.

Whether Dahlgren's complaisance was calculated or not, it paid dividends. Four days after the Beardslee mine demonstration, Lincoln asked Secretary Welles to promote both Dahlgren and Captain Davis (he of the Permanent Commission) to the rank of rear admirals. The ambitious Dahlgren had realized at least half of his dream; and if rank came, could glory be far behind?

Washington's Birthday buried the capital in snow, and the Secretary of the Navy "did not venture abroad." Admiral Dahlgren, only five years younger, floundered through the drifts nevertheless to see Welles on some ordnance matter—as if to prove his physical fitness for sea duty. When the new admiral expressed gratitude for his promotion, Welles tartly suggested that he "thank the President, who had made it a specialty; . . . I did not advise it."

CHAPTER 17

Gunning for Charleston

IF A CITY IS MEASURED BY THE FEELING
it inspires, Charleston, South Carolina, was great indeed in 1863.
Pride in their town, in its manners and wealth and aristocratic
charm, had been the mark of Charlestonians for a century. Now
their pride was loftier than ever; for Charleston was to the War
for Southern Independence as Boston and Lexington together had
been to the Revolution.

Therefore, those who loved the Union, or most of them, hated
Charleston just as intensely. They hated its arrogant, elegant rulers,
hated its fine town houses built on two centuries of brutal slavery,
hated the very stones of its battery and the Spanish moss that con-
descended from its languid oaks. From the day that crowds on
Charleston's roof tops exulted at the shelling of Fort Sumter, the
North longed for vengeance; and every dead or wounded Union
soldier sharpened the point of that determination. Halleck wrote
to Sherman:

Should you capture Charleston, I hope that by some accident the
place may be destroyed; and if a little salt should be sown upon its
site, it may prevent the growth of future crops of nullification and
secession.

Charleston *delenda est!*

Here was a clash between cold military strategy and hot feeling.
Charleston had no great war industry, no natural resources, no im-

portant railroad junctions. The Ashley and Cooper Rivers, which, as Charlestonians saw it, joined there to form the Atlantic Ocean, tempted no gunboats. In short, except as the destination of an occasional blockade runner, Charleston had no practical strategic value. Yet the humbling of that proud little metropolis remained a prime Union military objective, for not even the prosiest of textbook generals could overlook the psychological impact such a stroke would have on both North and South.

The man who had saved the border slave states for the Union knew the value of the psychological factor in warfare and could calculate it as a master. Abraham Lincoln was anything but a vindictive man, but he craved to see Charleston laid low. And in tracing Lincoln's weapons policy, one sees the depth of his craving as never before.

An attack on Charleston from the sea would run up against Fort Sumter, now in rebel hands, heavily armed and rising sheerly from the water at the entrance to Charleston Harbor. A Federal attack by the "back door" was stalled eight miles south of the city in June 1862. But in the first year of the war, the carelessness of some Negroes cooking their supper on a Cooper River wharf had been memorialized by a sweep of desolation from the Cooper to the Ashley through the heart of the town, a "desert space" which more than a year later reminded a British traveler of "the Pompeiian ruins," and which suggested that the city might be vulnerable to at least one weapon: fire.

"President sent for me," Dahlgren noted in his diary on February 16, 1863. "Some inflammable humbug had been poked at him; from it he went off easily to Charleston matters." The "inflammable humbug" was the incendiary fluid of one Alfred Berney of Jersey City, New Jersey; and the poking had been done by Oliver Spencer Halsted, Jr., of Newark, who may be recalled as the "Pet" Halsted of the Dingee affair.

Whether Berney should be called an inventor or not is a moot point. A reputable New York dealer in lamp oil claimed convincingly that the incendiary formula was his, and that Berney had stolen it from him. The Berney (or Callender) fluid had been fired from a gunboat against the defenses of Yorktown in the spring of 1862, at which time Lincoln's friend Lieutenant Wise had jauntily predicted that it would "puzzle the Devil himself even in his own Dominions to put out, should one crack over or into Hell." A year and a half later, Wise was referring to "that man Berney" as "a cheat, humbug—as is his liquid fire—and a most arrant coward and liar." So perhaps Mills Callender, the lamp-oil dealer, was telling the truth.

The character of Berney's advocate was not much more savory; but in view of his apparent influence with Lincoln, it deserves a closer inspection.

Halsted, Sr., was a Princeton graduate, former mayor of Newark and chancellor of New Jersey, author of legal and theological works and a close student of philology and the Bible. One wonders what he thought of his erratic offspring. Born in 1819, the boy had the vivacity and charm which later distinguished the man. His aunts, with whom he was a favorite, gave him his nickname "Pet"; around the White House in Lincoln's time, he was scarcely known by any other name. Like his father, "Pet" Halsted graduated from Princeton and entered the law. In 1849 he took passage for the gold fields of California; but when the crew of the bark ran off at San Francisco, "Pet" bought her and ran her along the coast for a while instead. Two years later he was back in Newark and dabbling unsuccessfully in politics. Curiously enough, he supported Bell for President in 1860, which explains why he was not one of the Newark delegation which met Lincoln on his way to Washington in 1861.

Pet's hair was thin and somewhat curly, and his beard and mustache were so long as to draw notice even in those shaggy days. Though small, he was sinewy and agile. He made a hobby of boxing and could take on two untrained men heavier than himself with a good chance of whipping them. This hobby led him into rather disreputable company, as was inevitable in those times.

The wild whiskers did not conceal a likable quality. The gallant one-armed warrior Phil Kearney owed (or thought he owed) his first Civil War command to Halsted's lobbying talents, and so took Halsted into his confidence. Kearney regarded his friend as "a brilliant, kind-hearted, dashing adventurer," just the sort Kearney liked. Kearney soon found Halsted to be "not so straightforward as you suppose. He plays many hands at the same time, at a full consideration of his own best chances." Presently Kearney had "learned to pity, & not admire" him. "As an assistance," wrote Kearney, "I believe him dangerous, for he has so many interests ever in charge that he kneads them up to suit himself."

"Gifted with matchless assurance," the *New York Tribune* said of Pet Halsted, "he succeeded in making himself a familiar in the councils of men of note." Mrs. Lincoln may have given him his entrée to the White House. She and the Lincoln children vacationed in New Jersey in the summer of 1861, at which time Halsted wrote Lincoln on terms of easy familiarity to give him advice on Navy steamer purchases. He would, he promised Lincoln, make it a point to call about the matter. "Mrs. Lincoln, children, & suite," he concluded, "are well, & leave this afternoon. *Tad* has entirely recovered & is as light as a lark."

This was Halsted's cue to shut up shop in Newark and join the new gold rush to Washington. "No public character was so well known in Washington as he," recalled the *New York Tribune*. "Nor was he a mere unconscionable braggart; his was a swagger which was more than magnificent. He went everywhere, knew everybody, and cut a large figure in social as well as political life. There was nothing he did not know—nothing he could not do. There were no bounds to his ambition and no limit to his glowing imagination. He was lavish in his expenditure and as generous as a prince, when he had money; and when money failed him, his credit was liberally bestowed."

Halsted had not been idle since the Dingee affair. His friend General Kearney had written him letters bitterly criticizing Mc-

Clellan, adding that they must not "get in any shape into print." A few weeks after Kearney died of his wounds on the rain-swept field of Chantilly, Halsted injected himself into the limelight by publishing the letters. "Brave Phil will be out of his grave with a horsewhip yet, for the ghouls who have maligned his memory," growled the *Boston Post*. Kearney's widow was said to have cut Halsted dead after the betrayal.

To all appearances, Lincoln was not repelled by Pet's antics. In October 1862 Halsted and Governor Sprague of Rhode Island had an interview with Lincoln, at which (said Halsted) "letters were read, criticisms and opinions on the Generals, and conduct of the war freely made and interchanged." When McClellan fell permanently from grace soon after, Halsted's stock rose among the knowing. Lincoln was presently asking Secretary Welles to see Halsted about some steamer purchases.

This was the man who came to Lincoln in the following February to "poke" Alfred Berney's "inflammable humbug" at the President. "Humbug" or not, incendiary warfare fitted in with Lincoln's thinking about Charleston; and the President was ready to give it a chance. He gave orders, therefore, for Captain Benét to test the Berney liquid fire at West Point.

Levi Short, the "Greek Fire" man, meanwhile kept his memory green in Lincoln's mind. Armed with a letter from three prominent Philadelphians urging a field trial of Greek Fire in the name of "humanity and duty alike," Short appeared in a White House anteroom late in March. He failed to see Lincoln, but he left his letter of recommendation; and when Lincoln came across it some days later, he called Short back to Washington for a conference and another Greek Fire demonstration.

Whatever the subject of his conversation with Short, Lincoln talked freely and at length with Pet Halsted about ways to take Charleston and Vicksburg (the stronghold which blocked full Federal control of the Mississippi), and Halsted finally convinced Lincoln that incendiary bombardment was the answer in both cases.

But Assistant Secretary Fox had great faith in the power of conventionally armed ironclads to defy land forts, and so Lincoln waived his own views in favor of Fox's. On April 7 a squadron of monitors was sent into Charleston Harbor.

Lincoln had not been as hopeful as Fox; with his "intuitive sagacity," Secretary Welles wrote, the President had "spoken discouragingly of operations at Charleston during the whole season." And Lincoln turned out to be right. The monitors steamed apprehensively toward the city, only to slink away a few minutes later, mauled and battered by the guns of Sumter and the other forts. "We have met with a sad repulse," confessed Admiral Du Pont.

The experts had been given their chance. Now Lincoln felt inclined to try his own plan. After Du Pont's failure, however, it seemed that a purely naval attack might not do the job. And since a land approach was apt to be slow and difficult, Lincoln began thinking in terms of incendiary bombardment by guns of great range and power. This was why he now took notice of Horatio Ames and his wrought-iron cannon.

Horatio Ames was not the sort of man who is easily ignored. Despite a pleasant roundness about his face, Ames's features dispelled any illusion of softness or pliancy. The broad, tight-lipped mouth, the deep creases that rose from its corners to a bold nose, the brows that angled belligerently over narrowed eyes, all combined to give Horatio Ames the look of a man about to charge a stone wall headfirst, with odds no better than even on the wall. And he was built to match, standing six-feet-six in his stocking feet and weighing over three hundred pounds. He was nearing sixty, to be sure, but an observer might still have guessed, and guessed rightly, that Ames had spent many years as a blacksmith.

Born in Massachusetts, Ames quit school at the age of eleven and took up blacksmithing. A few years later he moved to Falls Village, in the famous Salisbury iron district of Connecticut, and built up a good business in wrought-iron products, mostly shafts and cranks for large steam engines. Ames's brother Oakes outdid him back in the Bay State, making a fortune from his shovel works while Horatio lost ground to more progressive foundries. Galled by this, Horatio looked about for some new product to revive his fortunes and came across a wrought-iron rifled cannon invented by Patrick Danvers of New York City.

Ames got a manufacturing license from Danvers and set to work on a small 12-pounder. The Danvers gun was built up from annular wrought-iron cross sections, like flat rings, imposed one against the other and welded together. In his Falls Village foundry Ames set up two huge hammers or steam rams, one horizontal for welding the rings together, the other upright "to make the iron close and sound." With characteristic grim humor Ames nicknamed them "Thor" and "Odin."

When the war broke out, Ames hastened to Washington and put his claims before General Ripley. But the irresistible force had met an immovable object and had to change direction. Thenceforward, Ames's chief target was the Navy Ordnance Bureau.

In the summer of 1861 Commander Harwood ordered five 50-pounders from Ames at the exalted price of seventy-five cents a pound; and when the guns were tested in the following spring, they proved remarkably strong. Unfortunately for the Yankee ironmaster, Dahlgren took over Harwood's post soon after, and he felt that Ames's price was out of the question. This conflict led to one of the liveliest correspondences in the files of the Bureau. Both men were spirited controversialists, proud, stubborn and quick-tempered. Meager schooling and years of hard labor at plough and forge had left Horatio Ames with a churlish disposition and a rich command of invective. Moreover, he had acquired his knowledge of guns, in his words, "pretty much by myself"; and he had nothing but contempt for books and the men who wrote them. "We have devils to fight," he wrote a fellow inventor, "of the meanest of the scientific, educated class, whose god is meanness, deception, and fraud."

When the two opponents each hinted at chicanery and bad faith on the part of the other, they were merely skirmishing. By the start of 1863 Ames had accused Dahlgren of subjecting the nation's welfare to his own ends. "Must the Honor & Glory of this country be shaped to promote one mans vanity?" Ames asked Secretary Welles. Dahlgren's objections to the Ames gun were "the merest common place Twaddle," he insisted.

Late in January 1863 Ames interested Lincoln briefly in his case. The President asked Dahlgren for information on it, and Dahlgren shrewdly dispatched copies of all the correspondence, which by now occupied a volume. Lincoln had no time for anything so involved, and after two weeks he returned the papers without comment. Baffled, Ames subsided until spring came and the armies stirred. Early in April his towering bulk loomed again at the door of the Navy Ordnance Bureau, to the dismay of badgered clerks. Still he got nowhere, nor did a brisk encounter with General Ripley gain him anything. Ames grew more violent in his denunciations of Dahlgren. "To make a mockery of War is criminal," he wrote Welles, "to sacrifice the Nations Life for Dollars is Treason." Dahlgren replied in kind. "The coarse, reckless and insolent invective which is addressed to me," he wrote Ames, "can find no excuse or pretext in anything I have previously written or said to you." An impasse had been reached.

Ames broke it by exploiting Du Pont's failure at Charleston. Connecticut's representatives in Washington were mustered in a body for the assault: Senators Dixon and Foster, Congressman Hubbard and Congressman-elect Augustus Brandegee. By now, Brother Oakes, an energetic, ambitious and shrewdly calculating man, was a Congressman and growing rapidly in influence. Finally —for Horatio Ames knew his way around Washington by this time—Pet Halsted was enlisted.

On April 25 Pet Halsted demonstrated his ability to "play many hands at the same time," as the late Phil Kearney had put it. He wrote a long letter to Lincoln, reminding the President of their talks about Charleston and Vicksburg and urging him to "insist & demand that your own plans & views be carried out."

By a marvelous coincidence three of Halsted's clients between them offered the ingredients of success: Robert Parrott had three 300-pounder rifled cannon he wanted to sell; Horatio Ames had sold the Navy six 50-pounder wrought-iron guns* which he wanted brought to public notice; and Alfred Berney had his liquid fire. Halsted wrote grandly:

We now offer to take two Monitors, and being allowed to fit them up, under the direction & supervision of Berney & myself, with the guns, fire, & shell as referred to & otherwise acting on the President's plan of attack, will guarantee to take or destroy Sumpter & Charleston in from one to three days after operations are opened.

Lincoln knew perfectly well that Pet Halsted was in this for something more than just the glow of duty done; but the argument seemed plausible, and Lincoln made up his mind to look into it.

On the rainy afternoon of April 28, 1863, Lincoln strode into the Navy Ordnance Office, determined to find out what was what in the case of Horatio Ames. Dahlgren and Wise were both there, and Lincoln put Ames's story to them as he had heard it from Horatio himself: that Harwood had promised Ames unlimited orders at seventy-five cents a pound if the first six guns succeeded, and that Ames had consequently spent a huge sum in enlarging his plant and machinery. Dahlgren could scarcely control his temper. No such promise had ever been made, he explained; and even if it had been, the Navy lacked the funds with which to honor it. The admiral had more in his mind, but he saved it for his diary:

It is unfortunate that the President will meddle in such matters. No adventure on the Treasury now stands on its merits. Projects for new cannon, new powder, and devices of all kinds are backed by the highest influences.

That amiable raconteur Harry Wise carried the day for the Bureau. Having been present at all of Harwood's talks with Ames, Wise could testify that, so far as he could recall, no such promise of future orders had been made. Then Wise gently led the conver-

---

* He had sold one more after the original order for five.

sation round to other topics, and before long Lincoln was in his usual easy good humor. In a rare moment of reminiscence he spoke of the hard struggle he had had to finance the education of his son Bob. He himself had had only one year of education, he added, but he guessed that Bob would not do better than he had. Presently, satisfied with what he had heard, Lincoln strolled back to the White House through the drizzle.

In the Ordnance Bureau Dahlgren and Wise breathed easier, as did Captain Harwood when he heard the story. "I thank you for doing that little bit of fighting for me 'in re Ames,' " wrote Harwood to Wise later in the day.

That was not all Lincoln did that day. Captain Benét had reported on the Berney trial more than two weeks before, but the Ordnance Office had held his report instead of sending it to the President. Having learned of its existence from Halsted's letter, Lincoln now called for the report and read it over. "Every shell that struck the target & exploded," reported the captain, "did ignite the incendiary fluid, & set the target in a blaze." He had not only bombarded a large target of heavy oak timbers, but had also burst shells of various calibers under piles of logs, all with spectacular effect. More than that, he had seen Berney set a stream of fluid blazing simply by holding a torch to the hose nozzle. There was no backfire, and the flame could be cut off by removing the torch. Benét thought the shells would "prove very destructive to all wooden & other combustible structures"; and as for the flame thrower, "even when the object attacked is not combustible, the burning fluid itself with its volumes of flame & clouds of black smoke would make its use of great effectiveness." He recommended the preparation without hesitation.

This sounded like quite a spectacle, and Lincoln wanted to see it for himself. Halsted hastily arranged for a demonstration in the Treasury Park, not, as in Short's case, for the vulgar multitude, which let no contracts anyway, but for Lincoln, Stanton and a select half dozen of Pet's clients—including the redoubtable Horatio, to whom Halsted referred as "Admiral Ames."

Lincoln and Stanton walked down together from the White

House in the cool, clear twilight of May 9. They found Berney waiting with his props and paraphernalia: a pile of water-soaked wood, barrels of fluid, some eleven-inch shells and a hand pump. Cheered on by Halsted's little claque, he made the Treasury Park shake and burn as if it had itself caught the ague from its pestilential environs. While Lincoln and Stanton looked on, the inventor sent the woodpile flying into the air in a burst of smoke and flame, detonated two shells in the middle of the lot to suggest their effect on an enemy position and squirted fire from his hand pump. Lastly, he played a stream of fire on three hundred gallons of the fluid, representing the amount thrown in a minute from the nozzle of a steam pump. The black pool blazed up, and fire billowed into the spring twilight, playing its glare over the lanky President and his stocky war minister. At last the flames dwindled down, and night closed in around them.

So pleased was Lincoln with the weird show that he personally arranged to have General Hooker try a 100-pounder shell or two on the enemy, and had actually left for Hooker's camp to witness the experiment when Lee's invasion of the North disrupted the plan. Even so, Lincoln forced the reluctant General Ripley to order a thousand Berney shells for trial in actual service.

The battle between Dahlgren and Ames, however, continued unabated. Congressman-elect Brandegee tried to mediate between the two; but Dahlgren's concessions were minor, and Ames was unreceptive. Presently Dahlgren was huffily protesting that Ames had "*publicly* applied certain abusive terms to me, such as scoundrel." Late in June the Navy refused Ames's offer to make fifty 200-pounders at a dollar a pound. "What is the matter with Pet Halsted and Horatio?" someone asked Wise the next day. And the *Scientific American,* getting wind of Ames's proposal some weeks later, commented pointedly: "We presume there are a great many forges willing to make such guns on similar terms."

Three weeks after Berney's Treasury Park exhibition, Lincoln and Stanton attended the trial of a breech-loading rifled cannon designed for just the sort of long-distance work called for at Charleston.

The inventor, George Ferriss of Utica, New York, was a large-eyed, gaunt-faced man, from whose square jaw descended a fringe of grizzled beard. As a maker of fine sporting arms, Ferriss had few equals; as a writer and a talker, his skill was negligible. That deficiency, however, was supplied by his partner. David O. Macomber, son of a sea captain, had started out as a sign painter in Utica and then had succumbed to his father's wanderlust. He and Ferriss complemented each other neatly. Ferriss was quiet and unassuming; Macomber was brash, expansive and glib, the writer of letters and deliverer of sales talks. The pair seemed inseparable.

A year before, Macomber had been introduced to Lincoln by Horatio King, Buchanan's last Postmaster General, and had shown the President a model of Ferriss's cannon. It was a massively built-up gun, with a coiled wrought-iron bore enclosed in steel rings and a screw-type breech piece worked by a crank. Ferriss's idea was to get great range and penetration by means of an unusually heavy charge of powder. At that time Lincoln had agreed to have a full-size gun built by the government on one condition: that a working model of the Ferriss gun, with a 1½-inch bore, demonstrate double the penetration of a conventional model with the same size bore.

Now Ferriss and Macomber were back with the stipulated models; and on May 29 Lincoln and Stanton accordingly went down to the Navy Yard to see them fired. If all Macomber claimed for the gun's range should be borne out, here might be the means of humbling Charleston.

A surprise awaited them. Ferriss and Macomber had taken advantage of Lincoln's failure to require something like equality in the weights of the two guns, as well as in their bores. With a bore of only an inch and three quarters, the Ferriss gun's *external* diameter ran from 14.78 inches at the breech to 7.78 inches at the muzzle; and the gun weighed fifteen hundred pounds! Moreover, the Ferriss gun's performance was mediocre. Considering the charge used—a pound and a half of powder for a two-and-a-half-pound shell—the range was not great. And when two shells were fired at an iron target from two hundred yards, one missed, and the other made a dent about an inch deep. To be sure, the Ferriss gun performed somewhat better than its conventional rival, but then it had a powder charge six times as great as the latter.

Stanton's comments were caustic, and Lincoln good-humoredly pointed out that the gun had not yet sent its shells nine miles as Macomber had promised it would.

During August and early September, Ferriss and Macomber fired their small gun for range on Fire Island beach, off Long Island; and when one of the shells went nine and a quarter miles, Macomber whooped up the gun in the New York papers. "Verily," marveled the *Herald*, "we live in a wonderful age!" Lincoln's conditions had been met, and the President accordingly had the War Department formally invite a proposal. Here Macomber stretched his luck too far: his asking price for a 100-pounder Ferriss gun was enough to buy no less than forty-five 100-pounder Parrotts. The proposition was declined, and Lincoln looked elsewhere for weapons against Charleston.

Late in May Lincoln, Stanton and Welles agreed that the next attack on Charleston would have to be the joint work of army and navy. Fort Sumter had been too much for monitors alone; it must be destroyed by land batteries. Remembering how effectively Fort Pulaski had been pulverized a year before, Lincoln sent for the author of that work, General Quincy Adams Gillmore. Gillmore confidently undertook to render an encore against Sumter from near-by Morris Island. That left the problem of who was to command the naval squadron which was to steam into the harbor and chastise Charleston after Sumter had been knocked out.

In the days following, Secretary Welles mulled over possibilities. Du Pont, able as he was, had caught the McClellan "slows," and, worse still, had convinced himself that Charleston Harbor was no place for the Navy under any circumstances. Porter was too young; Gregory was too old. Lincoln wanted Dahlgren to have the job, but

Frank Leslie's Illustrated History
of the Civil War

A LINCOLN WEAPONS PROJECT PAYS OFF
Mortar boats firing on Island No. 10, in the Mississippi, on the night of March 18, 1862.

THE MACHINE GUN WHICH LINCOLN INTRODUCED INTO WARFARE

A specimen of the Union Repeating Guns or "Coffee-mill Guns," nicknamed, tested and purchased by Abraham Lincoln in 1861.

Welles felt that the cry of favoritism would be raised to the injury of the service and Dahlgren himself. At last, Welles settled on Andrew Foote. Since Dahlgren had his heart set on sea duty, Welles offered him the post of second in command. Dahlgren declined to go at all unless he could be first in command, not only of naval but of land operations too. "This," wrote Welles, "precludes farther thought of him. I regret it for his own sake. . . . It is doubtful if he ever will have another so good an opportunity." Welles was wrong.

The summer of 1863 began on a Sunday, and Rear Admiral Dahlgren attended church in a mood of mingled sadness and speculation. Rear Admiral Foote, so lately engrossed in preparations for his new mission, had suddenly taken sick and now lay dying in New York. As the church service began, Dahlgren's thoughts dwelt on the possibilities opened by the impending tragedy. Presently a messenger summoned him from his devotions to the home of Secretary Welles, where he learned that his great ambition had at last been realized: he was to command the coming attack on Charleston. With a show of resignation the disgruntled Secretary remarked that "it seemed destined that no one else should do so." Still, not even destiny could bring Welles to accept defeat with perfect grace. "Full and unreserved" was his own description of his talk with Dahlgren. He told Dahlgren bluntly that this new appointment was Lincoln's doing, and that it would aggravate the discontent already caused by Dahlgren's promotion to rear admiral.

The plain speech of Gideon Welles did not disturb Dahlgren, who had heard it often enough before. He turned his thoughts rather to the glory he saw ahead.

Levi Short won the race to hurl fire shells into Southern towns, and he did it through a stroke of policy worthy of Pet Halsted.

Rear Admiral David D. Porter commanded the Mississippi squadron, which could throw shells into beleaguered Vicksburg. His mother, Mrs. Evalina D. Porter, took it into her head to rent part of the old Porter family mansion "Green Bank" on the Dela-

ware to a cartridge firm. Hearing of this somehow, Levi Short rented the rest of the place as a workshop in which to make up his new
"Solidified Greek Fire." (This now came in tin cylinders three
inches long and five-eighths of an inch in diameter.) And not long
after, the Navy, at Admiral Porter's request, ordered ten gross of
Short's canisters for the Mississippi flotilla.

One night, Porter's gunboats sent a few Short shells into the air
over Vicksburg. Great flakes of fire drifted down, "setting the town
on fire in three places . . . burning up a considerable quantity of
stores, and the houses burned to the ground." Vicksburg fell before
much of Short's Greek Fire reached the squadron; but Porter gave
Short a glowing testimonial, which the inventor featured in his advertising circulars.

The force of Porter's testimonial is somewhat weakened by what
the admiral said in private correspondence. Some time later he
wrote his mother:

I would be very glad to oblige you in the case of Short, but my
conscience will not permit me to recommend his greek fire, which
I know to be good for nothing. If he wants me to do anything for
him, let him first pay you what he owes you, and when I see the
receipt I may perhaps change my mind.

And in another letter:

I expect to hear of Green Bank going up in the air some of these
days with the powder arrangements, and if that old humbug with
his greek fire could be on top of it when it does go it would serve
him right.

Eventually, reverberations from the banks of the Delaware gave
notice to the neighbors that the Porter place had indeed ascended.
Levi Short, however, had preceded it by some months.

Meanwhile, by a remarkable feat of rough-and-ready engineering, General Gillmore's troops built a gun emplacement in a Mor-

ris Island quagmire within range of Charleston, and there in a sort of sandbag pulpit they planted a 200-pounder Parrott gun which gained the nickname of "the Swamp Angel." Berney and Pet Halsted came down with five hundred of their incendiary shells, and Levi Short sent down forty gross of his little tin canisters from the Porter mansion. Under orders from Lincoln himself, the Swamp Angel at last opened fire on Charleston with both Berney and Short incendiary shells, beginning at one-thirty in the morning of August 22, 1863.

In the heat of the August night, as Confederate guns on James Island boomed dully away at Union positions, a wakeful British visitor lay reading by candlelight in the Charleston Hotel. He had just reached the Battle of Waterloo in *Les Miserables* when a noise like "the whirr of a phantom brigade of cavalry" sounded overhead, followed by a crash and a deafening explosion down the street. From his window the startled Briton saw flames and smoke billowing from a near-by warehouse, while in the street below, an excited watchman pounded his stick against the curb in the Charleston manner of sounding an alarm. Speculators, in town to buy up blockade-runner cargoes, rushed about the hotel corridors in wild alarm and little else. Another shell whirred overhead, "and down on their faces went every man of them, into tobacco-juice and cigar ends, and clattering among the spittoons." Outside, as a Negro fire company put out the warehouse blaze, frantic citizens jammed the sidewalks in their flight.

After the work of that sweltering night General Pierre G. T. Beauregard, the Confederate commander, denounced Gillmore for throwing "a number of the most destructive missiles ever used in war into the midst of a city, taken unawares and filled with sleeping women and children." He also set about acquiring phosphorus shells to fire back. Some Northerners, including Commodore John Rodgers, joined in Beauregard's denunciation of the weapon; most exulted at the news. The *Washington Star* reminded its readers that the people of Sodom must likewise have thought their brimstone shower bath a villainous device, "but the hand of retribution was not stayed on that account." And the *Nashville Union* lampooned Beauregard's protest, with special reference to certain side effects of the Greek Fire:

> 'Tis sweet to draw one's dying breath
> For one's dear land, as Horace saith,
> But dreadful to be stunk to death.

After the shouting had died down, the fiery missiles turned out to have been more destructive to Union gun crews than to rebel property. Twelve Berney and four Short shells were fired the first night, and twenty more Short shells on the day after. Six of the last exploded in the Swamp Angel. On the thirty-sixth round the breech blew out, and the rest of the gun landed on the parapet. When other guns came within range of Charleston, thirteen more Short shells were fired with similarly poor results. Of thirty-seven Short shells tried in the Swamp Angel and other guns, twenty burst in or near the gun or did not burst at all.

Hurrying down to Morris Island from Philadelphia, Short feverishly juggled powder charges, Greek Fire charges and layers of cartridge paper, but without restoring confidence in his shells among those who had to stand the consequences of a premature burst. Sick and despondent, the old man went back to Philadelphia. In October he came up with a new scheme. Having seen the rebels dig in at Fort Sumter, Short proposed "stinking them out" by adding noxious ingredients to his Greek Fire. The Chief of Ordnance made no reply; and early on the day before Thanksgiving, 1863, death silenced Levi Short's importunities.

Berney's reputation fared little better than Short's in the Charleston experiment. Pet Halsted maintained that all the bad incendiary projectiles had been "worthless shells known as the Short shell which I predicted a failure in advance"; and someone, probably Halsted, published an enthusiastic but spurious endorsement of the Berney shell over the signature of General Gillmore. After Fleet Commander Ammen had ordered five hundred Berney shells on the strength of the false endorsement, Gillmore told him that the shells "were entirely useless, exploding within a mile of the gun," and so Ammen canceled his order.

After the affair at Charleston the Navy agreed with a writer in the *United States Service Magazine* that "investigations of this kind are in pursuit of an *'ignis fatuus.'* " The Army's Chief of Ordnance commented wryly that "Charleston is in existence still." And Abraham Lincoln gave no further thought to incendiary warfare.

Some weeks later, success rewarded the fanatical persistence of Horatio Ames.

Augustus Brandegee paid a flying visit to Willard's Hotel to arrange quarters for himself during the approaching session of Congress. As he passed through the crowded lobby, the Congressman-elect from Connecticut was disturbed to see his burly constituent from Falls Village bearing down upon him. Before Brandegee could escape, the "admiral" had buttonholed him and exacted a promise of help in reopening the Ames case with President Lincoln.

Pet Halsted arranged for the interview, and the two men presented themselves at the White House. Hulking Horatio Ames dwarfed his political escort, as they mounted the stairs. At Lincoln's office Brandegee's card gained them immediate admittance. What followed is best told by Brandegee himself:

As he rose—and seemed to keep on rising—before me, his hair was black, coarse and of an unkempt appearance, his nose prominent, his cheek bones high, his cheeks very hollow, his complexion swarthy, his manner gracious but subdued, while his eyes had an expression that I find myself incapable of describing, as though they lay in ambush in their deep caverns, ready to spring forth or retreat further within, as occasion required. He was awkward, but it was the awkwardness of nature, which is akin to grace. The expression of his face was earnest, with a shade of sadness, and his voice was soft, and at times as tender as a woman's.

I had prepared what I thought a neat little speech of introduction, but he at once put my rhetoric and embarrassment to flight by taking me by the hand and saying, "Well, what does little Connecticut want?"

The tone, the familiar address, the friendly manner, the gracious smile at once put me at my ease, and I stated my case as to a friend, and almost an equal. As I proceeded with gathering warmth, commenting upon the unfairness of submitting the Connecticut invention to a rival gun-maker, the unfriendly tests adopted and the supreme importance of a gun which would do more execution at the muzzle than at the breech, Mr. Lincoln listened with evident interest. Ames had stated that a record existed of the various charges, the number of firings, and the respective results to each gun, and that it would vindicate all he claimed, but he had been denied access to it. Mr. Lincoln closed the interview by requesting me to procure it, and bring it to him at 8 o'clock that evening. And to my suggestion that I was unknown at the department, he took an Executive envelope from a bundle which lay always on his table and wrote the following: "Let Mr. ———, of Connecticut, have a copy of such record as he indicates. A. Lincoln."

At the Navy Ordnance Bureau Lincoln's note acted as an open sesame. Brandegee and Ames were back in Lincoln's office at eight o'clock sharp with the records they wanted. As they talked, Brandegee noticed Lincoln's long legs, sticking out from under his desk. At first the President had on a pair of carpet slippers; but as the talk progressed, he worked his feet out of them, disclosing "what seemed to be a pair of dark yarn stockings." His big toe protruded from a hole in one of the socks, and this he kept "in almost perpetual motion." The record seemed to bear out Ames's contentions; and after much discussion and some searching questions, Lincoln wrote a few words on the back of an executive envelope: "If Horatio Ames will make ten wrought iron guns after his method, which will answer satisfactorily such tests as I shall order, I will see that he gets paid $1 per pound for each gun." So ended the interview.

Toward the end of September, Lincoln modified the terms somewhat and then made his offer formally, agreeing to pay eighty-five cents a pound for fifteen Ames guns, 100-pounders or larger, *provided* that a board appointed by the President judged them superior to any of equal caliber then in use. "Pet Halsted walked up with me [to the White House]," recorded John Hay in his diary about a month later. "He says the President won over Ames and Brandegee by his friendly candid manner and the fair way in which he met their complaints and requests."

A few days before the Swamp Angel opened on Charleston, Gillmore's guns on Morris Island began to batter Fort Sumter. Seven days later the Fort was, in the words of its engineer in chief, "a desolate ruin, a shapeless pile of shattered walls and casemates, showing here and there the guns disabled and half-buried in splintered wrecks of carriages, its mounds of rubbish fairly reeking with the smoke and smell of powder." But its garrison dug in and lived; and when Dahlgren sent a landing party against it, the assault failed. As the weeks passed, Sumter became more and more powerful as an earth work. With its defenders active and the harbor reputedly sown thickly with mines and obstructions, Dahlgren would not take his squadron in.

Late in October, Lincoln had a long talk with two high-ranking officers just up from Gillmore's army. Still hopeful of retribution for Charleston, he asked them pointedly why that spawning-ground of rebellion was not shelled. The callers replied that they "preferred to save their fire for service against [Forts] Johnson & Moultrie when the Navy moves, rather than burst their guns now by throwing a few shell into the city." To John Hay, who was listening, this sounded like "a very sensible conclusion"; and if Lincoln thought otherwise, he seems not to have pressed his views. At any rate, the two officers came away "much pleased with the Tycoon."

One wonders what might have happened if Lincoln had read and remembered a letter written to him in May 1862 by a New York schoolteacher named John W. Doughty. Perhaps Doughty taught chemistry; he certainly knew the properties of chlorine. His proposal was to use heavy shells filled with liquid chlorine. This, he explained to the President, would immediately expand into a choking gas of many times its original volume, which, being denser than air, would sink irresistibly into trenches and bombproofs. But there is no evidence that Lincoln actually read Doughty's letter. Someone, probably a White House secretary, referred it to the War Department; and thence it went to General Ripley, who ignored it. Doughty wrote Ripley and was told that the Ordnance Department was too busy to test the idea. Two years later Doughty wrote again, repeating his suggestion and enlarging on it. Nothing was done to develop it—until 1915, when the Germans, using a cruder version, produced an astonishing collapse in the Allied lines at Ypres.

The defenders of Sumter wintered cosily in uncontaminated air. And waiting helplessly outside Charleston Harbor as the old year died in violent wind and rain, Admiral John Dahlgren, sick and discouraged, wrote:

Thus endeth the old year 1863—one that has witnessed my highest advancement, but not my happiness, for I have been loaded with responsibilities that no one could hope to lead to a favorable issue; the best possible result of which would ruin the reputation of any man. And now what is there to look forward to?

CHAPTER 18

Ripley's Last Stand

THE RESTLESS AMBITION WHICH BESET CAP-
tain Dahlgren in January 1863 had no counterpart in General Ripley. For more than a year Ripley had been established with his wife
and daughters in a house of his own at Jackson Place, just off Lafayette Square; and there he seemed content to stay. Through all
the ebb and flow of carnage, the general regularly, if perhaps not
altogether serenely, woke in his own bedroom, breakfasted at his
own table, followed a familiar morning route across Pennsylvania
Avenue past the White House and down Seventeenth Street, and
took up his daily vigil as preserver of the Union Army from newfangled gimcracks. Perhaps, as he walked austerely through winter
rains on his way to the Winder Building, Ripley felt an occasional
twinge at the sight of Andrew Jackson's effigy astride an ever-
rearing charger in the sodden park. But by then, the old hero who
once threatened to hang young Ripley for his excessive devotion to
red tape had been almost twenty years in the grave; and for all
Stanton's bluster, no such retribution menaced the Union Army's
Chief of Ordnance.

The climactic new year of 1863 brought little rest to the watch-
dog of weapons. New follies arose and old ones persisted. Ripley's
representations and misrepresentations of 1862 had not, for example, completely scotched the coffee-mill guns. Undismayed by
setbacks in the Peninsula, the American Arms Company brought
out an improved model of its machine gun and looked about for

other markets. Its secretary, the resourceful J. D. Mills, took some prominent Kentuckians out to Staten Island one day for a demonstration of the new model; and on the ferryboat he met a soldier of fortune just about to leave for Venezuela, which, like the United States, was then racked by civil war. Mills's sales talk on that occasion led to a Venezuelan trial order for one gun, although what came of the trial is not recorded.

Toward the end of 1862 a company agent persuaded Captain David Porter to try his luck with a coffee-mill gun. At a hundred and forty yards the delighted captain hit the head of a small barrel six times out of ten, and he saw the agent hit it eighteen out of twenty-four times in rapid firing. Some few trifling mechanical defects could be easily fixed, thought Porter; and he ordered four of the guns through the Navy Ordnance Bureau. After they reached his Mississippi Squadron, however, Porter decided that light howitzers throwing shrapnel would do just as well for most river work. Perhaps the captain had heard about an incident on the Yazoo River, when a shaving of lead flew sidewise from one of the new machine guns and embedded itself in the leg of General William T. Sherman. The errant fragment, which had to be extracted with pincers, may have given Sherman added grounds for his famous definition of war, but it did not raise his esteem for machine guns.

In the East that spring the *Scientific American* reported sadly that the coffee-mill guns had "proved to be of no practical value to the army of the Potomac, and are now laid up in a store-house in Washington." Nevertheless, the commander of a Negro regiment about to leave New York for Louisiana asked for eight of the guns and got them, over the protests of General Ripley, who refused to furnish proper ammunition until Assistant Secretary Watson flatly ordered him to do so. Ripley might have spared himself this skirmish, for the regiment in question found no occasion to use the guns.

A new threat to Ripley's equanimity arose in June, when General Rosecrans saw a coffee-mill gun fired successfully and requested more such guns for his Army of the Cumberland. After a surly account of the gun's shortcomings, Ripley admitted there were some on hand, "if you still desire to have any sent to you." Rosecrans did so desire, and ten guns were sent. Ordnance officers along the way seemed to forward them with extraordinary deliberation, however, and at last they went astray in Nashville, thus missing out on the Battle of Chickamauga.

Lincoln knew nothing about this sabotage of the coffee-mill guns, and in any case he had shifted his support to the Rafael Repeater. After three weeks of testing at 6th Corps Headquarters in Virginia during April, the Rafael machine gun won hearty praise from a board of two brigadier generals and a colonel, all able men. In its "simplicity of construction, accuracy, range, and frequency of fire," the board found the gun to be "all that is claimed for it," and they recommended an initial use of from eight to twelve guns per brigade. Brigadier General (formerly Colonel) Pratt, whose battle experience with the coffee-mill gun had been unhappy, glowingly endorsed the Rafael Repeater and asked that at least twenty-four of them be attached to his division. After studying the report, Lincoln wrote:

The within are additional testimonials in favor of what is called the "Rafael Gun" of which I thought favorably some time ago. Will the Sec. of War please refer it to the Ordnance Bureau, with reference to the propriety of introducing the "Rafael Gun" into the Service?

In spite of all this, Ripley never bought a single Rafael Repeater.

One who did not appreciate Ripley's ingrained abhorrence of all new weapons might well agree with several Navy officers, who told the Rafael Repeater's owners "that they should regard the answer of the government officials to our proposals as a test of their patriotism. If they refused these guns, they should believe they were traitors & did not want or desire the termination of the war."

Ripley could no longer cite the small arms shortage as an argument against converting to new weapons. As early as June 1862, the Ordnance Department had a third of a million arms in storage, besides having issued nearly a million to the troops. To be sure, an acute and unexpected shortage developed in September and October after the great battles of late summer; but by 1863 the Springfield Armory was turning out twenty thousand first-class rifles a month and had thirty thousand on hand waiting to be called for.

Late in 1862 opportunity once more hammered at the door of the Ordnance Office. The Union Firearms Company had failed, for lack of investors, to fill Lincoln's order for twenty-five thousand Marsh breechloaders. Now Samuel Marsh had severed connections with his old partner, Robert Gallaher, and had made a fresh start with an entirely new company, the Marsh Patent Fire Arms Company, which enjoyed the support of such solid citizens as Moses Grinnell, Mayor George Opdyke of New York City and General Dan Sickles.

But when the new company offered to make up to a hundred thousand Marsh breechloaders, Ripley made no reply; and when Marsh wrote again in January 1863, Ripley confused, or pretended to confuse, the new company with the old one. Pointing out haughtily that nearly seven thousand breechloaders remained deliverable on the President's old order to the Union Firearms Company, Ripley refused to consider any further orders. Marsh wrote again in February to explain that he had no present connection with that moribund firm and obviously could deliver no rifles in its name. General Ripley seemed unable to understand. "There are, *now,* 5800 of these arms deliverable to the Government," he insisted inexorably. "In my opinion it is not adviseable to *purchase* any of them at any price."

And not a single Marsh breechloader was ever purchased.

Ripley fought off the Spencer repeating rifle with equal determination. To demands from the field, which mounted in volume and feeling as 1863 progressed, Ripley replied that repeating and breech-loading arms could be furnished only to mounted men, and

there were not enough even for that purpose. Besides, added Ripley, the original order for Spencer rifles had been largely forfeited
"owing to the non-delivery of the arms within the times specified
in the contract." In short, Ripley's acquiescence in the purchase of
breech-loading carbines from the Spencer Company gave him an
excuse for blocking the production of breech-loading rifles.

Even while the Chief of Ordnance was thus pulling a long face,
for the benefit of field commanders, over the scarcity of Spencer
rifles, he was recommending to the War Department that existing
orders be canceled. In February, for example, he told Assistant
Secretary Watson that it was not "expedient to continue the manufacture under the contract." In March, after a delivery of two
hundred Spencers, Ripley complained about their cost and insisted
that their "practical value and utility for the military service have
yet to be ascertained." And in May Ripley told Fisher and Cheney
of the Spencer Company that he could give them no further orders
for rifles without special authority from Secretary Stanton. Not
unnaturally, the two men thereupon applied to Stanton, who flew
into a rage and demanded to know why Ripley burdened him with
business belonging to the Ordnance Department. To this, Ripley
replied lamely: "I did not send them to you, at all, for any purpose."

The Spencer Company did its best to counter Ripley's opposition to its rifles. Early in 1863 it sent Christopher Spencer west to
explain the proper use of his gun to troops which already carried it
and to the commanders of troops not yet so fortunate. In April the
young inventor dined with General Grant and Flag Officer Foote
not far from Vicksburg.

The Spencer rifle's most effective promoter in the West, however, was a black-bearded Confederate cavalry leader named John
H. Morgan, who in the late summer and early fall of 1862 hovered
over Tennessee and Kentucky "like an eagle on the wing, ready to
pounce upon any weak point." Strategically, Morgan's raiders were
of slight account, but their nuisance value was high. "In no other
way," commented Lincoln, "does the enemy give us so much

trouble, at so little expence to himself." During the fall of 1862 General Rosecrans, whose Army of the Cumberland was the principal sufferer from Morgan's depredations, noted that Morgan moved his men swiftly on horseback to the point of attack, where they dismounted and fought as infantry. Two could play at that game, thought Rosecrans, and he wrote the War Department for Colt revolving rifles to arm some mounted infantry of his own. Governor Morton of Indiana, whose state felt the threat of Morgan's raids with particular keenness, took up the idea and demanded no less than fifty such regiments.

General Ripley and his ally, General in Chief Halleck, did not share Morton's enthusiasm. Halleck wrote Rosecrans in February 1863:

You are not the only general who is urgently calling for more cavalry and more cavalry arms. The supply is limited, and the demands of all cannot be satisfied. . . . In regard to "revolving rifles," "superior arms," &c., every one is issued the moment it is received.

Nevertheless, the mounted infantry idea had powerful support. On Lincoln's fifty-fourth birthday Stanton authorized the formation of such a regiment, to be armed as prescribed by the President. And just then, Major General Lovell H. Rousseau arrived in Washington from Rosecrans's army, all afire with zeal for mounted infantry.

Rousseau, a tall Kentuckian of elegant manners and great strength, had been, in Lincoln's own words, "our first active practical Military friend in Kentucky," and he had stood well with the President ever since. Now he was back at the White House to tell Lincoln that only mounted infantry could deal with men like Morgan's. "I propose to organize and use such a force . . . to be furnished with Sharps rifles," he declared. "If I do not make this pay at the end of three months from today, I will cheerfully relinquish the command." Lincoln was convinced, and immediately wrote Rosecrans a letter in support of the idea.

Rousseau did not depart at once. On March 2 he appeared at the last White House levee of the season, a highly successful affair at which "hats, coats, dresses, crinoline, and corns suffered terribly." Evidently he endured the hardships of Washington society long enough to win his point, for in mid-April General Ripley notified Rosecrans that two thousand Spencer rifles would be on their way in a month or so, this being "as soon as they can be made."

Rosecrans waited not upon the Spencers before following Lincoln's suggestion: in March he authorized Colonel John T. Wilder to impress mounts for his infantry brigade.

Born in New York's Catskills in 1830, John Thomas Wilder rose from poverty until his Indiana foundry and millwrighting firm was doing business in six states. By June 1861, when he became lieutenant colonel of the 17th Indiana Infantry, Wilder was a recognized expert in hydraulics, the holder of three turbine patents and the employer of a hundred men. In the service he invented a device for twisting iron rails, a useful gadget for hit-and-run raids.

Unwilling to wait for the Spencers promised by Ripley, Wilder bought some directly with money borrowed from bankers in his home town; his men paid him for their rifles in installments, and the Federal Government later reimbursed them. Wilder's impatience paid off at Hoover's Gap on June 24, 1863. After months of querulous inaction, Rosecrans had begun the brilliant Tullahoma campaign which was to maneuver Bragg out of Tennessee. Rosecrans ordered Wilder's "First Mounted Rifles," leading the advance, to "trot through" Hoover's Gap, pushing Confederate pickets before them. Wilder obeyed orders literally, paying no heed to rebel rear-guard opposition. At last the Confederate general sent Bushrod Johnson's brigade against Wilder's men. Although Rosecrans's army was six miles to the rear, the Yankees already possessed the confidence bred by breechloaders. Holding firm until the main body of Rosecrans's forces came up, Wilder's men fired their Spencer rifles into the rebel brigade until Johnson felt sure he was outnumbered five to one. Wilder lost fifty-one men killed and wounded to Johnson's one hundred and forty-six. From then on, the 1st Mounted Rifles were universally known as "Wilder's Lightning Brigade."

On that June day in 1863 the eyes of the nation were not turned toward Hoover's Gap; nor did they rest on Admiral Dahlgren, who left Washington that morning for his South Atlantic squadron.

At Chancellorsville in May Berdan's men had given part of the Stonewall Brigade its first taste of disordered retreat; but the battle as a whole had been a bloody defeat for the Army of the Potomac and its sanguine, ruddy-cheeked commander, General Joseph Hooker. Now Lee's army was once more swarming northward, and all Washington cocked its ears for the rumble of guns. Pennsylvania already shrank before the impending blow; and Lieutenant Commander Jeffers, testing Diller's powder at Philadelphia, wrote Harry Wise that the city was "full of sound and fury signifying nothing. Very few join the various companies notwithstanding the clamorous appeals to their patriotism and state pride." While the opposing armies sidled watchfully northward through Maryland, Hooker yielded his command to austere, quick-tempered George Meade; and on the first day of July, the Battle of Gettysburg began.

As the men of Meade's army fell back through the little Pennsylvania town, General Ripley, in the Winder Building at Washington, was writing the Spencer Company that no more of its rifles were wanted.

On the second day of the battle Longstreet's men, pushing toward Little Round Top, ran into a hundred Berdan men, supported by two hundred Maine troops with muzzle-loaders. In the twenty-minute action that ensued, the Sharpshooters fired an average of ninety-five rounds each from their single-shot breechloaders. The Confederates mistook them for "two Federal regiments." One Sharpshooter was captured and taken back through the enemy lines. "It is impossible for me to describe the slaughter we had made in their ranks," he said after the war. "In all my past service, it beat all I had ever seen for the number engaged and for so short a time. They were piled in heaps and across each other. .... The doctor would hardly believe that there were so few of us fighting them, thought we had a corps, as he said he never saw lead so thick in his life as it was in those woods."

The stand of the Sharpshooters had the effect of delaying Longstreet's corps forty minutes. Had the delay been only thirty-five minutes, Longstreet might have taken the Peach Orchard and the ridge and thus changed the outcome of the battle.

In the Peach Orchard, Gardiner explosive bullets popped on both sides. Major French had persuaded Assistant Secretary Watson to order more than a hundred thousand, of which twenty-four thousand were issued to the 2nd New Hampshire in June. Ten thousand of these were abandoned to the rebels in Virginia and thus reached Gettysburg in enemy hands. While Corporal Thomas Bignall of the 2nd New Hampshire fought in the Peach Orchard, a shell struck his cartridge box of Gardiner bullets. "The cartridges," recalled a horrified witness, "were driven into his body and fired, and for nearly half a minute the devilish 'musket shells' issued at Washington were exploding in his quivering form. But death was mercifully quick."

Lee's men struck hard at both flanks of the Union Army that day, without decisive effect. On July third, as Meade had shrewdly anticipated, Lee hit the Federal center with the splendid although vain effort known as Pickett's charge. With it the rebel bolt was shot. Throughout the nation's birthday, the rebels remained sullenly defiant on Seminary Ridge. Early on the morning of the fifth, they were found to be in full retreat through the mountain passes. And meanwhile, unknown to either army, the Fourth of July had been gloriously observed in the West by the capture of Vicksburg.

Back in Washington on Independence Day, Abraham Lincoln analyzed dispatches and wondered if General Meade would now go on to destroy the rebel army and end the war. As he sat on the White House stairs pondering the future, a friend from his Springfield past appeared before him. Lincoln hailed Archimedes C. Dickson cordially as "Dick" and talked with him for some time, learning among other things that his one-time crony was now in the lumber business at St. Louis. At last the President remarked that he was "busy just then" but wanted to see Dickson again, and he asked Dickson how long he would be in town. This gave Dickson his cue to introduce Lincoln to the Absterdam shell, which was to become Lincoln's last notable project in the field of weapons.

Arriving from France nearly twenty years before, one John Absterdam had set himself up as a mechanical engineer, and in May 1862 had patented a mixture of sulphur and plumbago as a lubricant for journal boxes. Presently it occurred to him that his mixture would do to lubricate projectiles also. Thumbing through the Army Ordnance Manual, Absterdam came across a description of Major Alexander Dyer's rifle shell, distinguished chiefly by a cup or sabot of soft metal at the base, which was supposed to expand and take the grooves like a Minié bullet. In August 1862, at about the time of Second Bull Run, the Frenchman patented a shell based on the Dyer model but girdled with two or three raised bands of the Absterdam lubricant, intended both to lubricate the gun and to keep the shell in line with the bore.

In the spring of 1863 Absterdam went to St. Louis and persuaded Colonel Callender, the chief ordnance officer of that military department, to try a few of his patent shells. The colonel did not like them. The grooves which held the lubricating bands weakened the shell, he insisted; the shells were hard to load after a few rounds; and worst of all, fragments of the bands flew off one shell in flight—not an effect which Union troops underneath would be apt to applaud.

So Absterdam changed his approach and began trading shares in his shell for influence in selling it. James Eads, the gunboat designer, for example, was to get a share in profits from Navy orders. Orloff A. Zane, a quartermaster clerk at St. Louis who claimed acquaintance with General Rosecrans and other officials, received a half interest in future sales to the Western armies. When Archimedes Dickson got a half interest in Eastern orders on the grounds of his influence with Lincoln, Dickson and Zane consolidated their allotments into a half share of all Army orders for the shell. This was the business which had brought "Dick" Dickson to the White House on the momentous Fourth of July, 1863.

After Dickson had explained the alleged excellences of the Absterdam shell to the President, Lincoln assured him that "if there was any virtue in it he would do all he could." Confirmation of the President's good will came a day or two later. William Butler of Springfield, another old friend of Lincoln's who had been offered a cut of Absterdam profits, scrupulously withdrew from the venture on being told by Lincoln that he would do as much for Dickson "as for any other man that lived." And the President left orders for Dickson to be admitted at any time, although he advised his friend to come early in the morning if possible.

Dickson was quick to capitalize on Lincoln's attitude. When he asked the President for "a little order to test my shell," Lincoln told him he would have it. On July 10, as Lincoln grew increasingly despondent over Meade's failure to follow up the recent victory, Dickson, Zane and Absterdam all talked with the President at the Soldiers' Home; and next day Lincoln called at the Navy Ordnance Bureau and ordered a trial of the Absterdam shell "as soon as possible."

Shocking news came to Lincoln on the morning of July 14: Lee and his army had escaped unmolested across the Potomac. "There is bad faith somewhere," he burst out to the Secretary of the Navy. "What does it mean, Mr. Welles? Great God! what does it mean?" Two hours later, Welles found him lying on a sofa at the War Department, "completely absorbed, overwhelmed with the news . . . dejected and discouraged." Yet, on that very day, he went down to the Navy Yard and watched the firing of twenty Absterdam shells out over the river from a 6-pounder Army field gun. The officer in charge considered the results "admirable" and thought that Absterdam's patent bands would lubricate the gun just as well as grease. Lincoln threw his influence behind the shell; and after beating down the price by a third, General Ripley ordered a thousand Absterdam shells for extensive trials at West Point.

Now that the Confederacy had been sundered at Vicksburg and brought to a shuddering stop at Gettysburg, the final triumph of the Union was no longer in doubt, only the time of its coming. A month after Gettysburg, John Hay went with Lincoln to the photographic studio of Alexander Gardner. Lincoln, noted Hay was "in very good spirits"; and he told Hay "that the rebel power is at last beginning to disintegrate, that they will break into pieces if we only stand firm now." The new aspect of affairs had its bearing on ordnance policy. At last there was some validity to Ripley's long-standing contention that large orders for "fancy arms" would have to be received and paid for after the need for them had passed. And while Lincoln never voiced that idea in so many words, it must have been in his mind after Gettysburg and Vicksburg.

Ironically, it was just then, as Ripley's weapons policy began to come into its own, that Ripley himself began to slip. Captain George T. Balch, an ambitious officer more than thirty years Ripley's junior, had been attached to the Ordnance Office early in 1862 and had earned a reputation for hard efficiency. Ripley later heard rumors, "apparently well-founded," that Balch had begun plotting his chief's removal as early as August 1862. And Balch's machinations were not to be scorned, for something about the energetic captain took the fancy of both Stanton and Watson. By the summer of 1863 Watson was sending for Balch daily for information on Ordnance Office business and was making no secret of the fact that he had "no confidence whatever in General Ripley." Despite Balch's half-hearted protests against this undercutting of his superior, the practice continued while Ripley remained.

There were other straws in the wind. Reports began to come in during the summer, especially from Vicksburg, of defective artillery ammunition. The Parrott shells were said to be pitted with sand holes, some of which were filled with putty, others left undisguised. Small arms ammunition sent from Indianapolis was "rascally," the powder "worthless." Stanton was angry; and later in the summer, when Ripley reported against enlarging a contract for Gibbs carbines, the Secretary significantly referred the subject to Watson "for more careful examination."

Not even the multiplying signs of his own official doom could shake Ripley in his opposition to breech-loading rifles. Soon after Gettysburg, Colonel Berdan made a final effort to get Spencer rifles for his Sharpshooters. But his pushing ways had made too many enemies; and charges of cowardice, although dismissed by a court-martial, had cast a shadow on his reputation. Ripley found it easy to snarl the friendless colonel in red tape till he ceased to struggle. And while the Spencer rifles of Wilder's Lightning Brigade were spreading the breechloader gospel through the Army of the Cumberland, General Halleck suddenly began to insist that mounted infantry be armed only with such guns "as the Ordnance Department can furnish."

A week after this War Department backsliding, General Rousseau checked in again at Willard's; and a few days later, Christopher Spencer came on to Washington bearing a request from his company that Lincoln witness another demonstration of the Spencer rifle by its inventor. "We would suggest," added the company, "that as the Hon. Secretary of War, Gen. Halleck and others were knowing to the mishaps of our gun at its former trials before you . . . they should be present if possible."*

When he arrived at the White House with the aforementioned letter and a new Spencer rifle for the President, the inventor was ushered into the reception room, where he found Lincoln alone. Spencer took the gleaming repeater from its cloth case and handed it to Lincoln. After a thorough and knowing inspection, Lincoln asked Spencer to take it apart and show him "the inwardness of the thing." This done to Lincoln's satisfaction, he invited Spencer to

---

* This suggests that Lincoln had witnessed Berdan's accident with a Spencer rifle on Christmas Day, 1861. Christopher Spencer was in Washington and seeing Lincoln at that time.

come over at two the next afternoon, when "we will go out and see the thing shoot."

That same day General Rousseau called on Lincoln with the draft of an order giving Rousseau authority, with Rosecrans's consent, to mount his division and arm it with Sharps or Spencer rifles. Without formally signing the order, Lincoln sent it to Stanton with the endorsement "Sec. of War please see Gen. Rousseau at once"; and Stanton immediately ordered Ripley to find out how soon five thousand Sharps or Spencers could be procured for Rousseau, consistent with existing carbine contracts. Ripley wrote the two companies next day.

Tuesday, August 18, 1863, was a quiet day in the war. Meade and Lee watched each other warily in Virginia. Dahlgren's naval squadron lay outside Charleston Harbor in simmering futility. Rosecrans had finished the Tullahoma campaign and, after the usual interlude of bickering with the War Department, had set off along the road which would bring him to disaster at Chickamauga. In Washington the sun was bright and the sky blue, but the temperature stayed in the seventies most of the day; and when it did edge higher in midafternoon, a light breeze from the north picked up enough force to rustle trees and start the stars and stripes dancing over the Winder Building.

At two that afternoon Lincoln set out with his son Robert, his private secretary John Hay and Christopher Spencer along the shade-dappled walk that led from the White House to the War Department. While Robert went in to invite Stanton along, Lincoln entertained the others with some of his stories. Noticing a torn pocket in his black alpaca coat, he mended it with a pin taken from his waistcoat. "It seems to me," he said smiling, "that this does not look quite right for the Chief Magistrate of this mighty Republic." Robert emerged from the War Department and reported that Stanton was too busy to join them. "Well," commented Lincoln philosophically, "they do pretty much as they have a mind to over there." And off went the party to the Treasury Park.

The target was a board about six inches wide and three feet long with a black spot painted at each end. Lincoln placed his first shot to the left of the bull's eye and five inches low. His next hit the bull's eye, and working the lever rapidly, he put five more close to it. "Now," said he, "we will see the inventor try it." The board was reversed, and Spencer did what Hay called "some splendid shooting." "Well," said Lincoln, "you are younger than I am and have a better eye and steadier nerve." Young Hay's marksmanship was "lamentably bad," as he himself admitted, blaming it on his eyes. Hay noted in his diary:

An irrepressible patriot came up and talked about his son John who, when lying on his belly on a hilltop at Gettysburg, feeling the shot fly over him, like to lost his breath—felt himself puffing up like a toad—thought he would bust. Another, seeing the gun recoil slightly, said it wouldn't do; too much powder; a good piece of audience should not rekyle; if it did at all, it should rekyle a little forrid [forward].

General Rousseau left for the West that day, "the object of his mission . . . having been accomplished." But halcyon weather continued through the following day, and in the evening Lincoln was down in the Treasury Park again with his new rifle. Spencer never tired of describing in later years the "almost boyish eagerness with which the President . . . examined and tested 'the machine' in the White House grounds."

Rousseau presently had reason to believe that he had left a little too soon. The Sharps Company reported that it could supply no arms before January; and the Spencer Company wrote that while two thousand rifles would soon be available, they had been promised to the state of Massachusetts. The Bay State was willing to settle for the use of four thousand late model Springfields till January, when twenty-five hundred more Spencers would be ready; but although government warehouses were jammed with Springfields, Ripley ignored the offer and advised Stanton against buying any Spencer rifles at any time. A few days later, the dogged old

Chief of Ordnance coolly informed Rousseau that his Spencers could not be delivered before January and ought not to be ordered even for that date because of the need for carbines. "The authorities here," he added blandly, "will keep your request in mind."

Fortunately for Rousseau's plans, Lincoln, Stanton and Halleck had finally decided to remove Ripley, a step made easier by an act of Congress giving the President authority to retire officers of more than forty-five years service without recourse to a retiring board. Only the matter of Ripley's successor remained to be settled. Halleck suggested Major Rodman, but once again, as in 1862, the major's cannon patents were held to disqualify him. Stanton and Watson wanted to appoint the hard-driving Captain Balch. Lincoln favored his genial friend at the Washington Arsenal, Colonel George D. Ramsay.

The final choice was put off for more than two weeks, during which time Ripley's fate ceased to be a secret. A *New York Times* dispatch of September 2, 1863, reported the exile of "the old fogy Ripley . . . who combatted all new ideas in the fabrication of firearms, artillery and projectiles." Charles F. Raymond of Norwalk, Connecticut, whose ideas about bifurcated cannon had been coldly received by the outgoing chief, wrote Stanton to thank him "and congratulate the Country on the removal of that *old Fossell Fogy.*" At last, on September 15, 1863, at the age of sixty-nine, Brigadier General James W. Ripley was formally retired from active duty and assigned the nominal task of periodically inspecting the coastal defenses of New England.

With all that has been said of Ripley's shortcomings, perhaps there is room for a kinder verdict, that of Ripley's chief assistant, the gentle Captain James G. Benton. General Ripley (said Benton) had done his job "with integrity and with great zeal . . . He may have erred sometimes; and he may have created a great many enemies by refusing to adopt inventions which he thought were unfit or not suited to the service, or were too expensive. But I am very confident, in fact I know, that he was actuated solely by the interests of the service, because I have been in a position to know the fact."

As for the disagreement between Lincoln and Stanton over Ripley's successor, it had ended in a curious and, as it proved, an unworkable compromise.

Colonel Ramsay had long been *persona non grata* to Stanton. Back in May 1862, the irascible Secretary of War had ordered the removal of one of Ramsay's assistants after a misunderstanding about a shipment of ammunition. Boldly and at once, Ramsay took the young officer's part, got the Secretary to reconsider and had the satisfaction of seeing the officer prove his ability in later service. More serious and more daring was Ramsay's action just after Second Bull Run, when Stanton in a panic ordered all arsenal stores to be shipped to New York forthwith. Conscious of the disastrous effect such an order would have on Union morale, Ramsay deliberately disobeyed it, at the risk of his career and perhaps his life. All remained quiet at the arsenal. When General McClellan heard of Stanton's order, he had it countermanded at once; and next day Lincoln himself thanked Ramsay warmly for running his fearful risk. The weapons thus kept available to McClellan helped stave off defeat at Antietam two weeks later; and on the strength of that narrowly won victory, Lincoln issued his preliminary emancipation proclamation.

Now that Lincoln favored Ramsay as Chief of Ordnance, Stanton professed to have no confidence in the colonel's fitness for the post. When Lincoln brought up the question of seniority in opposition to Captain Balch, Stanton at last consented to Ramsay's appointment. But the Secretary insisted that Balch be made Ramsay's principal assistant and the real Chief of Ordnance in all but name. This suggestion seems to have been more of a gambit than a retreat. To be sure, Stanton had been successful with such an arrangement in the Adjutant General's office, but in that case the titular chief had been assigned to duties away from Washington. With Ramsay and Balch working side by side, a clash was inevitable; and Stanton doubtless hoped to have Ramsay at his mercy when the test came. The Stantonian proposition was so unfair to Ramsay that even Captain Balch, who had long been a close friend of the Ramsay family, had qualms of conscience when he heard of it. But Watson called on him to make the sacrifice for the nation's sake, and Balch patriotically consented.

Thus, to his astonishment, Colonel Ramsay was ordered to "take charge" of the Ordnance Office. No one told him that he was to be only a figurehead. He knew nothing of Stanton's plans for Balch. Ramsay entered upon his duties, he said later, "with all the zeal and honesty of disposition that a man could have, feeling the extraordinary responsibility which had been so unexpectedly devolved upon me, and which I should have declined if an opportunity had presented itself." But Captain Balch, having assumed the role of puppeteer, gathered the strings in hand immediately by assigning Captain Benton to command the Washington Arsenal and Colonel Maynadier to duty outside the capital. When Ramsay first took his seat at General Ripley's old desk, therefore, he faced a stack of unsigned papers on which only Balch could now advise him.

Ramsay had not been made Chief of Ordnance, as Stanton explicitly pointed out to him; he had only been ordered to relieve General Ripley; and so, for official business, he adopted the style of "Acting Chief of Ordnance." At dusk a week or so later Stanton summoned him on routine business. In the Secretary's murky office Ramsay managed to identify Governor Andrew of Massachusetts. Indulging his taste for theatrics, Stanton turned to Andrew and said, "Let me introduce you to our new Chief of Ordnance." This was how Ramsay first learned that he was to be more than a temporary stopgap.

Afterward the colonel went home to the arsenal and broke the news to his wife. The couple sat alone in the gathering night. "I remember," said Ramsay later, "how sad the fact made us: that we were about to lose our place to go into this other position." Theirs was a prophetic sadness.

General Rousseau, at least, was a decided gainer by the recent change. Two weeks after Ripley's removal, Watson ordered Ramsay to accept the offer of Massachusetts and send Rousseau half of the two thousand Spencers thus acquired. Since the War Department, as late as the following December, was opposed to arming mounted infantry with such guns, it is not hard to see the hand of Abraham Lincoln in that order.

CHAPTER 19

Farewell to Arms

ON JUNE 25, 1863, THE DAY AFTER DAHL-
gren left for his new command, Harry Wise took over as Chief of
the Navy Ordnance Bureau. Like Dahlgren, the merry little globe-
trotter dreamed of maritime glory, but he had suffered an injury in
the service which would have made sea duty difficult. Besides, in
appointing him, Lincoln felt that he had "got the right peg in the
right hole." Despite his incorrigible levity, Wise made an excellent
administrator—much better than Dahlgren, in the opinion of nearly all Navy officers. Moreover, he worked well in that sphere of
policy now called "public relations." Most inventors, according to
the *Scientific American,* liked Wise and found in him a "willingness and favorable disposition toward new inventions which it
would be well for others [meaning Ripley] to adopt."

Still, Dahlgren's departure cost Lincoln his right-hand man in
ordnance matters. Only once more was there a revival of the old
relationship, early in 1864, when Lincoln sent a New York sea
captain named Lavender down to Charleston with a device for removing underwater obstructions.* Harry Wise was a pleasant companion and a good administrator, yet he had no reputation for professional brillance. This may have been one reason why Lincoln

---

* Dahlgren liked the device and was "much pleased" to get Lincoln's note, but
nothing came of it.

seldom consulted him on new weapons. Another may have been that Lincoln took little interest in new weapons after the summer of 1863, what with Ripley out of the way and the war in its latter stages.

One inventor to feel the change was Joseph Francis, who had done much to save lives with his corrugated iron lifeboat. Francis had also devised an amphibious pontoon wagon with iron sides thick enough to deflect bullets. In April 1863, after being knighted by Czar Alexander II and the Emperor Napoleon III for his inventions and services, he offered his pontoons to the American Emancipator. Nearly a year later, when Francis came back to report that the War Department would do nothing for him, Lincoln tried to open a way for the inventor. But when Stanton proved obstinate, Lincoln promptly let the matter drop.

Professor Henry Wurtz, a well-known chemist and geologist who had been one of Joseph Henry's star pupils at Princeton, had developed a chemical compound which, he claimed, would cause gunpowder to generate increasingly greater pressure as the projectile moved along the bore of the cannon—an effect much to be desired. After what seemed like encouraging experiments in the summer of 1863, Wurtz ran into opposition from the Ordnance Department. Perhaps because of Joseph Henry's intercession, Lincoln ordered still another trial, which was made near Philadelphia in December. On the fourth firing with about fifty spectators gathered around it the test gun, an eight-inch columbiad, burst into small fragments. Miraculously, no one was injured. After the report went to Lincoln, he bothered no more with "accelerating cartridges," and the professor turned his undoubted talents to more peaceable uses.

The trial of Professor Wurtz's cartridge was the last such new project undertaken by Lincoln. One sweltering June night in 1864, however, he did drive out to the Navy Yard with ex-Senator Browning, Assistant Secretary Fox and others, to see the firing of signal rockets from field artillery. Several went up with good results, trailing fire across the night sky, but the last one exploded halfway in its course and fell to the water. "Well," said Lincoln, "small potatoes and few in a hill."

That phrase would also have fitted the affair of Captain Isaac Diller's powder, which after high promise had fizzled out as dismally as the Navy Yard rocket.

To his cheerful predictions for the Diller powder, Lieutenant Commander Jeffers had attached the condition "if it preserves its properties after graining." That "if" turned out to be a big one. The powder had to be packed into hard grains in order to be transported and stored safely. Dr. Wetherill labored to grain it, but the process was prohibitively expensive. He modified the formula to make graining easier, but experiments in October 1863 with forty pounds of the new formula showed it to be too unstable for safe storage. Jeffers and Laidley, the Army and Navy representatives, suggested that experiments with larger amounts might change their findings. Captain Diller had spent all the money allotted him by Lincoln and had gone into debt on his own account. So, for the eighth time since April, he called at the White House for instructions.

This time, Lincoln showed scant enthusiasm. Prodded by Dahlgren, American firms were now making gunpowder out of Chilean sodium nitrate instead of saltpeter from British India. The Army's niter stock pile had reached a comfortable eight million pounds. A month before, the last real threat of war with England had ended. In short, Diller's chlorate-based powder was no longer needed. Although not rejecting Diller's request for funds in so many words, Lincoln shifted the conversation to Springfield politics. "So that party is settled," commented Lieutenant Commander Jeffers.

In contrast, the "Absterdam party" (as it came to be called) was far from settled.

Unable to interest field commanders in his shell during the summer of 1863, Absterdam had enlarged his following in the usual way: by promising contingent fees to persons of influence. Ex-

Senator Browning, Senator Lane of Kansas and even young Lieutenant George Ramsay, nephew and namesake of the new Chief of Ordnance, were mustered into the Absterdam service. Congressman John A. Bingham of Ohio, having some influence with Stanton, undertook to get a large order if Lincoln would sign a certain prescribed note. Early one morning Archimedes Dickson found Lincoln in his office; and after the President had drunk a cup of coffee, he obligingly copied off Bingham's note on a card and signed it. Stanton, to Bingham's surprise, blocked the deal—as Lincoln had doubtless anticipated he would.

There were others in the "Absterdam party." Ben Butler heard of twelve, and remarked in mock awe that it was "the same number as the apostles." Next to Dickson, Absterdam's most diligent henchman was Thomas H. Ford, a Mexican War veteran and former lieutenant governor of Ohio. Ford had long been intimate with party leaders—Thurlow Weed, among others—but his luck and his health had both failed him by 1861, and he had appealed piteously to Lincoln for an office. Unfortunately for both Ford and the Union, Lincoln did not find him a place. As a clerk, Ford could have done little worse than misfile correspondence. Denied a Federal clerkship, he pulled strings to get an Ohio volunteer commission; and as the sickly commander of two thousand troops on Maryland Heights near Harper's Ferry in 1862, he yielded the Heights to Stonewall Jackson. Ford was censured and dismissed from the service, and spent the few years left to him as a second-rate Washington attorney. His usefulness to the Absterdam party came from his employment as political errand boy for Ben Butler, a function which gave him access to Lincoln.

The Absterdam party discovered, long before Ramsay did, that "Mr. Balch was the man we had to deal with." They also found the testy captain hard to get at. Indirect influence failed. So did the direct approach by Zane, Ford and Browning, who made the winter of 1863-1864 exceedingly unpleasant for Balch. After some of the Absterdam shells ordered by Ripley had been tested, the President himself sent along the report to be examined "for my friend

A. C. Dickson." But because four of the shells had lost their sulphur-plumbago bands in flight, Balch would not give an order for more.

Dickson and Zane next made a flank attack by way of Major Theodore T. S. Laidley, commandant of the Frankford Arsenal, who wanted his own fuse igniter adopted and thought he saw the way to this when Dickson flaunted a Lincoln letter before him. Balch fought against the partners' demand for trials at Frankford, until Lincoln walked over to the Winder Building with Dickson and personally ordered the trials made. "It made Balch mad and General Ramsay mad," recalled Dickson gleefully. The maneuver backfired, however. Laidley praised the fundamental design of the shell—Major Dyer's design—and took pains to state that "the fuze is lighted (with certainty) by means of the device recently proposed by me." But like Colonel Callender months before, Laidley deprecated the weakening effect of Absterdam's grooves and the fragmentation of the Absterdam lubricating bands.

After the Laidley report came through, ex-Senator Browning paid a call on Lincoln and a few days later went with him to the Ordnance Office. Lincoln wanted "to have some understanding about this thing," recalled Balch in later years. "We put it on technical grounds, and he wanted to understand, if possible, what those grounds were. . . . He had had a full understanding of the other side, and he proposed to get our view." After swapping pleasantries with Ramsay, Lincoln asked the general to "take up those papers now, and go on and explain this whole matter." When Ramsay explained that Balch knew more about it, Lincoln sat down purposefully at Balch's desk, spread "those papers" out before him, and spent fully an hour going over the affair with the captain. Lincoln was not content to discuss it from the angle of public business alone. He wanted enlightenment on various technical expressions in the Laidley report—the "drift of the projectile," for instance—and he listened attentively to Balch's elaborate explanations of them. At last Lincoln rose to leave, expressing himself, according to Balch, as "perfectly satisfied with the course which General Ramsay and myself, representing the bureau, had taken in the matter. . . . He said that he was very anxious to have these gentlemen get an order, but he did not wish to interfere in the regular course of business; that we were the judges of its value, and he would leave the matter there."

Meanwhile, unknown to Dickson and Zane, their friend and client Absterdam was busily hoodwinking them. The Frenchman added antimony to his sulphur-plumbago mixture so that the untrustworthy bands would expand in cooling and thus grip the shells more tightly. Enjoining Balch to secrecy, he persuaded the captain to order fifty of the new type for trial. Then he took steps to secure a separate patent on the improved shell. Absterdam's scheme was to let Dickson and Zane pressure Lincoln into ordering still another trial, which the wily Frenchman would see was made with the improved shell. Then, when an order had been given, Absterdam would inform his partners that the shell tested was his exclusively, and that they had no rights or interest in it.

Events fell out just as the crafty inventor had planned. Early in February 1864, having digested Balch's lesson in ballistics, Lincoln ordered new trials of the Absterdam shell at the Washington Arsenal, where he could see them for himself.

The first day of the trials dawned gray and chill. Gale winds whistled through Washington in midmorning, and Major Benton wired from the arsenal to ask if the President would indeed be down that afternoon. By three o'clock the winds, although still strong, had slackened; and pallid sunlight broke through now and then. Lincoln and Ramsay drove down on schedule, to be joined presently by Dickson, Zane, Browning, Ford and others of the faithful. Absterdam had not yet arrived from Philadelphia, but his fifty improved shells were on hand. After a dozen had been fired out over the river, further testing was postponed for a calmer day. On February 8 Benton fired ten more rounds. On the following day, Lincoln came down again. Only a few ragged cirrus clouds

drifted across the winter sky, and the breeze was scarcely percep-
tible. Ten more of the new shells were fired with results that "very
much gratified" Lincoln and even impressed Ramsay.

A few days later Absterdam enlightened Dickson and Zane as to
their status, only to find the partners more resourceful than he had
supposed. They got Lincoln to have Major Benton "finish the trial
of the Absterdam projectile"; and on March 2 Benton fired ten
shells of the *old* type, furnished by Dickson and Zane. Unaware of
the difference, Benton unwittingly played the partners' game by
referring to all the shells in all three trials as "the Absterdam projectile," ranking them with "the best rifle projectiles now used in
our service," and recommending a trial of them in the field. Before
the day ended, Dickson and Zane proposed to furnish 720,000 of
the "Absterdam projectile," slyly omitting to specify which type.
Lincoln, still unaware of the plot and counterplot, was, fortunately,
not prepared to be so extravagant. He merely wrote a note to Ramsay: "Will a number of the Absterdam shells, or projectiles, be
placed in the hands of the troops for trial, as recommended by Captain Benton in his report of March 3d?"

By now, Ramsay knew about the schism in the Absterdam party,
and he gave this as one reason for not ordering any "Absterdam
projectiles" just then. His other was the price asked—fifteen per
cent above the price of Hotchkiss shells. Lincoln was no respecter
of red tape. On Ramsay's letter he wrote:

I think the Absterdam projectile is too good a thing to be lost to
the services, and if offered at the Hotchkiss prices, and not in excessive quantities, nor unreasonable terms in other respects, by
either or both parties to the patent controversy, take it, so that the
test be fully made—I am for the government having the best articles, in spite of patent controversies.

This memorandum never reached Ramsay. What the Chief of
Ordnance actually received two days later was a note, written by
Lincoln in Dickson's presence, in almost the same words—except
for one significant change. Instead of writing "if offered . . . by

either or both parties to the patent controversy," Lincoln now wrote "if offered by Dickson and Zane." Ramsay took this as a command; and so, over the strenuous objections of both Absterdam and Balch, he gave Dickson and Zane an order for four thousand shells at Hotchkiss prices.

Balch declared open war on Dickson. "He would not ask me to take a seat when I went into his office," complained the latter. More damagingly, Balch put a clause in the Dickson-Zane contract requiring the shells to be "similar in every respect" to those fired in Lincoln's presence—in other words, those covered by Absterdam's second patent. Absterdam followed through with an injunction restraining Dickson and Zane from making that type of shell. Nevertheless, the partners went ahead, counting on Lincoln to sustain them. "President Lincoln . . . told me," said Dickson, "if I got into trouble to come to him, and if there was anything wrong he would see that I was righted; he had seen the shell tested here and liked it, and said he was willing to see me have a fair show with it."

While Absterdam grappled with Dickson and Zane, General Ramsay was coming to grips with Captain Balch.

The Ordnance Corps had speedily recognized the work of Captain Balch in a series of arrogant and officious decrees innocently signed by General Ramsay. The good-hearted general was slower in awakening. It took him all of four months to discover that Balch was something more than his old friend and chief administrative prop. He found this out in February 1864, when he disagreed with his "assistant" on an endorsement and Balch tendered his resignation. Secretary Stanton taught Ramsay his place, first by vetoing every name that Ramsay suggested as a replacement for Balch, then by giving Ramsay just one week in which to make up with Balch or be relieved from command. After being apprized of all this by Stanton, Balch "had a friendly conversation" with Ramsay, and "the matter was adjusted."

It was a fragile adjustment, and Ramsay's position grew increasingly precarious. Assistant Secretary Watson's fluctuating health at last seemed permanently broken. By January 1864 he was declining to walk across Seventeenth Street because of his "very sore lungs," and at the end of June he took final leave of the War Department. Stanton had depended on Watson in ordnance matters. "While Mr. Watson was there," said Stanton, "I considered him to be an expert. I was not an expert myself." Now Stanton had to leave more to the discretion of the head of the Ordnance Department. Yet who *was* head of the Ordnance Department? Ramsay and his fellow officers of the Ordnance Corps regarded Captain Balch as an enemy and shunned him as far as they could. Ramsay, in turn, was bombarded with searching inquiries about powder, niter, cartridges, ammunition and arsenal operations, all implying negligence on Ramsay's part, all signed by Stanton and all in Balch's handwriting. "I think," said Ramsay later, "that no man could have sustained himself under the pressure which was brought to bear upon me."

"There is a row between General Ramsay and Balch," wrote Major Laidley to his friend Archimedes Dickson early in August. "Cannot you do something to render certain the result? Do for mercy's sake." Since Laidley and Balch were bitter enemies, Dickson knew what the major meant. And since Dickson likewise detested Balch, he was quick to take Laidley's hint. "I would go and tell Mr. Lincoln I thought something was wrong," related Dickson afterward. "I just talked to him like I used to at Springfield. Says I, 'I think there is stealing going on. I think you had better turn some of them out.' Says he, 'Dick, I would do it, but I am afraid I might get a worse set in.' "

Presently Captain Balch again offered his resignation. Again it was not accepted. Instead, on September 12, 1864, Ramsay was relieved of his command and assigned, as Ripley had been, to the sinecure of inspecting coastal armaments.

Balch sped Ramsay on his way with what the latter called "an array of statistics" to prove that the Ordnance Department had been badly managed since the start of the war. This stung Ramsay to a spirited valedictory. "No department of the government," he informed Stanton, "has since and during the rebellion furnished its supplies more fully, more promptly, or more satisfactorily to the troops in the field. Not a cent . . . has been misapplied or wasted, so far as the Ordnance Bureau has had the power to control its application." And in later years, the old general insisted that "if I had been allowed my own assistants, the aid I required and the sympathy I required, I should have conducted that office in the most perfect manner; and I will say that when I left it I left it in perfect condition."

Archimedes Dickson's advice to Lincoln on how to deal with the Ordnance Department had included a suggestion as to the proper chief: Major Alexander B. Dyer, commandant of the Springfield Armory, the same man who had been offered the post two years before and had declined it. Laidley assured Dickson that Major Dyer would deal fairly with the Absterdam shell; and this seemed logical, for after all, the shell was based on Dyer's own design. "I went and told Mr. Lincoln what I thought," testified Dickson. "Says he, 'I think I will make that move.' " Next day Dyer was appointed, and this time he accepted—"in obedience," as he put it, "to the orders of my superior and from a sense of duty." Dickson recalled, "When we got General Dyer in there we thought we had the thing pretty square."

But Dickson had read too much into Lincoln's remark. For Dyer had actually been chosen as Ramsay's eventual successor as far back as March, when Watson began his gradual withdrawal from the Department; and the choice had been made by Stanton and Watson, not Lincoln. Stanton, in fact, had rather brusquely notified Lincoln that the appointment was based on merit, not personalities or politics, and that he wanted no interference with it on political grounds. Lincoln had no quarrel with that proposition. He took care, however, to interview Watson on the subject. "He wished to know," recalled Watson, "if I had fully examined the question . . . and if I was very clear in my opinion that . . . Dyer was the proper officer; because he was aware, as well as the Secretary of War and myself, that a very efficient and active man was required in the Ordnance Office. . . . He said he had some reluctance, upon one ground only, viz., that he did not believe there was another officer in the ordnance corps who was capable of managing the Springfield armory as efficiently as General Dyer had, and he did not like to take him away from there." Watson assured Lincoln that the rifle supply was now ample, that the armory was "fully organized and in efficient operation" and that Dyer was needed in Washington. This satisfied Lincoln.

Events conspired to make Dickson and Zane believe that Dyer was their man. The new chief assigned Balch to special duty at West Point, away from the Ordnance Office; and Laidley was given Dyer's coveted post as commandant at Springfield. Still more to the point was an order from Dyer for twenty thousand "Absterdam shells" at a price of more than forty thousand dollars. Interpreting this as Dyer's payment to them for his promotion, the two partners set about swindling the government—and as fast as possible, for Absterdam's injunction was hanging over them. Although the sample given them to follow was of Absterdam's second type, the partners' shells were all of the first type. The lubricating bands were of "a most brittle and miserable alloy . . . more of the character of sand than of any metal." At least four-fifths of the fuse plugs were so loose that the flame communicated directly with the bursting charge, and some could be pulled out by the fingers without unscrewing. Most of the shells were underweight by as much as a third; and since the contract did not specify that the case shot had to be filled with bullets (which were what made it "case shot"), Dickson and Zane delivered them empty and charged full price. Because of these and similar economies, Dickson and Zane made the shells for less than half what they charged the government. Unfortunately for the government, a sub-inspector, through what Dyer called "gross carelessness or fraudulent complicity," passed more than twelve thousand of the shells; and so the government eventually had to pay for them.

While the partners were thus occupied, unfavorable reports be-

gan coming in on the four thousand shells ordered from them by
Ramsay in March: reports from Captain Balch at West Point, from
Captain Benét at Frankford, and most damaging of all, from the
Petersburg front, where the firing was stopped because "it was
feared that the bad practice might encourage the rebels." Dickson
found General Dyer "rather out of humor," and scornful of Dickson's offer of political influence toward his Senate confirmation. "I
did not make much headway with him afterwards," said Dickson,
"none, in fact. . . . I told General Dyer on one or two occasions I
supposed I would have to call on the President."

But Dickson's influence with Lincoln was about played out. Late
in December shells made by the partners under Dyer's order began
arriving at the Washington Arsenal and proved to be incredibly
bad. Early in January 1865 Dyer suspended further receipt of the
Dickson-Zane shells. Since Absterdam's new shells had just done
well in testing, Dyer ordered twenty thousand from the inventor
instead, and in March about thirty thousand more.* It turned out, in
other words, that Lincoln had picked the right shell but the wrong
men.

One more Lincoln-sponsored weapon remained to be judged:
the built-up, rifled, wrought-iron cannon of Horatio Ames.

Lincoln had given Ames and Brandegee his word, and so when
the first seven-inch Ames gun was ready at the end of August 1864,
Lincoln accordingly set up a three-man Army-Navy board to test
it at Bridgeport, Connecticut. The bureaucrats took a petulant view
of the case. "What does Lincoln know about a gun?" asked one,
not pausing for an answer. And Captain Wise wrote privately to
the Navy's representative: "We wish to keep clear of this Ames
matter. We have had quite enough of it and as a million of dollars
is of some importance we would rather the Army paid the bill."

Whatever the bureaucrats thought, Lincoln was no easy mark.
While Ames prepared to bombard Long Island Sound, General

---

* Actually forty-eight thousand, but more than a third of the order was canceled in postwar retrenchment.

Ben Butler asked Lincoln for one or two of the guns to use immediately against an enemy ironclad on the James River. Lincoln replied firmly: "The Ames guns I am under promise to pay, or rather to advise paying, a very high price for, provided they bear the test, and they are not yet tested, though I believe in process of being tested. I could not be justified to pay the extraordinary price without the testing. I shall be happy to let you have some of them so soon as I can." Butler kept pressing for Ames guns, spurred on by Pet Halsted, but before any were ready he had vanished forever from the military scene.

Late in October Major General Quincy A. Gillmore, president of the board, transmitted the report, a formidable sheaf which included minute data on every one of the seven hundred rounds fired. Glancing at the bulky documents, Lincoln exclaimed, "I should want a new lease of life to read this through!" He threw the report down on the table. "Why can't a committee of this kind occasionally exhibit a grain of common sense? If I send a man to buy a horse for me, I expect him to tell me his *'points'*—not how many *hairs* there are in his tail."And he had Gillmore summoned to Washington "without delay." When Gillmore arrived, he told the President that Ames's cannon were stronger and tougher than any of their size, in or out of the service. They would be exceedingly useful as long range guns; and they would not burst—as some of the heavy Parrotts had started to do, killing some men and demoralizing all their gun crews. After that Lincoln must have felt that he had bought the right horse. So did Assistant Secretary Fox and even Captain Wise, who in the face of the Parrott-gun disasters finally turned to the Ames guns as the Navy's only hope.

Lincoln's conditions had been met; and by the end of May 1865 thirteen Ames guns had been accepted, the other two having burst in proof because of imperfect welds at the breech. Eventually Ames was paid a little more than $215,000. But the war had already ended before any of the big guns could fire a shot against the Confederates. Late in 1865 the Chief of Ordnance condemned the guns as unreliable. And presently the Bessemer and open hearth processes outmoded wrought-iron guns by making steel cheap, dependable and easy to handle.

Did Horatio Ames make a good thing out of the money paid him on Lincoln's order? His own testimony is sufficient answer. "If you," he wrote a fellow contractor in 1868, "had worked seven years with these puppies, and had lost $300,000 and the use of your works that could have made $300,000 more, you would have felt weak in the knees, too." By the time he died in 1871, Horatio Ames had lost his ironworks and was living on the largess of his nephew Oliver.

Although Lincoln himself turned away from them, certain new weapons for which he stood as godfather went on in their military careers—some obscurely, some bizarrely, some triumphantly.

The war record of the Woodruff guns, bought by Lincoln for the 6th Illinois Cavalry, fell short of the heroic. If any of the little cannon went along with the 6th Illinois on Grierson's famous raid in April 1863, their performance was evidently not worth reporting. The 4th Iowa Cavalry somehow acquired three Woodruff guns, and Private "Cy" Washburn took charge of them with great pride. But Private Washburn's little battery was "never known to hit anything, and never served any useful purpose, except in promoting cheerfulness in the regiment." In Arkansas one day a detachment of the 4th Iowa in search of provisions spied a party of rebels on the other side of an impassable creek and sent over a few shots from a Woodruff gun. The only Iowa casualty was Private Benoni Kellogg, who was killed. His body, lashed to the gun, was brought into camp and buried with honors. Confederate casualties in the encounter were unknown; and when the 4th Iowa moved on shortly afterward, Private Washburn was deprived of his guns. The only word of them thereafter is an ordnance return from the Department of the Missouri, showing two on hand late in 1864.

The Ellsworth guns were gone, but not forgotten. Major Kingsbury, exiled to the Great Plains by Ripley, told his commanding general, Alfred Sully, about the little cannon; and General Sully asked the Ordnance Department for some early in 1864. He wrote:

From their description, I should judge [that] . . . I could make good use of them in arming the block houses erected & about to be erected in the Upper Missouri river, and as an armament to the boats expected to be sent up the Missouri river from St. Louis next spring.

But the Plains Indians were safe from the Honorable Eli Thayer's "little breech-loading cannons," none of which could be found at the Washington Arsenal.

The Ellsworth guns have their place in history, nevertheless. Except for a single 70-pounder Whitworth, bought in England by Minister Adams in May 1862, Lincoln's little cannon were the only breech-loading artillery purchased by the Federal Government during the Civil War.

As for explosive bullets or "musket shells," General Grant denounced their alleged use by the rebels at Vicksburg as "barbarous, because they produce increased suffering without any corresponding advantage to those using them," and the *Scientific American* was of like mind. Both were still unaware, it seems, of Watson's Yuletide order of 1862 for the Gardiner bullets, which were used later both in Sherman's march through Georgia and in Grant's Richmond campaign. Watson's order was the last by Union authorities. After the Civil War, European nations outlawed such bullets; and in 1868 General Dyer, as Chief of Ordnance, condemned them as "inexcusable among any people above the grade of ignorant savages."

The coffee-mill guns died hard. In October 1863 John H. Schenck, an associate of Edward Nugent, announced himself as their new proprietor and complained that those ordered by Rosecrans had not yet reached that officer's successor, General George H. Thomas, "who highly approves of them." Although sixteen of the machine guns remained on hand at the Washington Arsenal, the Ordnance Office ignored Schenck's complaints, as well as his suggestion that the guns be carried on horseback by cavalry and mounted infantry, ready for swift dismounting and use. Ten, however, were sent to General Butler in February 1864 when he requested them for use on boat service up and down the James River.

Lincoln's last recorded comment on the coffee-mill guns had to do with the specimen given Colonel Van Wyck at the start of the Peninsula Campaign. As Frederick Avery had feared, that gun was not paid for while Ripley headed the Ordnance Office. In October 1864 the dispute came before Lincoln who said, according to Avery's representative, "that if it can be shown that the gun has been used in the service, it ought to be paid for; to the end that innocent parties may not suffer for doing what was really for the good of the service." Avery furnished the required proof, and on August 3, 1865, the American Arms Company at last received payment of $788.58. That, oddly enough, was the very day on which thirteen coffee-mill guns fetched from $5 to $8 apiece in a sale of old ordnance at Fortress Monroe.

Despite the Swamp Angel fiasco, incendiary warfare was not quite dead. In January 1864, by way of a last fling, twenty incendiary shells were thrown into Charleston, "causing a considerable conflagration" according to one report. A month or so later, some rebel guerrillas fired incendiary shells into the steamer *Emma*, fifteen miles south of Helena, Arkansas, but the ensuing blaze was doused in good time. And in July Ben Butler, that insatiable patron of military novelties, enlivened the siege of Petersburg by having incendiary mortar shells fired from a railroad flatcar.

It was Butler to whom Pet Halsted turned when Lincoln lost interest in incendiary shells. In October 1864 Halsted introduced Alfred Berney to Butler and suggested that "a small sprinkling of Hell-fire will do the Imps on the other side a power of good just about this time." Butler was receptive; and in November Halsted arranged a formidable concentration of generals—Grant, Meade, Butler, Crawford, and Warren, among others—to see a demonstration of Berney's liquid near Dutch Gap in Butler's command. (Butler invited Admiral Porter also, but Mrs. Porter's burnt child now shunned the Greek fire.) When darkness came, a shell was exploded among some bushes, setting them all ablaze. "They've got the fuses to work well now," remarked Grant in his placid way. "They tried the shells on three houses, the other side of the river, and burnt them all without difficulty." ("Good thing for the owners!" thought an ironic colonel.) Then Berney turned his flame thrower on a little stream and transformed it into a rivulet of fire. "It was a beautiful sight," recalled the meditative colonel, "and like the hell of the poets, with an unquenchable fire and columns of black smoke rolling up." Butler insisted that he could hold a redoubt with only five men and a small garden engine, to which Meade objected that the flame thrower had a rather limited range as compared to infantry rifles.

Notwithstanding the gibes of Meade, Butler ordered about fifteen hundred gallons of Berney's fluid and eight rotary pumps complete with couplings, hoses, nozzles and other appurtenances. These reached Bermuda Hundred early in February 1865 and may therefore have seen action. But the unkind fate that hovered over incendiary inventors had swooped down a month before and carried Ben Butler off to civil life. The day of the Berney shell was over, and its inventor passes from the stage of history as publisher of a short-lived magazine devoted to household hints.

One momentous development wiped out the score of all these disappointments. Lincoln lived to see himself proved tremendously right about breech-loading rifles.

Three years of hard campaigning demonstrated to Berdan's men that they had been wise to insist on the Sharps, even to the point of mutiny. After their bumptious founder resigned early in 1864, the Sharpshooters and their breechloaders continued to refute the arguments of the muzzle-loader faction.

To begin with, the gun was safe for its users. "I never knew of an accident occurring by premature discharge of a Sharps rifle," wrote the regimental historian after the war.

It consistently outdid the Springfield rifle in range. Although the

Sharps was sighted only up to a thousand yards, some of Berdan's men experimented with whittled sights at Todd's Tavern, Virginia, in 1864 and managed to fire with fair accuracy at fifteen hundred yards. The tighter-fitting breechloader bullets came out of the muzzle with greater speed than those of muzzle-loaders. Rebels opposite the Sharpshooters in the Petersburg trenches could tell the "forced balls" by their sound and the fact that they hit before the report of the gun came along; and, said one Confederate, "you can just bet your boots we were mighty careful how we got in their way."

The Sharps were accurate. At Kelly's Ford on the Rappahannock in November 1863 two Sharpshooters in different companies aimed at and hit the same retreating rebel at seven hundred yards. An Alabama rifleman, captured in the following year, told the Sharpshooters ruefully that in his lines a man could get a furlough just by holding up his hand, and was lucky if he got to the rear without an extension.

Although other companies and regiments were later armed with Sharps by their state governments or at their own expense, it was Berdan's corps that caught the public's fancy, stirred the envy of fellow soldiers and aroused an irresistible demand for breechloaders among Union troops. By his support of Berdan in the fight for breechloaders, Abraham Lincoln had thus helped to open the way for a revolution in the tools of war.

In Northern Georgia, near a dark stream which the Indians had named "Chickamauga," the River of Death, there was a small field bordered by woods and traversed by a drainage ditch. One fine day in September 1863, as the veterans of Longstreet's corps pushed warily across the open field, a blast of rifle fire tore out of the woods and through the September sunlight. While they lived, the startled Confederates heard a new and terrible sound, not the familiar volleying of muzzle-loaders, rattling and rolling and dying away like the intermittent crash of brick walls in a fire, but a steady roar, a torrent of fire and lead. They had run up against the Spencer repeating rifles of Wilder's Lightning Brigade. And as Wilder's men worked their Spencers in the woods, they saw a strange sight: "the head of the column, as it was pushed on by those behind, appeared to melt away or sink into the earth, for, though continually moving, it got no nearer." The rebels broke and fell back, were rallied and pushed forward, and at last found shelter in the drainage ditch—until a pair of Federal 10-pounders scoured its length with double-shotted canister. "They fell in heaps," said Colonel Wilder, "and I had it in my heart to order the firing to cease to end the awful sight." But he gave no order, and when silence fell at last, broken only by the moans of the wounded, "one could have walked for two hundred yards down that ditch on dead rebels without touching the ground."

Lovell Rousseau's men, after getting their Spencers, likewise became famous for their exploits. In July 1864 eight companies from Sherman's army went out on a raid in Alabama, supported by two companies of Rousseau's brigade. At Chehaw Station they ran into a strong force of rebels, who ensconced themselves in a ravine and turned a heavy fire on their attackers. Rousseau's men flanked the rebels, "pouring in a murderous fire with their Spencer rifles," while the 5th Iowa made a frontal assault. The rebels fled, leaving over forty dead and many wounded; the 5th Iowa lost one killed and four wounded.

A feeling spread through the Union Army that Spencer rifles could end the war in a hurry, and some who carried them seemed of a mind to do the job alone. In July 1864, during the Battle of the Crater, First Sergeant Barnard A. Strasbaugh of the 3rd Maryland Infantry took a firm grip on his Spencer rifle and singlehandedly captured eleven prisoners, wounding two of them. So good were the Spencers that one might even be carried away by them and get into trouble, as Captain Benjamin Skinner of the 7th Connecticut discovered at Olustee, Florida, in February 1864. Captain Skinner led four unsupported companies, armed with Spencers, against five Confederate regiments. By the time their ammunition began to run low, Skinner's men were so deep in the enemy lines that they were receiving enemy fire from three sides and had to pull out in a hurry.

The possession of Spencers brought other hazards. The 63rd Pennsylvania were happy to turn in Austrian muzzle-loaders for Spencers in 1864. Their joy was tempered when they began hearing the order "Spencers to the front" and found that "their place was on the skirmish line much more often than was agreeable."

Even so, Spencer rifles were universally coveted. Ben Butler asked for three thousand and promised to give them only to "tried and deserving regiments" as "the prize of gallantry and good behavior." During Jubal Early's raid on Washington, General Ramsay asked an officer of the 6th Corps, which had come to help relieve the capital, if there was anything he could do for him and his men. "Yes," answered Colonel Edwards, "you can arm Colonel Montague's regiment [37th Massachusetts] with the Spencer rifle." Ramsay replied, "Make out your requisition for them, and I will"; and a few days later the Bay State boys had their repeaters.

The Spencer carbine, like the Spencer rifle, was the favorite of the Army from privates to generals. In April 1864 General George Thomas called it "the most effective weapon in use." A few days later General Ramsay wrote: "The demand for them is constant and for large quantities. It seems as if no soldier who had seen them used could be satisfied with any other." General James H. Wilson, the brilliant young chief of the new Cavalry Bureau, persuaded Ramsay to order all the Spencer carbines that could be turned out. So at Spencer's Tremont Street factory, rifles yielded still further to carbines.

The drays that rumbled over Boston cobblestones from Chickering's Building to the docks were fraught with victory. On July 4, 1864, forty Spencer carbines were issued to each company of the 4th Iowa Cavalry. From then on, the Iowans "*expected* to win, and even acquired a sort of habit of looking upon every approaching fight as 'a sure thing.'" The 2nd Iowa Cavalry got Spencer carbines too, and a rebel prisoner told them: "It is no use for us to fight you'ens with that kind of gun."

Men like General Ripley might persuade themselves that breech-loading carbines were good and breech-loading rifles bad, but the distinction was rather too fine for most to see. Through 1864 the *Scientific American* belabored the War Department for its failure to adopt breech-loading rifles as infantry weapons, and the *New York Times* took up the cry in June. That summer the British War Office set up a special committee to consider the subject; and on the basis of American experience—the experience of Berdan and Wilder and Captain Skinner—the committee recommended arming British infantry entirely with breech-loading arms. At last the United States War Department fell into line. In October 1864 General Ramsay's first annual report* announced that a breech-loading rifle would be adopted as the standard arm of the infantry, "so soon as the best model . . . can be established by full and thorough tests and trials, and the requisite modifications of the present machinery for fabricating that model can be made."

Abraham Lincoln had won his point—or rather the battle record of breechloaders had won it for him.

---

* Issued after Ramsay was relieved of command.

CHAPTER 20

A Peal of Ordnance

WINTER, THE FOURTH AND LAST WINTER
of the war, brought mud to Washington as usual; but it brought
hope too, and a dispatch from General Sherman to President Lincoln: "I beg to present you as a Christmas-gift the city of Savannah . . ." Guns boomed triumphantly in Franklin Square, and
bunting mocked the rain. Behind Sherman's army lay a track of
devastation from Atlanta to the sea. The Confederacy was in fragments, and the fragments grew smaller; while at Petersburg,
Grant's well-fed divisions pinioned Lee's wasting army in a grim
bear hug. The long misery was almost over.

At the New Year's Day reception in the White House, held on
Monday, January 2, 1865, a correspondent of the *Scientific American* pushed through the cheerful crowd for a brief talk with the
President, whom he found maintaining "a constant flow of genial
mirth." Appropriately, their talk was of the future. The correspondent was "much pleased to learn that in the midst of the many
cares that press upon the President he is not indifferent to the
claims of our inventors. Himself an inventor and patentee, he readily discerns the intrinsic value of all good inventions, not only to
the public service, but also in their application to the industrial
arts generally, and he will do all in his power to encourage and to
promote the progress of these arts, by sanctioning all wise legislation in behalf of inventors." Although Abraham Lincoln had
suffered defeats in his struggle for better weapons, he could still

289

foresee the contributions technology would make in future years to the realization of his long-cherished dream: "the progressive improvement in the condition of all men everywhere."

And although he had suffered setbacks, proof kept piling up that Lincoln's fight for new weapons had not been in vain. On the very day that Lincoln chatted with the *Scientific American* reporter, Major General James H. Wilson wrote to Brigadier General Dyer from his cavalry corps headquarters in Alabama:

There is no doubt that the Spencer carbine is the best fire-arm yet put into the hands of the soldier, both for economy of ammunition and maximum effect physical and moral. Our best officers estimate one man armed with it equivalent to three with any other arm. I have never seen anything else like the confidence inspired by it in the regiments or brigades which have it. A common belief among them is if their flanks are covered they can go anywhere.

It was on that day also that the *Scientific American* carried a further sign of the times: "BREECH-LOADERS TO BE ADOPTED.— The Government has appointed a commission of seven military officers, to meet at Springfield Armory on the 4th of January, for the purpose of testing breech-loading carbines and muskets, in order to select the best for army use."

Signs even began to appear that Lincoln's support of the coffee-mill guns might some day be vindicated. During Ripley's last year in office, the dogged old bureaucrat succeeded nobly in blocking consideration of Dr. Richard Gatling's multibarreled, crank-operated machine gun. The Indianapolis inventor did not think to write Lincoln until early 1864, by which time Lincoln had lost his zeal for new weapons. Nor did Gatling's Copperhead reputation help him. Still, the Gatling gun was a good weapon, and it began to make headway. Near the end of the war, Admiral Porter acquired one for his Mississippi Squadron, and General Butler used eight on gunboats and two in the Petersburg lines. At the Washington Arsenal in February 1865 Gatling demonstrated an improved model of his gun before Dyer, Wise and Major General

Winfield Scott Hancock to such good effect that Hancock ordered a dozen for his corps.

"I assure you my invention is no 'Coffee Mill Gun,'" Gatling had written Lincoln in 1864. But while Lincoln lived, the public persisted in calling the Gatling a coffee-mill gun, and the public was not far wrong. Gatling's 1862 model was built fundamentally on the coffee-mill principle, even to its separate steel chambers and hopper feed. And whatever Dr. Gatling may have thought, he profited from the similarity. Coffee-mill guns had already seen action. To the bureaucratic mind, this meant that the Gatling guns were "improved" weapons, not "new" weapons; and that made a difference. Thanks to Lincoln, in other words, machine guns were no longer "new-fangled gimcracks." So in August 1866, after Captain Benét had subjected the improved Gatling guns to extensive trials at the Frankford Arsenal, the United States Army officially adopted the weapon and ordered a hundred as a starter. In purchasing his sixty coffee-mill guns, Abraham Lincoln had helped to blaze another broad new trail in ordnance.

A new day had dawned in the Winder Building. Secretary Stanton found his new Chief of Ordnance "diligent and accomplished," and the two men got along famously. Intramural bickering had largely vanished, and such as cropped up was decidedly more innocuous than in the time of Ripley and Ramsay. A new efficiency was evident, too. In August 1864 Ramsay had complained that he was short of clerks; in January 1865 Colonel Maynadier, back from exile, was preparing to dismiss a number because of "reforms in the system of office operations." Those to be kept included several disabled veterans, like young James Tanner, who at eighteen had lost both legs in the Second Battle of Bull Run.

Abraham Lincoln had ceased to be a familiar figure in the Ordnance Office. There were no more "champagne experiments," and Pet Halsted's letters to Lincoln now concerned themselves with such objects as "a practical way to get out Cotton" and "the placing

& keeping of gold at par." Lincoln's Second Inaugural Ball was held in the new north wing of the Patent Office; but the careworn President was too much occupied with the duties of a host to stroll reminiscently among glassed-in models of Chaplain Jones's gun carriage, S. Wilmer Marsh's breechloader, John Absterdam's improved shell or the ship model left years before by a one-term Congressman from Illinois. And the only ironclad models to receive much attention that evening were those among the sugar decorations on one of the confectioner's monumental cakes.

Gideon Welles was worried about his chief. A few days after the Second Inaugural and its shining promise of malice toward none and charity for all, Lincoln's health forced him for the first time to receive the Cabinet in his bedroom. "There is no doubt he is much worn down," thought the Secretary; and Welles was pleased when at the end of March Lincoln departed for Grant's headquarters at City Point, leaving behind him a horde of favor seekers who had been draining his strength by degrees. Once more Lincoln drove down to the arsenal, jolting across the extension grounds and past the grim penitentiary, now long used as a storehouse for the tools of war. This time he paused for no gun trials. Instead he boarded the steamer *River Queen* at the new wharf built during his friend Ramsay's command of the arsenal.

By one day, Lincoln missed seeing a final champagne experiment. "General" Robert Fleming had been pressing the claims of his incendiary fluid ever since his adventure on the Peninsula in 1862. He made no impression on Ripley; but Captain Benét tested and praised the stuff at West Point in September 1863; and in the fall of 1864 Stanton had twenty of Fleming's shells fired from the Petersburg lines. At City Point, the day before Lincoln arrived there, a board set up by General Grant tried the Fleming shells once more. As his adviser, Fleming had dropped the eccentric Dr. Worster in favor of a New York lawyer named Chester Alan Arthur, who tried a few days later to get a copy of the City Point report. He failed to get it, but the frustration of a future President made little difference to Fleming's fortunes. Presently the long, hard war was over, and with it the need for anyone's liquid fire.

From City Point on April 2, Lincoln wired news to Stanton of Grant's final crushing assault on the Petersburg lines. Next day the President sent word that Petersburg was in Federal hands; and a little later, a shout from the windows of the War Department told Seventeenth Street that "Richmond has fallen!" Exultant clerks poured out of the Ordnance Office or hobbled, smiling, to the windows. All that day, guns roared in salute, church bells danced, and crowds swarmed cheering through the city. Next evening, as dusk fell, men with matches stood at the darkened windows of the War Department and the Winder Building; and at the sound of trumpets and the blare of a band, Seventeenth Street was swept by a wave of candlelight.

On Palm Sunday, April 9, Lincoln returned to the White House. Before he went to bed, he learned that Lee had surrendered at Appomattox. An earsplitting tumult of artillery salutes shook the city awake next morning, and no one had to ask what it meant. Flags were dampened by an April rain, but spirits were not; and a crowd of Navy Yard workmen, roaming the muddy streets with bands and firing salutes from Dahlgren howitzers, drew the smiling President briefly to a White House window. By Thursday, while the capital of the restored nation made ready for an illumination to outshine all before, General Grant was in town to see about cutting down Army expenditures, and General Dyer was notifying all contractors that no more deadlines would be overlooked, that any delay would mean forfeiture. Retrenchment was in the air.

At this sad hour for contract hunters, there was at least one who nursed a feeble hope. Archimedes Dickson, still hanging on in Washington, had finally wangled an appointment with the President. The appointment was for April 15, 1865.

Good Friday, April 14, was the fourth anniversary of Fort Sumter's surrender; and the flag that had been lowered in 1861 was to be raised at the fort that day with speeches and ceremony. In Washington the management of Grover's Theater seized upon the occasion to hold a patriotic gala. Competition was slight: a torch-light procession of the arsenal employees; and at Ford's Theater on Tenth Street, a shopworn comedy called *Our American Cousin*. Abraham Lincoln chose Ford's; but young James Tanner, the leg-less Ordnance Office clerk, preferred Grover's, with its Grand Oriental Spectacle of *Aladdin; or, The Wonderful Lamp*, supple-mented by fireworks and a reading of "The Flag of Sumter," an original poem by Commissioner of Public Buildings Benjamin French.

A little after ten that night, the news that President Lincoln had been shot at Ford's Theater burst like a Parrott shell over the light-hearted audience at Grover's. The play broke off; and the stunned crowd streamed, half incredulous, out of the theater. James Tanner limped after them and through the jammed streets to his lodgings on Tenth Street, next door to the house where President Lincoln lay dying. The crippled clerk painfully mounted the stairs to his second floor rooms and clumped out onto his balcony. From it he could look down at the great men of the nation passing, stony-faced and pale, up the front steps of the Peterson house. One of Tanner's friends, a government clerk, happened to hear a call for someone to take testimony; he mentioned that Tanner knew shorthand; and General Halleck sent for the young veteran. Thus, as Abraham Lincoln drifted toward death, chance brought a representative of the Ordnance Office to stand with the others by his side.

The story of the long night has been told often, and told much as James Tanner told it to his co-workers in the Ordnance Office during that April of unforgettable joy and sorrow. The sobbing of Mary Lincoln, the labored breathing of the dying man, the faint creak of careful footsteps, the scratch of Stanton's pen, the sound of a door opening on a hushed crowd and a sodden sky—all these James Tanner heard, and all linger in the American mind. But in the Peterson house, silence came at last.

On the afternoon of April 18 the clerks of the Ordnance Office assembled on Seventeenth Street with those of other bureaus and walked in procession to the East Room of the White House, where they filed soberly past the silk-draped catafalque on which Lincoln's body rested in state. Like all government establishments, the Ordnance Office closed next day for the funeral procession down Pennsylvania Avenue. At noon church bells tolled beneath a cloudless sky, and minute guns began to boom in the forts around the city. The guns were still sounding at two, when old Major General Ethan Allen Hitchcock, to whom Stanton had once in desperation offered Ripley's command, wrote in his journal: "Now I hear the solemn music as the procession moves from the President's mansion with all that remains of Mr. Lincoln."

The guns fell silent, the music passed away, and the crowds dispersed. Next day, work was resumed in the Ordnance Office. Before April was over, the War Department had ended all arms purchases and directed that expenditures be cut to a minimum. Washingtonians, wondering what was different in the air, realized suddenly that the rumble of army wagons had come to a stop at last.

In Garrett's barn, John Wilkes Booth fell with a Spencer carbine by his side, thus paying an unintended tribute to the good judgment of his victim; and a memo came to the Chief of Ordnance: "Sergeant Boston Corbett, Co I, 16th New York Cavalry having satisfactorily accounted for the loss of one Colt's revolver, he is relieved from all responsibility therefor, and the Ordnance Department will issue another in place of the one lost." Booth's body, sewn in a gray army blanket, came to the Navy Yard on the monitor *Montauk;* and crowds gathered at the great stone gate to clamor for a sight of infamy requited. Enraged when curiosity seekers got aboard the vessel, Stanton had Booth's body hustled away to the old penitentiary in the arsenal grounds; and at midnight in a ground-floor room, as lantern light flickered over gun boxes and packing crates, the assassin's corpse was secretly buried beneath the earthen floor. Above, on the third floor, the murderer's accomplices, actual or alleged, were presently incarcerated; and there a vindictive trial was held. In a cramped, whitewashed room near their cells, the eight manacled prisoners sat listening hopelessly to the proceedings and looking out through grated windows at the sunny sky and the green treetops under which Lincoln had once driven on his way to witness gun trials.

While Stanton's work of vengeance proceeded, so did his Department's transition to peace. In the Ordnance Office the clerical force was cut by a fourth. The criterion for those remaining was the value of their services, Dyer informed Stanton, except for wounded veterans and "four young men whose fathers are understood to hold office." Young Tanner was promoted from temporary to permanent clerk.

Toward the end of 1864, Isaac Diller had tried to revive his powder project; and according to Samuel Ricker, Lincoln had been about to order a new board for further experiments when Booth's bullet intervened. Now, with Lincoln dead and the Ordnance Office on a peacetime basis, Diller saw no point in going on; and so he went back to his real estate business. Months later he was mildly astonished to receive a visit from Ricker, who felt "sore" about the powder fiasco. The captain was not very sympathetic. "He has spent much money in this powder matter," Diller wrote Dr. Wetherill, "but he will not allow that others have spent money, time, and risked much."

Archimedes Dickson likewise resigned himself to the inevitable. "As soon as Mr. Lincoln died," he said, "I quit and went home, and went to work at something else. I did not intend to give it up if he had lived, because he told me he would investigate it." Perhaps Dickson should have been thankful that Lincoln's investigation never came.

In Texas, as May ended and the summer of 1865 came on, Kirby Smith surrendered the last rebel army. Calls for cannon now were mostly from towns wanting to borrow them for Independence Day, but the Department's rules did not permit the loaning of ordnance even for so patriotic a purpose. One lazy day in June a request came in from the Methodist Episcopal church in Mattoon, Illinois: a church bell had cracked while being tolled for the funeral of

President Lincoln, and the congregation wondered if General Dyer could give them a worn-out rebel cannon to cast into a new bell. Dyer's decision is not on record, so it is possible to hope that he relaxed the rules for so neatly symbolic an end. But, as Major Laidley had once pointed out to Archimedes Dickson, the general was "a business man."

The world forgot about Lincoln's work with the tools of war. Dahlgren kept a diary, but in that respect he was alone among those who knew the story. All others concerned left memoir writing to the warriors and the politicians.

Hiram Berdan's creative imagination turned to other fields than literature. In 1874 a disturbed official of the American Legation in Berlin wrote the Secretary of State:

Do you know anything about a gentleman who styles himself "General Berdan?" I have no doubt that the man is a charlatan. Berdan and his wife and a very pretty daughter represented to [George] Bancroft [the American Minister] that they had been presented in Russia, upon which he was induced to present them here. It afterwards turned out that they had not been presented in Russia at all. But the mischief had been done, and the Berdans had got their position.

Pet Halsted thought of setting down the story. "The inside and true history of this war is yet to be written," he once asserted; "I propose to have a small share in making up the 'Chronicles.'" But in the summer of 1871, before any Halsted "Chronicles" had appeared, Pet Halsted was shot by a rival for the affections of his mistress; and instead of carrying an inside account of the Civil War, the *Newark Daily Advertiser* was apprizing its eager readers of the "Shocking Results of Guilty Love, Jealousy, Rum and Passion."

Harry Wise could have told much and told it well, but he died at Naples in 1869, worn-out at the age of forty-nine. For some years after the war, General Ripley had now and then been seen walking slowly, but still erectly, about the streets of Hartford,

Connecticut, his last home. He died in March 1870; and in the
same year Dahlgren succumbed to a heart attack. Soon after the
war ended, Captain Balch resigned from the Army, an embittered
man; his success in private life was limited, but he never returned
to the service. Stanton presently gave Ramsay the brevet rank of
major general, and when Ramsay was "little expecting it," restored him to command of the Washington Arsenal. "All of this,"
said Ramsay, "I believe was done as the *amende honorable.*" Major
General Ramsay remained at his beloved arsenal until his retirement in 1870. When he retired, Ramsay was "straight as a rush"
and "active as anybody," and he lived until 1882, still treasuring
the "familiar notes" he had received from his commander in chief.
But the old soldier was not the sort of man who considers his personal reminiscences as indispensable to the happiness of posterity.

General Dyer died in harness, and while he lived he had more
to do than cultivate memories of the past. A new age of ordnance
had arrived and was to be reckoned with; and besides, guns were
needed on the western plains. Dyer's successor, Brigadier General
Stephen Vincent Benét, had literary experience. But he knew the
story of Lincoln and the tools of war chiefly as hearsay, except perhaps for one rainy June day in 1862 when Lincoln toured the Cold
Spring Foundry.

Of all those who figured in the story, the *Scientific American*
delivered the only memorable epilogue in the weeks after Lincoln's
death. Lincoln's own invention had not revolutionized navigation
on the Western Waters, the magazine remarked. Nevertheless, the
dead inventor's "skill in buoying the great vessel of state over dangerous breakers has made his name honored throughout the whole
civilized world."

The development of weapons and of power went on, indifferent
to the philosophical Greek chorus which alternately rejoiced and
foreboded. General Phil Sheridan, who had made good use of
breechloaders in the last months of the war, expressed the opinion
some years later "that the improvement in the material of war was

so great that nations could not make war, such would be the destruction of human life." As the twentieth century dawned, Henry
Adams returned home from the great Paris exposition of 1900,
where the discoveries of the Curies about a certain new source of
energy had not relieved him from his fears of 1862. "Power
leaped from every atom," he mused, "and enough of it to supply
the stellar universe showed itself running to waste at every pore of
matter. Man could no longer hold it off." He saw disastrous possibilities in store for the next generation or two. "But," he added,
"bombs educate vigorously."

The scientists themselves, unchaining their thunderbolts and
worse than thunderbolts, could no more agree on the ultimate consequences than could the laymen. Perhaps the ultimate consequences
will never be certain till the sun—or the earth—is a cinder. Yet if,
as seems presently possible, the very power of weapons enforces a
lasting peace among nations, then Abraham Lincoln will have
helped, in more ways than he knew, to keep alive the last best hope
of earth.

Notes

TEXT to which the notes refer is indicated below by page and paragraph, the number of the page followed in parentheses by the *final word* of the paragraph. When a paragraph carries over from one page to another, the number of the second page is given here.

Notes referring to passages longer than a single paragraph are located by the numbers of all pages involved and by the final words of all paragraphs covered.

CHAPTER ONE (pages 3-21)

3 (air): Margaret Leech, *Reveille in Washington* (New York, 1941), p. 31.

3 (avenue): *Ibid.,* p. 43; *Washington Sunday Morning Chronicle,* Jan. 19, 1862; *New York Times,* Sept. 22, 1861; William H. Russell, *My Diary North and South* (New York, 1863), p. 20.

4 (inscrutable): Leech, *Reveille in Washington,* p. 43; Benjamin P. Thomas, *Abraham Lincoln* (New York, 1952), p. 245.

4 (served): Manuscript memoir by John A. Dahlgren, belonging to Joseph Dahlgren of Charlottesville, Virginia, p. 63; Madeleine V. Dahlgren, *Memoir of John A. Dahlgren* (Boston, 1882), pp. 328, 352.

4 (last): M. V. Dahlgren, *Memoir,* p. 328; Leech, *Reveille in Washington,* pp. 44-45; James G. Randall, *Lincoln the President: Springfield to Gettysburg* (2 vols.; New York, 1945), I, 294.

5 (Yard): Leech, *Reveille in Washington,* p. 45.

5-6 (transformation, Factory, imitation, dignity): Taylor Peck, *Round-Shot to Rockets* (Annapolis, 1949), pp. 105-107, 110; M. V. Dahlgren, *Memoir,* p. 314; Russell, *My Diary,* p. 27; *Scientific American,* April 6, 1861.

6 (*Merrimac*): Dahlgren ms. memoir, p. 57; "Journal of Occurrences," I, 56-57, David D. Porter Mss., Library of Congress (hereafter referred to as "L. C.").

7 (siege): Dahlgren ms. memoir, pp. 74-75, 59-60; Peck, *Round-Shot to Rockets,* p. 115.

7-8 (everywhere, category): Russell, *My Diary,* p. 27.

8 (quietness): *Idem.;* M. V. Dahlgren, *Memoir,* p. 328; W. H. Russell to H. A. Wise, Jan. 5, 1862, Henry Augustus Wise Mss., New York Historical Society.

8 (that): Dahlgren ms. memoir, p. 65.

8-9 (establishment, establishment): U. S. Naval Observatory Meteorological Journal (hereafter cited as "Observatory Journal"), National Archives (hereafter referred to as "N. A."), April 2, 1861; *Washington Evening Star,* April 3, 1861; M. V. Dahlgren, *Memoir,* p. 329; Casimir Bohn (publisher), *Bohn's Hand-Book of Washington* (Washington, D. C., 1858), pp. 51-53.

9 (alighted, countenance): Observatory Journal, N. A., April 3, 1861; Dahlgren ms. memoir, p. 65.

10 (President): *Ibid.,* pp. 65-66; H. A. Wise to J. A. Dahlgren, Sept. 1, 1863, John A. Dahlgren Mss., L. C.

10 (war): Dahlgren ms. memoir, pp. 65-66; M. V. Dahlgren, *Memoir,* pp. 352-353.

11 (west): Carl Sandburg, *Abraham Lincoln: The Prairie Years* (2 vols.; New York, 1926), I, 472.

11 (young): Paul M. Angle, *"Here I Have Lived"* (New Brunswick, N. J., 1950), p. 178; Ida M. Tarbell, *The Life of Abraham Lincoln* (4 vols.; New York, 1924), II, 57.

11 (involved): Charles S. Zane, "Lincoln As I Knew Him," *Sunset Magazine,* October 1912.

12 (phenomena): David H. Bates, *Lincoln in the Telegraph Office* (New York, 1907), pp. 4-5.

12 (expense): Albert J. Beveridge, *Abraham Lincoln, 1809-1858* (2 vols.; Boston, 1928), I, 520 n; *Scientific American,* March 30, 1861; Fred B. Joyner, *David Ames Wells, Champion of Free Trade* (Cedar Rapids, Iowa, 1939), p. 20.

13 (war): George B. McClellan, *McClellan's Own Story* (New York, 1887), p. 162.

13-14 (talk, door, before): Roy P. Basler (ed.), *The Collected Works of Abraham Lincoln* (8 vols.; New Brunswick, N. J., 1953), II, 437-442, III, 356-363; Harry E. Pratt (ed.), *Concerning Mr. Lincoln* (Springfield, Ill., 1944), pp. 21-22.

14 (me): Lincoln, *Works,* III, 374; William H. Herndon and Jesse W. Weik, *Herndon's Lincoln* (3 vols.; Chicago, 1890), III, 449 n.

14 (somewhere): Noah Brooks, *Washington in Lincoln's Time* (New York, 1895), p. 306.

14 (things): Tarbell, *Lincoln,* II, 97; David C. Mearns (ed.), *The Lincoln Papers* (2 vols.; New York, 1948), I, 159.

15 (self-possessed): M. V. Dahlgren, *Memoir,* p. 329.

16 (later): Robert U. Johnson and Clarence C. Buel (eds.), *Battles and Leaders of the Civil War* (4 vols.; New York, 1888), I, 5, 36 n; George A. Magruder to Montgomery Blair, June 20, 1865, Blair Family Mss., L. C.; "Letters to Secretary & Bureaux," II, 83, Records of the Navy Bureau of Ordnance (hereafter cited as "Nav. Bur. Ord."), N. A.; Henry A. Wise to Edward Everett, May 3, 1861, Edward Everett Mss., Massachusetts Historical Society.

16 (Dahlgren): Letterbook of Captain Henry A. Wise, 1862-1864, p. 35, Naval Records Collection of the Office of Naval Records and Library (hereafter cited as "Nav. Rec. Coll."), N. A.

16 (defense): "Washington Navy Yard Orders Issued, Nov. 1, 1860-Dec. 16, 1861," p. 115, Nav. Rec. Coll., N. A.; Peck, *Round-Shot to Rockets,* pp. 117-118.

17 (power): Dahlgren ms. memoir, pp. 76, 86; Tyler Dennett (ed.), *Lincoln and the Civil War in the Diaries and Letters of John Hay* (New York, 1939), p. 11.

17 (received): John A. Dahlgren to Abraham Lincoln, July 16, 1862, Robert Todd Lincoln Collection (hereafter cited as "Lincoln Mss."), L. C.; M. V. Dahlgren, *Memoir,* p. 341.

17-18 (accepted, occasion, delighted, flagstaff): Observatory Journal, May 9, 1861; *Washington Star,* May 10, June 4, 1861; *Washington Sunday Morning Chronicle,* May 12, 1861; John G. Nicolay to Therena Bates, May 9, 1861, Nicolay Mss., L. C.; Dahlgren ms. memoir, p. 88; "Memorandum Book: Navy Yard, Washington," May 9, 1861, Dahlgren Mss., L. C.; clipping dated "May 12th, Washington," *ibid.;* Hay, *Diary,* pp. 21-22.

19 (fanfare): *Boston Transcript,* May 25, 1861; Commandant's Memorandum Book, Dahlgren Mss., L. C.

19 (howitzers): Russell, *My Diary,* p. 141; *Scientific American,* June 22, 1861; *Washington Star,* June 25, 1861.

19 (Yard): M. V. Dahlgren, *Memoir,* pp. 336, 338-339.

20 (foundry): Dahlgren ms. memoir, pp. 102-103; Peck, *Round-Shot to Rockets,* p. 127; Edward Everett to Francis P. Blair, Sr., April 2, 1864, Everett Mss., Mass. Hist. Soc.

20 (Abe): Dahlgren ms. memoir, pp. 88, 110; M. V. Dahlgren, *Memoir,* p. 333; *National Intelligencer* (Washington, D. C.), March 26, 1862.

20 (himself): Russell, *My Diary,* pp. 186-187.

21 (responsibility): M. V. Dahlgren, *Memoir,* pp. 288-289; John T. Morse (ed.), *The Diary of Gideon Welles* (3 vols.; Boston, 1911), I, 62, 341.

21 (politicians): M. V. Dahlgren, *Memoir*, p. 351; Dahlgren ms. memoir, p. 111.

CHAPTER TWO (pages 22-36)

22 (world): Leech, *Reveille in Washington*, pp. 8-9; Russell, *My Diary*, p. 20.

22 (fifty): Leech, *Reveille in Washington*, p. 63; Thomas, *Lincoln*, p. 263.

23 (present): *Washington Star*, April 20, 1861; my description of Ripley is based on portraits, photographs and contemporary allusions.

23 (1818): Sarah D. Ripley (ed.), *James Wolfe Ripley* (Hartford, 1881), p. 3.

23 (with): Claud E. Fuller, *Springfield Muzzle-Loading Shoulder Arms* (New York, 1930), p. 100.

24 (Army): Ripley, *James Wolfe Ripley*, pp. 25-26; James Gadsden to James W. Ripley, Feb. 25, 1826, April 16, 1830, James W. Ripley Mss., belonging to Robert B. Bartholomew, Hoboken, N. J.

24 (indulgence): Ripley, *James Wolfe Ripley*, p. 25; conversation with Miss Zelina Bartholomew, granddaughter of General Ripley, in New York City, Nov. 20, 1952; letters from Dorothea Dix to James W. Ripley, 1832-1833, James W. Ripley Mss.

25 (Charleston): *Hartford Courant*, March 17, 1870.

25 (flagpole): *Springfield* (Mass.) *Sunday Republican*, Dec. 22, 1878; Derwent S. Whittlesey, "The Springfield Armory: A Study in Institutional Development" (unpublished Ph. D. dissertation, University of Chicago, 1920), pp. 179, 181-183, 204 (citations are based on a carbon copy in the library of the Springfield Armory, the pagination of which may not coincide with that of the final draft); *Springfield Gazette*, April 22, 1846 (the hostile paper was the *Independent Democrat*).

26 (arm): Whittlesey, "Armory," pp. 189, 199.

26 (works): Jacob Abbott, "The Armory at Springfield," *Harper's Monthly*, July 1852.

27 (Boston): *Springfield Republican*, Oct. 18, 1854; Whittlesey, "Armory," pp. 208, 210, 215, 219.

27 (me): *Hartford Courant*, March 17, 1870.

27 (too): Alfred Mordecai to Samuel Mordecai, June 2, 1861, Mordecai Mss., L. C.

27 (inevitable): A. Howard Meneely, *The War Department, 1861* (New York, 1928), p. 109; BB Book 10, p. 337, Office of the Secretary of War (hereafter cited as "Off. Sec. War"), N. A.

28 (Department): Meneely, *War Department*, pp. 76, 78, 81-84; Russell, *My Diary*, p. 23.

28 (nation): Meneely, *War Department*, pp. 105, 83 n, 107.

28 (war): "Letters Received, 1861," WD319, Office of the Chief of Ordnance (hereafter cited as "Ord. Off."), N. A.

29 (others): Ord. Off., Letters Rec'd 1863, WD513.

29 (did): *New York Herald,* May 8, 1862; Ripley was appointed to the superintendency at Springfield by a Whig administration, he promptly dismissed the Jacksonian paymaster, he feuded with the *Independent Democrat,* and he was removed under a Democratic administration and replaced by a Democratic politician.

29 (chief): *Official Records of the Union and Confederate Armies* (130 vols.; Washington, D. C., 1880-1901) (hereafter cited as "*O. R.*"), series 3, I, 102.

29 (himself): Ord Off., Letters Rec'd 1863, WD513; Meneely, *War Department,* p. 113 n; Off. Sec. War, Irregular Book I, 095; Simon Cameron to Henry K. Craig, May 4, 1861, Letters Sent: Military Affairs, Off. Sec. War.

30 (also): Lincoln, *Works,* IV, 394-395, 398.

30 (triumph): Meneely, *War Department,* p. 113; Cameron to Craig, May 4, 1861, Letters Sent: Military Affairs, Off. Sec. War.

31 (street): Ms. paper on the Winder Building by Mrs. Ruth B. Shipley, Washington, D.C.

31 (Ordnance): Ord. Off., Letters Rec'd 1864, WD305; and numerous allusions in Ordnance Office files.

32 (clerks): *Proceedings of a Court of Inquiry Convened at Washington, D.C., November 9, 1868 . . . to Examine into the Accusations against Brig. and Bvt. Major General A. B. Dyer, Chief of Ordnance* (2 vols.; Washington, D. C., 1869) (hereafter cited as "*Dyer Inquiry*"), II, 452; James W. Ripley to George T. Balch, Sept. 19, 1864, Elihu B. Washburne Mss., L. C.; Donald A. Mac-Dougall, "The Federal Ordnance Bureau, 1861-1865" (unpublished Ph. D. dissertation, University of California at Berkeley, 1951), pp. 105, 175, 208, 213.

33 (Department): *O. R.,* series 3, V, 144, I, 22, 292, series 1, XII, part iii, 95; Theodore F. Rodenbough and William L. Haskins (eds.), *The Army of the United States* (New York, 1896), pp. 32, 132; Emory Upton, *The Military Policy of the United States* (Washington, D.C., 1912), p. 262.

33 (business man, expended): MacDougall, "Federal Ordnance Bureau," pp. 35-36, 99, 157, 157 n; *O. R.,* series 3, II, 351; Daniel M. Roche, "The Acquisition and Use of Foreign Shoulder-arms in the Union Army, 1861-1865" (unpublished Ph. D. dissertation, University of Colorado, 1949), p. 60 n.

33 (swindled): MacDougall, "Federal Ordnance Bureau," pp. 216, 49; *O. R.,* series 3, I, 538-539.

34 (equivalent): Quoted in Roche, "Foreign Shoulder-arms," p. 120 n.

34 (it): Frank Moore (ed.), *The Rebellion Record* (11 vols.; New York, 1861-1868), V, 406 (Doc.).

34 (production): Felicia J. Deyrup, *Arms Makers of the Connecticut Valley* (Northampton, Mass., 1948), pp. 179-181.

35 (PRESIDENT): Ord. Off., Special File: Inventions (hereafter cited as "Inventions"), classes 4 and 5, No. 391.

35 (endorsed): Lincoln, *Works,* IV, 505-506.

35-36 (him, be): *Ibid.,* IV, 540, V, 458.

36 (Lincoln): *Washington Star,* Oct. 25, 1862; *National Republican* (Washington, D.C.), Oct. 22, 1862.

CHAPTER THREE (pages 37-58)

37 (hands): Thomas, *Lincoln,* p. 258; *O. R.,* series 3, I, 162, 164; Lincoln, *Works,* V, 20.

37 (come): *O. R.,* series 1, II, 42-43, series 3, I, 260; MacDougall, "Federal Ordnance Bureau," pp. 30-31.

38 (States): Wells, *Annual of Scientific Discovery for 1855,* pp. 23-24.

39 (locks): *O. R.,* series 3, I, 244.

39 (demand): Tarbell, *Lincoln,* I, 6; Lincoln, *Works,* IV, 62, I, 9.

39 (*Lincoln*): Ord. Off., Letters to Ordnance Officers, James W. Ripley to George D. Ramsay, June 18, 1861; *Scientific American,* Oct. 11, 1862; Alfred R. Waud Collection, Division of Prints and Photographs, L. C.

39 (matters): Ord Off., "Inventions," class 1c, No. 307.

40 (buckshot, further): William O. Stoddard, *Inside the White House in War Times* (New York, 1890), p. 42.

40-41 (Office, boys, wanted, Regiment, changed, President, boyhood, property, incident): Lucius E. Chittenden, *Recollections of President Lincoln and His Administration* (New York, 1891), pp. 151-154.

42 (it): Ord. Off., Misc. Letters Sent, LIII, 93.

42 (rifles): *O. R.,* series 1, II, 42-43.

42 (month): *O. R.,* series 3, I, 260, series 1, II, 604; table of monthly output during 1861 in Springfield Armory Library scrapbook.

42 (rifles): *O. R.,* series 3, I, 544, 525, II, 191, 855; Deyrup, *Arms Makers,* pp. 179-181; *Boston Transcript,* May 13, 1861; *Scientific American,* Dec. 21, 1861, Jan. 4, 1862.

43 (home): *O. R.,* series 3, I, 245, 322; Meneely, *War Department,* p. 148.

43 (deal): *O. R.,* series 3, I, 245, 263; Meneely, *War Department,* p. 280.

43 (powder): M. V. Dahlgren, *Memoir,* p. 333.

44 (earnest): Lincoln, *Works,* IV, 362, 419, 536; **Ord. Off.,** Register of Letters Rec'd 1861, WD1802.

44 (Kentuckian): Thomas, *Lincoln,* pp. 3-4, 8.

45 (me): Lincoln, *Works,* IV, 69-70.

45 (Tennessee): Off. Sec. War, Irregular Book I, R40, M158.

45 (nation): Lincoln, *Works,* IV, 532.

45 (Nelson): *Ibid.,* IV, 368-369.

46 (country): *Battles and Leaders,* I, 375-376; Daniel Ammen, *The Old Navy and the New* (Philadelphia, 1891), p. 340; Russell, *My Diary,* p. 26.

46 (mission): Daniel Stevenson, "General Nelson, Kentucky, and Lincoln Guns," *Magazine of American History,* Aug., 1883, p. 118.

46 (howitzer): *Ibid.,* pp. 118-119, 123; Ord. Off., Register of Letters Rec'd 1861, WD640; Lincoln, *Works,* IV, 395; Nav. Bur. Ord., Navy Dept. Letters, III, 126-127.

47 (proportion): Mearns, *Lincoln Papers,* II, 625; Stevenson, "Lincoln Guns," pp. 126, 132.

47 (Yankee): *Ibid.,* 132; Mearns, *Lincoln Papers,* II, 619-620.

48 (mob): Dahlgren ms. memoir, p. 98; Thomas, *Lincoln,* pp. 271-272.

48 (need): Diary of Mrs. Gustavus V. Fox, Feb. 28, 1863, Blair Family Mss., L. C.; Francis B. Carpenter, *Six Months at the White House with Abraham Lincoln* (New York, 1866), p. 255.

48 (immediately): *O. R.,* series 3, I, 355.

49 (campaigns): Whittlesey, "Armory," pp. 223-224; James W. Ripley to George Dwight, May 15, 1861, transcript in Springfield Collection, Springfield (Mass.) City Library; Springfield Armory Library scrapbook.

49 (arms): *O. R.,* series 3, I, 702.

49 (arms): Ord. Off., "Purchases of Ordnance," p. 216; *O. R.,* series 3, II, 855.

49 (guns): Draft of an unaddressed letter, March 8, 1862, Simon Cameron Mss., L. C.; 37th Cong., 2nd sess., Senate, Executive Document 72, pp. 40-41, 47.

49 (price): *Dyer Inquiry,* II, 453, 467.

50 (complied): *O. R.,* series 3, II, 193; Henry Wikoff to Simon Cameron, Sept. 7, 1861, Cameron Mss., L. C.; draft of an unaddressed letter, March 8, 1862, Cameron Mss., L. C.

50 (uproar): 37th Cong., 2nd sess., House, Report 2, p. 192; Roche, "Foreign Shoulder Arms," p. 60 n; *Boston Transcript,* Dec. 24, 1861; 37th Cong., 2nd sess., House, Executive Document 67, p. 35.

50 (discharged): Ord. Off., Letters Rec'd 1862, WD1781.

51 (trouble): Roche, "Foreign Shoulder Arms," Appendix A, p. 157; William W. H. Davis, *History of the 104th Pennsylvania Regiment* (Philadelphia, 1866), p. 36; *History of the Twenty-Third Pennsylvania Volunteers* (Philadelphia, 1904), pp. 126-127.

51 (them): William E. Doster, *Lincoln and Episodes of the Civil War* (New York, 1915), p. 24; Stoddard, *Inside the White House,* pp. 40-41.

51 (sharpers): Lincoln, *Works,* IV, 509; MacDougall, "Federal Ordnance Bureau," p. 130.

51 (particularity): Lincoln, *Works,* IV, 512-513.

52 (done): *Ibid.,* V, 163, 165; George Ashmun to Lincoln, March 19, 1862, Lincoln Mss., L. C.

52 (do): Noah Brooks, "Personal Recollections of Abraham Lincoln," *Harper's Monthly,* July 1865, p. 228; *New York Times,* Oct. 25, 1861.

53 (heart, Department): Ord. Off., "Inventions," class 8, No. 158.

54 (record, Chace): Ord. Off., Register of Letters Rec'd 1861, WD1711.

54-56 (deeply, serviceable, President, category, construction, accepted, contract): 37th Cong., 2nd sess., House, Executive Document 67, pp. 120-121, 123-125, 130; 37th Cong., 2nd sess., Senate, Executive Document 72, pp. 105-110, 113-118; Oliver S. Halsted, Jr., to Lincoln, Dec. 20, 1861, Lincoln Mss., L. C.; Ord. Off., "Purchases of Ordnance"; the quoted characterizations of Hagner and Crispin are from the ms. autobiography of James W. Benét, pp. 22, 39 n, at Yale University.

57 (each): Off. Sec. War, Irregular Book I, R88, IV, V39; Ord. Off., Register of Letters Rec'd 1861, WD1023; Lincoln, *Works*, IV, 481.

57 (Missouri): *Ibid.*, IV, 529-530.

57 (distance): *Ibid.*, IV, 485, 537, 541; *O. R.*, series 3, I, 539; William B. Wilson, *Acts and Actors in the Civil War* (Philadelphia, 1892), pp. 110-111.

58 (Union): *O. R.*, series 1, LII, part i, 188; Joshua F. Speed to Joseph Holt, Dec. 8, 1861, Joseph Holt Mss., L. C.; Lincoln, *Works*, V, 50.

CHAPTER FOUR (pages 59-74)

59 (themselves): *New York Times*, Dec. 10, 1863.

60 (world): Lewis Campbell and William Garnett, *The Life of James Clerk Maxwell* (London, 1884), pp. 250-252; Worthington C. Ford (ed.), *A Cycle of Adams Letters, 1861-1865* (2 vols.; Boston, 1920), I, 135.

60 (city): Henry Adams, *The Education of Henry Adams* (Modern Library edition, New York, 1931), p. 44.

61 (majority): W. P. A. Guide Series, *Washington, City and Capital* (Washington, D.C., 1937), pp. 950, 976, 977; Charles Dickens, *American Notes*, chap. viii (I cite no page reference because my source, like most available copies, is an undated edition of Dickens's collected works); 30th Cong., 1st sess., House, Executive Document 54, p. 9.

62 (invented): *Ibid.*, pp. 7, 16; Patent Office reports, 1837-1847, *passim;* Mearns, *Lincoln Papers*, I, 4-5.

62 (1850s): Tarbell, *Lincoln*, II, 42-43, and photograph of model, opposite p. 42.

62 (inventor): *Scientific American*, Dec. 1, 1860.

63 (Office): Leech, *Reveille in Washington*, pp. 66-69.

63 (themselves): *Scientific American*, May 18, June 15, 1861.

64 (July): Augustus Woodbury, *A Narrative of the Campaign of the First Rhode Island Regiment* (Providence, 1862), pp. 26-27, 158-159, 164-165.

64 (city): Ben: Perley Poore, *The Life and Public Services of Ambrose E. Burnside* (Providence, 1882), pp. 97-98.

64 (dawned): J. L. B. Blizard, "The Future of Discovery and Invention," *Technology Review*, June 1954, LVI, 395-397.

65 (Cumberland): *Boston Transcript*, Sept. 1, 1862; *Scientific American*, Jan. 11, 1862.

65 (him): *Ibid.,* May 25, 1861; *The American Annual Cyclopedia and Register of Important Events of the Year 1862* (New York, 1868), p. 699; Edward W. Jones to Joseph Holt, Aug. 26, 1861, Joseph Holt Mss., L. C.; Alfred Holmead to Chambré, Oct. 21, 1861, Titian R. Peale to J. E. Holmead, Sept. 6, 1861, Lincoln Mss., L. C.

66 (war): Lincoln, *Works,* V, 45; *Scientific American,* March 22, Nov. 22, 1862.

66 (Washington): Moore, *Rebellion Record,* I, 55 (Incidents); *Scientific American,* May 11, 1861; Benjamin F. Butler, *Butler's Book* (Boston, 1892), pp. 201-202.

66 (days): *Battles and Leaders,* II, 7 n.

67 (therefrom): *Scientific American,* Nov. 1, 1862.

67 (1861): *Ibid.,* June 2, 1849.

67 (industry): E. Merton Coulter, *The Confederate States of America, 1861-1865* (Louisiana State University, 1950), pp. 210, 274, 276-277; Emerson D. Fite, *Social and Industrial Conditions in the North During the Civil War* (New York, 1910), pp. 91, 93 n.

67 (wartime): Coulter, *Confederate States,* p. 274; *Battles and Leaders,* I, 115.

68 (Union): *Ibid.,* pp. 217-218.

68 (apple): Quoted in *Scientific American,* Aug. 3, 1861.

68 (man): John Ericsson to Lincoln, Aug. 2, 1862, Lincoln Mss., L. C.

69 (kinds): MacDougall, "Federal Ordnance Bureau," pp. 6-7; *Scientific American,* March 2, July 6, 1861; *American Annual Cyclopedia* for 1861, p. 562.

69 (infantry): *O. R.,* series 3, I, 264.

70 (Lincoln): A copy of the form is in Ord. Off., "Inventions," class 8, No. 183.

70 (persons): *Dyer Inquiry,* I, 513; 38th Cong., 2nd sess., Senate, Rep. Comm. 121, p. 108.

71 (witness): *Dyer Inquiry,* II, 466-467.

71 (suffers): *Scientific American,* Sept. 19, 1863; see also issues of May 24, July 19, 1862, and Jan. 17, Feb. 28, 1863.

71 (doing): Dahlgren to O. B. Pierce, Aug. 2, 1862, Nav. Bur. Ord., Letters Sent Misc.; Dahlgren to Gideon Welles, June 27, 1863, Dahlgren Mss., L. C.; 37th Cong., 2nd sess., House, Executive Document 126, p. 1.

72 (active): MacDougall, "Federal Ordnance Bureau," pp. 48-49, 216; *O. R.,* series 3, I, 538-539; Ripley to George B. McClellan, July 7, 1862, Ord. Off., Misc. Letters Sent.

72 (power): Russell, *My Diary,* pp. 151-152, 153.

73 (Army): F. Stansbury Haydon, *Aeronautics in the Union and Confederate Armies* (Baltimore, 1941), I, 109; *Scientific American,* July 30, Aug. 6, 1864; *Butler's Book,* p. 258; Edward W. Serrell to Benjamin F. Butler, July 8, 21, Dec. 28, 1864, Jan. 2, 1865, Benjamin F. Butler Mss., L. C.; Off. Sec. War, Irregular Book III, p. 615.

73 (Congressmen): *Scientific American,* Feb. 7, 1863; Ord. Off., Letters Rec'd 1864, WD387.

74 (taken): Ord. Off.: Register of Letters Rec'd 1862, WD907, H516, WD205, B174; "Inventions," class 8, No. 260; Letters Rec'd 1861, B636; Letters Rec'd 1864, C622; Alexander B. Dyer to Schuyler Colfax, Dec. 12, 1864, Misc. Letters Sent.

CHAPTER FIVE (pages 75-88)

75 (this): Mearns, *Lincoln Papers,* I, 35; Sandburg, *Prairie Years,* II, 401.

76 (secretaries, office): Mearns, *Lincoln Papers,* I, 38-41; *Washington Star,* April 3, 1861.

76 (war): More than two hundred letters from inventors escaped Stoddard's wastebaskets and are preserved in the National Archives; of these, one in every six or seven bears some notation in Lincoln's hand. Many of the surviving letters suggest that Stoddard's winnowing was extremely lenient. Yet even if we assume that as many as half of the incoming letters were discarded without referral, we must conclude that at least one in fourteen of the inventors' letters was put into Lincoln's hands, as against only one in fifty of those on other subjects. Ord. Off. and Nav. Bur. Ord. files, *passim;* David P. Holloway to John G. Nicolay, Nov. 1, 1862, Nicolay to William A. Grimshaw, Aug. 12, 1864, Nicolay Mss., L. C.

76 (plague): Ord. Off., "Inventions," classes 4 and 5, No. 785.

77 (promptly): *Ibid.,* class 1c, No. 262, classes 4 and 5, Nos. 828, 830.

77 (gun): *Ibid.,* class 8, No. 292, class 1a, Nos. 161, 253, class 1c, No. 274; "Minutes of War Board, March, 1862," p. 10, Edwin M. Stanton Mss., L. C.

78 (President): Ord. Off., "Inventions," James E. Littlefield to Lincoln, Nov. 2, 1861; William Foster to Samuel Hooper, March 22, 1862, Hooper to Nicolay, May 15, 1862, Nicolay Mss., L. C.

78 (shell): Ord. Off., "Inventions," classes 4 and 5, Nos. 671, 371, 484, class 1a, No. 181.

79 (files): *Ibid.,* class 1c, Nos. 283, 286.

79 (it): *Ibid.,* classes 4 and 5, No. 612.

79 (them): John Hay, *Addresses of John Hay* (New York, 1906), pp. 323-324.

80 (day): Thomas, *Lincoln,* p. 457; Anthony Trollope, *North America* (3 vols.; Leipzig, 1862), II, 141; Carl Sandburg, *Abraham Lincoln: The War Years* (4 vols.; New York, 1939), II, 217.

80 (application, silent): Allen Thorndike Rice (ed.), *Reminiscences of Abraham Lincoln by Distinguished Men of His Time* (New York, 1886), pp. 237-238.

81 (adopted): E. D. Townsend, *Anecdotes of the Civil War in the United States* (New York, 1884), pp. 89-90.

81 (tables): Hay, *Addresses,* p. 327; William O. Stoddard, *Abraham Lincoln and Andrew Johnson* (New York, 1888), pp. 213, 223.

82 (Herndon): *Scientific American,* Sept. 19, 1863; William H. Herndon to Edward McPherson, Feb. 22, 1866, Edward McPherson Mss., L. C.

82 (age): Allen Johnson and Dumas Malone (eds.), *Dictionary of American Biography* (20 vols.; New York, 1928), XVIII, 598-599.

83 (experiment): Joseph G. Totten to Lincoln, Jan. 2, 1862, Lincoln Mss., L. C.

83 (science): David Starr Jordan (ed.), *Leading American Men of Science* (New York, 1910), pp. 119, 124-126; Joseph Henry to Henry Wurtz, July 26, 1861, Wurtz Mss., New York Public Library.

84 (smile): Thomas Coulson, *Joseph Henry: His Life and Work* (Princeton, N. J., 1950), pp. 241-242; *Washington Star,* Jan. 4, 1862; Sandburg, *War Years,* I, 401.

84 (matters): Henry to Nicolay, May 5, 1862, May 10, 1864, George Harrington to Nicolay, March 1, 1865, Nicolay Mss., L. C.; Henry to Lincoln, April 22, 1861, Lincoln Mss., L. C.; Coulson, *Henry,* p. 244; Chittenden, *Recollections,* p. 237.

84 (also): John G. Nicolay and John Hay, *Abraham Lincoln: A History* (10 vols.; New York, 1890), VI, 358-359; Joseph Henry to Frederick Seward, Sept. 5, 1862, Lincoln Mss., L. C.; Warren A. Beck, "Lincoln and Negro Colonization in Central America," *Abraham Lincoln Quarterly,* Sept. 1950; Coulson, *Henry,* 308-309; Sandburg, *War Years,* III, 345-346.

85 (Navy): Bates, *Lincoln in the Telegraph Office,* pp. 264-265; Observatory Journal, Aug. 24, 1864.

85 (vigilance): Brooks, *Washington in Lincoln's Time,* pp. 11-13.

85 (gasbags): Jeremiah Milbank, Jr., *The First Century of Flight in America* (Princeton, N. J., 1943), pp. 33, 98; e.g. E. D. Tippett to Lincoln, Jan. 27, 1862, Nicolay Mss., L. C., John Merlett to Lincoln, May 28, 1861, Lincoln Mss., L. C.

86 (demonstrations): Milbank, *First Century of Flight,* pp. 119-122; F. Stansbury Haydon, *Aeronautics in the Union and Confederate Armies* (Baltimore, 1941), pp. 170-172.

86 (LOWE): T. S. C. Lowe to Lincoln, June 16 [*sic*—correct date is June 18], 1861, Lincoln Mss., L. C.

86 (mounted): Haydon, *Aeronautics,* pp. 175-176; *Boston Transcript,* June 21, 1861.

87 (corps, LINCOLN, hat): Haydon, *Aeronautics,* pp. 194-195.

87 (Army): *Idem.;* Milbank, *First Century of Flight,* pp. 123-127.

88 (nonetheless): *Scientific American,* Jan. 16, 1864; Milbank, *First Century of Flight,* pp. 124-126; T. S. C. Lowe to A. J. Myer, July 13, 1863, Off. Sec. War, Irregular Book IV.

CHAPTER SIX (pages 89-97)

89 (fussy): Russell, *My Diary,* p. 204.

89 (experiments): *Dyer Inquiry,* I, 525.

90 (Potomac, university): Ord. Off., Misc. Letters Rec'd, 1-W-42; *Washington Star,* Jan. 16, 1863; William J. O'Brien, "The Washington Arsenal," *Army Ordnance,* July-August, 1935; see photographs in Francis T. Miller (ed.), *Photographic History of the Civil War* (10 vols.; New York, 1911), V, 127, 131, 135, 175.

90 (points): *Dyer Inquiry,* I, 437, II, 298; 38th Cong., 2nd sess., Senate, Rep. Comm. 121, p. 10.

91 (war): Ord. Off., Misc. Letters Rec'd, 1-W-42; Frederick W. Seward, *Reminiscences of a War-Time Statesman and Diplomat* (New York, 1916), p. 228; Lincoln, *Works,* V, 429-430; *Washington Star,* Nov. 4, 1862.

91 (trees): Off. Sec. War, Irregular Book V, G21; *O. R.,* series 3, V, 141; *National Intelligencer,* Feb. 11, 1862; Ord. Off., Letters Rec'd 1865, W190.

91 (field): Off. Sec. War, Irregular Book V, S85.

92 (mothers): *Idem.; Washington Sunday Morning Chronicle,* June 30, 1861.

92 (Washington): *Washington Star,* Jan. 31, 1863.

92 (major): *Dictionary of American Biography,* XV, 340.

93 (me): Photograph in N. A., Office of Chief Signal Officer, B2447; James W. Benét, autobiography, p. 43; *Dyer Inquiry,* I, 513.

93 (high): Joshua F. Speed to Joseph Holt, Oct. 18, 1861, Joseph Holt Mss., L. C.

93 (co-operation): Ord. Off., Letters Rec'd 1861, WD1400; Off. Sec. War, Irregular Book V, G21; Moore, Rebellion Record, V, 406 (Doc.).

94 (presidents): *Washington Sunday Morning Chronicle,* June 30, 1861.

95 (trial): *Dyer Inquiry,* II, 522; Lincoln, *Works,* IV, 556; Ord. Off., "Inventions," class 6, No. 580.

95 (carriage): *Dyer Inquiry,* II, 179.

95 (merits): N. A., Patent Office Records, No. 33,891; Ord. Off., "Inventions," Misc., No. 250.

96 (Totten's): Joseph G. Totten to Lincoln, Jan. 2, 1862, P. Franklin Jones to Lincoln, Jan. 4, 1862, Lincoln Mss., L. C.; Ord. Off., "Experiments," classes 8 and 3, No. 2-63½.

96 (ordered): Theodore C. Pease and James G. Randall (eds.), *The Diary of Orville Hickman Browning* (2 vols.; Springfield, Illinois, 1925), I, 548-549.

97 (imagery): Benét, autobiography, pp. 8, 11-13, 23, 43; Stephen V. Benét to Alfred Mordecai, May 13, 1861, Mordecai Mss., L. C.

97 (proving): Benét, autobiography, p. 58; S. V. Benét to J. W. Ripley, Sept. 17, 1863, Lincoln Mss., L. C.

CHAPTER SEVEN (pages 99-116)

99 (grass): Stoddard, *Inside the White House,* p. 42; Stoddard, *Lincoln and Johnson,* p. 223.

100 (clean): W. J. Hardee, *Rifle and Infantry Tactics* (2 vols.; Mobile, Alabama, 1863), I 36-41.

100 (order): Theodore T. S. Laidley, "Breech Loading Musket," *United States Service Magazine,* Jan., 1865, III, 69.

101 (it): Charles B. Norton, *American Breech-loading Small Arms* (New York, 1872), p. 10-11; *Boston Gazette,* Dec. 16, 1776; exhibit in Arts and Industries Building, Smithsonian Institution, Washington, D.C.

101 (breechloaders): Claud E. Fuller, *The Breech-loader in the Service* (Topeka, Kansas, 1933), pp. 65-66.

101 (Virginian): Off. Sec. War, Letters Sent to President, VI, 15, 230-231; Fuller, *Breech-loader in the Service*, p. 77.

102 (Hooker): E. P. Alexander, *Military Memoirs of a Confederate* (New York, 1907), p. 53.

102 (weapon): Roche, "Foreign Shoulder Arms," p. 8; Off. Sec. War, Letters to the President, VI, 230-231.

102 (destination, track): Robert W. McBride, *Personal Recollections of Abraham Lincoln* (Indianapolis, 1926), pp. 27-28; Stoddard, *Inside the White House*, pp. 41-42; photograph in N. A., Office of Chief Signal Officer, B5147.

103 (*Star*): Leech, *Reveille in Washington*, pp. 7, 83; Trollope, *North America*, II, 154-155; *Washington Star*, Aug. 8, 1862.

103 (duration): *Ibid.*, June 18, 1862, Sept. 2, 1863; Thomas Chamberlin, *History of the One Hundred and Fiftieth Regiment Pennsylvania Volunteers* (Philadelphia, 1895), p. 43.

104 (competition): Hay, *Addresses*, p. 327; *Washington Star*, Nov. 20, 1862; Charles O. Paullin, "President Lincoln and the Navy," *American Historical Review*, Jan. 1908, XIV, 300; Ord. Off., Letters to War Dept., XIV, 45, 127, 341; Tarbell, *Lincoln*, III, 96-97. The account quoted by Miss Tarbell identifies Lincoln's usual shooting companion only as "a certain messenger of the Ordnance Department"; but Mullikin was the only such messenger, and his military background implies familiarity with the use of guns.

104 (him, shooting): Stoddard, *Inside the White House*, pp. 41-44; Stoddard, *Lincoln and Johnson*, pp. 223-224; *Washington Star*, May 9, 1861.

104 (equal): "Rifled Guns," *Atlantic Monthly*, Oct. 1859, IV, 453; William Y. W. Ripley, *Vermont Riflemen in the War for the Union* (Rutland, Vermont, 1883), p. 186.

105 (blackberries): James L. Bowen, *History of the Thirty-Seventh Regiment Mass. Volunteers in the Civil War of 1861-1865* (Holyoke, Massachusetts, 1884), p. 355; Charles A. Stevens, *Berdan's United States Sharpshooters in the Army of the Potomac, 1861-1865* (St. Paul, Minnesota, 1892), pp. 343, 348-349.

105 (firing): *Army and Navy Journal*, Dec. 24, 1864.

106 (ammunition): Ripley, *Vermont Riflemen*, p. 58; *O. R.*, series 1, XII, part iii, pp. 767-768; MacDougall, "Federal Ordnance Bureau," pp. 51-52.

106 (muzzle-loaders): *O. R.*, series 3, I, 264.

107 (States): Nav. Bur. Ord., Letters to Secretary and Bureaux, II, 33.

107 (breechloaders): *O. R.*, series 3, I, 869-870.

107 (check): Ord. Off., "Inventions," class 6, No. 526.

107 (operation): *Idem.;* Ord. Off., "Experiments," class 6, No. 302.

108 (Lincoln): *Idem.*

108 (interests): 37th Cong., 2nd sess., Senate, Executive Document 72, p. 256, House, Executive Document 67, p. 100; Ord. Off., Letters Rec'd 1861, WD1177; Richard W. Thompson, *Recollections of Sixteen Presidents* (2 vols.; Indianapolis, 1894), II, 389; Lincoln, *Works,* VI, 259; Simon Cameron to Richard W. Thompson, Aug. 30, 1861, Collections of the Lincoln National Life Foundation, Fort Wayne, Indiana.

108 (men): 37th Cong., 2nd sess., House, Executive Document 67, p. 102.

108 (muzzle-loaders): *Ibid.,* p. 103; Ord. Off., "Inventions," class 6, No. 549; Ord. Off., Letters Rec'd 1861, WD1818, WD1827, WD1838.

109 (war): *O. R.,* series 3, I, 270; Off. Sec. War, Irregular Book I, R135; *Dyer Inquiry,* I, 431.

109 (suit): Stevens, *Sharpshooters,* p. 526; New York City directory, 1860-1861; *Washington Star,* June 4, 1861; Ord. Off., "Inventions," class 8, No. 130; *O. R.,* series 3, I, 270; Hiram Berdan to Lincoln, July 21, 1861, Lincoln Mss., L. C.

109 (in): Ripley, *Vermont Riflemen,* pp. 9-10; Ord. Off., Letters Rec'd 1861, B418.

109 (enemies): *O. R.,* series 3, I, 477; *Boston Transcript,* Sept. 5, 1861.

110 (Mansfield, audience): *Ibid.,* Sept. 11, 1861; Stevens, *Sharpshooters,* pp. 9-10; Observatory Journal, Sept. 20, 1861; *New York Times,* Sept. 21, 1861.

110-111 (yards, breechloaders): Stevens, *Sharpshooters,* pp. 10-11.

111 (rifle): Ripley, *Vermont Riflemen,* p. 12.

111 (muzzle-loader): Winston O. Smith, *The Sharps Rifle* (New York, 1943), pp. 3, 6, 51, 102.

112 (efficient): *Ibid.,* pp. 8, 9, 11, 16; Ord. Off., Letters Rec'd 1861, W136.

112 (more): *Ibid.,* M701; Ripley, *Vermont Riflemen,* pp. 12-13.

112 (Rifles): Off. Sec. War, Irregular Book I, W236.

113 (men, wield): *New York Evening Post,* Dec. 20, 1861.

114 (Hartford): *Scientific American,* Dec. 1921, p. 103; *Dictionary of American Biography,* XVII, 446.

114 (lever): *Idem.; Scientific American,* Dec. 1921, p. 102.

114 (Navy): Nav. Bur. Ord., "Examination of Inventions," III, 9-10; Nav. Bur. Ord., Misc. Letters Sent, III, 211.

114 (form): M. V. Dahlgren, *Memoir,* p. 336.

115 (alone, paper): Tarbell, *Lincoln,* III, 96-97.

115-116 (seen, successful): Ord. Off., Special Files, "Decisions of the Commission on Ordnance Contracts," Case 93.

116 (infantry): *O. R.,* Series 3, I, 733-734.

116 (rifles): *Scientific American,* Dec. 1921, p. 102; Ord. Off., Misc. Letters Sent, LIV, 278.

116 (it): Ord. Off., Letters Rec'd 1861, WD2135; 37th Cong., 2nd sess., Senate, Executive Document 72, p. 419.

CHAPTER EIGHT (pages 118-123)

118 (himself): *Washington Star,* June 6, 1861; Theodore Lyman, *Meade's Headquarters, 1863-1865* (Boston, 1922), p. 249; Leech, *Reveille in Washington,* p. 301; Allan Nevins, *The Emergence of Lincoln* (2 vols.; New York, 1950), II, 454; Ord. Off., Letters Rec'd 1862, WD1505, Letters Rec'd 1861, B312; John J. Astor to Hamilton Fish, Dec. 19, 1861, Hamilton Fish Mss., L. C.

119 (faction): Ord. Off., "Inventions," class 6, No. 439; see voluminous records filed in N. A., Patent Office Records, Nos. 32,887, 41,017, 41,857; also Ord. Off., Letters Rec'd 1861, WD864, Letters Rec'd 1862, S720; and Nav. Bur. Ord., "Index to Inventions Tested at the Washington Navy Yard."

119 (war): Ord. Off., "Inventions," class 6, No. 439; Nav. Bur. Ord., "Examination of Inventions," IV, 255-257; Ord. Off., Letters Rec'd 1862, WD834.

120 (one, Government): Ord. Off., Misc. Letters Sent, LIII, 174; Ord. Off., Letters Rec'd 1861, WD756; Ord. Off., "Inventions," class 1c, No. 153; Lincoln, *Works,* IV, 399.

120 (trials): Ord. Off., Letters Rec'd 1861, WD323, WD756; James W. Ripley to J. D. Mills, June 28, 1861, Ord. Off., Misc. Letters Sent.

120 (comment): Ord. Off., "Inventions," class 6, No. 439.

121 (idea): Ord. Off., Letters Rec'd 1861, D561; Ord. Off., Misc. Letters Sent, LIV, 172.

121 (engineer): Ord. Off., Letters Rec'd 1861, B375; *Boston Transcript,* Sept. 9, 1861; Off. Sec. War, Irregular Book I, W230.

121 (it): Ord. Off., "Inventions," Misc., No. 240.

121 (regiment): *Ibid.,* class 1c, No. 223.

122 (each): Lincoln, *Works,* V, 4-5; Ord. Off., Register of Letters Rec'd 1861, W858.

122 (buoyantly): Hay, *Diary,* p. 31.

122 (November): Lincoln, *Works*, IV, 468-469.
123 (pieces, worth): N. A., Adjutant General's Office, Department of the Gulf, Letters Sent, I, 25-26, 64; Off. Sec. War, Irregular Book III, p. 137.
123 (order): Ord. Off., Letters Rec'd 1862, WD241; George B. McClellan to Simon Cameron, Nov. 30, 1861, Lincoln Mss., L. C.; Lt. Col. George M. Chinn, U. S. M. C., *The Machine Gun* (3 vols.; Washington, D. C., 1951), I, 39; Lincoln, *Works*, V, 75-76.

CHAPTER NINE (pages 124-130)

124 (mark): Ord. Off., Misc. Letters Sent, LVI, 64.
124 (hand): Off. Sec. War, Letters Rec'd 1864, B303.
125 (unmistakable): George W. Nichols, *The Story of the Great March* (New York, 1865), p. 44; Off. Sec. War, Letters Rec'd 1864, B303; Russell, *My Diary*, p. 203.
125 (balls): *Portrait and Biographical Record of Adams County, Illinois* (Chicago, 1892), pp. 152-153; Browning, *Diary*, I, 197, 264, 446; Henry Asbury, *Reminiscences of Quincy, Illinois* (Quincy, Illinois, 1882), pp. 146-147; Ord. Off., "Inventions," class 1a, No. 178.
125 (howitzers): *Idem.;* Ord. Off., Misc. Letters Sent, LIII, 618.
126 (each): Lincoln, *Works*, V, 18; Ord. Off., Letters Rec'd 1863, WD498; Ord. Off., Register of Letters Rec'd 1861, WD1842.
126 (tactics): Ord. Off., "Inventions," class 1b, No. 67, 194; 38th Cong., 2nd sess., Senate, Rep. Comm. 121, p. 46; Russell, *My Diary*, p. 211; "Rifled Guns," *Atlantic Monthly*, Oct. 1859, p. 454; *New York Tribune*, June 9, 1861; Ord. Off., Misc. Letters Rec'd, 1-W-240.
126 (along): Ord. Off., "Inventions," class 1b, Nos. 68, 89, 93.
126-127 (device, fire): *Idem.;* U. S. Patent No. 38,110; Nav. Bur. Ord., "Examination of Inventions," III, 143-144, 187-192.
127 (Department): Ord. Off., "Inventions," class 1b, No. 78.
127 (bothered): James W. Ripley to Walter G. Sherwin, Aug. 5, 1861, Ord. Off., Misc. Letters Sent.
127 (surprised): Ord. Off., Register of Letters Rec'd 1861, WD1084; Ord. Off., "Inventions," class 1b, No. 85.
128 (disposal): *Ibid.*, No. 93; James A. L. Fremantle, *The Fremantle Diary* (Boston, 1954), p. 141.
128 (history): *O. R.,* series 3, I, 447.
128 (fifties): Samuel S. Cox, *Three Decades of Federal Legislation* (Providence, Rhode Island, 1885), p. 91.

128 (Gun): William Woodward, "Firearms—Their Evolution and Worcester's Part Therein," Worcester Historical Society *Publications*, New Series, I, part iv, p. 272; *New York Tribune*, June 13, 1861.

129 (manpower): *Idem.;* Sabin P. Pond to George B. McClellan, July 29, 1861, McClellan Mss., L. C.; Eli Thayer to Lincoln, Sept. 21, 1861, Lincoln Mss., L. C.; *Scientific American*, Dec. 21, 1861.

129 (for): Eli Thayer to Lincoln, Sept. 21, 1861, Lincoln Mss., L. C.; Lincoln, *Works*, IV, 534-535; certificate of Col. Charles P. Kingsbury, Nov. 30, 1861, Lincoln Mss., L.C.; Ord. Off., Misc. Letters Sent, LIV, 179.

129 (mistaken): Lincoln, *Works*, V, 85; Ord. Off., Letters Rec'd 1862, R603.

130 (results): Ezra S. Stearns, *Genealogical and Family History of the State of New Hampshire* (New York, 1908), III, 1297-1298; ·Off. Sec. War, Letters Rec'd 1861, R107; Ord. Off., "Inventions," class 1b, Nos. 125, 135.

130 (gun): *Ibid.,* No. 125.

130 (ordered): Off. Sec. War, Letters Rec'd 1861, R107; Ord. Off., "Inventions," class 1b, No. 135; Ord. Off., Register of Letters Rec'd 1862, R418.

CHAPTER TEN (pages 131-144)

131 (business): John G. Nicolay to Therena Bates, April 29, 1863, Nicolay Mss., L. C.

132 (Crazy-man): E. D. Tippett to Lincoln, Jan. 27, 1862, Nicolay Mss., L. C.; E. D. Tippett to Lincoln, Feb. 9, 1863, Lincoln Mss., L. C.

132 (*bite*): Wisconsin State Historical Society *Collections*, IX, 433; Peter Yates to Lincoln, Oct. 4, 1864, Lincoln Mss., L. C.

133 (End): Yates to Lincoln, Feb. 18, 1861, *ibid.*

133 (fame): Nav. Rec. Coll., "Inventions Referred to Permanent Commission, 1862-1864," No. 11; Peter Yates to Lincoln, Feb. 18, 1861, Lincoln Mss., L. C.

133 (for): Herndon and Weik, *Herndon's Lincoln*, III, 524-525.

134 (life): *Dictionary of American Biography*, XVII, 123.

134 (balance): Howard K. Beale (ed.), *The Diary of Edward Bates* (*Annual Report of the American Historical Association*, 1930, IV), p. 212; Observatory Journal, Dec. 21, 1861.

135 (armies): *Scientific American*, Nov. 9, 1861, April 11, Aug. 22, 1863.

135 (thrusts): *Ibid.,* Oct. 26, 1861.

135 (yards): *Ibid.,* March 8, 1862; *New York Herald,* Jan. 3, 1862.

135 (been): *Washington Star,* May 16, 1862; Moore, *Rebellion Record,* V, 232 (Doc.).

136 (ended): Stoddard, *Inside the White House,* p. 39; Sandburg, *War Years,* II, 295; *Scientific American,* Feb. 8, 1862, March 4, 1865.

136 (cottage): John D. Billings, *Hardtack and Coffee* (Boston, 1887), p. 275; Francis H. Buffum, *A Memorial of the Great Rebellion* (Boston, 1882), pp. 65-67.

137 (grave): Ord. Off., "Inventions," Misc., No. 440; Chittenden, *Recollections,* pp. 419-420.

137 (door): Ord. Off., "Inventions," Misc., Nos. 234, 379, 430, 439, 332.

137 (tread): *Ibid.,* Nos. 336, 355, 370; *Scientific American,* June 1, 1861, Oct. 11, 1862, Oct. 24, 1863, July 9, 1864; *Battles and Leaders,* II, 374, IV, 577, 487.

138 (been): *Scientific American,* June 15, 1861.

138 (credence): Ord. Off., "Inventions," class 1c, No. 219; James W. Ripley to Pliny Miles, Sept. 23, 1861, Ord. Off., Misc. Letters Sent.

138 (ended): Ord. Off., "Inventions," class 1c, No. 219; Benjamin F. Isherwood to Lincoln, Dec. 4, 1861, Lincoln Mss., L. C.

139 (Dickinson, fire): *Boston Transcript,* May 20, 1861; *Scientific American,* May 25, 1861; Moore, *Rebellion Record,* I, 98 (Incidents); Ord. Off., "Inventions," class 1c, No. 276.

139 (accepted): *Scientific American,* May 25, 1861; Ord. Off., "Inventions," class 1c, No. 276.

140 (offshore): *Scientific American,* May 25, 1861; *New York Tribune,* June 20, 1861.

140 (uncomfortable): Charles Latimer to Ethan A. Hitchcock, May 11, 1863, Ethan A. Hitchcock Mss., L. C.

141 (Washington): *Idem.;* Hay, *Addresses,* p. 327.

141 (it): Nav. Bur. Ord., Letters to Navy Dept., II, 17-18, IV, 73; George Green to John A. Dix, Oct. 4, 1864, Ethan A. Hitchcock Mss., L. C.

141 (mule): N. A., Adjutant General's Office, Letters Rec'd 1864, A195; undated memorandum by Ethan A. Hitchcock, Hitchcock Mss., L. C.

141 (nation): Ord. Off., "Inventions," class 1c, No. 315, classes 4 and 5, No. 606; Ord. Off., Register of Letters Rec'd 1864, WD1231.

141 (declared): Ord. Off., "Inventions," classes 4 and 5, Nos. 238, 421; *Scientific American*, Aug. 9, 1862.

142 (subject): Ord. Off., "Inventions," class 1c, Nos. 133, 214, 306, 328, 354, 356, 366, 371; James W. Ripley to Charles F. Raymond, Aug. 8, 1864, Ord. Off., Misc. Letters Sent.

142 (enemy): MacDougall, "Federal Ordnance Bureau," p. 76; Ord. Off., "Inventions," class 1c, No. 206, classes 4 and 5, No. 606; George D. Ramsay to Edwin M. Stanton, Jan. 6, 1864, Ord. Off., Letters to War Dept.

142 (alone): *Scientific American*, Dec. 1921, p. 102.

143 (to): Wells, *Annual of Scientific Discovery* for 1856, p. 38; Nav. Rec. Coll., "Letters on Inventions Referred to the Board of Examiners, 1861-1862," No. 164; Sandburg, *War Years*, II, 294.

143 (unlikely): Off. Sec. War, Letters Rec'd 1862, E. B., Prst 158.

143 (miles): *Scientific American*, March 14, 1863.

144 (meanwhile): Orpheus C. Kerr (Robert H. Newell), *The Orpheus C. Kerr Papers, First Series* (New York, 1862), pp. 84-87.

CHAPTER ELEVEN (pages 145-150)

145 (Union): Thomas, *Lincoln*, pp. 281-282.

146 (Shogunate): Off. Sec. War, Letters to the President, VI, 193; John A. Dahlgren to William Seward, Dec. 26, 1861, Lincoln Mss.; *New York Times*, June 23, 1869.

146 (worrying): *O. R.*, series 3, III, 429; Ord. Off., Letters to the War Department, XIII, 297; Alfred D. Chandler, Jr., "Dupont, Dahlgren, and the Civil War Nitre Shortage," *Military Affairs*, Fall, 1949, p. 144; M. V. Dahlgren, *Memoir*, p. 333.

147 (exports): Chandler, "Civil War Nitre Shortage," p. 145.

147 (cheerful): Thurlow Weed to Simon Cameron, Dec. 16, 1861, Cameron Mss., L. C.; *New York Evening Post*, Dec. 19, 1861.

147 (obsolete): Thomas, *Lincoln*, p. 282; 38th Cong., 2nd sess., Senate, Rep. Comm. 121, p. 44.

148 (year): Frederick V. Longstaff and A. Hilliard Atteridge, *The Book of the Machine Gun* (London, 1917), p. 2; *Dyer Inquiry*, I, 442; 38th Cong., 2nd sess., Senate, Rep. Comm. 121, pp. 66-68, 106, 177.

148 (better): Clipping in James W. Ripley Mss., Hoboken, New Jersey; Ord. Off., Misc. Letters Sent, LIII, 111; Ord. Off., Letters to the War Department, XIII, 443.

148 (support): Lincoln, *Works,* IV, 343; *Boston Transcript,* Nov. 16, 1861; James W. Ripley to Lincoln, June 24, 1861, Lincoln Mss., L. C.; *Washington Star,* June 25, 1861.

148 (Parrotts): Off. Sec. War, Letters to the President, VI, 383; *Scientific American,* July 6, 1861; 38th Cong., 2nd sess., Senate, Rep. Comm. 121, p. 67.

148-149 (fortifications, calibers, firing, device): Ord. Off., Special Files, "Ordnance Board Reports, 1860-1870," 109E; *Scientific American,* March 8, 1862.

150 (Lincoln): Joseph G. Totten to Lincoln, Dec. 13, 1861, Lincoln Mss., L. C.

150 (released): Chandler, "Civil War Nitre Shortage," p. 145.

150 (piles): 38th Cong., 2nd sess., Senate, Rep. Comm. 121, p. 179; Chandler, "Civil War Nitre Shortage," p. 145.

CHAPTER TWELVE (pages 151-170)

151 (with): M. V. Dahlgren, *Memoir,* p. 354; *Dictionary of American Biography,* VI, 569; Brooks, *Washington in Lincoln's Time,* pp. 32-33; Lincoln, *Works,* IV, 363.

151 (Department): *Washington Star,* Jan. 3, 1862.

152 (feeling): Dahlgren ms. memoir, p. 112.

152 (living): Observatory Journal, Jan. 2, 3, 1862; Benjamin B. French to H. F. French, Feb. 7, 1862, Benjamin B. French Mss., L. C.; Henry L. Dawes to Mrs. Henry L. Dawes, Jan. 6, 1862, Henry L. Dawes Mss., L. C.

153 (man): Lincoln, *Works,* V, 90, 92; *Washington Star,* Jan. 8, 1862.

153 (do): Observatory Journal, Jan. 10, 1862; Lincoln, *Works,* V, 95; Montgomery C. Meigs, "General M. C. Meigs on the Conduct of the Civil War," *American Historical Review,* XXVI, 292.

153 (resignation): Bates, *Diary,* p. 223; Lincoln, *Works,* V, 96-97.

154 (newspaperman): Frank A. Flower, *Edwin McMasters Stanton* (Akron, Ohio, 1905), p. 125.

154 (heretofore): Joshua Speed to Joseph Holt, Feb. 4, 1862, Joseph Holt Mss., L. C.

154 (direction): Thomas A. Scott to James W. Ripley, Jan. 20, 1862, Ord. Off., Letters Rec'd, 1862; Off. Sec. War, Irregular Book V, B103.

155 (compromise, itself mutiny): *Idem.*

155 (*possible*): *Idem.;* Edwin M. Stanton to William P. Fessenden, Feb. 2, 1862, Civil War Collection, New York Historical Society; Ord. Off., Misc. Letters Sent, LIV, 392.

156 (affair): *Tribune* dispatch quoted in *Boston Transcript,* Feb. 8, 1862; Ripley, *Vermont Riflemen,* p. 13.

156 (breechloaders): Off. Sec. War, Irregular Book V, B103; Ripley, *Vermont Riflemen,* pp. 15, 29; Stevens, *Sharpshooters,* p. 163.

156 (quarters): Entry for Feb. 18, 1862, diary of Mrs. Gustavus Fox, Blair Family Mss., L. C.

157 (boats): *Battles and Leaders,* I, 283-284; Ord. Off., Letters to the War Department, XIII, 208.

157 (purpose): Enclosure dated Dec. 31, 1861, in Henry W. Halleck to Lorenzo Thomas, Jan. 9, 1862, Lincoln Mss., L. C.

157 (schooner): Ord. Off., Letters to War Dept., XIII, 208; Richard S. West, Jr., *The Second Admiral: A Life of David Dixon Porter* (New York, 1937), pp. 113-114.

158 (of): *Ibid.,* 114-116; George W. Brown, "The Mortar Flotilla," in New York Commandery, Military Order of the Loyal Legion, *Personal Recollections of the War of the Rebellion* (New York, 1891), I, 173; David D. Porter to George B. McClellan, Nov. 24, 1861, McClellan Mss., L. C.

158 (York): West, *Porter,* p. 118.

158 (Bureau): Allan Nevins, *Abram S. Hewitt; with Some Account of Peter Cooper* (New York, 1935), pp. 199-200.

158 (Ripley): Henry Augustus Wise to Henry Alexander Wise, July 13, 1856, Henry Alexander Wise Mss., L. C.; *Dictionary of American Biography,* XX, 425; Henry A. Wise to Hamilton Fish, Nov. 24, 1859, Hamilton Fish Mss., L. C.; Allan B. Cole (ed.), "Private Journal of Henry A. Wise, U. S. N., on Board Frigate *Niagara* 1860," *Pacific Historical Review,* September 1942.

159 (tipplers): *Dictionary of American Biography,* XX, 425; "Journal of Occurrences," I, 195, David D. Porter Mss., L. C.; Henry Augustus Wise to Henry Alexander Wise, March 3, 1857, Wise Mss., L. C.; Russell, *My Diary,* p. 187 and *passim.*

159 (it): Henry A. Wise to Hamilton Fish, May 2, 1861, Fish Mss., L. C.

159 (where): "Journal of Occurrences," I, 194-196, David D. Porter Mss., L. C.; *Official Records of the Union and Confederate Navies in the War of the Rebellion* (hereafter cited as *"O. R., Navies"*) (30 vols.; Washington, D. C., 1894-1927), series 1, XXII, 469; Nevins, *Hewitt,* pp. 199-200; *National Intelligencer,* Feb. 10, 1862.

160 (Louis): Bates, *Diary,* p. 223.

160 (follies, them): James M. Hoppin, *Life of Andrew Hull Foote* (New York, 1874), p. 182; Andrew H. Foote to Henry A. Wise, Dec. 15, 1861, Wise Mss., N. Y. Historical Society.

161 (them): Bates, *Diary*, p. 223.

161 (made): *O. R., Navies*, series 1, XXII, 491, 497.

161 (way): Ripley to Lincoln, with enclosures, Jan. 11, 1862, Lincoln Mss., L. C.

161-162 (there, bombs, orders): *O. R., Navies*, series 1, XXII, 497, 516, 518; Hoppin, *Foote*, p. 193; Andrew H. Foote to Henry A. Wise, Jan. 22, 23, 1862, Wise Mss., N. Y. Historical Society; Lincoln, *Works*, V, 108.

162 (him): *O. R., Navies*, series 1, XXII, 650.

162 (DEATH): *Ibid.*, 522; Lincoln, *Works*, V, 110; John Symington to Lincoln, Feb. 3, 1862, Lincoln Mss., L. C.; Nevins, *Hewitt*, pp. 201-204; Charles Knap to Lincoln, Jan. 29, 1862, Nicolay Mss., L. C.

162 (*time*): E. M. Shield to Salmon P. Chase, Feb. 1, 8, 1862, Chase Mss., L. C.; Robert B. Warden, *An Account of the Private Life and Public Services of Salmon Portland Chase* (Cincinnati, 1874), p. 414; E. M. Shield to Salmon P. Chase, Feb. 15, 1862, Lincoln Mss., L. C.

163 (work): John Symington to Lincoln, Jan. 25, 1862, *ibid.;* Off. Sec. War, Irregular Book V, S85; *Washington Star*, Jan. 30, 1862; T. A. Scott to E. M. Stanton, Feb. 2, 1862, Edwin M. Stanton Mss., L. C.

163 (brimstone, him): *O. R., Navies*, series 1, XXII, 526-527.

164 (beheld): Trollope, *North America*, II, 293-295.

164 (boats): *O. R., Navies*, series 1, XXII, 549.

164-165 (inches, mortars): Moore, *Rebellion Record*, IV, 118-119 (Doc.); T. A. Scott to E. M. Stanton, Feb. 11, 1862, Stanton Mss., L. C.

165 (men): *Battles and Leaders*, I, 433-435, 437.

165 (metre): *O. R., Navies*, series 1, XXII, 650; see index to Lincoln Mss., L. C., under "Henry A. Wise," for dozens of such telegrams, January-March, 1862; A. H. Foote to H. A. Wise, March 3, 5, 1862, Lincoln Mss., L. C.; Nav. Rec. Coll., Letter-book of Henry A. Wise, 1862-1864, p. 56.

166 (explosion): Quoted in *Washington Star*, March 27, 1862.

166 (burst): *Frank Leslie's Illustrated History of the Civil War* (New York, 1895), p. 177.

166 (Orleans): Brown, "Mortar Flotilla," p. 173; *Battles and Leaders*, II, 38.

166 (neglected): Bates, *Diary*, p. 223.

167 (did): *O. R., Navies*, series 1, XXII, 523.

167 (had): *Ibid.*, 522; A. H. Foote to H. A. Wise, Jan. 24, 1862, Wise Mss., N. Y. Historical Society.

167 (boats): Entry for Jan. 26, 1862, diary of Mrs. Gustavus Fox, Blair Family Mss., L. C.; *O. R., Navies,* series 1, XXII, 522.

168 (Ordnance): Lincoln, *Works,* V, 110; *Dyer Inquiry,* II, 443; National Archives Record Group 94, "Register of Officers Arriving in Washington, 1861-1867," entry under Jan. 25, 1862; *Boston Transcript,* Jan. 29, Feb. 1, 1862.

168 (compulsion, contracts): *Dyer Inquiry,* I, 193.

168 (office): Ethan A. Hitchcock, *Fifty Years in Camp and Field* (William A. Croffut, ed., New York, 1909), pp. 438-439; "Mem. 19 March. 1862," in Ethan A. Hitchcock Mss., L. C.; *Dyer Inquiry,* II, 399.

169 (War): Flower, *Stanton,* pp. 116, 293; Doster, *Episodes,* p. 125; *Washington Star,* Jan. 24, 1862; *Dyer Inquiry,* II, 400, 523.

169 (service, Ripley, crowd): Hitchcock, *Fifty Years,* pp. 441; "Minutes of the War Board, March, 1862," Stanton Mss., L. C. (especially pp. 11, 14); Doster, *Episodes,* p. 119.

169 (treatment): Donn Piatt, *Memories of the Men Who Saved the Union* (New York, 1887), p. 63.

170 (22): Lincoln, *Works,* V, 111-112, 115.

170 (Peninsula): McClellan, *McClellan's Own Story,* pp. 229-237.

170 (present): Hay, *Diary,* p. 36; memorandum by John C. Ropes of a conversation with Edwin M. Stanton, dated Feb. 8, 1870, Horatio Woodman Mss., Mass. Hist. Soc.

170 (proceedings): Dahlgren ms. memoir, March 1862.

CHAPTER THIRTEEN (pages 171-178)

171 (details): *Battles and Leaders,* I, 730.

171 (grant): 29th Cong., 2nd sess., House Report 36, pp. 1-3, 5-6, 12; 20th Cong., 1st sess., House Report 252, p. 1; 30th Cong., 1st sess., House Executive Document 8, pp. 1306-1309; N. A., Legislative Records Section, Records of U. S. House of Representatives, 30th Cong., Committee on Naval Affairs; 30th Cong., 1st sess., House Report 294.

172 (flotilla): Stoddard, *Inside the White House,* pp. 38-39.

172 (her): James B. Eads to Lincoln, Sept. 19, 1863, Lincoln Mss., L. C.

172 (it): *Battles and Leaders,* I, 748.

172 (Roads): Gustavus V. Fox to Lincoln, March 4, 1862, Lincoln Mss., L. C.

173 (side): John A. Dahlgren to Ulric Dahlgren, March 11, 1862, Dahlgren Mss., L. C.

173 (unhindered): Leech, *Reveille*, p. 132; *Battles and Leaders*, I, 737.

174 (heart): Jeriah Bonham, *Fifty Years' Recollections* (Peoria, Ill., 1883), pp. 339-342.

174 (Dahlgren): George C. Bestor to Lincoln, April 17, 1861, Nicolay Mss., L. C.; Andrew H. Foote to John A. Dahlgren, Nov. 14, 1861, Dahlgren Mss., L. C.

174 (yielded): Lincoln, *Works*, V, 82, 162; Browning, *Diary*, I, 540; E. M. Shield to Salmon P. Chase, April 12, 1862, Chase Mss., L. C.; 37th Cong., 2nd sess., House Executive Document 150, p. 6.

174 (Washington): John I. Weed to John G. Nicolay, March 19, 1863, Nicolay Mss., L. C.; Bonham, *Fifty Years' Recollections*, pp. 342-343.

175 (Hay): *Washington Star*, April 4, 1862; J. B. Brigham to Lincoln, March 11, 1862, "Misc. Ordnance Papers," Nav. Bur. Ord.

175 (defense): *Washington Star*, May 21, 1862.

175 (them): 38th Cong., 2nd sess., Senate, Rep. Comm. 128, pp. 26, 46-47; Benjamin Severson to Lincoln, March 31, 1862, Lincoln Mss., L. C.; Joseph G. Totten to Lincoln, April 12, 1862, *ibid.;* Ord. Off., "Inventions," classes 4 and 5, No. 289; James W. Ripley to Benjamin Severson, May 15, 1861, Ord. Off., Misc. Letters Sent.

176 (aqueduct): *Hutchinson's Washington and Georgetown Directory* (Washington, D. C., 1863); Off. Sec. War, Letters Rec'd, 1864, Prst 485.

176-177 (lock, time, unknown): Louis H. Bolander, "The *Alligator,* First Federal Submarine of the Civil War," *U. S. Naval Institute Proceedings,* June 1938, pp. 847-850; Nav. Rec. Coll., Office of the Secretary of the Navy, "Misc. Letters Rec'd," XIII, 121.

177 (ship): Bolander, "The *Alligator,*" pp. 851-854.

177 (knot): W. B. Shubrick to Gideon Welles, April 21, 1862, Nav. Rec. Coll., "Reports from Board of Examiners, 1862," p. 81; Joseph Smith and Samuel Pook to Gideon Welles, May 5, 1862, Lincoln Mss., L. C.

177 (submarine): Lincoln, *Works*, VI, 209.

178 (trial): *Ibid.,* V, 156; Nav. Bur. Ord., Misc. Letters Rec'd, XXXI, 53; Nav. Rec. Coll., "Reports from Board of Examiners, 1862," p. 64.

178 (ship): Henry A. Wise to John A. Dahlgren, Oct. 20, 1862, Nav. Bur. Ord., "Letters, Washington"; Nav. Bur. Ord., "Examinations of Inventions," IV, 265-266; *Washington Star*, Dec. 11, 1862.

178 (Lincoln's): Nav. Bur. Ord., "Examinations of Inventions," V, 51-52.

CHAPTER FOURTEEN (pages 179-192)

179-180 (lash, shell): Ord. Off., "Inventions," class 8, No. 176; *New York Herald,* Jan. 3, 1862.

180 (1848): Ord. Off., "Inventions," classes 4 and 5, No. 792; for sources of information on Uriah Brown, see citations for 171 (grant) in Chapter XIII, above.

180 (crowded): *O. R.,* series 3, I, 606; Ord. Off., Misc. Letters Sent, LIII, 10.

181 (him): Ord. Off., "Inventions," classes 4 and 5, Nos. 569, 790; original of Lincoln's note to Ramsay is in Illinois State Historical Library.

181 (Department): Ord. Off., "Inventions," class 8, No. 176; Lincoln, *Works,* V, 99.

181 (clear, impressed): *Washington Star,* Jan. 16, 17, 1862; *Washington Sunday Morning Chronicle,* Jan. 19, 1862; Observatory Journal, Jan. 16, 1862.

182 (expedition): *Ibid.,* Jan. 22, 1862; *Washington Star,* Jan. 24, 1862; *National Intelligencer,* Jan. 23, 1862; Ord. Off., Letters Rec'd., 1862. WD236; Ord. Off., "Inventions," class 8, No. 176.

182 (Worster): *National Intelligencer,* Sept. 25, 1861, Mar. 19, 25, 1862; C. L. Leary to "Dear Sir," c. March 1862, in Civil War Collection, N. Y. Historical Society; Elisha Whittlesey to Lincoln, April 2, 1862, in *ibid.*

182 (preservative): J. Rutherford Worster to Lincoln, Oct. 20, 1860, Lincoln Mss., L. C.

183 (hand): *National Intelligencer,* March 12, 1862; *Washington Star,* March 12, 1862.

183 (Bloomington): E. A. Carr to J. R. Worster, April 7, 1862, Civil War Collection, N. Y. Historical Society.

183 (recorded): Copy of endorsement dated April 4, 1862, on J. McDougall to Henry W. Halleck of same date, in *ibid.*

184 (cartridge): U. S. Patent 35,311.

184 (superfluous): Ord. Off., "Inventions," class 1b, No. 139; *National Intelligencer,* May 7, 1862.

184 (10-pounders): Lincoln, *Works,* V, 198; G. D. Ramsay to E. M. Stanton, Dec. 30, 1863, Ord. Off., Letters to War Department; Ord. Off., Register of Letters Rec'd, 1864, WD413.

185 (Cannon): *The Biographical Encyclopedia of Ohio of the Nineteenth Century* (Cincinnati, 1876), pp. 419-420.

185-186 (air, rest, heels, cylinder, *off*): Ord. Off., "Inventions," class
    1b, No. 135; Observatory Journal, May 3, 1862; Nav. Bur. Ord.,
    "Examinations of Inventions," III, 143-144.
186-187 (calibers, giant): *Battles and Leaders,* II, 1-2, 9.
187 (nothing): Ord. Off., "Inventions," class 1a, No. 237; Nav. Bur.
    Ord., "Examinations of Inventions," III, V, and VI, *passim;* Ord.
    Off., Misc. Letters Sent, LIX, 227.
187 (place): *New York Herald,* June 26, 1862; John D. Brandt to
    Henry A. Wise, July 9, 1862, Wise Mss., N. Y. Historical Society.
188 (cannon): Description of firing range from *National Intelligencer,*
    June 27, 1865; *New York Herald,* June 26, 1862; account of Lin-
    coln's tour of the works taken from story of a similar tour in *ibid.,*
    March 8, 1862.
188 (Richmond): *New York Tribune,* June 26, 1862; John D. Brandt
    to Henry A. Wise, June 27, 1862, Wise Mss., N. Y. Historical So-
    ciety.
189 (of): 33rd Cong., Special Session, Senate, Report 1, p. 121; Nav.
    Rec. Coll., Executive Letters, July-August 1864, No. 156.
189 (him): 33rd Cong., Special Session, Senate, Report 1, pp. 14-18,
    129, 159.
189 (attempt): Horace Greeley to Samuel Strong, Feb. 20, 1861, Hor-
    ace Greeley Mss., L. C.; *Washington Star,* Jan. 18, Dec. 11, 1862.
190 (position): Ord. Off., "Experiments," class 6, No. 316.
190 (serviceability): Ord. Off., "Inventions," class 6, No. 492.
190 (number): James W. Ripley to Lincoln, May 5, 1862, Lincoln
    Mss., L. C.
190 (field): Ord. Off., Register of Letters Rec'd, 1862, WD1052; Ord.
    Off., "Experiments," class 6, No. 316.
190 (adopted): *Ibid.,* No. 353; Ord. Off., "Inventions," class 6, No.
    545.
191 (bullet): Benjamin B. French to his sister Pamela, Oct. 9, 1861,
    and to H. F. French, Oct. 13, 1861, Benjamin B. French Mss., L. C.;
    Ord. Off., "Inventions," class 8, No. 182.
191 (another): *Scientific American,* Feb. 2, 1861; James G. Benton, *A
    Course of Instruction in Ordnance and Gunnery* (New York,
    1861), pp. 83-84; Rev. Horace E. Hayden, "Explosive or Poisoned
    Musket or Rifle Balls . . . during the Civil War," *Southern His-
    torical Society Papers,* VIII, pp. 20-21 (Jan. 1880); Lyman,
    Meade's Headquarters, p. 112; Thomas H. Parker, *History of the
    51st Regiment of Pennsylvania Volunteers* (Philadelphia, 1869),
    pp. 227-228; *History of the Corn Exchange Regiment* (Philadel-
    phia, 1888), p. 199.

191 (heard): *Washington Star,* June 6, 1862.

192 (exploding): Harold L. Peterson, "Explosive Bullets," *The American Rifleman,* Feb. 1948, p. 30; U. S. Patent 40,468.

192 (battle): Ord. Off., Misc. Letters Rec'd, 1-F-108; Lincoln, *Works,* V, 257.

192 (projectile): Ord. Off., "Inventions," class 8, No. 194; Ord. Off., Letters Rec'd, 1862, B778.

CHAPTER FIFTEEN (pages 194-206)

194 (Arsenal): Ord. Off., Letters Rec'd, 1862, G198.

195 (bridgehead): *Re-union of the 28th & 147th Regiments, Pennsylvania Volunteers* (Philadelphia, 1872), p. 4.

195 (Middleburg): *Washington Star,* April 5, 1862.

195 (guns): *Scientific American,* May 10, 1862.

196 (mouth): Ord. Off., Letters Rec'd, 1862, G198.

196 (day, report, ordered, dispatch): *Ibid.,* F138, F140; Ord. Off., Misc. Letters Sent, LV, 140.

196 (Guns): Ord. Off., Letters Rec'd, 1862, N47.

197 (files): *Ibid.,* F144, and corresponding item in Register; James W. Ripley to John G. Nicolay, May 16, 1862, Nicolay Mss., L. C.

197 (Army): Ord. Off., "Open Purchases, 1861-1867," p. 2.

197 (guns): *Washington Star,* Sept. 24, 1862.

197 (now): Ord. Off., Letters Rec'd, 1862, R527; Moore, *Rebellion Record,* V, 446 (Doc.); *Washington Star,* Sept. 19, 1862.

198 (Dixie): Ord. Off., Letters Rec'd, 1862, P240.

198 (fifty guns): Nav. Bur. Ord., Misc. Letters Rec'd, XX (new series), 67.

198 (gun): Ord. Off., Letters Rec'd, 1863, A437; *New York Herald,* April 21, 1862; Hay, *Diary,* p. 15.

199 (houses): Luther S. Dickey, *History of the Eighty-fifth Regiment Pennsylvania Volunteer Infantry 1861-1865* (New York, 1915), p. 33.

199 (consideration): *New York Evening Post,* April 25, 1862.

199 (Yorktown): Ord. Off., Letters to War Dept., XV, 327.

199 (have): Ord. Off., Letters Rec'd, 1862, K174; Oliver W. Norton, *Army Letters, 1861-1865* (Chicago, 1903), p. 87.

200 (gunner): Robert S. Westbrook, *History of the 49th Pennsylvania Volunteers* (Altoona, Pa., 1898), p. 115.

200 (hopper): Ord. Off., "Inventions," class 1c, No. 277; Ord. Off., Letters Rec'd, 1862, K174; Nav. Bur. Ord., "Examinations of Inventions," IV, 255-257.

200 (wrong): Ord. Off., Letters Rec'd, 1863, A401.

200 (paid): Chinn, *The Machine Gun*, I, 40.

201 (Monroe): Lincoln, *Works*, V, 181; *O. R.*, series 1, XI, part iii, p. 98; W. F. Barry to S. Williams, April 24, 1862, George B. McClellan Mss., L. C.; Ord. Off., Letters Rec'd, 1862, B1030.

201 (materials): Ord. Off., "Inventions," classes 4 and 5, No. 569; Ord. Off., Misc. Letters Rec'd, 1-WD-194.

201 (Washington): Ord. Off., Letters Rec'd, 1862, WD1275, WD-1440.

201 (buried): *Ibid.,* B1030; *ibid.,* 1863, F521.

201 (objected): Nav. Bur. Ord., "Examinations of Inventions," III, 187-192; Ord. Off., Misc. Letters Sent, LV, 437; Ord. Off., Letters Rec'd, 1862, R865.

202 (cannon, Ripley): Ord. Off., Letters Rec'd, 1863, WD676; Ord. Off., Misc. Letters Sent, LVIII, 398.

202 (publicity): 37th Cong., 2nd sess., Senate, Executive Document 72, pp. 256-257, 273; *New York Herald,* Jan. 4, 1862.

202 (canceled): Chittenden, *Recollections,* pp. 186-187; 37th Cong., 2nd sess., Senate, Executive Document 72, p. 262.

203 (delivered): Ord. Off., Letters Rec'd, 1863, WD683, 1862, U18.

203 (treasurer, Armory): 37th Cong., 2nd sess., Senate, Executive Document 72, p. 419; *Scientific American,* Jan. 25, 1862.

204 (July): 37th Cong., 2nd sess., Senate, Executive Document 72, pp. 420, 425, 427, 429-430; Nav. Bur. Ord., Misc. Letters Sent, XXXI, 69.

204 (rifles): Ord. Off., "Purchases of Ordnance," p. 201.

204 (Battles): Stevens, *Sharpshooters,* p. 103.

204 (work): *Ibid.,* pp. 119, 125-126; *O. R.,* series 1, XI, part ii, p. 278.

205 (muzzle-loaders): Stevens, *Sharpshooters,* p. 134; Ripley, *Vermont Riflemen,* pp. 53-54.

205 (rifles,): Roche, "Foreign Shoulder Arms," p. 120 n.

205 (country): Ord. Off., Letters Rec'd, 1863, WD1097; 38th Cong., 2nd sess., House, Executive Document 15, p. 29.

206 (sun): Stevens, *Sharpshooters,* pp. 202-203, 211; Lincoln, *Works,* V, 431.

206 (well, avail): Off. Sec. War, Irregular Book V, B103; Hiram Berdan to Lincoln, Nov. 27, 1862, Lincoln Mss., L. C.

206 (obvious): *Scientific American,* Jan. 3, 1863.

CHAPTER SIXTEEN (pages 207-227)

207 (admiral): Lincoln, *Works,* V, 262; John A. Dahlgren to Lincoln, July 10, 1862, Lincoln Mss., L. C.

207 (view): Welles, *Diary,* I, 164.

208 (Bureau): Lincoln, *Works,* V, 112-113.

208 (me): Dahlgren ms. memoir, pp. 121-122, 135-136.

208 (fall): Welles, *Diary,* I, 164.

208 (inventions): Ord. Off., "Purchases of Ordnance, 1861-1867," p. 169; Ord. Off., "Inventions," class 1c, No. 278.

208 (gun): Lincoln, *Works,* V, 263.

209 (danger): James R. Haskell, *Reports on the Rafael Repeater* (Washington, D. C., 1862), pp. 4-6; Ord. Off., "Inventions," class 1c, No. 277.

209 (civilization): *Idem.;* Nav. Bur. Ord., "Examinations of Inventions," IV, 17-19.

209 (Yard): John Ericsson to Lincoln, Aug. 2, 1862, Lincoln Mss., L. C.

210 (impressed, establishments, carriage): Carpenter, *Six Months in the White House,* pp. 113-114, 155, 165; M. V. Dahlgren, *Memoir,* p. 378; *Washington Star,* Aug. 8, 1862; *New York Tribune,* Aug. 8, 1862.

210 (service): Ord. Off., "Inventions," class 1c, No. 277. (A copy with minor variations is printed in Lincoln, *Works,* V, 365.)

211 (concession, regiment): Ord. Off., Register of Letters Rec'd, 1862, F235; James R. Haskell to Thurlow Weed, Oct. 8, 1862, Weed Mss., University of Rochester Library.

211 (Repeaters): Thurlow Weed to John G. Nicolay, Nov. 14, 1862, Nicolay Mss., L. C.

211 (stocks): Chandler, "Civil War Nitre Shortage," pp. 144-145.

212 (Republican): Photo of Diller in Illinois State Historical Library; Isaac Diller to Col. Francis Pickens, Oct. 7, 1860, in *ibid.;* J. F. Ringwalt, *The Diller Family* (New Holland, Pa., 1942), pp. 62-63; Angle, *"Here I Have Lived,"* p. 176.

212 (1862): Samuel Ricker to Jeremiah S. Black, Sept. 23, 1860, Feb. 15, 1861, Jeremiah Black Mss., L. C.; Edgar F. Smith, *Charles Mayer Wetherill* (reprinted from the *Journal of Chemical Education,* 1929), p. 46.

212 (Liebig): Isaac Diller to Lincoln, Oct. 31, 1861, Lincoln Mss., L. C.; Smith, *Wetherill,* pp. 2, 8, 35, 45, 59.

213 (Wetherill): *Ibid.,* p. 47; Nav. Bur. Ord., "Examination of Inventions," IV, 128-130; Isaac Diller to Lincoln, Sept. 10, 1862, Lincoln Mss., L. C.

213 (friend): Thomas Ewing, Sr., to Mrs. William T. Sherman, Dec. 12, 1862, Ewing Family Mss., L. C.; Isaac Diller to Lincoln, Oct. 31, 1863, Lincoln Mss., L. C.

213 (pay): Lincoln, *Works*, VI, 3.

214 (battles): M. V. Dahlgren, *Memoir*, pp. 383-384.

214-215 (myself, States, condition): Nav. Bur. Ord., Letters to Navy Department, III, 11-12; M. V. Dahlgren, *Memoir*, p. 372; Welles, *Diary*, I, 163-164.

215 (railroads): Herman Haupt and Frank A. Flower, *Reminiscences of General Herman Haupt* (Milwaukee, 1901), pp. xiii-xvi.

216 (Lincoln): Miller, *Photographic History*, V, 277, 280; Hay, *Diary*, p. 46.

216-217 (questioned, attacks, generally): *Boston Transcript*, Nov. 17, 1862.

217 (scoundrels): Welles, *Diary*, I, 511.

218 (Key, Chapultepec): Paul D. Olejar, "Rockets in Early American Wars," *Military Affairs*, Winter, 1946, pp. 22-23, 28-31; Reuben H. Walworth, *Hyde Genealogy* (2 vols.; Albany, 1864), II, 711.

218 (Monroe): Ord. Off., Register of Letters Rec'd, 1861, WD570; Ord. Off., Letters Rec'd, 1861, B778, 1863, F537; J. W. Ripley to C. P. Kingsbury, April 15, 1862, Ord. Off., Misc. Letters Sent; John Donaghy, *Army Experience of Capt. John Donaghy* (Deland, Fla., 1926), p. 84; Luther S. Dickey, *History of the 103d Regiment Pennsylvania . . . Infantry* (Chicago, 1910), p. 34.

219 (service): *Washington Star*, April 23, 1862.

219 (head): U. S. Patent 40,041.

219 (case, stand, Fredericksburg, party): Nav. Bur. Ord., "Examinations of Inventions," IV, 215; Nav. Bur. Ord., "Index to Inventions Tested by Capt. Dahlgren 1848-1863 at the Washington Navy Yard," memorandum at p. 6; M. V. Dahlgren, *Memoir*, p. 382.

220 (musket): Nav. Bur. Ord., "Examinations of Inventions," IV, 215, 217; Ord. Off., Register of Letters Rec'd, 1864, WD1.

220 (gun): Browning, *Diary*, I, 535-536; Nav. Bur. Ord., Misc. Letters Sent, V, 389-391; Nav. Bur. Ord., Misc. Letters Rec'd, XIX (new series), part ii, No. 36; Nav. Bur. Ord., Reports on Inventions, II, 17.

220-221 (muzzle, firing): Ord. Off., "Inventions," class 8, No. 238.

221 (yards): Ord. Off., "Experiments," class 8, No. 194½

221 (dangerous): Nav. Bur. Ord., "Examinations of Inventions," IV, 225-227.

221 (invention, Peckham): Ord. Off., Letters Rec'd, 1862, WD2031, WD2034-5, WD2037.

222-223 (inventor, 1862, President, answer, desirable): Ord. Off., "Inventions," class 8, No. 238.

223 (possible): *Idem.;* Nav. Bur. Ord., Misc. Letters Rec'd, XIX (new series), 10; Nav. Bur. Ord., "Examinations of Inventions," IV, 291-294.

223 (Government): *Scientific American,* July 19, 1862.

223 (anyway): Nav. Rec. Coll., "Letters Referred to Permanent Commission: Unfinished Business, 1864-1865," p. 69.

224 (Board): Ord. Off., Letters to War Dept., XIII, 139-140; *Scientific American,* Aug. 3, 1861, Jan. 4, 25, Feb. 16, May 17, 1862; 38th Cong., 2nd sess., Senate, Rep. Comm. 121, p. 108.

224 (statement): *Boston Transcript,* Jan. 3, 1862; Gideon Welles to R. C. Bristol, Aug. 28, 1862, Nav. Bur. Ord., Letters Rec'd, "Inventions, Rifle & Smoothbore, 1862-'4"; Charles H. Davis, *Life of Charles Henry Davis, Rear Admiral* (Boston, 1899), pp. 286, 289-290; Frederick W. True (ed.), *A History of the First Half-Century of the National Academy of Sciences* (Washington, D. C., 1913), pp. 1-2; the records of the Permanent Commission are in Nav. Rec. Coll.

224 (Academy): *New York Times,* May 21, 1863; Nav. Rec. Coll., "Minutes of the Permanent Commission, Feb. 11, 1863-Feb. 24, 1864," p. 115.

225 (Secretary): M. V. Dahlgren, *Memoir,* p. 386; Lincoln, *Works,* VI, 59; Welles, *Diary,* I, 240; Nav. Rec. Coll., Navy Department, Executive Letters, Feb., 1863, p. 117.

225 (Ridge): Isaac Diller to Lincoln, April 25, Oct. 31, 1863, Lincoln Mss., L. C.; Charles Wetherill to Isaac Diller, Oct. 31, 1863, *ibid.*

226 (powder): William N. Jeffers to Henry A. Wise, June 18, 1863, Wise Mss., New York Historical Society.

226 (work): M. V. Dahlgren, *Memoir,* p. 387; Observatory Journal, Feb. 4, 1863.

227 (us): Nav. Bur. Ord., Misc. Letters Rec'd, XXXIV, 136, Letters Sent, XXIX, 236; John G. Barnard to Lincoln, Feb. 13, 1863, Lincoln Mss., L. C.; *Chronicle* account quoted in *Scientific American,* March 14, 1863.

227 (summer): Nav. Bur. Ord., Misc. Letters Rec'd, XXIV (new series), part ii, No. 45.

227 (him, behind, it): Welles, *Diary,* I, 238-240.

CHAPTER SEVENTEEN (pages 228-248)

228 (secession): William T. Sherman, *Memoirs of General William T. Sherman* (2 vols.; New York, 1875), II, 223.

229 (before): Welles, *Diary*, I, 247.

229 (fire): Fremantle, *Diary*, p. 143.

229 (affair): M. V. Dahlgren, *Memoir*, p. 388.

230 (truth): Ord. Off., "Inventions," classes 4 and 5, No. 751; New York City directories, 1861-1863; Nav. Rec. Coll., Letterbook of Capt. H. A. Wise, 1862-1864, pp. 79, 236-237.

230 (1861): *National Cyclopedia of American Biography*, XIII, 91-92; *Newark* (N. J.) *Daily Advertiser*, July 3, 1871.

231 (times): *Idem.*

231 (himself): Philip Kearney to Cortlandt Parker, Aug. 14, Oct. 1, 1861, Philip Kearney Mss., L. C.

231 (lark, bestowed): *Newark Daily Advertiser*, July 3, 1871; Oliver S. Halsted, Jr., to Abraham Lincoln, Aug. 27, 1861, Nicolay Mss., L. C.

232 (betrayal): Philip Kearney to Cortlandt Parker, May 27, 1862, Philip Kearney Mss., L. C.; *Washington Star*, Oct. 16, 22, 1862; Oliver S. Halsted, Jr., to John G. Nicolay, Nov. 7, 1862, Nicolay Mss., L. C.; *Washington Star*, Nov. 25, 1862.

232 (purchases): Halsted to Nicolay, Nov. 7, 1862, Nicolay Mss., L. C.; Lincoln, *Works*, V, 498.

232 (Point): Ord. Off., "Inventions," class 8, No. 225.

232 (demonstration): Lorin Blodgett and others to Lincoln, March 23, 1863, Lincoln Mss., L. C.; Lincoln, *Works*, VI, 145.

233 (Harbor): O. S. Halsted, Jr., to Lincoln, April 25, 1863, Lincoln Mss., L. C.

233 (Du Pont): Welles, *Diary*, I, 265; *Battles and Leaders*, IV, 40.

233 (blacksmith): *New York Tribune*, Jan. 23, 1887.

234 (City): *Dyer Inquiry*, II, 65, 190; petition of Oliver Ames in *re* Horatio Ames's estate, Supreme Court of the District of Columbia, January Term, 1872; Nav. Rec. Coll., Executive Letters, Sept. 1863, No. 37.

234 (Odin): Ord. Off., "Inventions," class 1a, No. 162; 38th Cong., 2nd sess., Senate, Rep. Comm. 121, pp. 70, 133; *New York Tribune*, Jan. 23, 1887.

234 (Bureau): Ord. Off., "Inventions," class 1a, No. 162.

234 (fraud): Nav. Bur. Ord., "Ames Wrought Iron Gun," pp. 1-4; 38th Cong., 2nd sess., Senate, Rep. Comm. 121, p. 132; Nav. Bur. Ord., Misc. Letters Sent, V, 18-19; *Dyer Inquiry*, II, 58, 155.

235 (insisted): Nav. Rec. Coll., Subject File BG, "Correspondence about . . . cannon made by Horatio Ames," Horatio Ames to Gideon Welles, Jan. 3, 1862 [actually 1863].

235 (reached): Nav. Bur. Ord., Misc. Letters Sent, V, 481, VI, 442-
    446; H. A. Wise to J. G. Nicolay, Feb. 6, 1863, Lincoln Mss., L. C.;
    H. A. Wise to J. A. Dahlgren, April 4, 1863, Dahlgren Mss., L. C.;
    H. Ames to E. M. Stanton, April 3, 1863, J. W. Ripley to E. M.
    Stanton, April 11, 1863, H. Ames to P. H. Watson, April 16, 1863,
    Ord. Off., "Ames Papers"; Nav. Rec. Coll., Subject File BG, "Cor-
    respondence about . . . cannon made by Horatio Ames," H. Ames
    to G. Welles, March 17, 1863.

235 (enlisted): H. Ames to L. F. S. Foster, March 14, 1863, Nav. Bur.
    Ord., "Ames Wrought Iron Gun"; A. A. Harwood to H. A. Wise,
    April 28, 1863, Wise Mss., N. Y. Hist. Soc.; Nav. Bur. Ord., Misc.
    Letters Rec'd, XXII (new series), 106; O. S. Halsted, Jr., to Lin-
    coln, April 25, 1863, Lincoln Mss., L. C.

235-236 (out, opened, it): *Idem.*

236 (influences): M. V. Dahlgren, *Memoir,* pp. 390-391; Nav. Bur.
    Ord., Letters to the Navy Department, III, 133-138; Observatory
    Journal, April 28, 1863.

237 (drizzle): Nav. Bur. Ord., Letters to the Navy Department, III,
    133-138; entry for April 29, 1863, in Diary of Virginia Fox, Blair
    Family Mss., L. C.

237 (day): A. A. Harwood to H. A. Wise, April 28, 1863, Wise Mss.,
    N. Y. Hist. Soc.

237 (hesitation): P. H. Watson to Lincoln, April 28, 1863, Lincoln
    Mss., L. C.; Ord. Off., "Inventions," class 8, No. 225; S. V. Benét
    to J. W. Ripley, April 10, 1863, Lincoln Mss., L. C.

237-238 (Ames, them): Ord. Off., Misc. Letters Rec'd, 1-WD-550;
    Ord. Off., Letters Rec'd, 1863, H278.

238 (service): E. M. Stanton to J. W. Ripley, May 12, 1863, Stanton
    Mss., L. C.; Lincoln, *Works,* VI, 255, 270-271; Ord. Off., Letters
    to the War Department, XIV, 253-254.

238 (terms): Nav. Bur. Ord., Misc. Letters Rec'd, XXII (new series),
    106, Misc. Letters Sent, VI, 427, IX, 332; J. D. Brandt to H. A.
    Wise, June 25, 1863, Wise Mss., N. Y. Hist. Soc.; *Scientific Amer-
    ican,* Aug. 29, 1863.

239 (inseparable): Photograph of Ferriss in the Oneida Historical So-
    ciety, Utica, N. Y.; Raymond G. Ferriss, Ilion, N. Y., to the writer,
    May 9, 1954; M. M. Bagg, *Pioneers of Utica* (Utica, N. Y., 1877),
    pp. 74-75; Utica directories, 1827-1829; Ord. Off., "Inventions,"
    classes 4 and 5, No. 349.

239 (bore): D. O. Macomber to Lincoln, April 7, 1864, Lincoln Mss.,
    L. C.; Charles B. Norton and W. J. Valentine, *Report on the Muni-*

tions of War (Reports of the U. S. Commissioners to the Paris Universal Exposition of 1867, Washington, 1868), pp. 79-83.

239-240 (Charleston, latter, would) : Nav. Bur. Ord., "Examinations of Inventions," V, 303-307; Ord. Off., Letters Rec'd, 1863, WD637; D. O. Macomber to Lincoln, April 7, 1864, Lincoln Mss., L. C.

240 (Charleston): *Idem.; New York Tribune,* Sept. 3, 1863; *New York Herald,* Sept. 16, 1863; Ord. Off., Letters to the War Department, XIV, 395-396, 548-550.

240 (out): Welles, *Diary,* I, 309; *Battles and Leaders,* IV, 54-55.

241 (wrong): Welles, *Diary,* I, 309-317.

241 (admiral): M. V. Dahlgren, *Memoir,* p. 395; Welles, *Diary,* I, 337.

242 (flotilla): Bound Volume VII, 237-238, David D. Porter Mss., L. C.; D. D. Porter to Mrs. Evelina Porter, Nov. 13, 1863, May 18, 1864, *ibid.;* U. S. Patent 38,424; Nav. Bur. Ord., Misc. Letters Rec'd, XXI (new series), part i, No. 94, part ii, No. 14.

242 (circulars): *O. R., Navies,* series 1, XXV, 518.

242 (mind, months): D. D. Porter to Mrs. E. Porter, Nov. 13, 1863, May 18, 1864, David D. Porter Mss., L. C.; Bound Volume VII, 237-238, *ibid.*

243 (1863): Off. Sec. War, Irregular Book V, H79; *O. R.,* series 1, XLVII, part ii, p. 58; Ord. Off., Misc. Letters Sent, LVIII, 521; *Scientific American,* Sept. 19, 1863; *Battles and Leaders,* IV, 73.

243 (flight): *Army and Navy Journal,* July 30, 1864.

244 (death): Quincy A. Gillmore, *Engineer and Artillery Operations Against the Defense of Charleston Harbor in 1863* (New York, 1865), p. 314; 38th Cong., 2nd sess., Senate, Rep. Comm. 121, p. 81; *Washington Star,* Sept. 3, 1863; Moore, *Rebellion Record,* VII, 62-63 (Incidents).

244 (all): *Battles and Leaders,* IV, 73-74; *O. R.,* series 1, XXVIII, part i, p. 34.

244 (importunities): *Idem.; Scientific American,* Oct. 24, 1863; Ord. Off., "Inventions," class 8, No. 250; *Philadelphia Public Ledger and Daily Transcript,* Nov. 27, 28, 1863.

245 (order): *O. R.,* series 1, XLVII, part ii, p. 58; D. Ammen to H. A. Wise, Wise Mss., N. Y. Hist. Soc.

245 (warfare): Capt. E. C. Boynton, "Greek Fire and Other Inflammables," *U. S. Service Magazine,* Jan. 1864, p. 55; Nav. Bur. Ord., Letters Sent, LXXIV, 5-6; Ord. Off., Misc. Letters Rec'd, 1-WD-194.

245-246 (Ames, Lincoln, Lincoln, interview): *New York Tribune,* Jan. 23, 1887. Brandegee's account places the episode in June 1863, but September is the time indicated by contemporary records, e. g., H. A. Wise to "Hon. A. Brandegee, Willard's Hotel," Sept. 25, 1863, enclosing "copies of the correspondence relative to Mr. Ames' wrought iron gun," Nav. Bur. Ord., Misc. Letters Sent, VII, 448-449.

247 (requests): Lincoln, *Works,* VI, 484-485; Hay, *Diary,* p. 107.

247 (in): *Battles and Leaders,* IV, 26.

247 (Tycoon): Hay, *Diary,* p. 107.

248 (Ypres): New York City directories, 1860-1863; Ord. Off., "Inventions," class 8, No. 191, classes 4 and 5, No. 859.

248 (to): M. V. Dahlgren, *Memoir,* p. 433.

CHAPTER EIGHTEEN (pages 249-267)

249 (Ordnance): R. B. Marcy to Mrs. George B. McClellan, Nov. 18, 1861, McClellan Mss., L. C.; Browning, *Diary,* I, 533-534; Washington, D. C., directories, 1862-1863.

250 (recorded): N. A., General Records of the Treasury Department, AB series, Letters from Executive Officers, 1863, War Dept., part 1, vol. III, No. 20; *ibid.,* H series, Letters to Collector at N. Y., vol. XVIII, pp. 62-63.

250 (guns): Nav. Bur. Ord., Letters on the Armament of the Mississippi Squadron, 1862-1863, pp. 135-136; Nav. Bur. Ord., Misc. Letters Rec'd, XX (new series), 84, 128, 149; Nav. Bur. Ord., Letters Sent, LIII, 36; W. T. Sherman to Thomas Ewing, Sr., Aug. 12, 1870, Ewing Family Mss., L. C.

250 (guns): *Scientific American,* March 28, 1863; Ord. Off., Letters Rec'd, 1863, WD315, A401; Ord. Off., Register of Letters Rec'd, 1863, WD285; Ord. Off., "Inventions," class 8, No. 172; Ord. Off., "Experiments," class 8, No. 232.

251 (Chickamauga): Ord. Off., Register of Letters Rec'd, 1863, R128; Ord. Off., Misc. Letters Sent, LVIII, 296, 335; Ord. Off., Letters Rec'd, 1863, S947.

251 (Service): Ord. Off., "Inventions," class 1c, No. 277.

251 (war): J. R. Haskell to Thurlow Weed, Oct. 8, 1862, Weed Mss., University of Rochester Library.

252 (for): *O. R.,* series 3, II, 858; MacDougall, "Federal Ordnance Bureau," p. 166; *Washington Star,* Jan. 1, 1863; table of monthly output, 1862-1863, Springfield Armory Library.

252 (Sickles): Ord. Off., "Inventions," class 6, No. 549; Ord. Off., Register of Letters Rec'd, 1862, WD1899.

252 (price): Ord. Off., "Inventions," class 6, No. 549; Ord. Off., Letters Rec'd, 1863, WD63, WD130.

253 (rifles): Ord. Off., Letters Rec'd, 1863, WD179, H72; Ord. Off., Misc. Letters Sent, LVII, 345-346.

253 (purpose): Ord. Off., Letters Rec'd, 1863, WD188 (filed with WD292), WD606; Ord Off., Letters to War Department, XIV, 158.

253 (Vicksburg): Nav. Bur. Ord., Misc. Letters Rec'd, XX (new series), 116; Scientific American, Dec. 1921, p. 103.

254 (regiments): Battles and Leaders, III, 66; Lincoln, Works, VI, 108; New York Tribune, Nov. 15, 1862; Ord. Off., Register of Letters Rec'd, 1862, WD1897; Washington Star, Jan. 7, 1863.

254 (received, infantry): O. R., series 1, XXIII, part ii, p. 38; ibid., series 3, III, 46.

254 (idea): William F. G. Shanks, Personal Recollections of Distinguished Generals (New York, 1866), p. 241; Lincoln, Works, V, 283, VI, 108; Browning, Diary, I, 554; Off. Sec. War, Irregular Book V, R48.

255 (made): Washington Star, March 3, 1863; Ord. Off., Misc. Letters Sent, LVIII, 16.

255-256 (brigade, raids, Brigade): Samuel C. Williams, General John T. Wilder (Bloomington, Ind., 1936), pp. 1-3, 11, 14, 18-19; Battles and Leaders, III, 636.

256 (began): Stevens, Sharpshooters, p. 264; William N. Jeffers to Henry A. Wise, June 18, 1863, Wise Mss., N. Y. Hist. Soc.

256 (wanted): Ord. Off., Misc. Letters Sent, LVIII, 366.

257 (woods, battle): Stevens, Sharpshooters, pp. 304-305, 307, 309-311.

257 (quick): Ord. Off., Letters to the War Department, XIII, 419; Hayden, "Explosive Rifle Balls," pp. 23-24; Martin Haynes, A History of the Second Regiment, New Hampshire Volunteer Infantry, in the War of the Rebellion (Lakeport, N. H., 1896), p. 172.

258 (weapons): Dyer Inquiry, II, 128, 536-537.

258 (bore): Ibid., I, 20, 28, II, 511, 546-547.

258 (applaud): Ord. Off., Special Files, "Misc. Letters Rec'd," 1-S-5.

259 (1863): Dyer Inquiry, II, 529, 537, 551.

259 (possible): Ibid., II, 537; Lincoln, Works, VI, 97.

259 (possible): Dyer Inquiry, I, 31, II, 537; Nav. Bur. Ord., "Reports on Inventions," VI, 7.

260 (Point): Welles, *Diary*, I, 370-371; *Dyer Inquiry*, I, 31, II, 380; Nav. Bur. Ord., "Examinations of Inventions," V, 331-334.

260 (Vicksburg): Hay, *Diary*, p. 77.

260 (remained): Galusha B. Balch, *Genealogy of the Balch Families in America* (Salem, Mass., 1897), p. 306; *Dyer Inquiry*, I, 194, 488-489, 499-500; J. W. Ripley to G. T. Balch, Sept. 19, 1864, Elihu B. Washburne Mss., L. C.

261 (examination): E. M. Stanton to J. W. Ripley, June 21, 1863, E. M. Stanton to George Opdyke, Sept. 19, 1863, Edwin M. Stanton Mss., L. C.

261 (furnish): Joseph Hooker to Lincoln, April 21, 1863, Hiram Berdan to Edwin M. Stanton, Aug. 19, 1863, Lincoln Mss., L. C.; Off. Sec. War, Irregular Book IV, p. 195; Ord. Off., Letters Rec'd, 1863, F406, F434, F451; J. W. Ripley to D. W. Flagler, July 30, 1863, Ord. Off., Letters to Ordnance Officers; *O. R.*, series 1, XXIV, part iii, p. 571.

261 (possible): N. A., Adjutant General's Office, Register of Officers Arriving in Washington, 1861-1867, Aug. 8, 1863; Warren Fisher, Jr., to Lincoln, Aug. 13, 1863, Lincoln Mss., L. C.

262 (shoot): *Scientific American*, Dec. 1921, p. 102.

262 (day): Lincoln, *Works*, VI, 394-395; E. M. Stanton to J. W. Ripley, Aug. 17, 1863; Stanton Mss., L. C.; Ord. Off., Misc. Letters Sent, LIX, 7.

262 (Building): Observatory Journal, Aug. 18, 1863.

262-263 (Park, forward): *Scientific American*, Dec. 1921, p. 102; Hay, *Diary*, p. 82.

263 (grounds): *New York Tribune*, Aug. 19, 1863; Observatory Journal, Aug. 19, 1863; Bowen, *37th Mass. Volunteers*, p. 356.

264 (mind): Ord. Off., Letters Rec'd, 1863, M437, S696, S714, WD845; Ord. Off., Misc. Letters Sent, LIX, 104.

264 (Ramsay): *New York Tribune*, Aug. 21, 1863; *Dyer Inquiry*, I, 500.

264 (England): Ord. Off., "Inventions," class 1c, No. 333; *Hartford Courant*, March 17, 1870.

265 (fact): 38th Cong., 2nd sess., Senate, Rep. Comm. 121, pp. 69-70.

265 (proclamation): Off. Sec. War, Irregular Book V, R14; George T. Curtis, *Life, Character and Public Services of General George B. McClellan* (Boston, 1887), pp. 99-103; James C. Welling to William C. Prime, Sept. 7, 1886, George B. McClellan Mss., L. C.

266 (consented): *Dyer Inquiry*, I, 500-501; Townsend, *Anecdotes of the Civil War*, pp. 79-80.

266 (him, stopgap, sadness): *Dyer Inquiry*, I, 124-126.

267 (order): Ord. Off., Letters Rec'd, 1863, WD947, M495; Adam
Gurowsky to John A. Andrew, Dec. 29, 1863, John A. Andrew
Mss., Mass. Hist. Soc.

CHAPTER NINETEEN (pages 268-288)

268 (adopt): Welles, *Diary*, I, 343; Nav. Rec. Coll., Letterbook of
Capt. H. A. Wise, pp. 33-36; Robert Townsend to H. A. Wise,
Sept. 15, 1863, Wise Mss., N. Y. Hist. Soc.; Edward Everett to F.
P. Blair, April 2, 1864, Everett Mss., Mass. Hist. Soc.; *Scientific
American*, Sept. 19, 1863.

269 (stages): Lincoln, *Works*, VII, 118.

269 (drop): John B. Ehrhardt, *Joseph Francis (1809-1893)* (Princeton, N. J., 1950), pp. 20-22; John A. Dix to Lincoln, April 17,
1863, Nicolay Mss., L. C.; Joseph Francis to Lincoln, March 4,
1864, Lincoln Mss., L. C.

269 (uses): Memorandum by Joseph Henry, Nov. 14, 1849, Henry
Wurtz Mss., N. Y. Public Library; *Dictionary of American Biogra-
phy*, XX, 571; Ord. Off., "Inventions," class 8, No. 245; Ord.
Off., "Experiments," Nos. 248, 250, 252, 253; T. T. S. Laidley to
George D. Ramsay, Dec. 15, 1863, Lincoln Mss., L. C.; *Scientific
American*, Jan. 16, 1864.

270 (hill): Browning, *Diary*, I, 673; Bates, *Lincoln in the Telegraph
Office*, pp. 265-266; *Washington Star*, June 27, 1864.

270 (instructions): W. N. Jeffers to H. A. Wise, June 18, 1863, Wise
Mss., N. Y. Hist. Soc.; Isaac Diller to Lincoln, and Charles M.
Wetherill to Lincoln, Oct. 31, 1863, Lincoln Mss., L. C.; Nav. Bur.
Ord., "Diller's Powder, 1862-1863," W. N. Jeffers to H. A. Wise,
Oct. 24, 1863.

270 (Jeffers): Chandler, "Civil War Nitre Shortage," pp. 148-149;
O. R., series 3, IV, 806; memorandum by Isaac Diller, Nov. 2,
1863, Lincoln Mss., L. C.; W. N. Jeffers to H. A. Wise, Oct. 30,
1863, Wise Mss., N. Y. Hist. Soc.

271 (would): Ord Off., Misc. Letters Rec'd, 1-S-5; *Dyer Inquiry*, I,
31, II, 530, 533, 537, 540-541.

271 (Lincoln): *Ibid.*, II, 527, 532-533; Albert B. Hart, *Salmon Portland Chase* (Boston, 1899), pp. 155-156; Benjamin F. Butler, *Private and Official Correspondence during the Civil War* (5 vols.;
Norwood, Mass., 1917), V, 9; Thomas H. Ford to Lincoln, March
7, 1861, Lincoln Mss., L. C.; *Battles and Leaders*, II, 612; Moore,
Rebellion Record, V, 443 (Documents); Leech, *Reveille in Wash-*

ington, p. 268; Thomas H. Ford to B. F. Butler, Aug. 13, 1864, Benjamin Butler Mss., L. C.

272 (more): *Dyer Inquiry,* I, 31, 493, II, 383, 546, 549.

272 (bands): *Ibid.,* I, 37-38, 132, 515, II, 537, 545, 557; Lincoln, *Works,* VII, 127.

273 (there): Browning, *Diary,* I, 656; *Dyer Inquiry,* I, 516.

273 (it): *Ibid.,* I, 516, 525, II, 383.

274 (Ramsay): Observatory Journal, Feb. 3, 8, 9, 1864; Ord. Off., Letters Rec'd, 1864, W112; *Dyer Inquiry,* I, 31, II, 381-382, 521, 523; Browning, *Diary,* I, 658, 660.

274 (3d): *Dyer Inquiry,* I, 28, II, 382-383; Ord. Off., Register of Letters Rec'd, 1864, A89; Lincoln, *Works,* VII, 216, 229.

274 (controversies): G. D. Ramsay to Lincoln, March 8, 1864, Lincoln Mss., L. C.

275 (prices): Ord. Off., Letters Rec'd, 1869, WD32; *Dyer Inquiry,* I, 514-515, 519, II, 541.

275 (it): *Ibid.,* I, 32, 514-515, 517, II, 537, 540.

275 (adjusted): *O. R.,* series 3, IV, 587; *Dyer Inquiry,* I, 126, 497, 501, II, 121, 126-127; Ord. Off., Letters to the War Dept., XIV, 497-498.

276 (me): *Dyer Inquiry,* I, 139, 194-195, 206, 507, II, 123, 126, 129, 400; *Scientific American,* May 30, 1863; P. H. Watson to Joseph Holt, Jan. 29, 1864, Joseph Holt Mss., L. C.; *O. R.,* series 3, IV, 582, 586-589, 592, 618; E. M. Stanton to G. D. Ramsay, June 15, 1864, Edwin M. Stanton Mss., L. C.

276 (in): *Dyer Inquiry,* II, 326, 537.

276 (armaments): Off. Sec. War, Irregular Book V, 034; *Dictionary of American Biography,* XV, 340.

277 (condition): Ord. Off., Letters to the War Dept., XV, 160; *Dyer Inquiry,* II, 126.

277 (square): *Ibid.,* II, 537-538, 593.

278 (Lincoln): *Ibid.,* I, 189, 193, II, 399.

278 (them): *Ibid.,* I, 171, 511, II, 310-311, 313-314, 316-317, 347, 390, 395, 534-535, 545, 592-593.

279 (President): *Ibid.,* I, 510-511, II, 337, 392, 538, 540, 542-544, 592.

279 (men): Ord. Off., "Purchases of Ordnance," pp. 19, 204; *Dyer Inquiry,* I, 46, II, 340, 395, 424, 560.

279 (bill): Ord. Off., Letters Rec'd, 1864, WD918; *Scientific American,* Sept. 19, 1864; Nav. Rec. Coll., Letterbook of Capt. H. A. Wise, Jan. 1862-Nov. 1864, pp. 218-219.

280 (scene): Lincoln, *Works,* VIII, 3; Ord. Off., Letters Rec'd, 1864, B523, B562.

280 (hope): 38th Cong., 2nd sess., Senate, Rep. Comm. 121, pp. 148-149, 170-171; Carpenter, *Six Months in the White House,* pp. 253-254; Ord. Off., Misc. Letters Sent, LXII, 496, LXIII, 65; Nav. Rec. Coll., Letterbook of Capt. H. A. Wise, Mar. 1864-Jan. 1865, pp. 181-182.

281 (handle): *Army and Navy Journal,* March 25, June 3, 1865; Ord. Off., "Purchases of Ordnance," p. 19; *O. R.,* series 3, V, 142.

281 (Oliver): *Dyer Inquiry,* II, 441; Petition of Oliver Ames in *re* Horatio Ames's Estate, Supreme Court of the District of Columbia, January Term, 1872.

281 (1864): William F. Scott, *The Story of a Cavalry Regiment* (New York, 1893), p. 62; Ord. Off., Letters Rec'd, 1864, S336.

282 (spring, Arsenal): *Ibid.,* S163, W119.

282 (War): Off. Sec. War, Irregular Book III, p. 22.

282 (savages): *Battles and Leaders,* III, 522; *Scientific American,* Sept. 12, 1863; Peterson, "Explosive Bullets"; Hayden, "Explosive Rifle Balls," p. 125.

283 (River): Ord. Off., Letters Rec'd, 1863, S947, 1864, WD258, W195; Ord. Off., Misc. Letters Rec'd, 1-S-11.

283 (Monroe): Ord. Off., Letters Rec'd, 1863, WD217; Ord. Off., Register of Letters Rec'd, 1865, WD448; *Army and Navy Journal,* Aug. 12, 1865.

283 (flatcar): Moore, *Rebellion Record,* VIII, 31, 41-42 (Diary); Butler, *Correspondence,* Butler to W. F. Smith, July 3, 1864.

284 (rifles): O. S. Halsted to B. F. Butler, Oct. 19, 1864, Benjamin Butler Mss., L. C.; Butler, *Correspondence,* V, 365, 369; Lyman, *Meade's Headquarters,* pp. 281, 283-284.

284 (hints): E. R. Bennet to B. F. Butler, Jan. 22, 1866, Butler Mss., L. C.

284 (war): Stevens, *Sharpshooters,* p. 236.

285 (way): *Ibid.,* pp. 417, 462.

285 (extension): *Ibid.,* p. 368; Ripley, *Vermont Riflemen,* p. 187.

285 (war): *O. R.,* series 3, I, 181, 331-332; Haynes, *2d New Hampshire,* p. 8; Chamberlin, *150th Pennsylvania,* p. 243.

286 (ground): Moore, *Rebellion Record,* VII, 58, (Incidents).

286 (wounded): *Ibid.,* XI, 190, 194-195.

287 (hurry): *O. R.,* series 1, XXXV, part i, pp. 307-308, XL, part i, pp. 541-542.

287 (agreeable): Gilbert A. Hays (compiler), *Under the Red Patch: Story of the Sixty Third Regiment Pennsylvania Volunteers, 1861-1864* (Pittsburgh, 1908), pp. 67-68.

287 (repeaters): *O. R.,* series 1, XXXVI, part iii, p. 201; Bowen, *37th Mass.,* pp. 354, 363.

287 (carbines): Ord. Off., Misc. Letters Rec'd, 1-T-24; Ord. Off., Letters to the War Dept., XIV, 559; James H. Wilson, *Under the Old Flag* (2 vols.; New York, 1912), I, 374; Ord. Off., Misc. Letters sent, LX, 283, LXIX, 204.

287 (gun): Cyril B. Upham, "Arms and Equipment for the Iowa Troops in the Civil War," *Iowa Journal of History and Politics,* Jan. 1918, pp. 26-27.

288 (made): *Scientific American,* March 19, May 28, 1864; *New York Times,* June 10, 1864; *Army and Navy Journal,* Oct. 1, 1864; *O. R.,* series 3, IV, 802.

CHAPTER TWENTY (pages 289-299)

289 (over): Leech, *Reveille in Washington,* p. 354.

290 (everywhere): *Scientific American,* Jan. 28, 1865; Thomas, *Lincoln,* p. 522.

290 (anywhere): *O. R.,* series 1, XLV, part ii, p. 488.

290 (use): *Scientific American,* Jan. 2, 1865.

291 (corps): Ord. Off., Misc. Letters Sent, LIII, 465, LVIII, 485; Ord. Off., Letters to War Dept., XIV, 31; Ord. Off., "Inventions," class 1c, No. 351; Ord. Off., Letters Rec'd, 1864, WD708; Nav. Bur. Ord., Misc. Letters Sent, VIII, 163; Chinn, *The Machine Gun,* I, 50; A. B. Dyer to H. A. Wise, Jan. 31, 1865, Wise Mss., N. Y. Hist. Soc.; Ord. Off., Special Files, "Misc. Letters Rec'd," 1-H-42.

291 (ordnance): *Scientific American,* Dec. 10, 1864; Chinn, *The Machine Gun,* I, 48, 54.

291 (Run): *Dyer Inquiry,* II, 400; G. D. Ramsay to George Harrington, Aug. 23, 1864, Ord. Off., Misc. Letters Sent; W. Maynadier to B. C. Hallin, Jan. 20, 1865, *ibid.*

292 (cakes): O. S. Halsted to Lincoln, Sept. 13, Oct. 1, 1864, Lincoln Mss., L. C.; Leech, *Reveille in Washington,* pp. 371-372.

292 (arsenal): Welles, *Diary,* II, 257, 264; Nav. Rec. Coll., Executive Records, March-May 1865, No. 55.

293 (fire): Ord. Off., Letters Rec'd, 1862, WD1452, WD1576, WD1594, 1864, F83, WD315; Ord. Off., "Inventions," classes 4 and 5, Nos. 744, 790; Ord. Off., Register of Letters Rec'd, 1864, WD992; Ord. Off., Misc. Letters Rec'd, 1-A-90, 1-S-199, 1-WD431.

293 (candlelight): Leech, *Reveille in Washington,* pp. 377-379.

293 (air): *Ibid.*, 381-382, 384; *Dyer Inquiry*, II, 427.

293 (1865): *Ibid.*, II, 536.

294 (French): Leech, *Reveille in Washington*, pp. 384, 387.

294 (side): James Tanner to H. F. Walch, April 17, 1865, in *Abraham Lincoln Quarterly*, Dec. 1942.

295 (Lincoln): Ord. Off., Letters Rec'd, 1865, WD194, WD201; Leech, *Reveille in Washington*, p. 402; Hitchcock, *Fifty Years in Camp and Field*, p. 476.

295 (last): *O. R.*, series 3, IV, 1280-1281.

296 (trials): Ord. Off., Letters Rec'd, 1865, WD219; Leech, *Reveille in Washington*, pp. 408-409; Brooks, *Washington in Lincoln's Time*, pp. 267, 270-271.

296 (clerk): Ord. Off., Letters Rec'd, 1865, WD235.

296 (much): Ord. Off., Misc. Letters Rec'd, 1-D-25; Samuel Ricker to J. S. Black, Feb. 5, 1867, Jeremiah Black Mss., L. C.; Smith, *Wetherill*, pp. 47-48.

296 (came): *Dyer Inquiry*, II, 538.

297 (man): Ord. Off., Register of Letters Rec'd, 1865, A357, WD422, and *passim* under War Dept., May-June 1865; Ord. Off., Misc. Letters Sent, LXIV, 193; *Dyer Inquiry*, II, 339.

297 (position): J. C. B. Davis to Hamilton Fish, Oct. 13, 1874, Hamilton Fish Mss., L. C.

297 (Passion): Clipping, in O. S. Halsted to J. G. Nicolay, Oct. 19, 1862, Nicolay Mss., L. C.; *Newark Daily Advertiser*, July 3, 1871.

298 (posterity): *Dictionary of American Biography*, XX, 425, XV, 340; N. A., Adjutant General's Office, Personal File of George T. Balch; *Dyer Inquiry*, I, 498, II, 127.

298 (Foundry): *Dictionary of American Biography*, V, 581.

298 (world): *Scientific American*, May 27, 1865.

299 (vigorously): George S. Boutwell, *Reminiscences of Sixty Years in Public Affairs* (2 vols.; New York, 1902), II, 242; Adams, *Education of Henry Adams*, pp. 494, 496.

Sources Cited

I. PRIMARY MANUSCRIPT SOURCES

A. National Archives.
Adjutant General's Office:
Department of the Gulf: Letters Sent.
Letters Received.
Personal File of George T. Balch.
Register of Officers Arriving in Washington, 1861-1867.
Legislative Records:
Records of the United States House of Representatives.
Naval Records Collection of the Office of Naval Records and Library
("Nav. Rec. Coll.") :
Executive Letters.
Executive Records.
Inventions Referred to the Permanent Commission, 1862-1864.
Letterbooks of Captain Henry A. Wise, 1862-1864, 1864-1865.
Letters on Inventions Referred to the Board of Examiners.
Letters Referred to the Permanent Commission: Unfinished
Business, 1864-1865.
Minutes of the Permanent Commission, 1863-1864.
Office of the Secretary of the Navy, Misc. Letters Received.
Reports from the Board of Examiners, 1862.
Subject File BG: "Correspondence about . . . cannon made by
Horatio Ames."
Washington Navy Yard: Orders Issued, 1860-1861.
Navy Bureau of Ordnance ("Nav. Bur. Ord.") :
Correspondence Regarding the Ames Wrought Iron Gun.
Correspondence Relating to Inventions and Patents: Inventions,
Rifle and Smoothbore, 1862-1864.
Examinations of Inventions.
Index to Inventions Tested at the Washington Navy Yard.
Letters on the Armament of the Mississippi Squadron.
Letters Received: Diller's Powder, 1862-1863.
Letters Received: Miscellaneous.
Letters Received: Navy Department ("Navy Dept. Letters").
Letters Received Relating to Ordnance Inventions ("Misc. Ord-
nance Papers").
Letters Sent: Miscellaneous.

Letters Sent: Navy Department.
Letters Sent: Washington.
Reports on Inventions.
Office of the Chief of Ordnance ("Ord. Off.") :
Ames Papers.
Letters Received.
Letters Sent: Miscellaneous.
Letters to Ordnance Officers.
Letters to the War Department.
Open Purchases, 1861-1867.
Purchases of Ordnance.
Registers of Letters Received.
Special Files:
Decisions of the Commission on Ordnance Contracts.
Experiments.
Inventions.
Miscellaneous Letters Received.
Ordnance Board Reports, 1860-1870.
Office of the Secretary of War ("Off. Sec. War") :
Irregular Books I, III, IV, V.
Letters Received.
Letters Sent: Military Affairs.
Letters Sent to the President.
Records of the Patent Office.
Treasury Department:
AB series, Letters from Executive Officers.
H series, Letters to the Collector at New York.
United States Naval Observatory:
Meteorological Journal ("Observatory Journal").
B. Library of Congress Collections.

Jeremiah S. Black
Blair Family
Benjamin F. Butler
Simon Cameron
Salmon P. Chase
John A. Dahlgren
Henry L. Dawes
Ewing Family
Hamilton Fish
Benjamin B. French
Horace Greeley
Ethan A. Hitchcock
Joseph Holt
Philip Kearney
Robert T. Lincoln ("Lincoln Mss.")
George B. McClellan
Edward McPherson
Alfred Mordecai
John G. Nicolay
David D. Porter
Edwin M. Stanton
Elihu B. Washburne
Henry Alexander Wise

C. Other Manuscript Collections.

John A. Andrew Mss., Massachusetts Historical Society.

Autobiography of James W. Benét, Yale University.

Civil War Collection, New York Historical Society.

Memoir by John A. Dahlgren ("Dahlgren ms. memoir"), belonging
to Lieutenant Commander Joseph F. Dahlgren (USNR).

Edward Everett Mss., Massachusetts Historical Society.

Production Scrapbooks, Springfield Armory Library.

James W. Ripley Mss., belonging to Robert Bradford Bartholomew.

Springfield Collection, Springfield (Mass.) City Library.

Richard W. Thompson Mss., Lincoln National Life Foundation.

Thurlow Weed Mss., University of Rochester Library.

Henry Augustus Wise Mss., New York Historical Society.

Horatio Woodman Mss., Massachusetts Historical Society.

Henry Wurtz Mss., New York Public Library.

II. CONTEMPORARY NEWSPAPERS AND PERIODICALS

Army and Navy Journal
Atlantic Monthly
Boston Transcript
Harper's Monthly
Hartford Courant
National Intelligencer (Washington, D. C.)
National Republican (Washington, D. C.)
Newark (N. J.) *Daily Advertiser*
New York Evening Post
New York Herald
New York Times
New York Tribune
Philadelphia Public Ledger and Daily Transcript
Scientific American
Springfield (Mass.) *Gazette*
Springfield (Mass.) *Republican*
Washington (D. C.) *Evening Star*
Washington (D. C.) *Sunday Morning Chronicle*

III. CONGRESSIONAL DOCUMENTS

20th Cong., 1st sess., House, Report 252.
29th Cong., 2nd sess., House, Report 36.

30th Cong., 1st sess., House, Executive Documents 8, 54, Report 294.
33d Cong., special sess., Senate, Report 1.
37th Cong., 2nd sess., House, Executive Documents 67, 126, 150, Report 2.
37th Cong., 2nd sess., Senate, Executive Document 72.
38th Cong., 2nd sess., House, Executive Document 15.
38th Cong., 2nd sess., Senate, Rep. Comm. 121, 128.

IV. BOOKS AND ARTICLES, PUBLISHED AND UNPUBLISHED

Abbott, Jacob, "The Armory at Springfield," *Harper's Monthly*, July 1852.
Adams, Henry, *The Education of Henry Adams* (Modern Library edition). N. Y., 1931.
Alexander, E. P., *Military Memoirs of a Confederate*. N. Y., 1907.
The American Annual Cyclopedia and Register of Events. 14 vols., N. Y., 1861-1875.
Ammen, Daniel, *The Old Navy and the New*. Phila., 1891.
Angle, Paul M., *"Here I Have Lived."* New Brunswick, N. J., 1935.
Asbury, Henry, *Reminiscences of Quincy, Illinois*. Quincy, Ill., 1882.
Bagg, M. M., *Pioneers of Utica*. Utica, N. Y., 1877.
Balch, Galusha B., *Genealogy of the Balch Families in America*. Salem, Mass., 1897.
Bates, David Homer, *Lincoln in the Telegraph Office*. N. Y., 1907.
Bates, Edward, *The Diary of Edward Bates*. Howard K. Beale, ed., *Annual Report of the American Historical Association*, 1930, IV.
Battles and Leaders. See Johnson, Robert U.
Beck, Warren A., "Lincoln and Negro Colonization in Central America," *Abraham Lincoln Quarterly*, Sept. 1950.
Benton, James G., *A Course of Instruction in Ordnance and Gunnery*. N. Y., 1861.
Beveridge, Albert J., *Abraham Lincoln, 1809-1858*. 2 vols., Boston, 1928.
Billings, John D., *Hardtack and Coffee*. Boston, 1887.
The Biographical Encyclopedia of Ohio of the Nineteenth Century. Cincinnati, 1876.
Blizard, J. L. B., "The Future of Discovery and Invention," *Technology Review*, June 1954.
Bohn, Casimir, *Bohn's Hand-Book of Washington*. Wash., D. C., 1858.
Bolander, Louis H., "The *Alligator*, First Federal Submarine of the Civil War," *U. S. Naval Institute Proceedings*, June 1938.
Bonham, Jeriah, *Fifty Years' Recollections*. Peoria, Ill., 1883.

Boutwell, George S., *Reminiscences of Sixty Years*. 2 vols., N. Y., 1902.

Bowen, James L., *History of the Thirty-Seventh Regiment Mass. Volunteers in the Civil War*. Holyoke, Mass., 1884.

Boynton, Capt. E. C., "Greek Fire and Other Inflammables," *U. S. Service Magazine,* Jan. 1864.

Brooks, Noah, "Personal Recollections of Abraham Lincoln," *Harper's Monthly,* July 1865.

Brooks, Noah, *Washington in Lincoln's Time*. N. Y., 1895.

Brown, George W., "The Mortar Flotilla," *Personal Recollections of the War of the Rebellion* (N. Y. Commandery, Mil. Ord. of Loyal Legion), I, 173-182. N. Y., 1891.

Browning, Orville H., *The Diary of Orville Hickman Browning*. Theodore C. Pease and James G. Randall, eds., Springfield, Ill., 2 vols., Springfield, Ill., 1925.

Buffum, Francis H., *A Memorial of the Great Rebellion*. Boston, 1882.

Butler, Benjamin F., *Butler's Book*. Boston, 1892.

Butler, Benjamin F., *Private and Official Correspondence during the Civil War*. 5 vols., Norwood, Mass., 1917.

Campbell, Lewis, and Garnett, William, *The Life of James Clerk Maxwell*. London, 1884.

Carpenter, Francis B., *Six Months at the White House*. N. Y., 1866.

Chamberlin, Thomas, *History of the One Hundred and Fiftieth Regiment Pennsylvania Volunteers*. Phila., 1895.

Chandler, Alfred D., Jr., "Dupont, Dahlgren, and the Civil War Nitre Shortage," *Military Affairs,* Fall, 1949.

Chinn, Lt. Col. George M., *The Machine Gun*. 3 vols., Wash., D. C., 1951.

Chittenden, Lucius E., *Recollections of President Lincoln and His Administration*. N. Y., 1891.

Coulson, Thomas, *Joseph Henry: His Life and Work*. Princeton, N. J., 1950.

Coulter, E. Merton, *The Confederate States of America, 1861-1865*. Baton Rouge, La., 1950.

Cox, Samuel S., *Three Decades of Federal Legislation*. Providence, R. I., 1885.

Curtis, George T., *Life, Character and Public Services of General George B. McClellan*. Boston, 1887.

Dahlgren, Madeline V., *Memoir of John A. Dahlgren*. Boston, 1882.

Davis, Charles H., *Life of Charles Henry Davis*. Boston, 1899.

Davis, William W. H., *History of the 104th Pennsylvania Regiment*. Phila., 1866.

Deyrup, Felicia J., *Arms Makers of the Connecticut Valley.* Northampton, Mass., 1948.

Dickens, Charles, *American Notes.*

Dickey, Luther S., *History of the Eighty-fifth Regiment Pennsylvania Volunteer Infantry.* N. Y., 1915.

Dickey, Luther S., *History of the 103d Regiment Pennsylvania Volunteer Infantry.* Chicago, 1910.

Dictionary of American Biography. Allen Johnson and Dumas Malone, eds., 20 vols., N. Y., 1928.

Donaghy, John, *Army Experiences of Capt. John Donaghy.* Deland, Fla., 1926.

Doster, William E., *Lincoln and Episodes of the Civil War.* N. Y., 1915.

Dyer Inquiry. See United States War Department.

Ehrhardt, John B., *Joseph Francis (1801-1893).* Princeton, N. J., 1950.

Fite, Emerson D., *Social and Industrial Conditions in the North during the Civil War.* N. Y., 1910.

Flower, Frank A., *Edwin McMasters Stanton.* Akron, Ohio, 1905.

Ford, Worthington C., ed., *A Cycle of Adams Letters, 1861-1865.* 2 vols., Boston, 1920.

Fremantle, James A. L., *The Fremantle Diary.* Walter Lord, ed., Boston, 1954.

Fuller, Claud E., *The Breech-loader in the Service.* Topeka, Kans., 1933.

Fuller, Claud E., *Springfield Muzzle-loading Shoulder Arms.* N. Y., 1930.

Gillmore, Quincy A., *Engineer and Artillery Operations against the Defense of Charleston Harbor in 1863.* N. Y., 1868.

Hardee, W. J., *Rifle and Infantry Tactics.* 2 vols., Mobile, Ala., 1863.

Hart, Albert B., *Salmon Portland Chase.* Boston, 1899.

Haskell, James R., *Reports on the Rafael Repeater.* Wash., D. C., 1862.

Haupt, Herman, and Flower, Frank A., *Reminiscences of General Herman Haupt.* Milwaukee, 1901.

Hay, John, *Addresses of John Hay.* N. Y., 1906.

Hay, John, *Lincoln and the Civil War in the Diaries and Letters of John Hay.* Tyler Dennett, ed., N. Y., 1939.

Hayden, Rev. Horace E., "Explosive or Poisoned Musket or Rifle Balls," *Southern Historical Society Papers,* Jan. 1880.

Haydon, F. Stansbury, *Aeronautics in the Union and Confederate Armies.* Baltimore, 1941.

Haynes, Martin, *A History of the Second Regiment, New Hampshire Volunteer Infantry, in the War of the Rebellion.* Lakeport, N. H., 1896.

Hays, Gilbert A., *Under the Red Patch.* Pittsburgh, Pa., 1908.

Herndon, William H., and Weik, Jesse W., *Herndon's Lincoln*. 3 vols., Chicago, 1889.

History of the Corn Exchange Regiment. Phila., 1888.

History of the Twenty-Third Pennsylvania Volunteers. Phila., 1904.

Hitchcock, Ethan A., *Fifty Years in Camp and Field*. William A. Croffut, ed., N. Y., 1909.

Hoppin, James M., *Life of Andrew Hull Foote*. N. Y., 1874.

Hutchinson's Washington and Georgetown Directory. Wash., D. C., 1863.

Johnson, Robert U., and Buel, Clarence C., eds., *Battles and Leaders of the Civil War*. 4 vols., N. Y., 1888.

Jordan, David Starr, ed., *Leading American Men of Science*. N. Y., 1910.

Joyner, Fred B., *David Ames Wells, Champion of Free Trade*. Cedar Rapids, Iowa, 1939.

Laidley, Theodore T. S., "Breech Loading Musket," *U. S. Service Magazine*, Jan. 1865.

Leech, Margaret, *Reveille in Washington, 1860-1865*. N. Y., 1941.

Leslie, Frank, *Frank Leslie's Illustrated History of the Civil War*. N. Y., 1895.

Lincoln, Abraham, *The Collected Works of Abraham Lincoln*. Roy P. Basler, ed., 8 vols., New Brunswick, N. J., 1953.

Longstaff, Frederick V., and Atteridge, A. Hilliard, *The Book of the Machine Gun*. London, 1917.

Lyman, Theodore, *Meade's Headquarters, 1863-1865*. Boston, 1922.

MacDougall, Donald A., "The Federal Ordnance Bureau, 1861-1865." Unpublished Ph. D. dissertation, University of California at Berkeley, 1951.

McBride, Robert W., *Personal Recollections of Abraham Lincoln*. Indianapolis, 1926.

McClellan, George B., *McClellan's Own Story*. N. Y., 1887.

Mearns, David C., ed., *The Lincoln Papers*. 2 vols., Garden City, N. Y., 1948.

Meigs, Montgomery C., "General M. C. Meigs on the Conduct of the Civil War," *American Historical Review*, Jan. 1921.

Meneely, A. Howard, *The War Department, 1861*. N. Y., 1928.

Milbank, Jeremiah, Jr., *The First Century of Flight in America*. Princeton, N. J., 1943.

Miller, Francis T., ed., *Photographic History of the Civil War*. 10 vols., N. Y., 1911.

Moore, Frank, ed., *The Rebellion Record*. 11 vols., N. Y., 1861-1868.

National Cyclopedia of American Biography. 37 vols., N. Y., 1921.

Nevins, Allan, *Abram S. Hewitt; with Some Account of Peter Cooper.* N. Y., 1935.

Nevins, Allan, *The Emergence of Lincoln.* 2 vols., N. Y., 1950.

Newell, Robert H., *The Orpheus C. Kerr Papers, First Series.* N. Y., 1862.

Nichols, George W., *The Story of the Great March.* N. Y., 1865.

Nicolay, John G., and Hay, John, *Abraham Lincoln: A History.* 10 vols., N. Y., 1890.

Norton, Charles B., *American Breech-loading Small Arms.* N. Y., 1872.

Norton, Charles B., and Valentine, W. J., *Report on the Munitions of War* (in *Reports of the United States Commissioners to the Paris Universal Exposition of 1867*). Wash., D. C., 1868.

Norton, Oliver W., *Army Letters, 1861-1865.* Chicago, 1903.

O'Brien, William J., "The Washington Arsenal," *Army Ordnance,* July 1935.

Official Records of the Union and Confederate Armies in the War of the Rebellion (cited as "*O. R.*"). 130 vols., Wash., D. C., 1880-1901.

Official Records of the Union and Confederate Navies in the War of the Rebellion (cited as "*O. R., Navies*"). 30 vols., Wash., D. C., 1894-1927.

Olejar, Paul D., "Rockets in Early American Wars," *Military Affairs,* X, 1946.

Parker, Thomas H., *History of the 51st Regiment of Pennsylvania Volunteers.* Phila., 1869.

Paullin, Charles O., "President Lincoln and the Navy," *American Historical Review,* Jan. 1909.

Peck, Taylor, *Round-shot to Rockets.* Annapolis, Md., 1949.

Peterson, Harold L., "Explosive Bullets," *The American Rifleman,* Feb. 1948.

Piatt, Donn, *Memories of the Men Who Saved the Union.* N. Y., 1887.

Poore, Ben: Perley, *The Life and Public Services of Ambrose E. Burnside.* Providence, R. I., 1882.

Portrait and Biographical Record of Adams County, Illinois. Chicago, 1892.

Pratt, Harry E., ed., *Concerning Mr. Lincoln.* Springfield, Ill., 1944.

Randall, James G., *Lincoln the President: Springfield to Gettysburg.* 2 vols., N. Y., 1945.

Re-union of the 28th & 147th Regiments, Pennsylvania Volunteers. Phila., 1872.

Rice, Allen T., ed., *Reminiscences of Abraham Lincoln by Distinguished Men of His Time.* N. Y., 1886.

"Rifled Guns," *Atlantic Monthly*, Oct. 1859.

Ringwalt, John L., *The Diller Family*. New Holland, Pa., 1942.

Ripley, Sarah D., ed., *James Wolfe Ripley*. Hartford, Conn., 1881.

Ripley, William Y. W., *Vermont Riflemen in the War for the Union*. Rutland, Vt., 1883.

Roche, Daniel M., "The Acquisition and Use of Foreign Shoulder-arms in the Union Army, 1861-1865." Unpublished Ph. D. dissertation, University of Colorado, 1949.

Rodenbough, Theodore F., and Haskins, William L., eds., *The Army of the United States, 1789-1869*. N. Y., 1896.

Russell, William H., *My Diary North and South*. N. Y., 1863.

Sandburg, Carl, *Abraham Lincoln: The Prairie Years*. 2 vols., N. Y., 1926.

Sandburg, Carl, *Abraham Lincoln: The War Years*. 4 vols., N. Y., 1939.

Scott, William F., *The Story of a Cavalry Regiment*. N. Y., 1893.

Seward, Frederick W., *Reminiscences of a War-Time Statesman and Diplomat*. N. Y., 1916.

Shanks, William F. G., *Personal Recollections of Distinguished Generals*. N. Y., 1866.

Sherman, William T., *Memoirs of General William T. Sherman*. 2 vols., N. Y., 1875.

Shipley, Ruth B., "The Winder Building." Unpublished article, 1953.

Smith, Edgar F., *Charles Mayer Wetherill*. Reprinted from *Journal of Chemical Education*, 1929.

Smith, Winston O., *The Sharps Rifle*. N. Y., 1943.

Stearns, Ezra S., *Genealogical and Family History of the State of New Hampshire*, N. Y., 1908.

Stevens, Charles A., *Berdan's United States Sharpshooters*. St. Paul, Minn., 1892.

Stevenson, Daniel, "General Nelson, Kentucky, and Lincoln Guns," *The Magazine of American History*, Aug. 1883.

Stoddard, William O., *Abraham Lincoln and Andrew Johnson*. N. Y., 1888.

Stoddard, William O., *Inside the White House in War Times*. N. Y., 1890.

Tarbell, Ida M., *The Life of Abraham Lincoln*. 4 vols., N. Y., 1924.

Thomas, Benjamin, *Abraham Lincoln*. N. Y., 1952.

Thompson, Richard W., *Recollections of Sixteen Presidents from Washington to Lincoln*. 2 vols., Indianapolis, 1894.

Townsend, E. D., *Anecdotes of the Civil War in the United States*. N. Y., 1884.

Trollope, Anthony, *North America.* 3 vols., Leipzig, 1862.

True, Frederick W., ed., *The First Half-Century of the National Academy of Sciences.* Wash., D. C., 1913.

United States War Department, *Proceedings of a Court of Inquiry . . . to Examine into the Accusations against Brig. and Bvt. Major General A. B. Dyer, Chief of Ordnance* (cited as *"Dyer Inquiry"*). 2 vols., Wash., D. C., 1869.

Upham, Cyril B., "Arms and Equipment for the Iowa Troops in the Civil War," *Iowa Journal of History and Politics,* Jan. 1918.

Upton, Emory, *The Military Policy of the United States.* Wash., D. C., 1912.

Walworth, Reuben H., *Hyde Genealogy.* 2 vols., Albany, N. Y., 1864.

Warden, Robert B., *An Account of the Private Life and Public Services of Salmon Portland Chase.* Cincinnati, 1874.

Welles, Gideon, *Diary of Gideon Welles.* 3 vols., Boston, 1911.

West, Richard S., Jr., *The Second Admiral: A Life of David Dixon Porter.* N. Y., 1937.

Westbrook, Robert S., *History of the 49th Pennsylvania Volunteers.* Altoona, Pa., 1898.

Whittlesey, Derwent S., "The Springfield Armory." Unpublished Ph.D. dissertation, University of Chicago, 1920.

Williams, Samuel C., *General John T. Wilder.* Bloomington, Ind., 1936.

Wilson, James H., *Under the Old Flag.* 2 vols., N. Y., 1912.

Wilson, William B., *Acts and Actors in the Civil War.* Phila., 1892.

Wise, Henry Augustus, "Private Journal of Henry A. Wise, U. S. N., on Board Frigate 'Niagara,' 1860" ed. by Allan B. Cole, *Pacific Historical Review,* Sept. 1942.

Woodbury, Augustus, *A Narrative of the Campaign of the First Rhode Island Regiment.* Providence, R. I., 1862.

Woodward, William, "Firearms—Their Evolution and Worcester's Part Therein," *Worcester Historical Society Publications,* n. s., I, 264-278 (1932).

W. P. A. Guide Series, *Washington, City and Capital.* Wash., D. C., 1937.

Zane, Charles S., "Lincoln As I Knew Him," *Sunset Magazine,* Oct. 1912.

Acknowledgments

My THANKS, first of all, to the History Department of Boston University, and especially to Professors Warren O. Ault and Robert E. Moody for a thorough grounding in history and historical techniques without which the zeal of a converted engineer would have been useless. From the moral support of Professor Warren S. Tryon I first drew nerve to think seriously of writing history. Professor Kenneth A. Bernard, who knows far more about Abraham Lincoln and his times than I am ever likely to, prompted my initial investigation of Lincoln's connection with Civil War technology and became principal reader for the doctoral dissertation which was the first fruit of my research. I am greatly indebted to his encouragement and counsel.

As research assistant to Dr. Benjamin P. Thomas for more than six months, I was able to discover much material useful to my own research as well. At many points in my own long quest, Dr. Thomas's cheerful advice and encouragement kept my spirits up; and he gave up a great deal of his limited spare time to reading both drafts of my book. I owe him more than I can ever repay.

Mrs. Stephen Vincent Benét, Lieutenant Commander Joseph F. Dahlgren (USNR) and Robert Bradford Bartholomew, grandson of General Ripley, welcomed me into their homes and generously gave me access to family papers. Though I have criticized some of General Ripley's official acts, his grandson's generosity has made it possible for me to record the general's fine personal qualities.

The hospitality of Lewis F. Davis, Harold Peterson, Roger Bragdon, Bruce Cowper and Bert Sheldon and the friendly interest of Miss Laura Benét, James Ripley Jacobs, Roy P. Basler and Lieutenant Colonel J. J. Reen have made the long search less lonely.

Among those who gave of their time and knowledge to lighten my labor at many points were Miss Fidelia N. Abbott, Mrs. Alitha

H. Andrew, Miss Zelina Bartholomew, Mrs. Elmer E. Count, Jr.,
Captain Wade De Weese (USNR), Mrs. Henry W. English, Ray-
mond G. Ferriss, Colonel Calvin H. Goddard, Dr. Harbeck Halsted,
Wilson Harwood, Colonel Berkeley R. Lewis, Roger Lewis, Francis
Lord, George Melcher, Schuyler Pardee, Mrs. Ruth B. Shipley,
Professor Bradley Stoughton, James L. Taylor, Jr., and Harry C.
Thompson. My thanks to all, and especially to Lieutenant Colonel
George M. Chinn (USMCR), Harry E. Pratt and Louis A. Warren.

I look back gratefully to the friendly aid I received in the Manuscript Room of the New York Public Library and from Wayne
Andrews, W. R. Leech and their associates in the New York Historical Society. Mr. Riley, Miss Collins and Mr. Wheeler of the
Massachusetts Historical Society have been unfailingly and cordially
helpful. My visits to the Connecticut Valley Historical Society, the
New Jersey Historical Society, the Springfield Armory Library and
the manuscript divisions of the Yale and Princeton Libraries were
made pleasant and fruitful by their staffs. For months, my calls for
truckload after truckload of National Archives records bore heavily
upon Richard G. Wood of the War Record Branch, Nelson M.
Blake of the Navy Record Section and their expert staffs. The physical labor of trundling out tons of documents was in itself enormous, yet performed from first to last with speed, accuracy and good
humor.

During six months of full-time research in the Manuscript Division of the Library of Congress, I came to know Dr. C. Percy Pow-
ell, Dr. Elizabeth McPherson, Frank White and Wilfred Langone,
not only as tireless and enthusiastic guides to that happy hunting
ground of historians, but also as good friends.

Years of using the public libraries of Malden and Boston, Massachusetts, and the library of Boston University, have contributed
much to this book and to my education generally. Boston University's rich Stone and Bullard collections of Civil War material have
been of immense assistance to me.

For researches undertaken in my behalf, my thanks go out:

To the Historical Societies of Connecticut, Missouri, New Hampshire, Pennsylvania and Wisconsin; of Quincy and Adams, McLean and Morgan Counties, Ill.; of Oneida County, N. Y.; and of Buffalo, N. Y., Litchfield, Conn., Nashua, N. H., and Worcester, Mass.

To the American Antiquarian Society, the Henry E. Huntington Library, the Historical and Philosophical Society of Ohio, the Lincoln National Life Foundation, the Ohio State Archaeological and Historical Society, the State Libraries of Illinois and Indiana, and the Illinois State Historical Library.

To the public libraries of Buffalo, N. Y., Jersey City, N. J., and Springfield, Mass.

And to the libraries of the United States Naval Academy, Lafayette and Oberlin Colleges, Princeton, Yale and Cornell Universities and the Universities of Rochester and North Carolina.

Last only in point of time is my debt of gratitude to Julius Birge, who read and saw possibilities in my first draft, to Harrison Platt, who read both drafts and gave me wise and kindly editorial guidance, and to all at Bobbs-Merrill.

Index

358